⁂ PSYCHOLOGY ⁂
AND THE CHURCH

CRITICAL
QUESTIONS

※

CRUCIAL
ANSWERS

DAVE HUNT AND T.A. MCMAHON

The **Berean Call**

BEND • OREGON
www.thebereancall.org

PSYCHOLOGY AND THE CHURCH
Critical Questions, Crucial Answers

Published by The Berean Call
Copyright © 2008

Library of Congress Control Number: 2008923559
ISBN: 978-1-928660-61-3

Unless otherwise indicated, Scripture quotations are from
The Holy Bible, King James Version (KJV)
Used by Permission

Printed in the United States of America

The Berean Call
PO Box 7019
Bend, Oregon, 97708-7019

PUBLISHER'S NOTE

Assembled for the first time in one place, this book is a revised and expanded compilation of articles, questions, and commentary from past issues of *The Berean Call* newsletter.

We believe this work fills an important void in the literature of the church, which has largely become saturated with the terms and tenets of psychology—both by osmosis and by assimilation.

For your convenience, the book is divided into several sections: Articles by T. A. McMahon, articles by Dave Hunt, and Q&A with Dave Hunt. An appendix also includes the transcript of the DVD production *Psychology and the Church: Critical Questions, Crucial Answers,* hosted by T. A. McMahon.

Because each chapter was originally published as an independent article, some duplication of content has been removed except where it is necessary to preserve the context. In most chapters, new material has been added to update, clarify, or further expound on the subject at hand. Although the chapters of this book are neither chronologically nor topically arranged, an extensive subject index is provided for those researching a particular item of interest.

Readers will note that in some instances, "self" is printed lowercase, and in others, is capitalized (even in the middle of a sentence). This is intended to differentiate between "self" in the common sense and "Self" as an autonomous entity—a designation that usurps the position of reverence and worship reserved for God alone.

We pray this compilation will be of help to pastors, layworkers, professors, parents, and students alike—indeed, to all believers whom the Lord leads to search the Scriptures for biblical insight pertaining to the field of psychology and its impact on society and the Body of Christ.

A dedicated website has also been established for topics covered in this volume, featuring portions of this book, related materials, research links, downloadable files, and audio and video media:

www.PsychologyAndTheChurch.com

INTRODUCTION

WHAT IS CHRISTIAN PSYCHOLOGY?

— Dave Hunt —

T HE ONLY POSSIBLE JUSTIFICATION for the existence of "Christian" psychology in the church would be if the Bible did not contain all of the counsel, wisdom, and guidance that Christians need for living sanctified lives pleasing to God in today's modern world. For literally thousands of years both Old and New Testament believers found God and His Word more than sufficient in every way. At least this is what the Bible tells us of those who triumphed by faith over every trial and circumstance that Satan could bring against them. Some of their lives are summarized briefly in Hebrews 11:

> And what shall I more say? For the time would fail me to tell of Gedeon, and of Barak, and of Samson, and of Jephthae; of David also, and Samuel, and of the prophets:
> Who through faith subdued kingdoms, wrought righteousness, obtained promises, stopped the mouths of lions, quenched the violence of fire, escaped the edge of the sword, out of weakness were made strong . . . turned to flight the armies of the aliens.
> Women received their dead raised to life again: and others were tortured, not accepting deliverance; that they might obtain a better resurrection: and others had trial of cruel mockings and scourgings, yea, moreover of bonds and imprisonment: they were stoned, they were sawn asunder, were tempted, were slain with the sword: they wandered about in sheepskins and goatskins; being destitute, afflicted, tormented; (Of whom the world was not worthy:) they wandered in deserts, and in mountains, and in dens and caves of the earth. . . . [1]

Isn't the Bible Sufficient?

The Bible itself, written by "holy men of God [who] spake as they were moved by the Holy Ghost" (2 Peter 1:21), declares that the heroes and heroines of Bible history all triumphed by faith in God and in His promises. They neither had nor needed any help whatsoever from "Christian psychology," which didn't even exist in their day. What would be the purpose of offering some new and extra-biblical help to today's Christians, whose lives (at least in the Western world) do not involve trials and challenges that even come close to those of biblical saints? Wouldn't faith in God and His Word, which has been proved thousands of times through the ages to be more than sufficient in every conceivable circumstance and in the deepest trials—wouldn't that be sufficient for Christians today, no matter what their trials and challenges in life might be? What could possibly persuade a Christian to look to psychology, invented by anti-Christians and only lately come upon the scene, for help in living a life pleasing to God?

Of course, even Christian psychologists (at least many of them) still claim to have a firm faith in the inerrancy of Scripture—though increasing numbers of Christians are joining the ranks of theistic evolutionists, who refuse to take the first eleven chapters of Genesis literally. But no matter how firmly a psychologist clings to inerrancy of Scripture, they all must deny its sufficiency. This is the only way to justify their profession. If any part of the Bible is in error, however, then where can the line be drawn? If the Bible has not given us all we need to live the Christian life, that fact alone would be enough to make all of it suspect in view of the many places where it claims to be sufficient for living triumphant lives pleasing to God.[2]

If, however, the Bible *is* sufficient and Christian psychology just points us to the Bible, as the argument goes, what could be wrong with that? First of all, Christian psychology doesn't "just point us to the Bible." If it did, and if Christian psychologists really believed that the Bible was sufficient (as it claims to be), why not call what they do "biblical counseling"? Why muddy the water of life by calling Bible study *psychology*? That word refers to an entire field of study that has nothing at all to do with the Bible—and, in fact, is not only *extra*-biblical but *anti*-biblical.

And what could this new way of knowing God's Word possibly be? How and why would psychology, invented by atheists and anti-Christians as a sub-stitute for God, the Bible, and Christianity, provide new insights into the Bible unknown to (and obviously unneeded by) millions of believers over the last four thousand years or more? And why would we need it now? There is neither a biblical nor rational answer to that logical question.

The Emperor Is Naked!

Furthermore, there is no psychology that is classified as "Christian" psychology. Textbooks and reference manuals list hundreds of psychologies (Freudian, Jungian, Rogerian, Skinnerian, behavioristic, humanistic, transpersonal, etc.)—each named after its founder or its founder's chief theory. But there is no school of psychology that was founded by a Christian and is therefore called "Christian" and recognized as such in textbooks or reference manuals. It just doesn't exist.

It is not easy to get Christians to face the facts. In spite of what we've pointed out above, the plaintive query still persists: "But if Christian psychology is Christian. . . ?" It isn't—and how could it be? It wasn't founded by Christians and is in fact *anti*-Christian. It doesn't come from the Bible but is simply an attempt to integrate the theories of atheists into the Bible in order to supply missing essentials for daily living that the Holy Spirit apparently failed to include. Does that sound reasonable?

Well, if it isn't Christian, why is it called that—and what is it? Here is what two leading Christian psychologists had to say in a paper delivered at a convention of Christian psychologists:

> We are often asked if we are "Christian psychologists" and find it difficult to answer since we don't know what the question implies. We are Christians who are psychologists, but at the present time there is no acceptable Christian psychology that is markedly different from non-Christian psychology.
>
> It is difficult to imply that we function in a manner that is fundamentally distinct from our non-Christian colleagues. Is there a distinct Christian dentistry, or surgery, or history or grammar. . . ? As yet there is not an acceptable theory, mode of research or treatment methodology [in psychology] that is distinctly Christian.[3]

Okay, so technically there is no such thing as Christian psychology. But there are hundreds of authors, conference speakers, pastors, and church leaders who call themselves, and are known as, Christian psychologists (James Dobson, Gary Collins, Clyde Narramore, et al.). It is a recognized label and among the most popular subjects in Christian universities and seminaries. That is true—but even in Christian universities and seminaries, the way it is taught and the content of the courses must be approved by atheists for accreditation. Consider the following ecstatic announcement by Fuller Theological Seminary nearly twenty years ago:

Accredited! The Graduate School of Psychology has received accreditation from the American Psychological Association [mostly anti-Christians] for a third five-year period after evaluation by two APA site visit teams. . . . The [APA] committee on accreditation . . . found the program's religious orientation not to adversely affect the quality of [psychological] training.

Now isn't that something to rejoice about! Our seminaries merit Satan's imprimatur of approval because his representatives find that, in spite of a "religious orientation," students are being well trained in the wisdom of the world that is foolishness with God (1 Corinthians 1:20).

Psychology is of rather recent origin. It wasn't even well known in the secular world until after Freud and Jung popularized it in the late 1800s and early 1900s. Nor did it enter the evangelical church until after World War II. For nearly nineteen hundred years, Christians did very well without "Christian Psychology." They triumphed over the world, the flesh, and the devil by faith in Christ alone and obedience to His Word. In fact, the greatest heroes of the faith all lived before psychology was merged with Christianity and entered the church. If the greatest men and women of God throughout history didn't need psychology, why would anyone need it today?

Enter the Trojan Horse

How did psychology get into the church? The man most responsible for the intrusion of that Trojan Horse was none other than arch heretic Norman Vincent Peale. Peale declared on national TV on the *Phil Donahue* show, "It's not necessary to be born again. You have your way to God; I have mine. I found eternal peace in a Shinto shrine . . . God is everywhere." Shocked, Donahue responded, "But you're a Christian minister; you're supposed to tell me that Christ is the way and the truth and the life, aren't you?" Peale replied, "Christ is one of the ways."[4] Among his many other heresies were the following:

The world you live in is mental and not physical. Change your thought and you change everything.[5]

Who is God? Some theological being. . . ? God is energy. As you breathe God in, as you visualize His energy, you will be reenergized![6]

Prayer power is a manifestation of energy. Just as there exist scientific techniques for the release of atomic energy, so are there scientific procedures for the release of spiritual energy through the mechanism of prayer. . . . New and fresh spiritual techniques are being constantly discovered . . . experiment with prayer power.[7]

Prayer . . . is a procedure by which spiritual power flows from God . . . releases forces and energies . . . one must learn step by step the formula for opening the circuit and receiving this power. Any method through which you can stimulate the power of God to flow into your mind is legitimate . . . [any] scientific use of prayer. . . . [8]

There is a powerful and mysterious force . . . a kind of mental engineering that works best when supported by a strong religious faith [it is called] imaging . . . it has been implicit in all the speaking and writing I have done. . . . Imaging is positive thinking carried one step further . . . one does not merely think about a hoped-for-goal; one "sees" or visualizes it with tremendous intensity, reinforced by prayer [it] is touching the kingdom of God within . . . releasing forces more powerful than [one] knows.[9]

So how did secular, anti-Christian psychology metamorphose into Christian psychology? It is not a recognized branch of psychology that was founded by a Christian. It isn't listed in the index of psychology textbooks. It doesn't come from the Bible and was unknown in the church until Peale brought it in. As reported on Peale's home page, here is how "Operation Trojan Horse in the Church" began:

In 1937, Peale established a clinic with Freudian psychiatrist Dr. Smiley Blanton in the basement of the Marble Collegiate Church. (Blanton brought with him the "extensive experience" of having undergone psychoanalysis by Freud himself in Vienna in 1929, 1935, 1936, and 1937.) The clinic was described as having "a theoretical base that was Jungian, with a strong evidence of neo- and post-Freudianism."[10]

It subsequently grew to an operation with more than 20 psychiatric doctors and psychologically-trained "ministers," and in 1951 became known as the American Foundation for Religion and Psychiatry. In 1972, it merged with the Academy of Religion and Mental Health to form the Institutes of Religion and Health (IRH). To his death [December 24, 1993], Peale remained affiliated with the IRH as president of the board and chief fund raiser.

Indeed, Peale pioneered the merger of theology and psychology which became known as Christian Psychology. [Emphasis added]

Peale applied Christianity to everyday problems and is the person who is most responsible for bringing psychology into the professing Church, blending its principles into a message of "positive thinking." Peale said, "through prayer you . . . make use of the great factor within yourself, the deep subconscious mind . . . [which Jesus called] the kingdom of God within you. . . . Positive thinking is just another term for faith."

He also wrote, "Your unconscious mind . . . [has a] power that turns wishes into realities when the wishes are strong enough."[11]

According to J. Harold Ellens, author of a section on Peale in the *Baker Encyclopedia of Psychology and Counseling*, "Peale's work was initially scorned by ministers and therapists alike. . . . Dr. Peale was three-quarters of a century ahead of the times with his emphasis on the relationship between psychology and Christian experience. He saw psychology and Christian experience as very compatible . . . he had the courage to stand pat on this position in spite of the opposition of the entire Christian church for nearly half a century. His genius was that he . . . translated psycho-theology into the language of the people."[12]

So the "entire Christian church" opposed "Christian psychology" for decades. Eventually, not only liberals but evangelicals succumbed to this appealing delusion that theology could be made "scientific" by merging it with psychology—though the latter is not a science. Peale was not only a master of heresies by the dozens but a master of persuasion. Much of that can be credited to Billy Graham, who repeatedly praised Peale and endorsed his writings.

The Virus Spreads

In 1968, Clyde Narramore and his nephew, Bruce Narramore, founded the Rosemead School of Psychology "to train clinical psychologists from a Christian perspective . . . with its primary focus on the integration of psychology and theology. . . . In 1977, Rosemead merged with Biola University in La Mirada, California where it gained accreditation from the American Psychological Association (APA) in 1980. Biola's undergraduate programs in psychology were merged with Rosemead's graduate programs in the fall of 1981, forming the present Rosemead School of Psychology. In 2000, Rosemead founded the Institute for Research on Psychology and Spirituality."[13]

Psychology cannot be legitimized or sanctified by linking it with "spirituality"—a word and concept that do not appear in Scripture even once.

Christian psychology is an attempted marriage of the Bible to theories of the atheistic inventors of psychology (who were committed not to righteousness but to unrighteousness). It is worse than trying to mix oil and water; it is the attempt to blend the Word of God with atheism and occultism. This is impossible to do honestly. Even "Christian psychologists" themselves admit they can't quite find a way to put that mixture together. Yet no one seems to care that the very term "Christian psychology" is a deceit. After trying for decades to mix this devil's brew, Gary Collins admitted: "It is too early to answer decisively if psychology and Christianity can be integrated."[14]

Then why keep trying? What is the motive? Why is anyone attempting this impossible and incompatible partnership? It has succeeded because those who call themselves Christian psychologists and promote it in the evangelical church want legitimacy and respect both in the world and in the church. But Scripture declares, "whosoever . . . will be a friend of the world is the enemy of God" (James 4:4).

The very foundation of Christian psychology is the belief that the Bible is insufficient to deal with the traumas and challenges of modern life: we need something more than the counsel God gives in His Word. Although one of Christ's names is Counselor (Isaiah 9:6), we supposedly need more today than His counsel alone. We need outside help from the alleged experts; we need to go to professionals, to the psychologists who have special training and new techniques. Believing that lie opened the door of the church to psychology. Dwight L. Moody would be shocked by the statement over his name that for those coming out of cults it is "imperative . . . to get professional [i.e., psychological] counseling . . . it could be harmful to survivors to expect them to rely totally on prayer and Bible study."[15] It couldn't be stated more bluntly that God, His Word, the Holy Spirit, and Christ living His resurrected life in the believer are insufficient!

Should we not consider it odd that God left some vital ingredients out of His Word that His people have had to get along without for thousands of years? And wouldn't it be even stranger if God inspired the mostly atheistic and certainly anti-Christian founders and theorists of psychology with essential "truth" hidden to the apostles and prophets and all of the leading Christians in the entire history of the church until the 1950s? Isn't it also too incredible that the Holy Spirit failed to include in the Scripture, inspired over a period of sixteen hundred years, theories and therapies essential to a Christian's spiritual and emotional well-being, thus leaving it to anti-Christians to eventually supply them?

No, we are told reassuringly, this is not strange at all because "All truth is God's truth" and there are many sources for it outside the Bible.

The atheistic founders of psychology's various schools presumably offer part of "God's truth" that either isn't included in Scripture or isn't explained there as well as psychology expresses it. This is the sand upon which Christian psychology is founded. It is not the kind of ground upon which one would want to build anything.

1. Hebrews 11:32-38.

2. See Deuteronomy 8:3; Psalm 1; Psalm 119:9; John 10:10; 2 Corinthians 2:14; Galatians 5:16, 22-26; 2 Timothy 3:15-17, and many other places.

3. J. Sutherland and P. Poelstra, "Aspects of Integration," a paper presented to the Western Association of Christians for Psychological Studies, Santa Barbara, CA, June 1976.

4. *Christian News,* May 12, 1997, 11.

5. Charles S. Braden, *Spirits in Rebellion: The Rise and Development of New Thought* (SMU Press, 1966), 387.

6. Norman Vincent Peale, *Plus: The Magazine of Positive Thinking*, Vol. 37, no 4 (Part II), May 1986, 23.

7. Norman Vincent Peale, *The Power of Positive Thinking* (Fawcett Crest, 1983), 52-53.

8. Norman Vincent Peale, *The Power of Positive Thinking*, New Condensed Edition (Center for Positive Thinking, 1987), 17.

9. Norman Vincent Peale, *Positive Imaging: The Powerful Way to Change Your Life* (New York: Fawcett Crest, 1982), Introduction, 1-3.

10. Carol V. R. George, *God's Salesman: Norman Vincent Peale and the Power of Positive Thinking* (New York, NY: Oxford University Press, 1993), 90.

11. http://normanvincentpeale.wwwhubs.com/.

12. Beth Ann Krier, "Prolific Norman Vincent Peale: Positively 90," *Los Angeles Times*, June 5, 1988, Part IV, 1, 13.

13. http://www.rosemead.edu/about/history.cfm.

14. Gary Collins, *Can You Trust Psychology?* (InterVarsity Press, 1988), 130.

15. *Moody Monthly*, March 1989, 23.

BLESSED IS THE MAN THAT WALKETH NOT IN THE COUNSEL OF THE UNGODLY, NOR STANDETH IN THE WAY OF SINNERS, NOR SITTETH IN THE SEAT OF THE SCORNFUL. BUT HIS DELIGHT IS IN THE LAW OF THE LORD; AND IN HIS LAW DOTH HE MEDITATE DAY AND NIGHT. AND HE SHALL BE LIKE A TREE PLANTED BY THE RIVERS OF WATER, THAT BRINGETH FORTH HIS FRUIT IN HIS SEASON; HIS LEAF ALSO SHALL NOT WITHER; AND WHATSOEVER HE DOETH SHALL PROSPER.

— PSALM 1:1-3 —

PART ONE

TO WHOM SHALL WE GO?

— T. A. McMahon —

Then said Jesus unto the twelve, Will ye also go away? Then Simon Peter answered him, Lord, to whom shall we go? thou hast the words of eternal life. —JOHN 6:67-68

HAVE YOU EVER BEEN CONVICTED by Peter's response to his Lord and Savior? I have. There are times when I catch myself not going to Jesus. It's not that I intentionally want to "go away" from the Lord; it's just that He's not always my first choice in everyday situations. So when John 6:68 comes to mind, especially after having turned elsewhere and reaped less-than-gratifying results, another thought pops into my head: I must be stupid!

Why didn't I turn to the One who has the "words of eternal life"? He is, after all, the God of all creation, Wonderful, Counselor, Mighty God, the Alpha and the Omega, perfect in all His attributes, which includes omniscience. By comparison, the best input I can get from the world is the equivalent of being handed a paddle while going over Niagara Falls.

Some would argue that going to God in certain circumstances is fine, but you wouldn't go to Him to learn how to fix your plumbing or rebuild the carburetor on your truck. Though there were times when I turned to Jesus for help in (literally) bailing me out of an "I'll-do-it-myself" plumbing solution, I recognize that His Word is not a manual for home repair, auto mechanics, open-heart surgery, and so forth. Even in those endeavors, however, it is a very good idea to seek the Lord for His grace and mercy.

Although not instructing mankind in everything, the Bible is the only true, objective source of information for knowing God and living one's life in the way He requires. Not only does it touch upon all aspects of how we live; it certainly bears upon everything having eternal value. The Apostle Peter tells us that "through the knowledge of God, and of Jesus our Lord . . . his divine power hath given unto us all things that pertain unto life and godliness . . . "

(2 Peter 1:2–3). That would seem to cover everything worth being concerned about. Again, Peter exclaimed, "You [Lord] have the words of eternal life." His "words" are found in the Holy Scriptures. So, if we call ourselves Bible-believing Christians, shouldn't we, then, be those who continually go to the Bible for "all things that pertain unto life and godliness"?

Sadly, that is not the case for most evangelicals. Mirroring the world around them, they seem to have an appetite for psychological counsel. A major reason for this attraction is that, along with the masses, they have the erroneous idea that the substance of clinical counseling is the stuff of science. Certainly the fact that the purveyors of this so-called medically related, scientific wisdom have advanced degrees and are professionals would cause one to think so. However, psychotherapy is not and cannot be a scientific endeavor. The most obvious reason for this is that its subject is human behavior, a study that defies scientific certainty.

True science can concern itself with only the physical side of man—those things governed by physical laws, e.g., physics or chemistry. The nonphysical (man's mind) is out of bounds to those in lab coats, for mankind's will and emotion mock the scientific method. Psychotherapy nevertheless maintains its clinical façade because of its pseudo-medical terminology. For example, one might think that a person's problematic "mental health" indicates that he is "mentally ill" and ought to see a doctor and possibly be committed to a "mental hospital." However, a mind (or anything mental), being nonphysical, cannot be ill; neither can it be examined by a doctor in a hospital for "mental patients." These terms sound scientific and have influenced multitudes to think of psychotherapy in terms of medical science, but in reality they're nonsensical.

If psychotherapy isn't truly the scientific pursuit of humanity's mental, emotional, and behavioral wellbeing, what is it? Bluntly put, it's talk. Rhetoric. Conversation! Research psychiatrist Thomas Szasz, in his book *The Myth of Psychotherapy: Mental Healing as Religion, Rhetoric, and Repression*, burns off clinical psychology's scientific mist:

> In plain language, what do patient and psychotherapist actually do? They speak and listen to each other. What do they speak about? Narrowly put, the patient speaks about himself, and the therapist speaks about the patient. . . . Each tries to move the other to see or do things in a certain way.

This, then, is neither brain surgery nor any other form of medical intervention; nor is it rocket science. In other words, a Ph.D. or M.D. is not a necessary requirement to handle the medium of "talk." Yet wouldn't advanced degrees make one more effective in the psychotherapeutic conversation process? No. The many research studies comparing the effectiveness of professional therapists versus nonprofessionals have given equivalent results. In other words, nonprofessionals do as well as professionals.

Physician, Heal Thyself

If the medium of psychotherapy—talking and listening—doesn't depend upon advanced classes in conversation in order to be effective, what does one study to earn a Ph.D. in clinical psychology? Theories about human behavior, mostly: what Sigmund Freud gleaned from Greek dramas, his speculations about infantile sex, psychic determinism, and the unconscious; Carl Jung's beliefs about archetypal images, the occult, and the collective unconscious; Alfred Adler's "masculine protest" and "inferiority complex" concepts; Abraham Maslow's humanistic psychology, "hierarchy of needs" theory, and New Age obscenities; B. F. Skinner's stimulus-response behavioral dogmas; Erich Fromm's godless view of love; Arthur Janov's primal scream; Carl Rogers' client-centered therapy; Fritz Perls' Gestalt, and a legion of other speculative ideas.

What then of these theories? Have they, over the years, formed an historic body of knowledge from which developed true and helpful insights regarding mankind's nature or provided remedies for the problems of life? To the contrary, the field of psychotherapy is its own lunatic asylum! If you think that's a little harsh, check out the lives of any of those mentioned above. Freud was a cocaine addict who lusted for his own mother. Jung was suicidal and communed with a demon. Rogers abandoned his cancer-stricken, dying wife for another woman but relieved his guilt by allegedly contacting his deceased wife's spirit through a Ouija board. Rogers later ended his own life through assisted suicide. And the list goes on. ("Physician, heal thyself" comes to mind.) In addition, there are more than four hundred fifty different (often contradictory and utterly bizarre) psychotherapeutic systems and thousands of methods and techniques.

Karl Popper, regarded as the preeminent scholar in the area of philosophy of science, concluded, after a lengthy study of psychotherapy, that its theories, "though posing as science, had in fact more in common with primitive myths than with science," and that "these theories describe some facts but in the manner of myths. They contain most interesting psychological suggestions, but not in testable form."[1] Eighty leading educators, writing in *Psychology: A Study of a Science*, edited by Sigmund Koch, concurred: "The entire subsequent history of psychology can be seen as a ritualistic endeavor to emulate the forms of science in order to sustain the delusion that it already is a science."[2] Martin and Deidre Bobgan, prolific authors and critics of psychotherapy, summarize the scene today: "The entire field is amassed in confusion and crowded with pseudo-knowledge and pseudo-theories resulting in pseudo-science."[3]

The information critical of psychotherapy is hardly hidden from public view. Neither is it the work of conspiracy groups or wild-eyed fundamentalists. The only mystery is why so few are paying attention, especially those who claim to be Bible-believing Christians—and pastors. Moreover, in psychotherapy, the values, favored theories, and beliefs of the therapist rule. The client must conform to what the therapist presents in order for the process to be effective, and a willing client is normally quite receptive to whatever is presented. So whether or not the client's problem is resolved, he has been influenced, even co-opted, by the value system of the *therapist*.

An Affair to Remember—Or Spiritual Adultery?

Many evangelical pastors are either intimidated by, or infatuated with, psychotherapy. Somehow these shepherds have been convinced that their lack of education and training in the therapeutic process has rendered them incapable of effectively addressing the mental, emotional, and behavioral problems of their flock. So what do they do? Most become referral services for their local psychotherapeutic community—"Christian psychologists" or otherwise—and others go back to school to add a psychology credential to their theology degree. They may preach and teach the Word on Sundays and Wednesday evenings, but, to their shame, they have, whether intentionally or not, communicated to their congregations that the Bible is inadequate when it comes to problems regarding how we live and relate to others.

But surely they wouldn't refer a person to a psychotherapist for something so mundane as not getting along with a spouse or another family member, or not feeling good about himself, or being depressed, or problems of lust or greed or bitterness or self-control—would they? Yes, that's mostly what psychotherapists deal with, and the church provides their clients!

Any problem that can't be "cured" through talk is out of psychotherapy's league. Evangelical pastors, who are usually good talkers and, better yet, talkers of "good," seem to have missed this. But what they also miss, which should be more obvious to them, and critically so, is the heart and soul of psychotherapy: self.

Secular counseling begins and ends with self; professional "Christian" counseling begins and ends with Christianity interpreted through "self" theories. The result of both is antithetical to what the Bible teaches. There is not a verse from Genesis to Revelation that gives one hint of support for the "self" concepts of psychology—even the Christianized versions that have flooded the religious marketplace throughout the last few decades. Self is the problem, and there is no manmade cure, talking or otherwise. Throughout its pages, the Word of God is both implicit and explicit on the subject. Matthew 16:24 issues the mandate: "If any man will come after me, let him deny himself, and take up his cross, and follow me," and 2 Timothy 3:1–2 warns the generation that makes self both its redemption and redeemer: "This know also, that in the last days perilous times shall come. For men shall be lovers of their own selves. . . . " Thanks to the overwhelming influence of psychology and Christendom's complicity, we are in those "perilous times."

Someone once observed, regarding Christianity's capitulation to psychotherapy, that "the church has sold its birthright for a pot of beans." Yes and no. There is definitely a sellout involved, but beans are nutritious and psychotherapy is toxic to its core. Its modern beginnings with Freud were based on deceit, as historians have well documented. His professional progeny have simply added and subtracted ingredients to his stew of delusion. Nevertheless, Christian psychotherapists assure us that there are healthy benefits involved because "all truth is God's truth," and some of the luminaries of psychology mentioned above have contributed such morsels of truth. What those extrabiblical truths are, we've yet to be told. Even if these so-called "truths" *were* real, they would have to be served up in the poisonous broth of psychotherapy.

Twice in Proverbs we are told, "There is a way which seemeth right unto a man, but the end thereof are the ways of death" (Proverbs 14:12; 16:25). God obviously wanted that repeated for us, perhaps especially for this humanistically oriented generation, which majors on what seems and feels right. But the critical issue is that "man" has become the judge of what is right, and the consequence is death, i.e., separation from God. This is the lie that the serpent fed Eve—that she herself could, like God, be the arbiter of what was good and what was evil. Just as God said it would, death resulted from the choice Adam and Eve made. We have a similar choice today: God's Word and His way, or the way that seems right to a man.

If we truly know and love the Lord, there *is* no other way for us. Not only is God's Word sufficient for all things that pertain to life and godliness, but He has also sealed every born-again believer with His Holy Spirit, the Spirit of Truth, to enable us to live our lives in a way that is fruitful and pleasing to Him. Furthermore, all believers are called and equipped to minister to one another. The Epistle to the Galatians (6:2) tells us that we are to bear one another's burdens, and 2 Timothy 3:17 declares that Scripture thoroughly prepares us for every good work. Jesus said, "If ye continue in my word, then are ye my disciples indeed; And ye shall know the truth, and the truth shall make you free" (John 8:31, 32). Later, in a prayer for us, Jesus said, "Sanctify them through thy truth: thy word is truth" (John 17:17). So where else are we going to go? He alone has the words of truth and eternal life.

1. Karl Popper, "Scientific Theory and Falsifiability," *Perspectives in Philosophy*, Robert N. Beck, ed. (New York: Holt, Rinehart, Winston, 1975), 344, 346.

2. Sigmund Koch, "The Image of Man in Encounter Groups," *The American Scholar*, Autumn 1973, 636.

3. Martin and Deidre Bobgan, *Psychoheresy*, (EastGate Publishers, 1987), 31.

CONTENDING FOR THE FAITH

— T. A. McMahon —

Beloved, when I gave all diligence to write unto you of the common salvation, it was needful for me to write unto you, and exhort you that ye should earnestly contend for the faith which was once delivered unto the saints. —JUDE 3

ORIGINALLY, JUDE WANTED TO SHARE those things of the faith with his fellow believers that were common to them all. But the Holy Spirit redirected him to a matter of greater urgency. Issues of the faith, "once delivered unto the saints," were being both subtly undermined and overtly perverted. As then, so today. All saints (i.e., Christians—Ephesians 1:1; Colossians 1:2, etc.) are to earnestly contend for the teachings of the faith "given by inspiration of God" (2 Timothy 3:16).

To *earnestly contend* for something is not a laid-back activity; the common cross-reference for that phrase is 1 Timothy 6:12: "Fight the good fight of faith. . . . " In both instances the meaning has to do with laboring fervently, or striving, just as an athlete would when participating in a sporting event. The sports analogy provides a very graphic illustration: good athletes must train vigorously, in keeping with the demands of their sport. Likewise, a committed Christian must spiritually condition himself in keeping with Paul's exhortation to "exercise thyself. . . unto godliness" (1 Timothy 4:7). Paul often used the correlation between athletic endeavors and the Christian walk to show that a born-again believer's life is not a passive proposition. It requires spiritual training that includes many of the qualities that a superior athlete demonstrates: diligence, commitment, self-discipline, teachability, etc. Yet, common to the sports scene today, many of us have dedicated ourselves to being spectators—not necessarily "couch potatoes," but definitely not players.

Too often the reaction to Jude's exhortation is that contending for the faith is "best left to the experts," i.e., to scholars, theologians, apologists, or cult authorities. There are at least two problems with such an idea. First, Jude's words were not written to theological experts but to "them that are sanctified by God the Father, and preserved in Jesus Christ, and called"—that is, *all* of His "saints" (Jude 1, 3). Second, a major aspect of contending for the faith has to do with *every saint's spiritual development.* In other words, contending for the faith isn't just for cult experts, nor does it necessarily involve arguing with or confronting others. It should be the lifelong spiritual regimen of every believer (1 Peter 3:15).

Earnestly contending for the faith requires *the desire to diligently study God's Word.* Jesus set forth the basis of a developmental program for everyone who is committed to Him: "If ye continue in my word, then are ye my disciples indeed" (John 8:31). Second Timothy 2:15 underscores the practical, everyday exercise for the believer: "Study to shew thyself approved unto God, a workman that needeth not to be ashamed, rightly dividing the word of truth." The heart of Christianity is a personal relationship with Jesus Christ. Studying and applying the Scriptures is the primary way our personal relationship with Him develops; it's predicated upon knowing Him through His revelation of Himself.

Earnestly contending for the faith requires *knowledge.* We needn't become experts before we share "the faith which was once delivered unto the saints," but we are to be diligent in our pursuit of the knowledge of the Lord. Though it's all too often attempted, it is nevertheless foolish to try to contend for something when one is uninformed. Solomon writes, "My son, if thou wilt receive my words, and hide my commandments with thee; so that thou incline thine ear unto wisdom, and apply thine heart to understanding; yea, if thou criest after knowledge, and liftest up thy voice for understanding; if thou seekest her as silver, and searchest for her as for hid treasures; then shalt thou understand the fear of the LORD, and find the knowledge of God. For the LORD giveth wisdom: out of his mouth cometh knowledge and understanding. He layeth up sound wisdom for the righteous: he is a buckler to them that walk uprightly. He keepeth the paths of judgment, and preserveth the way of his saints" (Proverbs 2:1–8).

Contending for the faith requires *the diligent practice of discernment.* In Hebrews 5:13–14 we find, "For every one that useth milk is unskillful in the word of righteousness: for he is a babe. But strong meat belongeth to them that are of full age, even those who by reason of use have their senses exercised to discern both good and evil." The "milk" and "meat" of these two passages are metaphors which refer to spiritual growth; limiting ourselves to a spiritual infant's diet and program inhibits our spiritual development. However, those who exercise their senses by studying the Word of God will grow in discernment, no longer remaining "children, tossed to and fro, and carried about with every wind of doctrine, by the sleight of men, and cunning craftiness, whereby they lie in wait to deceive. . . " (Ephesians 4:14).

The Need for Correction

Earnestly contending for the faith requires that *we willingly receive correction.* Correction, however, is not a "psychologically correct" endeavor today, either in the world or in the church. It is regarded as a threat to one's positive self-image by many who promote the humanistic theology of self-esteem. It's incredible how such a worldly mindset has impacted those who should be separate from the world and whose thinking is to reflect the mind of Christ. Even a cursory search of the Bible reveals example after example of correction that would be viewed today as potentially destructive of one's psychological well-being! Was Peter's "self-esteem" psychologically damaged and both his self-image and ministerial image irreparably harmed by Paul's public correction? Was Peter's ministry written off by most of the early church because Paul was not sensitive (or biblical—supposedly not heeding Matthew 18) enough to meet privately with Peter? Isn't that the way many in the church see things today? And what about the ego trauma felt by the publicly corrected Barnabas (Galatians 2:13), Alexander (2 Timothy 4:14–15), Phygellus and Hermogenes (2 Timothy 1:15), Hymenaeus and Philetus (2 Timothy 2:17–18), Demas (2 Timothy 4:10), Diotrephes (3 John 9–10), and others?

Correction is foundational to the life of every Christian. In Paul's second letter to Timothy, he counseled his young disciple concerning the value of using the Scriptures for correction (as well as for *reproof*!), "That the man of God may be perfect, thoroughly furnished unto all good works" (2 Timothy 3:17). Correction must begin at home; that is, there must be a willingness on the part of an individual not only to be corrected by another, but a desire to correct oneself. The admonition to "examine yoursel[f], whether ye be in the faith" (2 Corinthians 13:5) is not a public survey; it requires checking ourselves out and then doing what's necessary to make things right before the Lord. Without a willingness to consider the possibility of a "beam" in one's own eye, hypocrisy will take the reins in any correction of another.

Earnestly contending for the faith requires *playing by the rules*. While some go out of their way to avoid giving scriptural correction, others turn it into a big stick, swinging it at whoever seems to disagree with their views. The Scriptures tell us (in the context of heavenly rewards) that those who compete for a prize will disqualify themselves unless their conduct accords with the rules of the event (2 Timothy 2:5). This should also be applied to the way we go about contending for the faith, especially in regard to correcting one another. The first and foremost rule is love. Biblical correction is an act of love. Period. If one doesn't have a person's best interest at heart, love is not involved. If love isn't the motivating factor in correcting one another, the approach isn't biblical.

The manner in which we correct one another is an important part of "the rules" of contending for the faith. "And the servant of the Lord must not strive; but be gentle unto all men, apt to teach, patient, in meekness instructing those that oppose themselves; if God peradventure will give them repentance to the acknowledging of the truth" (2 Timothy 2:24–25). Yet a stern rebuke is also biblical; the Scriptures abound with examples of such reproofs and rebukes when the situation required it. But they are a far cry from correction accompanied by sarcasm, put-downs, attacks on personal character, and anything else that puffs up the corrector rather than ministering to the one being corrected. It's ironic that the prevailing humor (TV, comic strips, etc.) of this self-esteem-conscious, ego-sensitive generation is sarcasm, especially the put-down. Making someone else feel inferior has become the "in" way to boost one's own self-esteem.

A simple test for biblical correction here is the degree of smugness on the part of the corrector. If there's any at all—he fails. Another quick test is the "nastiness" barometer. If the one correcting treats another in a way he would object to being treated himself—he's part of the problem, not the biblical solution. To make that very point, we've been tempted to return some of the more malicious letters we've received to the writers with their own names superimposed over ours.

Contend—Don't Be Contentious

Earnestly contending for the faith involves *knowing what to contend for*. That which involves the direct subversion of the gospel, particularly the major doctrines related to salvation, demands our earnest concern and attention. The book of Galatians is a good example. The Judaizers were coercing believers into accepting a false gospel, i.e., adding certain deeds of the Law as a necessity for salvation. Paul earnestly contended with them, as he also instructed Titus to do (Titus 1:10–11,13). In a similar vein, we would and do contend with those who promote or accept a false gospel of salvation (e.g., Mormons, Christian Scientists, Jehovah's Witnesses, and Roman Catholics, among others).

Although some issues may not seem to be related to the gospel, they may indirectly subvert God's Word, turning believers away from the truth and thereby inhibiting the grace necessary for a life pleasing to the Lord. Psychotherapy, for example, is one of the most popular vehicles for turning Christians to the ungodly (and therefore grace-barren) solutions of men.

Contending for the faith also requires *knowing when to avoid contending*. Chapter 14 of Romans deals with matters where contending becomes contentiousness. Paul addresses situations where immature believers make issues of things that ought to remain nonissues. Some were bringing about division by contending over what foods should or should not be eaten or which day should be recognized as a day of worship. The scriptural counsel here is: there are some things that we should not judge, being peripheral issues that do not deny the faith, matters of decision for the individual conscience (v. 5). Only the Lord can judge one's heart and mind in such matters.

When Jesus discussed the signs of the last days with His disciples on the Mount of Olives (Matthew 24), the first sign He cited was religious deception. Its extent today is unprecedented in history. That fact alone ought to make our regard for earnestly contending for the faith a major concern. It also means that there are so many deviations from the faith (1 Timothy 4:1) to be considered, we may need to prioritize when and for what we contend. In regard to our own walk with the Lord, we are to examine everything that seems at odds with the Scriptures and make the necessary corrections. When it comes to biblically questionable teachings and practices being accepted and promoted by others, however, discernment may also include when and how to address them. These days, it's not uncommon to be wrongly perceived (or in fact to merit the reputation) as one who "finds fault with everything"; so seeking the Lord's wisdom and leading is always critical to our contending being fruitfully received.

Finally, earnestly contending for the faith is not *coercing* for the faith. Too often we forget that our eternal life in Christ came to us as a free gift, a gift of God's unfathomable love, which must be offered to others in love. Love is destroyed by coercion. Though we may not intend to force matters of the faith upon others, it's important to regularly check our motives and methods. Earnestly contending for the faith must be carried on as a love offering. We must remember that we are merely channels of that love, and if any change in the heart is to take place, it will be accomplished through the grace of God, who alone is the grantor of repentance (2 Timothy 2:25–26).

Acts 20:27–31 contains some thoughts that many today would regard as unbalanced in contending for "all the counsel of God," but they are God's words, passionately communicated by the Apostle Paul to those in the church at Ephesus *and to us: "Take heed therefore* unto yourselves, and to all the flock. . . . For I know this, that after my departing shall grievous wolves enter in among you, not sparing the flock. Also of your own selves shall men arise, speaking perverse things, to draw away disciples after them. Therefore *watch*, and *remember*, that by the space of three years *I ceased not to warn every one* night and day with tears."

In these "perilous" last days (2 Timothy 3:1), please pray that all of us, like Paul, demonstrate a passionate concern for the spiritual welfare of our brothers and sisters in Christ and for the purity of the gospel essential to the salvation of souls.

WHAT IS
"PSYCHOSPIRITUALITY"?

— T. A. McMahon —

THIS WORLD WE LIVE IN "AIN'T HEAVEN." Multitudes of problems that constantly beset believers and unbelievers alike make that very apparent. But Jesus said that He came that we might have life, even a more abundant life (John 10:10), and His words indicate His willingness to help those who commit their lives to Him. His offer is not only incredibly wonderful (after all, He's the almighty God!); it is the only true help available. God alone knows every thought, every action, every variable, how they interact, and what good or evil they will produce. The Spirit of Christ is our personal counselor. God's Word is our only true counseling manual, containing His insights, His corrections, His tender mercies, and His healing balm for whatever afflicts our heart and soul. Even so, a staggering number of His own want "a second opinion."

This ominous trend taking place among today's evangelicals is greatly diminishing an already threadbare reliance upon the Word of God. It's particularly dangerous because much of it sounds biblical, and its chief promoters are, for the most part, highly influential evangelical leaders. This trend involves approaching life, solving its problems, increasing its benefits, even enriching one's relationship with the Lord, through psychospiritual concepts, techniques, and methods.

The term "psychospiritual" will likely not be found in your dictionary, so here is our definition: Simply stated, it involves adding psychology to things spiritual. That would include one or more of the following innovations: *supplementing* spiritual content with psychological teachings; *interpreting* or explaining the spiritual through psychological concepts; *validating* the spiritual through the alleged science of psychology; *integrating* the spiritual with psychology. The term applies to the spiritualizing of psychology as well. For example, transpersonal psychology, the field's latest stage, has a vocabulary and concepts that are blatantly religious. Consider this quote in the *Association for Humanistic Psychology* (AHP) *Newsletter*: "AHP has always held spiritual concerns close to its heart. . . . We have championed the return of spirit to therapy."

As Christians, we reject all psychology that implicitly or explicitly professes: a) to have scientific understanding of the inner (mental, emotional, moral) workings of man; b) to have an objective knowledge of his nature, and/or c) to offer the cure for the problems of man's soul. We recognize that there are endeavors that would come under the umbrella of psychology and that fall outside the above description and its related concerns. However, the very few exceptions to the multibillion-dollar field of psychotherapy and its accompanying markets are hardly a redeeming factor. Psychological counseling is a religious wolf in pseudoscientific clothing. As Martin and Deidre Bobgan have stated (and impressively documented in their many books on the subject), "psychological explanations about life and psychological solutions to life's problems are questionable at best, detrimental at worst, and spiritual counterfeits at least." The bottom line regarding the psychospiritual approach is this: it is a delusion.

True spirituality has nothing to do with psychology (1 Corinthians 2:11), a fake science based primarily on man's rationalizations, i.e., self-deceptions. True spirituality isn't something to which man's wisdom (1 Corinthians 1:20) can *contribute*, nor can man *validate* the teachings of the Scriptures. As Christians, true spirituality is a product only of our submission and obedience by His grace to His Word (John 14:15). The idea that man can add anything to God's way is utter folly. Who would even dare? Yet, as obvious as that answer should be, the psychospiritual delusion continues to grow.

The Masculine Journey: Fallacy of the "Phallic Jesus"

One summer, not long ago, fifty thousand-plus gathered in Colorado for the Promise Keepers Christian Men's Conference. Colorado football coach Bill McCartney, founder of the organization, declared in his address, "We're going to contest anything that sets itself up against the name of Jesus Christ." Obviously, the coach hadn't "scouted" psychospirituality. Two of the main speakers at the conference were psychologist James Dobson and psychology popularizer Gary Smalley. Of even more concern than what attendees heard from the speakers was the fact that each man received a complimentary hardback copy of *The Masculine Journey: Understanding the Six Stages of Manhood* by psychotherapist Robert Hicks (foreword by psychologist John Trent).

The book, written to help "provide directions for a man's life so that he doesn't get lost along the way," consists primarily of psychologically biased conjecture centering around six Hebrew words. In chapter after chapter, subjective insights into manhood are offered through quotes by a host of secular authors with a psychological bent, including Carl Jung, inner-healing therapist Leanne Payne, transpersonal psychiatrist/spiritualist Elizabeth Kübler-Ross, and Sam Keen, former theologian in residence at Esalen, the New Age/Eastern mystical therapeutic center south of San Francisco. Keen's books feature vicious diatribes against biblical Christianity.

The author of *The Masculine Journey*, who is also a pastor and seminary professor of pastoral theology, demonstrates what a perverting influence a psychospiritual bias can have. Consider the following small sampling of quotes (his and others') related to just two of man's alleged stages.

The *phallic stage*:

> Possessing a penis places unique requirements upon men before God in how they are to worship Him. We are called to worship God as phallic kinds of guys, not as some sort of androgynous, neutered nonmales, or the feminized males so popular in many feminist-enlightened churches. . . .
>
> I believe Jesus was phallic with all the inherent phallic passions we experience as men.

This seems to be either the result of Freudian brainwashing or hanging out in locker rooms. Either way, it's blasphemous.

Regarding man's (emotionally) *wounded stage*:

> In order for men to discover what manhood is all about, they must descend into the deep places of their own souls and find their accumulated grief. . . .
>
> I am convinced many men in our society today are lashing out at women, at society, at bosses, even at God, all because they do not understand the wounding experience. . . .
>
> The story of Jacob . . . illustrates a young man having been severely wounded by a dysfunctional family system.

One would have to be totally indoctrinated by inner-healing psychobabble to derive even a jot of such nonsense from the Bible.

There are just too many biblically erroneous teachings in Hicks's book to cover here. Most involve his interpretations based upon psychology. Where do you find male and female *categories* of emotional woundedness? or anatomically related worship? Where do you find *understanding manhood* as a key to a godly life? You don't, if you simply take Scripture at its word: "There is neither Jew nor Greek, there is neither bond nor free, there is neither male nor female: for ye are all one in Christ Jesus (Galatians 3:28).

At the end of the book, we find this statement: "Promise Keepers wants to provide men's materials like this book. . . . " Dr. James Dobson, on a radio broadcast, held out great hope that Promise Keepers would stir the coals of revival among men in this country. That is indeed a worthwhile hope, but it grieves us deeply to see that the sparks of truth are being fanned into false flames by the winds of psychospirituality. The unbiblical preoccupation of this Christian men's movement is with man himself and from man's perspective. It could only truly live up to Coach McCartney's "contending for the faith" exhortation by getting back to the basics of the faith. The emphasis has to be focusing on God himself, getting to know Him and His way through His Word. If not, it is at best doomed to a grace-barren, fleshly form of godliness. Sadly, attendees were encouraged in a postconference follow-up letter to purchase the study guide and to form *The Masculine Journey* study groups.

Lonely No More: A Tobiah in the Temple?

Whereas Hicks's book is designed to appeal to men, an even more destructive psychospiritual offering has been published for women. As a prolific author, television personality (*Focal Point*), radio broadcaster (*The Chapel of the Air*), and popular speaker at Christian women's conferences, Karen Mains has few peers when it comes to influence upon evangelical women. She served for eight years as chairperson of the trustee board for InterVarsity Christian Fellowship/USA and on the Board of Reference of Renovaré (Richard Foster's Christian mysticism organization). Her heretical book *Lonely No More* is an exercise in journaling, i.e., writing down one's spiritual experiences, thoughts, emotions, dream interpretations, communications with God (and vice versa). In it she reveals her innermost "wounds," aspirations—and has an axe or two to grind.

The psychospiritual aspects of the book are reflected primarily in its *inner-healing* foundation—a mixture of Freudian/Jungian concepts and spiritual beliefs, practices, and techniques. Karen received training in inner healing at the School of Pastoral Care established by Agnes Sanford, and considers Sanford disciple and inner-healing/spiritual therapist Leanne Payne to be one of her personal "spiritual directors" (see *The Seduction of Christianity* regarding the occultic aspects of Agnes Sanford and inner healing).

Inner loneliness and deep soul wounds, resulting from husband David's workaholism and lack of sensitivity to her needs, from Christian males resenting her leadership qualities, and from past experiences of repressive evangelical restrictions (theological and cultural), are among the "emotional hurts" Mains attempts to deal with throughout her book. The route of psychospiritual self-therapy through which she leads the reader is a deadly swamp of subjectivity infested with Jungian dream analysis, symbolic imagery, shamanic visualization, interactive communication with dream entities, projections from the (Freudian) subconscious, and mystical contemplative prayer and fasting. Her Jungian "spiritual director," a Roman Catholic nun and director of novice training, becomes her guide on her soul journey.

Karen reassures her (more than likely evangelical) readers that "spiritual directors are a part of the Catholic tradition . . . who stand beside others in their spiritual pilgrimages and assist them . . . in the practice of gazing Godward. Some Catholic seminaries offer advanced degrees in spiritual direction." Rather than reassuring, it's particularly frightening that a woman who claims to be "a historical evangelical" and "well aware of the dangers of undisciplined subjectivity" would buy into such spiritual mockery, let alone try to pass it off as beneficial in knowing God.

In qualifying her admittedly "subjective experiences of the supernatural," she offers that the experiences "must not offend Scripture, orthodox doctrine or the traditions of the historical saints who have made the pilgrimage before me." The latter two "qualifiers" might be of value to Roman Catholics but certainly not to a Berean (Acts 17:10-11). And there is abundant evidence throughout the book that her penchant for the psychospiritual has corrupted whatever biblical sense she may have had. Consider the following:

> Through my hardships I discover there's a small part of myself that hasn't grown whole along with the rest of me. It's been maimed by neglect during years of married life. I call it my "idiot-self." I'm discovering that this malnourished orphan needs to be nursed and nurtured. I must find the idiot-self creeping about in the infrastructure of my soul. . . . Self of my self, this abandoned child is very much a part of me. . . . I understand that in some way, I, the intuitive, introverted, feeling-proficient female, have become the substitute for [my husband] David's own female self, his anima, to use the Jungian terminology. He . . . functions for me as my animus. . . . I have abdicated to my husband my own maleness.

In addition to the book's Jungian and mystical preoccupation with self, the author offers the basic thesis of humanistic and Christian psychology: "My great concern is loving David; my great concern is loving myself. I know I will not care for him well until I learn to care for myself well." That is *not* the way Jesus put it, nor is it the way of the sacrificial love He demonstrated and promises to live through us.

Although *Lonely No More* may be its author's most blatant exposure of what she believes, she and her husband David have championed psychospirituality for decades, from their radio and television shows to the material used in their 50-Day Spiritual Adventure for churches.

The books addressed above are merely two among hundreds like them currently offered in local Christian bookstores. Psychospirituality is being offered by and for Christians in every medium available. It is big-time. The two top-rated Christian radio programs are hosted by a psychologist and two psychiatrists: Drs. James Dobson, Frank Minirth and Paul Meier. Christian psychotherapeutic centers, the biggest advertisers on Christian radio, overflow with believers. Psychological evaluation of those desiring to go into the mission field is becoming the rule; some missions organizations even offer or require training in psychological counseling. And with the blessing of numerous evangelical luminaries, a psychology-influenced gospel is being exported worldwide.

Is psychospirituality what the body of Christ needs today, even though it was unknown to believers for nearly two millennia? What's the fruit of this new thing? Can it add anything of genuine spiritual value to what has been readily available from the Holy Spirit since the beginning of the church? Is it a necessary supplement in order to produce *love, joy, peace, longsuffering, kindness, goodness, faithfulness, gentleness, self-control* (Galatians 5:22–23) in the life of a believer?

Pray and encourage fellow believers in Christ to drink from the Lord's pure, life-giving, and grace-abundant waters rather than from spiritually toxic streams polluted by psychospirituality. Pray also that, just as Nehemiah was given the spiritual fortitude to throw the subversive Tobiah the Ammonite (Nehemiah 13:4–8) and all his belongings out of God's temple, so too will God's people have similar strength and courage to jettison from His church the psychospiritual approach with all of its destructive baggage.

"A Way Which Seemeth Right"

— T. A. McMahon —

There is a way which seemeth right unto a man,
but the end thereof are the ways of death. –PROVERBS 14:12

I RECENTLY ATTENDED THE Celebrate Recovery Summit 2005 at Saddleback Church in Southern California. The primary purpose of the conference was to train new leaders who would return to their churches and inaugurate the Celebrate Recovery (CR) program. Saddleback's pastor, Rick Warren, describes CR as "a biblical and balanced program to help people overcome their hurts, habits, and hang-ups . . . [that is] based on the actual words of Jesus *rather than psychological theory* [emphasis added]." [1]

As a long-time critic of psychological counseling and 12-Steps therapies in the church (see *The Seduction of Christianity*), I was pleased to have the opportunity to learn firsthand from those who are leading and/or participating in the program, to better understand what was intended in CR and to see how it is implemented. What I learned right away was that the three thousand or so in attendance had a tremendous zeal for the Lord and an unquestionable sincerity in desiring to help those who were struggling with habitual sin. This was my impression in all of my interactions—with individuals, in small groups, in workshop sessions, and in the general worship sessions. The CR Summit lasted three (eight- to nine-hour) days and covered nearly every aspect of Celebrate Recovery.

Other thoughts ran through my mind, however, as I reviewed whether I had missed something significant in my previous criticisms of 12-Steps recovery therapies. Is Celebrate Recovery's 12-Steps program truly different—that is, "biblical and balanced . . . rather than psychological"—as Rick Warren believes? Furthermore, is he simply naïve when he says in his "Road to Recovery" series of sermons, "In 1935 a couple of guys formulated, *based upon the Scriptures*, what are now known as the classic twelve steps of Alcoholics Anonymous and used by hundreds of other recovery groups. Twenty million Americans are in a recovery group every week and there are 500,000 recovery groups. *The basis is God's Word* [emphasis added]." Or is Celebrate Recovery another alarming example of *a way that seems right to a man* but is actually turning believers to ways and means other than the Bible to solve their sin-related problems? Let's consider these questions in light of some A.A. and 12 Steps background information.

Dubious Beginnings

To begin with, 12-Steps programs are not only a Saddleback Church issue. Increasing numbers of evangelical churches are sponsoring Alcoholics Anonymous (A.A.) and Narcotics Anonymous (N.A.) meetings and/or creating their own self-help groups based upon A.A.'s 12-Steps principles. Bill Wilson, one of the founders of A.A., created the 12 Steps. Wilson was a habitual drunk who had two life-changing events that he claims helped him achieve sobriety: 1) he was (mis)informed by a doctor that his drinking habit was a disease and was therefore not his fault, and 2) he had an experience (which he viewed as spiritual enlightenment) that convinced him that only "a Power greater than" himself could keep him sober. Attempting to understand his mystical experience, he was led into spiritism, a form of divination condemned in the Scriptures. His official biography indicates that the content of the 12-Steps principles came to him "rapidly" through spirit communication. It certainly didn't come from God through His Word.

Celebrate Recovery began fourteen years ago at Saddleback and is used in more than thirty-five hundred churches today, making it evangelical Christianity's most prominent and widely exported 12-Steps church program. Warren considers CR to be "the center of living a purpose-driven life and building a purpose-driven church" and recently announced that Chuck Colson's Prison Fellowship would begin implementing CR in every prison where the ministry is functioning.

Celebrate Recovery is a very complex methodology that attempts to bring biblical adjustments to the 12-Steps program originated by A.A. and utilized in numerous other "addiction" recovery programs. The complexity, however, applies to the setting up and implementation of the program as well as to the strict rules that govern its execution. Although there are many problems related to "making it work," there is only space in this article to address some fundamental issues. Let's begin with the implications regarding the name of the program.

Reflecting A.A.'s influence upon CR, the term "Recovery" is significant. All those in A.A. are "recovering" alcoholics, who, according to A.A., never completely recover. Recovery is a term that primarily denotes a process of physical healing. A.A. teaches that alcoholism is a disease for which there is no ultimate cure. Although CR rejects A.A.'s view of alcoholism as a disease and calls it sin, the title nevertheless promotes the A.A. concept in contradiction to what the Bible teaches. Sin is not something from which a believer is "in recovery." Sin is confessed by the sinner and forgiven by God. The believer is cleansed of the sin right then. "I said, I will confess my transgressions unto the LORD; and thou forgavest the iniquity of my sin" (Psalm 32:5).

At the 2005 Celebrate Recovery Summit, every speaker introduced himself or herself in the A.A. "recovery" mode, with this "Christianized" difference: "Hi, I'm so and so . . . and I'm a believer in Jesus Christ who struggles with issues of (alcohol, drug, codependency, sex, or whatever) addiction." The audience then applauded to affirm the individual for overcoming the "denial" of his or her habitual sin. Not to confess some "addiction" or specific sin struggle raises suspicions of "being in denial." Throughout the three-day conference there was never a hint from any of the speakers that anything about A.A., 12 Steps, or CR might not be biblical. Moreover, where Celebrate Recovery programs were not available, those "in recovery" were encouraged to attend A.A. or N.A. meetings.

From the Words of Jesus—or Bill Wilson?

Rick Warren, on video, reassured the Summit attendees that CR was no manmade therapy. He insisted that CR was based upon the "actual words of Jesus Christ from the eight Beatitudes, which parallel the 12 Steps" and identified his own "Higher Power: His name is Jesus Christ." I don't find "Higher Power," which is a misrepresentation of God, in the Bible. Nor can I fathom why a Bible-believing Christian would want to promote Bill Wilson's concept and methodology. Why not simply rely on what the Bible teaches?

Is God's way completely sufficient to set one free from so-called addictions? Did A.A.'s founders provide a more effective way? If so, what did the church do for the nearly two thousand years prior to Bill Wilson's "spiritually enlightened" way to recovery? Moreover, if Wilson's method really works, why are some in the church trying to add Jesus as one's Higher Power and the Beatitudes to it? On the other hand, if the effectiveness of the 12-Steps program is questionable and detrimental to the gospel and to a believer's life and growth in Christ, why attempt to "Christianize" such a program? It is imperative that all believers ask themselves whether they truly believe that the Scriptures and the enablement of God's Holy Spirit are sufficient for "all things that pertain unto life and godliness" (2 Peter 1:3). A rejection of this biblical teaching is the only possible justification for turning to ways the Bible condemns: "the counsel of the ungodly" (Psalm 1:1) and "a way which seemeth right unto a man."

How dependent is Celebrate Recovery upon (with minor modifications) A.A.'s 12 Steps? Completely! Those going through CR's small group take from twelve to sixteen months to complete the 12-Steps program. Many go through more than one small group and often become leaders in one while attending others. Without Bill Wilson's principles, the CR program would be reduced to a handful of misapplied Bible verses. Tragically, the most obvious biblical problem with such an approach to overcoming habitual sins seems to be dismissed by all 12-Steps advocates: the Bible never offers a by-the-numbers *self-help* methodology for deliverance from sin or for living a sanctified life. God's way involves obedience to His *full counsel* and maturity in Christ through the enablement of His Holy Spirit.

Warren's CR program views the 12 Steps as generally compatible with Scripture and seeks out verses that appear to biblically reinforce each step. In doing so, however, scriptural interpretations are forced upon concepts that either have no direct relationship to the Bible or that pervert the true interpretation of the scripture intended to support the particular step. CR's attempt to use the Beatitudes as biblical principles for overcoming habitual sins, for example, is a serious distortion of the Word of God.

Search as you may, you'll find no commentaries that even hint at such a use of the Beatitudes. Why? Simply because the Beatitudes have *everything* to do with seeking the Kingdom of God and *nothing* to do with solving an individual's so-called addictions. Again, why try to legitimize from Scripture Wilson's "ungodly counsel" from "seducing spirits [bringing] doctrines of devils" (1 Timothy 4:1)?

Consider, for example, the "Beatitudes-justified" first three steps: (1) We admitted we were powerless over our addictions and compulsive behaviors; that our lives had become unmanageable: "Happy are those who are spiritually poor." (2) Came to believe that a power greater than ourselves could restore us to sanity: "Happy are those who mourn, for they shall be comforted." (3) Made a decision to turn our life and our will over to the care of God (modified from A.A.'s "God as we understood Him"): "Happy are the meek."

This is more than a misdirected attempt to sanctify Bill Wilson's "biblically vague" (in Rick Warren's words) 12 Steps.[2] It both abuses the Scriptures and reinterprets Wilson.

In the first three foundational steps of A.A., Wilson is summarizing his beliefs based upon his experiences as a "recovering alcoholic." He felt "powerless" because he believed alcoholism was an incurable disease that consequently made his life "unmanageable." Since he couldn't "cure" himself (although millions manage to overcome this without 12-Steps or other therapies!), he put his faith in "a power greater than ourselves," whom he called God, and "understood" Him by fabricating Him out of beliefs discovered in his study of different religions and religious experiences. That's more than "biblically vague." It's a false religion.

If It Works, Don't Fix It—But Does It Work?

So why would Celebrate Recovery or the multitudes of other Christianized 12 Steps groups try to reconcile the Word of God with Wilson's definitely erroneous and demonically inspired methodology? The deluded response is: "Because it works!" But does it?

Pragmatism is the fuel that powers "the way that seems right" and governs much of what is being lauded in the church today. Not only is this unbiblical, but too often there is nothing beyond enthusiastic testimonials to support the claim that something actually works. The reality of the 12-Steps program of A.A. and N.A. is that there is *no research evidence proving that they are more effective than other treatments*. Furthermore, the most extensive studies related to "addictions" conclude that most drug and alcohol abusers recover without *any* psychotherapeutic treatment or self-help therapies.[3]

The many problems inherent within a Christianized 12-Steps program— and particularly Celebrate Recovery—are too numerous for this brief chapter. Yet, consider these observations: CR is highly promoted as completely biblical and not psychological, yet the key speakers for CR Summit 2005 were clinical psychologists Drs. John Townsend and Henry Cloud. Psychologist David Stoop, the editor of *Life Recovery Bible* (CR participants' mandatory paraphrase Bible, polluted with psychotherapy commentary), is a favorite speaker at Saddleback's CR Large Group meetings. The CR leadership manual advises, "Have Christian psychotherapists volunteer their time to help instruct and support your leaders."[4]

CR's entire program content is marbled with psychobabble such as this "solution" from its Adult Children of the Chemically Addicted group's dogmas: "The solution is to become your own loving parent. . . . You will recover the child within you, learning to accept and love yourself."[5] This is biblical?! Honoring the psychologically contrived "disorder" of codependency, CR's Codependency and Christian Living group made this humanistic and biblically false statement: "Jesus taught. . . . A love of self forms the basis for loving others."[6]

A.A.'s 12-Steps methodology, along with its antibiblical psychotherapeutic concepts and practices, permeates Celebrate Recovery, yet no one at the Summit with whom I spoke seemed concerned. CR's small group meetings are the antithesis of the way the Bible instructs mature believers to help those young or struggling in the faith to grow. Pastors and elders can be small group leaders but not for teaching purposes. No leader may biblically instruct or correct but may only affirm the "transparency" of the participant sharing his feelings. "Cross-talk," or comments by others, are prohibited to allow the freest expression possible. Much of this "expression" reinforces psychotherapeutic myths. The two-hour meetings usually open with the spiritually anemic Serenity Prayer and the recitation of the 12 Steps. Leaders are drawn from those who have completed one or more 12-Step groups. Some leaders work through one "addiction" in a small group while leading another group. It's not unusual for a leader to put in eight to ten hours in CR functions per week, every week. Serious Bible study and discipleship are not part of the Celebrate Recovery "biblical" emphasis.

Let no one think that presenting these critical concerns about Celebrate Recovery in any way lessens the biblical obligation (Galatians 6) of the church to minister to those struggling with habitual sin. The issue is not whether we *should* minister, but *how* we should minister: man's way or God's way? Man's way, or *a mixture of biblical teaching and ungodly counsel*, is contrary to God's way. Man's way leads to death. Applying Scripture to man's way leads to a slower death, akin to what would result when pure water is added to a toxic drinking fountain. We desperately need to take heed to God's admonition through the Prophet Jeremiah:

> *For my people have committed two evils; they have forsaken me the fountain of living waters, and hewed them out cisterns, broken cisterns, that can hold no water.* —JEREMIAH 2:13

---

1. *Celebrate Recovery Summit 2005* Handbook, 61.

2. *Celebrate Recovery Senior Pastor Support Video,* 2003.

3. *The Harvard Mental Health Letter,* Vol. 16, No. 12, 1-4; See also www.stats.org/issuerecord.jsp?issue=true&ID=8.

4. *Celebrate*, 31.

5. Ibid., 342.

6. Ibid., 350.

PSYCHOLOGY AND
THE EVANGELICAL CHURCH

— T. A. McMahon —

NOTHING IN THE HISTORY of the modern church has induced believers to abandon their faith in the sufficiency of God's Word like the pseudo-science of psychological counseling. Consider the following: the evangelical church is a primary referral service for counseling psychologists and psychiatrists. Many large churches have licensed psychotherapists on staff. Mission agencies are requiring their missionary candidates to be evaluated and approved by licensed psychological professionals prior to being considered for service. Christian psychologists and counselors are often better known and more respected by evangelicals than preachers and teachers.

Most evangelicals are convinced that psychotherapy is scientific and that it is necessary to supply what is lacking in the Bible regarding man's mental, emotional, and behavioral needs. When I use the term "psychotherapy," I am referring to psychological counseling, clinical psychology, and (non-biological) psychiatry. I may also use the general term "psychology." I recognize that there are some areas of psychology that are clearly distinct from psychotherapy and may have scientific merit and value, e.g., those fields that study perception, man-machine interface, ergonomics, some educational psychology, and so forth. They are, however, a very small percentage of the entire industry of psychology, which claims to have scientific insights into the mind of man.

So what's the problem with psychotherapy? According to numerous scientific studies, it rarely works (and then only superficially) and is known to be harmful. From a biblical perspective, it is an antichristian, religious counterfeit. Both conclusions will become quite apparent as we proceed.

Given the significant influence it has had on the church, the psychological way compared to the biblical way should be an issue of critical concern for all those who believe that the Word of God is their authority and that it is completely sufficient for "all things that pertain unto life and godliness" (2 Peter 1:3). How do these two ways compare?

They couldn't be more at odds. The basic theories of psychological counseling are contradictory to what the Bible teaches about the nature of man and God's solution for his mental, emotional, and behavioral problems. Psychotherapeutic concepts regard humanity as intrinsically good. The Bible says that—other than Jesus Christ—man is *not* good but was born with a sinful nature, "for all have sinned, and come short of the glory of God" (Romans 3:23).

Psychological counseling often promotes the belief that problems adversely affecting a person's mental and emotional welfare are determined by circumstances external to the person, such as parental abuse or environment. The Bible tells us that a man's evil heart and his sinful choices cause his mental, emotional, and behavioral problems. "For from within, out of the heart of men, proceed evil thoughts, adulteries, fornications, murders, thefts, covetousness, wickedness, deceit, lasciviousness, an evil eye, blasphemy, pride, foolishness: All these evil things come from within, and defile the man" (Mark 7:21–23).

Psychotherapy attempts to improve the self through concepts such as self-love, self-esteem, self-worth, self-image, self-actualization, etc. The Bible teaches that Self *is* humanity's main problem, not the solution to the ills that plague mankind. And it prophetically identifies the chief solution of psychological counseling, self-love, as the catalyst to a life of depravity. "This know also, that in the last days perilous times shall come. For men shall be lovers of their own selves. . . ." (2 Timothy 3:1).

The Bible teaches that reconciliation to God through Jesus Christ is the only way for man to truly remedy his sin-related mental, emotional, and behavioral troubles. "And you, that were sometime alienated and enemies in your mind by wicked works, yet now hath he [Jesus Christ] reconciled in the body of his flesh through death, to present you holy and unblameable and unreproveable in [God's] sight" (Colossians 1:21–22).

Psychotherapy has shipwrecked the faith of many regarding the sufficiency of the Bible. Because psychologists claim to have insights into the nature of man and also methods for change not found in the Bible, it follows that the Bible cannot be sufficient for counseling or addressing believers' mental, emotional, and behavioral needs.

Psychotherapy has sold the church the lie that psychology can be integrated with the Bible. That idea ought to be scandalous to any thoughtful believer. Since psychology and the Bible are fundamentally in opposition to one another, it should be obvious that there can be no real integration of their teachings. Moreover, if the Bible, the Manufacturer's handbook, isn't sufficient to cover all things that pertain to life and godliness, then His created beings must look elsewhere for their mental, emotional, and behavioral welfare. And if they must look elsewhere, then the Bible's claim to be authoritative, inerrant, and sufficient is also false.

How influential is psychotherapy in the church? It is becoming rare indeed to find a topical sermon with no supposed insights from psychology. Typical would be Willow Creek church near Chicago, whose influence is national and international through its ten-thousand-member association of churches. One researcher of church-growth methods who spent a year at Willow Creek observed, "[Pastor Bill] Hybels not only teaches psychological principles but often uses the psychological principles as interpretive guides for his exegesis of Scripture. . . . King David had an identity crisis, the apostle Paul encouraged Timothy to do self-analysis, and Peter had a problem with boundary issues. The point is, psychological principles are regularly built into Hybels' teaching." Rick Warren's record-breaking *The Purpose-Driven Life* furthers the acceptance of psychology in the church by including such psychobabble as "Samson was co-dependent" and "Gideon's weakness was low self-esteem and deep insecurities."

Why this psychologizing of Christianity? Well, primarily because the church has been sold three erroneous ideas:

1) Psychotherapy is a scientific endeavor
2) Counseling is for professionals only
3) Christian psychology reconciles science and faith

Let's look at each of these. *First*, psychotherapy is not a scientific endeavor. Martin and Deidre Bobgan report in their book, *The End of "Christian Psychology"*:

> Attempting to evaluate the status of psychology, the American Psychological Association appointed Dr. Sigmund Koch to plan and direct a study which was subsidized by the National Science Foundation. This study involved eighty eminent scholars assessing the facts, theories, and methods of psychology. The results of this extensive endeavor were published in a seven-volume series entitled *Psychology: A Study of a Science*.

Dr. Koch sums up the panel's findings in these words: "I think it is by this time utterly and finally clear that psychology cannot be a coherent science."

Dr. Karl Popper, regarded as one of the greatest philosophers of science, after a thorough study of psychotherapy, declared: "though posing as sciences [psychotherapy] had in fact more in common with primitive myths than with science [and] resembled astrology rather than astronomy."

Secondly, counseling is *not* for professionals only. Psychotherapy, thanks to Freud and some others with medical backgrounds, has terms and concepts that falsely give the impression that they have to do with medical science. An understanding of the term "illness" is key to seeing through this mirage.

Can one's mental process—that is, his thinking or behavior—literally be ill? Our brains, which are physical, can certainly be, but our *minds*, which are nonphysical, can't be ill. So the term "mental illness" is a misnomer—a myth. Furthermore, with exceptions in the area of psychiatry, psychotherapists do not address the organic or physical problems of their clients.

So, what do psychotherapists do? Well, mostly they talk and listen. Research psychiatrist Dr. Thomas Szasz spells it out for us: "In plain language, what do patient and psychotherapist actually do? They speak and listen to each other. What do they speak about? Narrowly put, the patient speaks about himself, and the therapist speaks about the patient. . . . Each tries to move the other to see or do things in a certain way."

I assume that most evangelicals, whether in the pulpit or pew, can certainly handle the medium of counseling—which is simply talking and listening! But, few of us are trained professionals. We don't have an advanced degree in talking and listening, nor have we studied theories about human behavior, which are nothing more than the opinions and speculations of godless men. Furthermore, there are more than five hundred different (often contradictory and sometimes utterly bizarre) psychotherapeutic systems and thousands of methods and techniques.

So, as nonprofessionals, we missed out on all of that knowledge-so-called. But still, aren't professionals more effective than nonprofessionals in helping people with their problems? No!

After reviewing the research comparing trained and untrained psychological counselors, researchers Truax and Mitchell report: "There is no evidence that the usual traditional graduate training program has any positive value in producing therapists who are more helpful than nonprofessionals."

Consider the conclusion of a lengthy research project conducted by Dr. Joseph Durlak:

> Overall, outcome results in comparative studies have favored non-professionals. . . . There were no significant differences among helpers in 28 investigations, but nonprofessionals were significantly more effective than professionals in 12 studies.
>
> The provocative conclusion from these comparative investigations is that professionals do not possess demonstrably superior therapeutic skills, compared with nonprofessionals. Moreover, professional mental health education, training, and experience are not necessary prerequisites for an effective helping person.

Best-selling author, psychologist Dr. Bernie Zilbergeld, writes in his book, *The Shrinking of America: Myths of Psychological Change*: ". . . most problems faced by people would be better solved by talking to friends, spouses, relatives or anyone else who appears to be doing well what you believe you're doing poorly. . . . If I personally had a relationship problem and I couldn't work it out with my partner, I wouldn't go and see a shrink. I would look around me for the kind of relationship I admire. . . . That's who I would go to. I want somebody who's showing by his life that he can do it."

Now that's just good commonsense advice from a man who understands the field of psychotherapy. Yet, in this "perilous time" for the church, many (and the numbers continue to grow) have abandoned not only "common sense," but worse yet, they have discarded their biblical mandate, which is to minister to one another through the Word of God and in the power of the Holy Spirit. They've been intimidated by myths and have turned from the truth.

Finally, Christian psychology cannot reconcile science and faith. Why not? Because psychology is not a science, nor can it be Christianized. Of course, there are Christians who are licensed professional psychotherapists, but there is no recognized branch or stream of psychology identified as Christian.

Consider this statement representing the view of the Christian Association for Psychological Studies:

> We are often asked if we are "Christian psychologists". . . . We are Christians who are psychologists but at the present time there is no acceptable Christian psychology that is markedly different from non-Christian psychology. It is difficult to imply that we function in a manner that is fundamentally distinct from our non-Christian colleagues . . . as yet there is not an acceptable theory, mode of research or treatment methodology that is distinctly Christian.

How then do licensed psychotherapists who are Christians function? They selectively draw from the concepts learned during their secular education and training and attempt to integrate them into their Christian belief system. Yet, the concepts are all antithetical to the biblical way of ministering to a believer's problems related to overcoming sin and living a life that is fruitful, productive, and pleasing to the Lord.

You have to wonder why a Christian would turn to any of these wisdom-of-men approaches that were conceived by people who were so obviously anti-Christian. Freud considered religion an illusion and was known to have a hatred for Christianity because of what he believed to be its anti-Semitic teachings. Others, such as Abraham Maslow and Carl Rogers, were blatant New

Agers and occultists. Yet, consider this quote from a leading Christian psychologist: "Under the influence of humanistic psychologists like Carl Rogers and Abraham Maslow, many of us Christians have begun to see our need for self-love and self-esteem. This is a good and necessary focus." Not according to the Scriptures!

The Book of Nehemiah gives us a picture of what's happening in the church. Nehemiah (his name means "Jehovah is our comforter") is a type of the Holy Spirit. God sends him to rebuild and strengthen Jerusalem. Under the guise of helping Nehemiah, enemies of Israel attempt to subvert the restoration. Incredibly, the priest gives one such adversary, Tobiah, a room within the Temple. So it is with so-called Christian psychology today.

How serious is this psychologizing of the church? Although devastating even now, Scripture tells us it will far exceed what we can imagine. The Apostle Paul is emphatic in his warning (2 Timothy 3:1–5) that "in the last days" man's condition will be "perilous." That warning begins with a characteristic that is the cornerstone of humanistic psychology and which Paul indicates (verses 2–5) is the source of a host of evils: self-love.

PSYCHOLOGY—THE "DOCTRINES OF DEVILS?"

— T. A. McMahon —

Now the Spirit speaketh expressly, that in the latter times some shall depart from the faith, giving heed to seducing spirits, and doctrines of devils. —1 TIMOTHY 4:1

IN PREVIOUS WRITINGS, I have addressed the destructive influence psychological counseling is having on the evangelical church. Simply put, the church has turned from God's Word to man's bankrupt theories in attempting to resolve mental, emotional, and behavioral problems. The greater part of the church no longer believes what the Scriptures proclaim: that God, in His Word, has given us "all things that pertain unto life and godliness, through the knowledge of him that hath called us to glory and virtue" (2 Peter 1:3). The results, sadly, are what one might expect: there is often little statistical difference between those who profess to be Christians and those who do not, regarding the number of divorces, the reliance upon psychological counseling theories and methods, living together outside of marriage, illegitimate childbirths, pornography, sexual and physical abuse, and so forth.

Although such consequences are shocking, they shouldn't be surprising to anyone who believes the Bible. Twice in the Book of Proverbs we are told, "There is a way which seemeth right unto a man, but the end thereof are the ways of death" (Proverbs 14:12; 16:25). Throughout Scripture, death implies separation, whether of the soul and spirit from the body in physical death or, in another sense, the separation of light from darkness and truth from error—and, ultimately and eternally, from God. Just as the body without life corrupts, so do one's life choices result in corruption when they are separated from God's truth.

Psychology, with its psychotherapeutic counseling, has been embraced by evangelicals more than almost any other unbiblical endeavor that has entered the church in the last half-century. "Christian psychologists" are generally more popular and influential than preachers and teachers of the Word. What evangelical in America doesn't know of psychologist Dr. James Dobson? The psychologically oriented American Association of Christian Counselors boasts fifty thousand members. The evangelical church is one of the leading referral services for secular counselors (whether they claim to be Christians or not!). Like their secular counterparts, the second-most popular career choice for students at Christian colleges is psychology. What makes this information truly shocking is the fact that the roots, concepts, and many of the psychological counseling practices come from "seducing spirits, and doctrines of devils."

First Timothy 4:1 is a prophetic verse. It foretells that "in the latter times" (that is, the time near the return of our Lord), "some shall depart from the faith." This departure is supported by other verses such as Luke 18:8, where Jesus asked, "When the Son of man cometh, shall he find faith on the earth?" The implied answer is no. Paul, in 2 Thessalonians 2:3, declares under the inspiration of the Holy Spirit that a "falling away" from the faith will characterize the Last Days. But haven't many professing Christians departed from the faith since the time of the apostles? Yes. The rest of the verse, however, indicates a condition that is unique to our present day. Those who profess to be Christians will give "heed to seducing spirits, and doctrines of devils."

There's a Snake in the Garden!

Doctrines of devils are designed to undermine what is taught in the Scriptures. They reflect the strategy that Satan instituted in the Garden of Eden when he seduced Eve into disobeying God. The chief of the seducing spirits began his direct communication with Eve by raising doubts in her mind as to what God had commanded: "Yea, hath God said. . . ?" (Genesis 3:1). The serpent's dialogue with her led her to believe that God had lied to her: "And the serpent said unto the woman, ye shall not surely die." Although God warned Adam and Eve that the punishment for disobeying Him by eating the fruit of a certain tree in the Garden would be death (Genesis 2:17), Satan twisted that clear warning around, making God not only a liar but also the one who was withholding what they needed for their self-improvement and for realizing a supposed higher potential.

Genesis 3:1–5 reveals Satan's basic strategy for the seduction and destruction of mankind. His deception began by *questioning* God's Word and offering tempting alternatives. Eve responded by believing Satan, *rejecting* God's Word, and turning to her own self-interests. The enticements were so desirable to the flesh, including immortality, enlightenment, godhood, and knowledge (Genesis 3:5), that she eagerly embraced the lie. At that tragic moment in the history of mankind, self became a god, an autonomous rebel bent on doing its own thing. What Satan offered to Eve, he likewise has presented to all of her descendants, with similar success. His deadly allurements—*immortality, enlightenment, godhood,* and *knowledge*—comprise the foundational teachings of "doctrines of devils."

Even in a cursory review of psychotherapeutic concepts, Satan's primary lies are clearly revealed. Teachings (i.e., doctrines) such as the following are found in nearly all psychotherapeutic theories:

> IMMORTALITY: There is no death in the sense that it should be feared. Materialist psychotherapists teach a judgment-free mortality; spiritually oriented counselors claim that we either evolve to a higher consciousness or reincarnate to improve our next temporal state of being.

> ENLIGHTENMENT: Knowing the self, who we are, why we do what we do, and how we change, all open the critical gate to establishing our mental wellbeing. Some systems teach that our problems of living are determined by traumas related to our past (including past lives), our parental upbringing, our environment, or our having been oppressed by religious dogmas.

> GODHOOD: The solution to humanity's problems is found within the self. Self is deified, whether directly or indirectly. For instance, psychology's "self-actualization" is a process that leads to self-deification, which ultimately replaces any need for salvation outside of man himself.

> KNOWLEDGE: The deification process for humanity involves methods of plumbing the depths of the unconscious, which is alleged to be the infinite reservoir that holds all mysteries of life.

Sadly, these doctrines of devils now permeate "Christian psychology." Few evangelicals realize that these demonic teachings were introduced to the "founding fathers of psychological counseling" *literally* by "seducing spirits."

The Freudian Spiritual Connection

It was Sigmund Freud who declared that "religion is the universal obsessional neurosis of humanity." Furthermore, there is evidence that Freud *hated* Christianity, which he erroneously regarded as anti-Semitic. How, then, would this atheistic rejecter of organized religion advance doctrines of devils? His master stroke would be founding the "religion" of psychoanalysis. None of Freud's theories, whether psychic determinism or psychosexual development or belief in the unconscious, have *any* scientific validity; moreover, they are religious beliefs that are antithetical to the doctrines of the Bible. Research psychiatrist Thomas Szasz had Freud primarily in mind when he declared, "Modern psychotherapy . . . is not merely a religion that pretends to be a science; it is actually a fake religion that seeks to destroy true religion."[1]

Given the fact that psychoanalysis and its associated concepts are so diametrically opposed to biblical Christianity, there's no doubt that Freud's "fake religion" is the product of "doctrines of devils." A strong case could further be made that Freud's theories came both directly and indirectly from "seducing spirits" through the techniques he employed in analyzing his patients. He put them into altered states of consciousness through hypnosis and the highly suggestible technique of "free association." Early on, when he was formulating some of his theories, Freud was a regular user of the mind-altering drug cocaine for his bouts with depression.[2] Calling it his magical drug, "he pressed it on his friends and colleagues, both for themselves and their patients."[3]

Psychiatrist and historian Henri F. Ellenberger's classic work, *The Discovery of the Unconscious*, reveals,

> Historically, modern dynamic psychotherapy derives from primitive medicine, and an uninterrupted continuity . . . through the exorcists, magnetists, and hypnotists that led to the fruition of dynamic psychiatry in the systems of Janet, Freud, Adler, and Jung.[4]

Psychotherapy is a modern form of shamanism, which explains why psychiatrist E. Fuller Torrey rightly observes,

> The techniques used by Western psychiatrists are, with few exceptions, on exactly the same scientific plane as the techniques used by witchdoctors [medicine men and shamans].[5]

Shamanism is all about contacting spirit entities to gain their help, wisdom, insights, and so forth. In an interview with a former Yanamamo shaman who resides in the Amazonian rain forest of Venezuela, I was told rather bluntly that his spirit guides were liars and deceivers, from his first contact with them through ingesting hallucinogenic drugs until they left him when he turned to Christ. Their lies reinforced what he wanted to hear. The same was true of Freud, whose concepts were a reflection not of science but rather removing his own guilt and satisfying his flesh. Freud's theories were based mainly upon his own personal problems, most of which were sexual perversions.

In Freudian thought, the *"unconscious"* is a God-replacement realm without laws and judgment; *morality* is an oppressive neurosis-generating structure imposed by society and organized religion; *sexual freedom* (including adultery, homosexuality, incest, etc.) is paramount for normal mental health; *dreams* are symbolic messages from the unconscious and can be scientifically interpreted through psychoanalysis. These beliefs represent doctrines of devils. Although a materialist, Freud acknowledged the existence of spirit entities. He was influenced from that source either indirectly, through his patients, or directly, through his own drug use, the replicas of pagan idols he used to help him write,[6] and other techniques he used to explore the unconscious.

Forever Jung

The life and works of psychiatrist Carl Gustav Jung clearly reveal that his psychological theories came directly from the "seducing spirits" Paul warns about in 1 Timothy 4:1. Jung is far more popular today among professing Christians than Freud (the atheist) because of his perceived affinity for religion and things spiritual. Although his father was a Protestant pastor (who seriously doubted his professed faith!), Jung was antibiblical and resentful of organized Christianity from his youth. His early symbolic visions revealed Jesus as a Dark Lord, and God defecating on a cathedral. His mother's side of the family was heavily involved in spiritualism. His grandfather, Pastor Samuel Preiswerk, conducted ongoing séances to commune with his deceased first wife while his second wife and daughter (Jung's mother) participated. The latter, who had bouts of insanity, reserved two beds in the Jung home for visiting ghosts. Jung's doctoral thesis (published in 1902) was based upon séances conducted by his thirteen-year-old cousin, whom he placed in an altered state of consciousness through hypnosis in order to contact his and her dead ancestors.

In 1916, Jung's household experienced an assault by demonic beings who claimed to be dead Christian Crusaders from Jerusalem. They were seeking counsel on redemption and were greatly distressed that their Christianity had left them in a hopeless condition. They would not leave Jung's home until he began writing advice to them, advice that he received from one of his many spirit guides, his mentor Philemon, the "old man with horns of a bull."[7]

Richard Noll, a lecturer in the History of Science at Harvard University and a clinical psychologist (who declares that he "is not a Christian of any sort"), makes some stunning observations in his book on Jung titled *The Jung Cult*. He argues that Jung's "psychological theories of the collective unconscious and archetypes are essentially masks—a pseudoscientific cover to hide the practices of what was essentially a new religious movement in which Jung taught people to have trance visions and to contact the 'gods' directly."[8]

Jung's teachings are doctrines of demons, gleaned directly from seducing spirits: the *unconscious* and the *collective unconscious* represent an impersonal form of God; *archetypes* are viewed as psychological rationalizations for demons, the *anima* and *animus* are terms for the female and male entities within each person; *psychological "types"* are determined characteristics within our makeup.

Jung promoted all things occult, including astrology, alchemy, the I-Ching, mysticism, necromancy, visualization, dream interpretation, the active imagination, yoga, meditation, etc. Incredibly, his theories and recommended practices are endorsed in the teachings of some of the most influential voices in the evangelical community. In many cases, ignorance is the principle reason, yet the demonic lies are nevertheless readily promoted and accepted among the sheep.

Spiritual Seduction within the Church

Rick Warren's 30 million copies of *The Purpose-Driven Life* include Jungian concepts, such as psychological "types." Saddleback Church's *Celebrate Recovery* program, which has been exported to forty-five hundred churches and Prison Fellowship Ministries, is based on A.A.'s "12-Step" principles. A.A. co-founder Bill Wilson received the "12 Steps" while he was in contact with spirit entities. He later wrote a personal letter to Carl Jung thanking him for his influence:

> [A.A.] actually started long ago in your consulting room, and it was directly founded upon your own humility and deep perception. . . . You will also be interested to learn that in addition to the "spiritual experience," many A.A.s report a great variety of psychic phenomena, the cumulative weight of which is very considerable. Other members have—following their recovery in A.A.—been much helped by [Jungian analysts]. A few have been intrigued by the "I Ching" and your remarkable introduction to that work.

Warren is not the only witting or unwitting promoter among evangelicals of what Jung learned from demons. He is just the most successful and the best known. Others include Christian psychologists, inner healers, and pastors. Jung's occult methodologies, especially his demonically inspired techniques of visualization, guided imagery, meditation, and working with spiritual directors, are foundational to the Emerging Church interests of evangelical youth and the contemplative movement supported by Richard Foster, Eugene Peterson, and a multitude of others.

This astonishing development in the evangelical church is symptomatic of the abandonment of God's Word. The result will be the advancement of the apostate "Christian" church. The antidote is found in Isaiah 8:20:

> *To the law and to the testimony: if they speak not according to this word, it is because there is no light in them.*

1. Thomas Szasz, *The Myth of Psychotherapy* (Doubleday, 1978), 27-28.

2. Martin Gross, *The Psychological Society* (Random House, 1978), 234-36.

3. Ernest Jones, *The Life and Work of Sigmund Freud, Volume I* (1856-1900) (New York: Basic Books, 1953), 81.

4. Henri F. Ellenberger, *The Discovery of the Unconscious* (Basic Books, 1970), 48; back cover.

5. E. Fuller Torrey, *The Mind Games: Witchdoctors and Psychiatrists* (Emerson Hall, 1972), 8.

6. Shirley Nicholson, *Shamanism* (The Theosophical Publishing House), 58, as cited in Martin and Deidre Bobgan, *The End of "Christian Psychology"* (EastGate Publishers, 1997), 105.

7. C. G. Jung, *Memories, Dreams, Reflections* (Pantheon Books, 1963), 182-83; 190-92.

8. Richard Noll, *The Jung Cult: Origins of a Charismatic Movement* (New York: Simon & Schuster, 1994), xi-xii.

IS PSYCHOLOGY MENTIONED
IN BIBLE PROPHECY?

— T. A. McMahon —

RECENTLY, I gave the title of this chapter as the topic for one of my messages to an individual who was putting together a prophecy conference. An obvious pause on his end of the phone line told me that he was trying to imagine how psychology might possibly fit in with the rebuilding of the Jewish Temple, the Great Tribulation, the Battle of Armageddon, the Antichrist and the False Prophet, and other events and individuals that are common subjects at prophecy conferences. When his lack of response began to approach that awkward stage, I slowly and deliberately quoted 2 Timothy 3:1–2: "This know also, that in the last days perilous times shall come. For men shall be lovers of their own selves. . . . "

"Go for it!" was his immediate response.

Although the conference organizer didn't know exactly how I was going to treat the subject, he immediately recognized the fit from the phrases: "the last days . . . perilous times . . . lovers of their own selves." It's very disturbing (yet understandable, as we will see) that most evangelicals (especially pastors) have missed the Apostle Paul's very clear, even strident, warning about the perils of self-love and its connection to psychology in the last days.

Me, Myself, and I

To better understand what Paul's concerns were, we need to start with a definition of the term "self." It simply means the person himself. It's *me*—and all that comprises me. Being a lover of my own self, then, means that I love *me*, first and foremost. Self fills up my heart, my mind, my will, my consciousness. Self, prior to salvation in Christ, is an autonomous being, doing its own thing in rebellion against God. For believers in Jesus who are new creatures in Christ (2 Corinthians 5:17), self should be in submission to Him. A true believer denies himself daily, takes up his cross, is crucified with Christ—and yet he lives, with his life being *in Christ* by faith (Matthew 16:24; Galatians 2:20).

Why did Paul put such an emphasis on *self* as an issue of critical concern in "the last days"? Hasn't "self" been mankind's common problem ever since the first act of disobedience against God in the Garden of Eden (Genesis 3)?

Wasn't Satan's seduction of Eve a lying appeal to enhance her "self"? Satan declared: "For God doth know that in the day ye eat thereof, then your eyes shall be opened, and ye shall be as gods, knowing good and evil" (3:5). And didn't Eve fall for his lies of *self-gratification* and *self-deification*? And wasn't *self-preservation* an obvious product of Adam and Eve's sin as they shifted the blame away from themselves? Hear Adam: "The woman whom thou gavest to be with me, she gave me of the tree. . . . " Then Eve: "The serpent beguiled me . . . " (3:12–13). Obviously, self took center stage in the life of mankind from sin's earthly birth and thereafter!

The Influence of Darwinian Thought

Yet Paul indicates a special emphasis on self in the "last days." Although self-seeking and self-serving have been dominant characteristics of mankind as far back as the Fall, it has only been *since the rise of modern psychology* that self has been proclaimed as the *solution* to all of our mental, emotional, and behavioral ills. This was a new development of the nineteenth century that became inevitable as Darwinian "scientists" began promoting their own theory of man's origin. Why inevitable? Because as God "lost" His position as mankind's Creator, He eventually was replaced altogether. Evolutionary theory eliminated any necessity for God, since all life, we were told, came about through *natural* processes. Taking God out of the picture of life left us with only Self, resulting in *humanity* becoming the measure of all things. That attempt, however, has left evolutionists/humanists with a dilemma.

On the one hand, man has been "relieved" of his accountability to his Creator; on the other hand, he's left by himself to solve all of his problems. This evolutionary and humanistic belief posits that within man is the ultimate and necessary potential for coming up with these solutions. The *Humanist Manifesto I* declares, "Man is at last becoming aware that he alone is responsible for the realization of the world of his dreams, that he has within himself the power for its achievement." If the solutions are not within self, then godless mankind has nowhere else to turn, and, consequently, humanity has no hope. We are assured by today's psychotherapists, however, that the cures for humanity's ills are indeed found within mankind. Thus, Paul's prophetic warning regarding the "last days" being "perilous times" and characterized primarily by men being "lovers of their own selves" is more fitting to our time than to any other period in history.

Replacing God with Self leads to the central dogma of the religion of psychology: *mankind is innately good.* Psychotherapy is an exercise in futility unless innate goodness resides within man at his very core. Why? Because if man has an evil nature, as the Bible teaches, then it's impossible for him to change himself. In other words, if I'm innately evil, I will *always* be evil because there is nothing within me to *enable me to change*. If, however, I'm good within but am experiencing problems of living, then through various psychological methods or techniques, I should be able to tap into, utilize, or realize that goodness, thus remedying those adversities. All the psychotherapeutic selfisms, from self-love to self-esteem to self-image to self-actualization to self-realization—and ultimately to self-deification—are predicated upon the innate goodness of man's nature.

Antichrist and Psychology

Humanistic psychology—to which all psychotherapies are related—is the pseudo-scientific belief system of the Antichrist, who is the personification of human evil. The basics of his religion were introduced to mankind by Satan in his seduction of Eve (turning her away from obedience to God and toward her own self-interests, and even to godhood–Genesis 3) and will culminate in a man, the Antichrist, setting himself up in the Temple of God to be worshiped as God (2 Thessalonians 2:4). It's all about the worship of Self.

This Humanist/Selfist religion of the Antichrist does not just suddenly appear on the scene when the Antichrist is revealed. As noted, the religion of Selfism has been in development since the Garden of Eden. Moreover, it can be seen in the Tower of Babel and the idolatry both of the Gentiles and of Israel throughout the Old Testament and is prevalent in all the religions of the world today.

Only biblical Christianity stands against the exaltation of self that ties all other religions together. The Bible declares self to be evil and hopeless and says that man's salvation can come only from God as it is received by faith in Jesus alone, who satisfied divine justice by His full payment for the sins of mankind, according to the Scriptures. All other religions look to *Self* to obtain salvation, ultimately through one's own efforts, whether by rituals, sacraments, meditation, liturgies, good works, or other means. Human achievement versus Divine accomplishment—this is the critical difference between man's way of salvation and God's way.

The Apostle Paul's caveat about the "last days" is directed at believers, warning them and indicating the peril that will follow the practice of self-love. Therefore, it's rather shocking to witness the humanistic "self" concepts of the apostate religion of the Antichrist taking hold in unprecedented fashion within evangelical Christianity. One well-known Christian psychologist has credited humanistic psychologists and New Agers Carl Rogers and Abraham Maslow for helping evangelicals to recognize their "need for self-love and self-esteem."

That certainly cannot be derived from the writers of Scripture! Nevertheless, there have been many influential professing Christians who have knowingly or unknowingly sown the seeds of the humanistic self-love teachings so far and wide and for so long among Christians that the heresies have taken root and their deadly fruit has been eagerly consumed throughout the church.

Are You *Positive?*

Norman Vincent Peale is widely recognized as the one who pioneered the merger of theology and psychology that became known as "Christian psychology." Consistent with his humanistic beliefs, which he spread through his nationally broadcast radio sermons and his highly popular *Guideposts* magazine, he explained that people "are inherently good; the bad reactions [sin?] aren't basic." Robert Schuller, whose "Possibility Thinking" reflected his mentor Peale's "Positive Thinking," both of which mirror the teachings of the Mind Science cults, sent two hundred fifty thousand copies of his book, *Self-Esteem: The New Reformation*, to pastors throughout the U.S.

Schuller's *Hour of Power* is the world's most popular religious television program. Yet to millions, his humanistic views presented under the guise of Christianity are not recognized for their blasphemy: "Jesus knew his worth, his success fed his self-esteem. . . . He suffered the cross to sanctify his self-esteem. And he bore the cross to sanctify your self-esteem. And the cross will sanctify the ego trip!"[1] Could the Antichrist himself add anything more unbiblical?!

Sadly, many conservative evangelical preachers and teachers of note such as Chuck Swindoll, Charles Stanley, Josh McDowell, Anthony Hoekema, Norm Geisler, and others, bought into, taught, Christianized, and further popularized the concepts of self-love, self-esteem, self-worth, and self-image. It is the "new priesthood" of Christian psychologists, however, with credentials that falsely imply the anointing of science, that has convinced both shepherds and sheep of the legitimacy of the theories and methods of humanistic psychology. Among the swelling numbers of highly regarded, degreed professionals who teach the church what they have gleaned from "the counsel of the ungodly" is Dr. James Dobson, who, no doubt, is and has been the most influential individual among evangelicals for the last quarter-century. Concerning self-love and self-esteem he writes:

> In a real sense, the health of an entire society depends on the ease with which its individual members can gain personal acceptance. Thus, whenever the keys to self-esteem are seemingly out of reach for a large percentage of the people, as in twentieth-century America, then widespread "mental illness," neuroticism, hatred,

alcoholism, drug abuse, violence, and social disorder will certainly occur. . . . [2]

If I could write a prescription for the women of the world, it would provide each one of them with a healthy dose of self-esteem and personal worth (taken three times a day until the symptoms disappear). I have no doubt that this is their greatest need. [3]

Right behind Dobson in terms of his influence in the church today is Rick Warren. Although he has distanced himself of late from one of his early mentors, Robert Schuller (Warren was a repeat speaker in the nineties at the Robert Schuller Institute for Successful Church Leadership), his article in *Ladies' Home Journal*, March 2005, titled "Learn to Love Yourself" is classic Schuller—and pure humanistic psychology. Warren lists "five truths," none of which is either a "truth" or biblical:

1) Accept yourself
2) Love yourself
3) Be true to yourself
4) Forgive yourself
5) Believe in yourself

Yet these humanistic, antibiblical doctrines have been taught so often from so many pulpits that most Christians, when presented with what the Bible actually teaches about self and the selfisms, are either shocked that they've been misled or bitterly resent hearing the truth.

Although I could not adequately cover in this brief article the details of how terribly subversive and destructive humanistic psychology (especially as championed in "Christian" psychology) is to Bible-believing Christians, here are a few concerns that we all need to seriously and prayerfully consider:

1) Humanistic psychology's theories came from the atheistic, anti-Christian founders of psychotherapy, whose concepts qualify for what the Scriptures condemn as "the counsel of the ungodly" (Psalm 1:1).

2) The humanistic emphasis upon loving and esteeming self rejects the biblical commandment to "deny self," which Jesus admonished us to do in Matthew 16:24.

3) The increasing focus on esteeming oneself gradually distorts a believer's understanding of the truth regarding the sinful nature of man and hides conviction of sin in a morass of humanistic rationalizations.

4) The subjective "feelings orientation" of humanistic psychology undermines the absolutes of God's objective truth.

5) As the leaven of humanism grows in the mind of a believer, his interpretation of the Scriptures gradually shifts from what God has indeed said (Genesis 3:1) to "a way which seemeth right unto a man . . . " (Proverbs 14:12).

Scripture tells us that man's ways, i.e., all his selfist and humanistic teachings, "are the ways of death," a death that separates a believer from the truth and robs him of his faith and fruitfulness.

How "perilous" will all of this become in these "last days"? Consider the following and, should the Lord tarry, weep for your children!

Evangelical youth usually recognize the pseudo-science and myths of evolution, thanks to the instruction of organizations such as the Institute for Creation Research and Answers In Genesis, as well as numerous other apologetics ministries, creation scientists, gifted teachers, and so forth. Although the battle continues to rage in this area, not many evangelical young people go off to college intent on becoming "evolutionists."

Yet what of the pseudo-science and myths of *psychology*? Who is teaching our children about that? Certainly not the rapidly growing, fifty-thousand-member American Association of Christian Counselors, whose main goal is the "integration" of psychotherapy and Christianity. How serious is this ignorance of the evil of psychology for our young people? The prestigious *Princeton Review* reports that psychology is the number two career choice for all those attending college. It's even more popular in professing Christian universities, from Liberty University on the East coast to Biola University and Fuller Theological Seminary on the West coast and nearly all that reside between.

Who is telling the truth to our children? Not Dr. James Dobson of Focus on the Family, who ironically advises, "Christian psychology is a worthy profession for a young believer, *provided his faith is strong enough to withstand the humanistic concepts to which he will be exposed* . . . [emphasis added]."[4] Weep and pray for our next generation of evangelicals who are being led into the humanistic priesthood of what is tragically and deceptively called Christian psychology.

1 Robert Schuller, *Living Positively One Day at a Time* (Revell, 1981), 201; *Self-Esteem, the New Reformation* (Word Books, 1982), 14-15.

2 James Dobson, *Hide or Seek* (Revell Pub., 1974), 12-13.

3 James Dobson, *What Wives Wish Their Husbands Knew about Women* (Tyndale House, 1975), 60.

4 James Dobson, *Dr. Dobson Answers Your Questions* (Wheaton, IL: Tyndale House, 1989), 497.

PART TWO

THE BATTLE FOR *THE TRUTH*

— *Dave Hunt* —

SCRIPTURE TEACHES US QUITE CLEARLY that it is not in denouncing the devil—much less by psychotherapy—but by believing and obeying the *truth* that one is set free from sin, self, and Satan: "If ye continue in my word, then are ye my disciples indeed; and ye shall know the truth, and the truth shall make you free" (John 8:31–32). Christ is the truth, "God's truth." Bringing correction and instruction to the Ephesians, Paul writes: "But ye have not so learned Christ; if so be that ye have heard him, and have been taught by him, as the truth is in Jesus. . . " (Ephesians 4:20–21).

Christ, who is the truth, has many names in Scripture. One of them is "Counselor." It is a tragedy that instead of sitting at the feet of Jesus to learn "the truth [as it] is in Jesus" from the greatest possible "counselor," Christian psychology has turned us to sit at the feet of Christ's enemies under the guise that all truth is God's truth, and surely these anti-Christians who couldn't make their own lives work must have some of the truth that is missing from the Bible to pass on to us!

Everyone knows what is meant in general by the word "truth"; but what is *the truth*? The definite article indicates exclusivity. This is not "*a* truth" among many, but *the* truth. Anything in disagreement must therefore be a lie.

Of course, *the* truth could be about an accident that occurred; it could be about any event or condition. There cannot, however, be conflicting statements or opinions about anything, all of which are *the* truth. That fact is axiomatic and understood by all.

Does *the truth* matter? Of course it does. The truth about one's physical condition and prospects for recovery is surely important. The truth about road conditions ahead, whether a bridge is out and one could lose one's life as a result or at least have to turn around and go another way is important. However, when Christ says "*the truth* shall make you free," He obviously is not talking about one's health, road conditions, or anything else having to do with this earthly life. Although He used earthly illustrations such as bread, water, shepherd, sheep, vine, branches, tree, fruit, etc., Christ was always illustrating eternal life or eternal punishment.

Jesus *Is* the Truth

When Jesus said, "I am *the way* . . . no man cometh unto the Father, but by me" (John 14:6), He certainly did not mean that He was only one of several ways to heaven. When He said "I am *the truth*," He was explaining that He was not the way *mystically* but there was something specific that those who would accept Him as *the way* must believe. Indeed, they must believe on *Him* because He is *the truth* as well as *the way*.

Right here we confront a huge conflict. What about all the other great leaders of world religions who are followed by millions and even billions of people? How could that many be so wrong? Who would dare to suggest that Christianity has a monopoly on God and heaven? How could anyone be so narrow-minded and dogmatic?

So goes the complaint of those who want to believe that "all roads lead to the same place"—a sure formula for disaster even in life on earth. Those complaining are simply too proud to examine the facts, to face the truth, and admit that they are wrong. Stubbornness is a common human trait. In this case, however, instead of the error involving directions to an earthly destination, it involves wrong directions to heaven, with disastrous results for eternity.

It was not a religion, a religious leader, or a church that said, "I am *the way* . . . *the truth* . . . *the life*." Buddha didn't dare to say that, nor did Confucius or Muhammad. No sane person dared to say this because any sane person knew he could not prove his claim. He could not die for the sins of the world and rise from the dead the third day. Nor could he fulfill *any* of the more than one hundred clear and specific prophecies given by Hebrew prophets that would identify the true Messiah recorded hundreds and even thousands of years before Christ.

Obviously, truth is not a magic formula to pronounce or a "positive confession" to make. It is a revelation from God—i.e., His Word, as Jesus said—to believe and obey. "The just shall live by faith" (Hebrews 10:38) in God and in His Word. Nor is faith a power of the mind or a magic "force," as the positive-confession and positive/possibility-thinking heretics claim. Faith is a conviction understood, firmly held, and acted upon. What and in whom one believes determines one's life on earth and one's eternal destiny.

There is a battle raging for man's soul and for control of the universe. It is a very real war between the "God of truth" (Deuteronomy 32:4; Psalm 31:5; Isaiah 65:16) and Satan, "the father of [lies]," in whom there "is no truth" (John 8:44). One either believes God's truth or Satan's lie. There is no neutral ground. The cosmic battle of the ages is the battle for truth.

What Is the Truth?

We are being told by the rapidly proliferating Christian psychologists that their profession, though begun and practiced by atheists, has been lately raised up by God to help Christians who struggle with personal problems to live triumphantly for Christ in a wicked and difficult world. Yet psychology is the invention of men who, no one can deny, were messengers of Satan and sworn enemies of God.

What Christian psychologists want us to believe about "truth" is as unlikely a story as one could imagine, yet it has deceived multitudes of Christian leaders and their followers.

An editorial entitled "Truth" in the *Los Angeles Times* noted that "in a contemporary eight-volume encyclopedia of philosophy, 'Truth' has only three lines—theories on how to talk about it." Yet in the King James Bible the word "truth" occurs two hundred thirty-five times in two hundred twenty-two verses. Jesus, who said of Himself, "I am . . . the truth" (John 14:6), is called "the Word of God" (Revelation 19:13)—and He declared, "Thy word is truth" (John 17:17). It is to God's Word, then, that we must turn to learn the truth.

"Truth" has two meanings in Scripture: 1) Temporal facts man may observe about himself, others, and the physical universe, including truthful reportage of contemporary events; and 2) Eternal and spiritual reality pertaining to God and the relationship that everything else bears to Him as found only in His Word. Decrying the lack of truthfulness in today's world, the *Times* editorial was all about Number 1. It knew nothing of Number 2. The Bible, however, when it speaks of the truth, almost always means the latter.

The Bible repeatedly declares that man does not like the truth—in fact, that he prefers Satan's lies to God's truth. Though speaking to the Jews in His day, Christ addressed all mankind when He said, "And because I tell you the truth, ye believe me not" (John 8:45). Isaiah wrote twenty-seven hundred years ago, "None calleth for justice, nor any pleadeth for truth: they trust in vanity, and speak lies . . . judgment is turned away backward, and justice standeth afar off: for truth is fallen in the street" (Isaiah 59:4,14). This description of Israel as it ripened for God's judgment fits today's world. In so many ways, our society has opted for lies. Unfortunately, that has become true of the church as well through the invasion of psychology.

The state promotes many lies, from evolution to "safe sex." It lies about AIDS, so that a highly contagious, deadly, and incurable disease is protected as a "minority right." Lenders lie about finance charges and salesmen about their product; TV commercials appeal to lust and ambition rather than to truth. Is there a politician who *always* tells the truth and never compromises what he knows is right in order to make a deal or to get votes? If so, he wouldn't rise very high in the political world.

Success/motivation/self-improvement and "personal empowerment" seminars and group therapies teach that one creates reality with the mind. Eve's descendants still love that lie of promised godhood invented by the Serpent. It's the heart of Hinduism and of such pseudo-Christian cults as Christian Science, Unity, and Religious Science. Norman Vincent Peale and his protegé, Robert Schuller, have even brought into the evangelical church the delusion that thinking or saying something makes it so. Kenneth Hagin (though now deceased), through his books and tapes, and Kenneth Copeland, Frederick Price, et al., teach the same lie but conceal it with biblical language. Bereans (Acts 17:11) are not deceived.

God designed us to personally know and love Him and His truth. Instead, many people allow a guru, the latest Mormon prophet, the Watchtower Society, the pope, a "professional psychologist," or some other deceiver to take the place of God. In the very act of surrendering one's God-given rational faculties to a guru, whether he or she leads a church or a cult, those who do so have lost the battle for truth!

Is All Truth God's Truth?

"Christian psychology" has brought more of Satan's lies into the church than one could count. Truth is exchanged for feeling good about oneself. Even among evangelicals, sin, repentance, and judgment are avoided as "negative." A false Christ is preached—one who loves us because we're valuable and who affirms our self-worth. Flattery is preferred to honesty, doctrine and correction are despised, and parents are told to praise their children, even when they need reproof, in order to "boost their self-esteem."

Clearly, when Jesus said "the truth shall make you free," He didn't mean facts, scientific or otherwise. Therefore, even if it were a science (which it is not), psychology could not be part of "God's truth." Freud, Jung, and the other fathers of psychology, all anti-Christians, knew nothing of the truth to which Christ referred when he told Pilate, "Everyone who is of the truth heareth my voice." That non-Christians are not "of the truth" is clear from His words: "My sheep hear my voice" (John 10:27).

Is "all truth God's truth," as we are being told by Christian psychologists? "His truth shall be thy shield and buckler" (Psalm 91:4): this surely doesn't refer to scientific knowledge—nor could it refer to psychology, "Christian" or otherwise. "Having your loins girt about with truth" (Ephesians 6:14) can hardly mean mere facts. When God said, "If ye can find a man [in Jerusalem] . . . that seeketh the truth . . . I will pardon it" (Jeremiah 5:1), He didn't mean a research scientist, much less a psychologist! Non-Christians know nothing of God's truth, for "the natural man receiveth not the things of the Spirit of God" (1 Corinthians 2:14). "God's truth" is only revealed by His Spirit to His own.

"All truth is God's truth" is a major lie of Satan designed to justify the godless theories taken from anti-Christians upon which "Christian psychology" is based. Jesus said: "The Spirit of truth; whom the world cannot receive (John 14:17) . . . when he, the Spirit of truth, is come, he will guide you into all truth" (John 16:13). If "the Spirit of truth" guides into all truth, and the world cannot receive Him, then Freud, Jung, et al., knew nothing of God's truth! Psychology is certainly no part of "God's Truth," which is our "shield and buckler" and with which our "loins are to be girt," and which only the Spirit of Truth, whom the world cannot receive, teaches!

What Is "God's Truth"?

Paul referred to "the gospel of your salvation" as "the word of truth" (Ephesians 1:13). He wrote of "the truth of the gospel" repeatedly (Colossians 1:5; Galatians 2:5, 14). Christ, who "came . . . to give his life . . . a ransom for many" (Mark 10:45; 1 Timothy 2:6), testified, "To this end was I born, and for this cause came I into the world, that I should bear witness unto the truth" (John 18:37). Salvation comes through believing the truth—the message of the Cross.

Paul declared, "Christ Jesus came into the world to save sinners" (1 Timothy 1:15) from the penalty God's justice demands (Psalms 9:8; 96:13; Ezekiel 18:4, etc.). Christ said that He had come "to seek and to save that which was lost" (Luke 19:10) and "to call . . . sinners to repentance" (Matthew 9:13). Christ saves only those who, believing on Him, admit to and repent of being lost, guilty sinners, unable to please God or to save themselves. This is the truth that sets free!

Didn't Jesus live the perfect life for us to follow? Yes, but we're unable to live up to His example. His sinless life "condemned sin in the flesh" (Romans

8:3) and is the standard by which mankind will be judged. His perfection both damns the sinner and qualifies Him to be our Savior, for only One who is perfectly holy could die for the sins of others. God's truth includes man's evil as well as God's holiness and His righteous provision for sinners.

God's love gave His Son to die; God's justice laid upon Him our sins and demanded the full penalty. And man's evil, self-centered, rebellious heart hated, rejected, and crucified Him. The Cross fully demonstrated both the limitless love and justice of God—and the horrifying evil that lurks in the depths of the human heart. Amazingly, the very nails driven into His hands and feet and the spear that pierced His side drew forth the blood that saves!

The salvation Christ purchased with His blood must be received directly from Him ("come unto me"– Matthew 11:28) as a free gift of God's grace (Romans 3:24), "not of works, lest any man should boast" (Ephesians 2:9). Acceptance of this gracious gift is by faith: "It pleased God by the foolishness of preaching to save them that believe" (1 Corinthians 1:21). Believe what? The gospel! It alone is "the power of God unto salvation to every one that believeth" (Romans 1:16) that "Christ died for our sins . . . was buried, and . . . rose again . . . according to the Scriptures" (1 Corinthians 15:1–4) that foretold it all. This is the proof God offers.

Sin's penalty could not be set aside. God's love cannot compromise His justice. Christ had to suffer the full punishment we deserved so that God "might be just, and the justifier of him which believeth in Jesus" (Romans 3:26). This "gospel of God" has been declared "by his prophets in the holy scriptures" (Romans 1:1–2). It must either be accepted on God's terms or rejected. It cannot be changed.

"God's truth" surely includes "the truth of the gospel" (Colossians 1:5), which Paul defended vigorously from error, publicly rebuking even the Apostle Peter when he strayed from it (Galatians 2:5, 14). We are under the same orders from our Lord today.

What Constitutes a False Gospel?

Here we confront a solemn question. How much distortion does it take to turn God's truth into a lie, to corrupt the gospel so that those who believe it are not saved but damned? No more important question could be asked. A Berean can accept nothing less than the biblical answer. The spiritual warfare that rages for the eternal destiny of souls is a battle for uncompromised and uncompromising truth!

To undermine the "truth of the gospel," Satan has invented clever counterfeit gospels that promise life but damn the soul. None is more successful than the false gospel of psychology. The church must awaken to this danger and throw it out forthwith. Those who preach these lies are cursed by Paul—and rightly so. These false gospels are like rat poison—very tasty (or the rats wouldn't touch it) and 98.6 percent nutritious but containing just enough hidden poison to kill. Bereans must be prepared to contrast the lie with God's truth and to warn the unwary earnestly and clearly.

We need to be aware of this deadly evil that comes from psychology: it is the one false religion common to all false religions. It replaces God's truth regarding sin and the Cross with humanistic diagnoses (addictions, dysfunctional families, compulsions, co-dependencies, neuroses, traumas buried in the unconscious, etc.) and pernicious therapies and selfist "remedies" (improve self-esteem and self-assertion; practice positive self-talk, visualization, et al.) unknown to and unneeded by heroes of the faith (Hebrews 11) who triumphed without them.

Roman Catholicism is a false gospel. It denies Christ's finished work and offers salvation through baptism, indulgences, and sacraments administered by the Church through her popes, cardinals, bishops, priests, and the intercession of Mary. Rome's gospel will not save but damn the soul. Evangelicals generally recognize at least some of Catholicism's false dogmas.

However, whether Catholicism, Mormonism, Hinduism, Buddhism, Islam, atheism, communism, humanism, positive thinking, positive confession, possibility thinking—all embrace and promote the lies of psychology. It is the great ecumenical lie that provides a common "faith" to bring all religions and cults together under the Antichrist.

An equally insidious false gospel was taught by Kenneth Hagin until his death, and is still taught by Kenneth Copeland, Joyce Meyer, and other TBN-promoted "positive confession" leaders. In spite of past exposés by ourselves and others, Copeland has defended this heresy repeatedly, declaring, "It must be preached because it's . . . the Truth and it sets people free." To support this lie, he insisted,

> The day that Jesus was crucified, God's life, that eternal energy . . . moved out of Him and . . . He allowed the devil to drag Him into the depths of hell as if He were the most wicked sinner who ever lived [and] to come under Satan's control . . . [or] His body would have never died. . . .
>
> For three days . . . every demon in hell came down on Him to annihilate Him . . . tortured Him beyond anything that has ever been conceived. . . .
>
> In a thunder of spiritual force, the voice of God spoke to the death-whipped, broken, punished spirit of Jesus. . . . God's Word . . . charged the spirit of Jesus with resurrection power!

Suddenly His twisted, death-wracked spirit began to fill out and come back to life. . . . He was literally being reborn before the devil's very eyes. . . .

Before His body even had time to decay . . . Jesus Christ dragged Satan up and down the halls of hell. . . . The day I realized that a born-again man had defeated Satan, hell, and death, I got so excited. . . !

He'd [Satan had] murdered Jesus to annihilate Him. . . .

The many blasphemous lies are obvious to any Berean. That God's life is "energy" is a New Age idea. Nor did death to Christ's body come because He was "under Satan's control." He was "dead already" (John 19:33) before He was taken down from the Cross. It is outright heresy to say that Satan "murdered Jesus." Christ laid His life down that He "might take it again" (John 10:17). And He gave up His life on the cross, not in hell. Nor could "time" decay His sinless body. God would not allow it "to see corruption" (Psalm 16:10; Acts 2:31).

Nor did "the devil drag Him into the depths of hell . . . [and] every demon in hell came down on Him to annihilate Him. . . . " Satan isn't hell's proprietor. He hasn't even been there yet, nor have his demons—nor will they torture lost souls in the Lake of Fire but will themselves be tortured there. The Bible says that God "laid on him the iniquity of us all" (Isaiah 53:6) and "It pleased the LORD [not Satan] to bruise him [Christ]; he [God] hath put him to grief [and made] his soul an offering for sin" (v. 10).

Christ told the believing thief, "Today shalt thou be with me in paradise" (Luke 23:43)—not in hell in Satan's clutches. As He died for our sins, Christ said, "Father, into thy hands I commend my spirit" (Luke 23:46). To say that rather than being in the Father's hands he fell into Satan's hands to be tortured three days and nights is to preach a false gospel. Copeland, Meyer, and others like them preach that Christ's suffering in hell at the hands of Satan is what paid the penalty for our sins and that this is the gospel that must be believed for salvation. It will damn the soul of those who believe it.

"It Pleased the Lord [Jehovah] to Bruise Him"

No greater blasphemy could be imagined than to say that Satan's torture of Christ in hell was the punishment that paid for our sins. The lie of Mel Gibson's *The Passion of the Christ* is heresy enough—that it was the beating administered by the Roman soldiers that God used to punish Christ for the sins of the world.

But the lie that Satan was God's executioner of His wrath against sin is even worse. Yet Joyce Meyer says that those who reject this "gospel" are not saved.

As He laid down His life, Christ cried in triumph, "It is finished!" He had paid in full the penalty God's justice demanded for sin—paid it not to Satan but to God (Isaiah 53:6). Instead, the false teachers say He had not paid for our sins in full on the Cross. They claim that it wasn't finished, though He said it was. Rome says His sacrifice wasn't finished on the Cross but must be continued on its altars. Hagin, Copeland, Meyer, et al., say that much remained to be suffered for sin—at the hands of Satan in hell. Neither of these false gospels will save anyone!

The Bible teaches that our redemption comes "through His blood" (Ephesians 1:7; Colossians 1:14, 20). Rome says that salvation comes in installments through their "unbloody sacrifice of Christ" on its altars and damns anyone to hell who denies that the sacrifice of the Mass is a propitiatory sacrifice offered for the sins of the living and the dead. Copeland et al. have long insisted that our redemption comes through Christ being tortured by Satan for three days and nights in hell. But if Satan didn't torture Christ quite enough (he's smart enough and evil enough to pull that trick), we're not saved. And if he did, do we thank him for the vital role he played in our salvation? What perversion! This is surely not the gospel that saves!

Without any doubt, however, psychology is the most successful false gospel in leading both the world and the church astray. Its followers outnumber Muslims, Roman Catholics, and all the cultists and occultists combined because it is embraced by every one of these groups. Indeed, its followers are found in every part of the world and in every strata of society. This is Satan's master stroke of genius.

The fact that a "Christianized" form of psychology could enter the church and there be hailed as the new liberating truth is staggering! It is Satan's greatest deception. The errors of Islam, Catholicism, occultism, and the cults are recognized by most Christians. Very few, however, recognize Christian psychology for the deadly lie that it assuredly is.

As we have often pointed out, since Christian psychology claims to offer what the Bible says it alone can supply and has already provided in the indwelling Christ and Holy Spirit. The tolerance—and even worse, highly honoring —in the evangelical church of this false religion invented and practiced by anti-Christians is a slap in God's face. It ought to be summarily thrown out as unneeded and unwanted. Nothing less is demanded by the Scripture and by all of the facts!

What must our response be to the false gospels that abound and are deceiving multitudes? It is not enough to grieve or even to pray. Ask God to show you what action to take to oppose heresy and to rescue the perishing! Be a Berean. Search the Scriptures. Know the truth for yourself. Be convinced of it and live it. Then "[speak] the truth in love" (Ephesians 4:15).

Love corrects. Surely the Bereans would have lovingly told Paul where he was wrong if their search of the Scriptures had uncovered that his teaching was false. Christ said, "As many as I love, I rebuke and chasten" (Revelation 3:19). John said, "I have no greater joy than to hear that my children walk in truth" (3 John 4). May that be our joy in abundance.

If we truly love others, we'll do all we can to rescue them from error. Nor is it loving to fail to point out where friends, acquaintances, or even enemies have gone astray.

Are We too "Negative"?

— Dave Hunt —

CRITICS HAVE LONG LEVELED the charge of "divisive" and "negative" against those who seek to warn the church of unbiblical teachings and practices. I prayerfully consider such accusations, for my heart echoes the same concern. I long just to preach the gospel and to put behind me the controversy that has become such an unwelcome part of my life. Yet in preaching the pure gospel, one must carefully distinguish it from the clever counterfeits all around.

How negligent it would be not to warn the sheep of poisoned pastures and false shepherds who promote lies in the name of truth, yet the odds are staggering. Norman Vincent Peale's magazines, for example, have 16 million readers monthly, four times the combined sales of all of my books over many years. The flesh faints with weariness and frustration. Then why persist in a task so lonely and burdensome? Yes, why this burning passion?

There are, praise God, the many letters of encouragement from those who offer their love, support, and prayers. There are, too, the grateful "thank-yous" from the thousands who have been set free from the delusion and bondage of false gospels—from Catholicism and "Christian psychology" to positive/possibility thinking and positive confession. Yet even without such encouragement, we would be compelled to carry on and would urge you to do the same.

Jeremiah was hated, maligned, imprisoned, and threatened with death because he preached repentance and warned of God's impending judgment when the "positive prophets" promised peace and prosperity "by the word of the Lord." Popular opinion opposed him. Jeremiah became so discouraged that he declared that he would no longer speak for God nor even mention His name, but God's Word was in his heart and burned like a fire in his bones, so that he *had* to speak (Jeremiah 20:7–11). Yes, above all, it is God's Word burning in our hearts that compels us.

Distressed by accusations of "negativism," I cry out to God and turn to His unfailing Word. And what do I find there? The very message I am constrained to preach! Christ himself was far more "negative" than I have dared to be. He continually warned of judgment and hell, exposed sin, demanded repentance, rebuked the religious leaders and indicted them as hypocrites, whited sepulchers, blind leaders of the blind, fools. That was strong language! Without doubt, He would be banned from most Christian pulpits and media today, nor would the major Christian publishers accept what He wrote if He offered it to them.

The Sermon on the Mount is not intended to enhance one's "self-esteem," though Robert Schuller and Christian psychologists attempt to interpret it this way. No, the Sermon on the Mount encourages one to be poor in spirit, to mourn, to be meek and merciful, and promises that those who are true to God and His Word will be hated, persecuted, and vilified (Matthew 5).

But didn't Jesus say, "Judge not, that ye be not judged" (Matthew 7:1)? Isn't it unbiblical, then, to accuse a Christian leader of any wrong? On the contrary, Christ could only have meant that we were not to judge motives, for He clearly told us to judge teaching and lives: "Beware of false prophets [i.e., teachers] . . . ye shall know them by their fruits [lives]" (vv. 15–20). How could we beware of what was wrong if we did not evaluate carefully what was said and done? Surely Christ is calling us to judge false doctrine and deeds!

Christian Psychology's Opposition to Truth

Paul warned of "vain talkers and deceivers . . . whose mouths must be stopped [from teaching false doctrine]." He urged Titus to "rebuke them sharply" (Titus 1:10–13). He told Timothy, "Them that sin rebuke before all [i.e., publicly], that others also may fear" (1 Timothy 5:20). Clearly, such reproof requires a judging that does not violate Christ's prohibition but which, in fact, He commanded and the apostles practiced—a judging that Satan hates because it unmasks his lies.

Only the very wise welcome correction. It is not pleasant to be told that one is wrong and has been leading others astray. The natural reluctance to face the truth about oneself when it is not flattering is enough to make the truth unpopular. That attitude, however, has been catered to and reinforced by Christian psychology to the point where the truth or falsity of the correction is not even considered. Correction is rejected out of hand because it is *negative*. That one word serves as a dishonest escape from truth.

Christian psychology has so popularized the delusion that positive is good and negative is bad that these clichés have nearly driven truth out of the church. The two most influential purveyors of this destructive delusion have been Norman Vincent Peale, with his perennial bestseller, *The Power of Positive Thinking*, and his chief disciple, Robert Schuller, with his many books that are all variations on exactly the same thing but that he calls Possibility Thinking.

This fear and even hatred of correction that hides behind the positive/negative fantasy is one of mankind's besetting sins and is found everywhere, from the youngest child and lowliest citizen to the world's most powerful religious and political leaders. Indeed, it is especially found in the corridors of power. Nor is it surprising that it is behind this plastic shield that the worst sinners attempt to hide, for they have neither moral nor rational defense.

Most reprehensible is the fact that Christian psychology, taking its authority from secular psychology, is a major promoter of the "always be positive, no matter what" avoidance of truth. Inasmuch as the Bible is "the word of truth" (Psalm 119:43; 2 Corinthians 6:7; Ephesians 1:13; 2 Timothy 2:15; James 1:18), Christian psychology must either avoid it or misinterpret it.

Evil Posing as Good

"The heart is deceitful above all things, and desperately wicked" (Jeremiah 17:9). Man's best intentions, which seem so noble, often turn into proof of the evil of his heart. The International Genocide Treaty signed by President Reagan is a prime example. On the one hand, it seems a good thing. Had it been in existence and honestly enforced in earlier days, would it not have prevented Islam's murder of millions of "pagans" from France to China through the centuries? Wouldn't it have prevented the Holocaust, the slaughter by Mao and Stalin of scores of millions of helpless and innocent people, and of Pol Pot's killing fields in Cambodia, had it only been enacted and in force in those days?

In fact, it would have done nothing of the kind. Islam is still slaughtering millions from Afghanistan and Iraq to Sudan and Indonesia. In Sudan, Islam is well on its way to a repeat of Hitler's Holocaust. Has the Genocide Treaty even slowed Islamic or any other genocide anywhere in the world? Have psychologists led an international outcry to denounce this greatest of evils the world has ever seen? The answer is a tragic NO.

This Treaty (ten-year term, automatically renewed every five years except for those countries denouncing it six months before a renewal date) was adopted by Resolution 260 (III) A of the UN General Assembly December 9, 1948, and went into force January 12, 1951. It made a law of the declaration by the General Assembly in Resolution 96 on December 11, 1946, proclaiming genocide a crime.

In the more than sixty years since then, what has been done? The only effect of the law has been threats and no action in the case of Rwanda, and the prosecution of Slobodan Milosevic, President of Serbia and Yugoslavia, "for crimes against humanity" in Kosovo and Croatia and genocide in Bosnia. No accounting was demanded of the Croatians or of the Muslims for their equal, if not greater slaughter, of Serbs. It was the air strikes of NATO that brought Serbia to its knees, together with the West's support of Muslims in Bosnia, in spite of their serving as sponsors of Muslim terrorists infiltrating Europe.

The UN, dominated by Muslims, has always proved to be a paper tiger in the case of genuine and obvious evil, but it can be very vicious against Christians and Israel. Under the treaty, genocide includes any defined action "with intent to destroy, in whole or in part, a national, ethnical, racial or *religious* group . . . causing serious . . . mental harm to members of the group [emphasis added]." This broad definition of "genocide" could be used to arrest and imprison those making "negative" statements reflecting upon any *religion*.

Could someone be prosecuted under this treaty for saying that homosexuality or Islam are condemned in the Bible?" Unquestionably, yes, though so far this has not been done. Although this provision has not been brought into play against preachers of the gospel who give the whole counsel of God, it could be implemented at any time the UN desires to do so.

The net is tightening around those who stand uncompromisingly for the truth of God's Word. Although not yet enforced, it is already a crime falling under the definition of "genocide" to try to convert anyone of another religion or to suggest that their beliefs are wrong. It is a serious crime to call homosexuality a sin. The day is coming when, to protect "minority rights," we will be prohibited by law from preaching the gospel except in the most "positive" manner. Sadly, much of the evangelical church has already conformed. And here, again, we must place much of the blame squarely on Christian psychology's shoulders for its support of the myth that "positive" is right and "negative" is wrong.

The Biblical Way—and the Unbiblical Way—to Preach or to Counsel

Since it is the truth of God's Word that sets the sinner free, those who preach the gospel and who seek to feed the new "babes in Christ" are compelled to do what Paul commanded Timothy: "Preach the word" (2 Timothy 4:2)! And how is that to be done? Is it with great care not to offend sinners but to give them what they would be pleased to hear? Absolutely not! In the next two verses, Paul tells Timothy: "Reprove, rebuke, exhort, with all longsuffering and doctrine. For the time will come when they will not endure sound doctrine . . . they shall turn away their ears from the truth, and shall be turned unto fables."

It is not enough to preach the truth "positively" when there are lies that counterfeit it so closely that many can't tell the difference. It is both logically and scripturally essential to expose and refute today's pernicious false gospels, yet to do so is to be opposed by church leaders and barred from most platforms. I am banned even from such evangelical networks as Moody Radio lest I expose the humanism they promote in the name of "Christian psychology." Why not allow an open discussion of vital issues before the whole church? Are church leaders concerned for truth—or with protecting their own interests?

"Christian psychology" may seem to help for a time, but it undermines our real victory in Christ by redefining sin as "mental illness." World-renowned psychiatrist Thomas Szasz pointed out that through the acceptance of psychotherapy as scientific, "the cure of [sinful] souls, which had been an integral part of the Christian religions, was recast as the cure of [sick] minds."[1] This heresy inspired a host of new terms such as obsessive-compulsive behavior, dysfunctional families, addiction—and, more recently, the increasingly popular co-dependency myths and 12-Step recovery programs spawned by Alcoholics Anonymous. In *12 Steps to Destruction,* Martin and Deidre Bobgan point out that Bill Wilson, founder of A.A., based his system upon what was a revolutionary new theory: that drunkenness was not a "moral defect" but an excusable "illness." Wilson was relieved to learn that he was not a drunk but an "alcoholic"—a new term at the time.

Enlarging upon this lie, Christian psychologists have excused as "mental disorders" all manner of behavior that Jesus, the Great Physician, diagnosed as sin. John MacArthur tells of hearing a woman call into a "Christian psychology" radio program to confess that she couldn't keep from having sex with anybody and everybody. She was told that her problem arose from an overbearing mother and milquetoast father and that it was an "addiction" that could take years of therapy to cure. So much for Christ's "Go, and sin no more" (John 8:11). Disobeying God is no longer sin if one has a compulsion or addiction or has had a traumatic childhood.

In his book, *Our Sufficiency in Christ*, MacArthur writes, "The depth to which sanctified psychotherapy can sink is really quite profound. A local newspaper recently featured an article about a 34-bed clinic that has opened in Southern California to treat 'Christian sex addicts.' According to the article, the clinic is affiliated with a large well-known Protestant church in the area." Several leading "Christian psychologists" interviewed for the article "scoffed at the power of God's Word to transform a heart and break the bondage of sexual sin." The director explained that his treatment center would serve to rescue many Christians who had been taught that "the Bible is all you need." But is that not what the Bible itself claims and what the entire church believed for nineteen hundred years until the advent of Christian psychology?

In *The Journal of Biblical Ethics in Medicine*, Dr. Robert Maddox warns that "all manner of sin . . . from gluttony to fornication, from stealing to bestiality . . . is [being] labeled as disease, to be cured with chemical, electrical and mechanical treatments."[2] The Bobgans also quote from University of California professor Herbert Fingarette's book, *Heavy Drinking: The Myth of Alcoholism as a Disease*: "I just don't understand why any churches would go for the disease idea . . . [it] denies the spiritual dimension of the whole thing."[3] They also quote Stanton Peele from his book, *Diseasing of America: Addiction Treatment Out of Control*: "Disease definitions undermine the individual's obligations to control behavior and to answer for misconduct . . . [and] actually increase the incidence of the behaviors of concern."[4]

Unheeded Warnings from the Secular World

No one could calculate the billions of hours and the prodigious effort and fortunes spent around the world by the untold millions of faithful believers (inside and outside the church) in consulting highly praised psychologists and psychiatrists. Freud's invention, with Jung's support, of the "unconscious mind" has provided a deep silk hat out of which modern magicians of the mind pull the solutions to numerous "diseases" that didn't exist until they invented their names along with their "cure"—for which they receive generous fees. University of Chicago philosophy professor Allan Bloom points out,

> Biologists can't even account for consciousness within their science, let alone the unconscious. So psychologists like Freud are in an impossible halfway house between science, which does not admit the existence of the phenomena he wishes to explain, and the unconscious, which is outside the jurisdiction of science.[5]

Even so, psychologists and psychiatrists continue their solemn pronouncements about the unconscious as though it were scientifically established and everyone ought to bow in reverence to their authority. The honored high priests and mediators of the omnipotent/omniscient unconscious have undergone the esoteric initiation that qualifies them to interpret the symbolic language of this "God within" through ink blots, dreams, Freudian slips of the tongue, hypnotic "regression" even into alleged past lives, and an almost endless list of other ingenious techniques invented by leaders of the craft for consulting this inner oracle. As investigative journalist Martin L. Gross has perceptively observed:

One of the most powerful religious ideas of the second half of the twen-tieth century is the Great Unconscious. . . . [Emphasis his]

In this religion of the Unconscious, our conscious mind is a second-class being . . . a mere puppet of the unknown true self. . . .

Is there an Unconscious. . . ? From a scientific point of view, it is a theological device which fills the gap in man's biological ignorance. . . . [6]

There is something insidious about the spectacular growth of psychology and the recent rise of its power over mankind, both in the secular world and in the church. Psychology has changed the world's thinking and standards through what Gross points out is a "new truth . . . fed to us continuously from birth to the grave"—a "truth" composed of unproven and contradictory theories. In *The Myth of Neurosis*, British psychiatrist Garth Wood bluntly charges that

. . . what has become big business is in fact fraud. The evidence does not support the claims of psychoanalysis and psychotherapy. . . . The situation is mind-boggling . . . psychoanalysis has never been validated by the scientific method. . . . Of course, many of us have known all along that psychoanalysis was scientifically bank-rupt. . . .

Why should the doctors who dispense this "therapy" be immune from the attentions of the government watchdogs who protect us from other scientifically disreputable "cures". . . ? Untested and unproved [this "pill"] is dispensed by the unscien-tific for the consumption of the unhappy.[7]

Analyzing a cross section of ideas presented at the Twenty-third International Psychoanalytic Congress in Stockholm, Nobel laureate in medi-cine-physiology Sir Peter Medawar found "the self-satisfied self-confidence in the importance of their insights [to be] sinister." After presenting examples of the unsupportable and wildly imaginative "interpretations" of dreams and behavior that rivaled their patients' most bizarre fantasies, Sir Peter asked the embarrassing question: "Where shall we find [in this congress] the evidence of hesitancy . . . that is commonplace in an international congress of, say, physiologists or biochemists? A lava-flow of *ad hoc* explanation pours over and around all difficulties. . . . "[8]

Booking Passage on a Sinking Ship

Psychiatrist Lee Coleman titled his exposé of psychiatry, *The Reign of Error*. Having testified in more than one hundred thirty criminal and civil trials, Coleman explained that his task was "to educate the judge or jury about why the opinions produced by these professionals [psychologists and psychiatrists] have no scientific merit."[9] In an article titled "Psychology Goes Insane, Botches Role as Science," psychologist Roger Mills writes: "I have personally seen therapists convince their clients that all of their problems come from their mothers, the stars, their biochemical make-up, their diet, their life-style and even the 'karma' from their past lives."[10]

This is nothing new. Jung had great respect for astrology and used it in his analysis. He wrote, "In cases of difficult diagnosis I usually get a horoscope." *Wholemind* newsletter has said, "A surprising number of today's psychotherapists are following Jung's advice." New York City therapist Susan LeMak says she finds "the symbols and archetypes of astrology" helpful in giving clients a new perspective on their problems.[11]

Research psychiatrist Thomas Szasz, a non-practicing Jew, called Freudianism "the clever and cynical destruction of the spirituality of man, and its replacement by a positivistic 'science of mind . . . ' not merely a religion that pretends to be a science [but] a fake religion that seeks to destroy true religion."[12] Another psychologist has written, "It appears that certain of the most influential pioneers in American psychology found in it an ideal vehicle for renouncing their own Christian upbringing in the name of science."[13] Yet at the same time, Christian psychologists claim that it is the ideal vehicle for enhancing God's Word. Something has gone badly amiss!

More than a hundred years ago, William James wrote, "I wish by treating Psychology as a science to help her become one."[14] Research psychiatrist E. Fuller Torrey declared, "The techniques used by Western psychiatrists are, with few exceptions, on exactly the same scientific plane as the techniques used by witchdoctors."[15] One test measuring psychotherapists against witchdoctors ended in a dead heat, the major difference being that the witchdoctors charged less and released their patients sooner. Nobelist Richard Feynman has described psychology as "not a science [but] more like witchdoctoring. . . . "[16]

How astonishing that as the secular world is pointing out the glaring holes in the badly listing and obviously sinking ship of psychotherapy, Christians are jumping aboard as though it were the ark of safety. How can Christians possibly imagine that this doomed vessel will not only stay afloat but add needed buoyancy to the ark God has provided—and finally bring passengers to a secure harbor?

It makes me weep to watch the growing deception—to cry out against it and to be heeded by so few and opposed by so many. Why is that essential correction, which Scripture so clearly demands, left to a few nobodies and largely shunned as "negative" by church leaders who might be heeded by millions if they would only speak out with a clear voice? Write to the most influential evangelical leaders and ask how they can "preach the Word" without involving themselves in the reproof and rebuke of rampant error that Paul said must be at the very heart of biblical preaching!

1. Thomas Szasz, *The Myth of Psychotherapy* (New York: Doubleday, 1978), xxiv.

2. http://www.psychoheresy-aware.org/sa&ph102.html.

3. Ibid.

4. Ibid.

5. Allan Bloom, *The Closing of the American Mind* (New York: Simon & Schuster, 1988), 199-204.

6. Martin L. Gross, *The Psychological Society: The impact—and the failure—of psychiatry, psychotherapy, psychoanalysis, and the psychological revolution* (New York: Random House, 1978), 43-44, 273-74.

7. Garth Wood, *The Myth of Neurosis: Overcoming the Illness Excuse* (New York: Harper & Row, 1987), 265, 268-69.

8. Cited in Wood, *Neurosis.*

9. Lee Coleman, *The Reign of Error* (Beacon Press, 1984), xii-xv.

10. Roger Mills, "Psychology Goes Insane, Botches Role As Science," *The National Educator*, 14.

11. *Wholemind Newsletter: A User's Manual to the Brain, Mind, and Spirit*, Vol. 1, No. 1, 5.

12. Szasz, *Myth*, 28, 139, 146.

13. Mary Stewart Van Leeuwen, *The Sorcerer's Apprentice* (InterVarsity Press, 1982), 49.

14. William James, *Collected Essays and Reviews*, 1920, "A Plea for Psychology As a Natural Science," (1982).

15. E. Fuller Torrey, *The Mind Game: Witchdoctors and Psychiatrists* (Emerson Hall Publishers, Inc., 1972), 8.

16. Richard Feynman et al., *The Feynman Lectures on Physics*, Vol 1 (Addison-Wesley, 1963), 3-8.

THE PROBLEM OF SELF-LOVE

— Dave Hunt —

FOR DECADES WE HAVE BEEN WITNESSING an accelerating and sad fulfillment of Paul's warning that in the last days prior to Christ's return sound doctrine would be scorned and in its place professing Christians would turn to myths. As a result, there is a diminishing biblical and increasing humanistic content in Christian books and sermons. Much of this unconscionable and destructive withdrawal from sound doctrine can unquestionably be traced to that Trojan Horse of psychology that Norman Vincent Peale brought into the church.

As a result, the very foundations of the Christian faith are being undermined by many of those who are looked up to as its chief defenders. Yet the shocking fact that "the faith which was once for all delivered unto the saints" (Jude 3) is now under not-so-subtle revision is hardly noticed because of the sterling reputations of the new purveyors of error. Adding to the confusion is the additional fact that most if not all of those involved in this polluting process stoutly and sincerely insist that what they teach is "biblical."

How is such delusion possible? It has been accomplished by a seemingly harmless redefinition. Whereas to be "biblical" used to mean that a teaching was *derived* from Scripture, it now means that it may be derived from anywhere as long as it can somehow be interpreted as being *compatible* with Scripture. Thus, the Bible and Christ, the Living Word, are no longer "The Truth" as Scripture so clearly claims. Instead, under the specious slogan that "all truth is God's truth," Holy Writ is now seen as only one of many ingredients in a new recipe for happiness to which anything may be added as long as the mixture still tastes somewhat "biblical." As a result, Christians are losing their taste and appetite for the unadulterated Truth of God's Word.

This accelerating erosion of spiritual discernment is compounded by the fact that exegesis of Scripture has fallen into disfavor with both shepherds and sheep. Ears are being tickled instead with humanistic concepts that are introduced as allegedly necessary and helpful supplements to God's Word, complete and sufficient though it claims to be. Far from being helpful, however, these "supplements" inexorably effect reinterpretations of Scripture—and a generation grows up with a "Christianity" whose foundations have been undermined without their knowing it.

The Deadly Process

Let's take a simple example to which we have often referred. Jesus commanded His disciples, "But seek ye first the kingdom of God, and his righteousness; and all these things [food, clothing, shelter] shall be added unto you" (Matthew 6:25–33). From humanistic psychology, however (now a legitimate source of revelation according to the "all truth is God's truth" thesis) so-called "Christian psychologists" have borrowed another myth: Abraham Maslow's "hierarchy of needs." It states that man's physical needs for such things as food, clothing, and shelter must first be met; then the so-called psychological needs; and, last of all, the spiritual needs. Although it blatantly turns Christ's command on its head, Maslow's theory and its derivatives now permeate the books, sermons, and counsel given by many church leaders and even influence evangelism. Biblical exegesis has been abandoned for new "interpretations" that have been derived from extra-biblical sources of presumed "truth."

Consider one further example. Paul solemnly warns, "In the last days perilous times shall come. For men shall be lovers of their own selves. . . " (2 Timothy 3:1–2). Then follows a list of sins that peculiarly characterize our world today and all of which have their root in self-love. Once again from humanistic psychology, however, "Christian" psychologists have borrowed the seductive myth that self-love (along with its concomitants self-esteem/worth/acceptance, etc.) is a vital ingredient for "mental health." Thus, instead of the problem being the iniquitous prevalence of innate self-love due to man's rebellion (as the Bible declares), a *lack* of it is now stated to be the root of the sins listed in verses 2–4. In the process, serious sins have been redefined as "behavior problems" requiring newly discovered "psychological solutions."

As we have so often noted and documented, this selfist myth of pop psychology, having been introduced into Christianity by leaders of supposedly impeccable reputations, has become so popular that today it is the prevailing belief throughout the church. It is as though Paul actually wrote, "In the last days perilous times shall come. For men shall be haters of their own selves, and as a consequence will need to undergo therapy and attend seminars in order to learn to love themselves properly. . . . " Such mutilations would be required before one could shoehorn the current self-love/self-worth fad into Scripture.

Acceptance of psychology's delusion that a lack of self-love is our major problem (promoted not only by Robert Schuller but by many others) meant that Christ's statement to "love your neighbor as yourself" had to be re-interpreted as a command to love ourselves first. Why would Christ command us, if we all lack self-love, to love our neighbors as we [fail to] love ourselves?

Christ's apparent error is now corrected by books and seminars teaching us how to first of all love self so that we can fulfill His command.

Simple exegesis of Christ's command to "love your neighbor as yourself," plus a little common sense, would agree with the rest of Scripture as follows:

1) We already love ourselves, or such a command would be foolish.

2) This is confirmed by Ephesians 5:29: "For no man ever yet hated his own flesh; but nourisheth and cherisheth it."

3) It is supported by conscience, which reminds us that we feed, clothe, and care for ourselves in satisfying our own desires, and ought to manifest love for our neighbors in the same way by caring for them as we care for ourselves.

4) The fact that this command is necessary indicates that, rather than lacking in self-love, our problem is an excessive amount of it, which causes us to be selfish and thus to neglect caring for others.

Surely, Christ would not be telling us to love our neighbor *as we love ourselves* if we didn't love ourselves enough or even hated ourselves, as some Christian psychologists have persuaded the church to believe is our natural state from birth. The inescapable truth is that we are naturally self-centered and seek our own happiness and welfare ahead of that of others. Obviously, it is this endemic selfishness that Christ's command is intended to correct.

Without a doubt, such had been the consistent interpretation of this Scripture for nineteen hundred years until humanistic psychology was embraced as a valid source of "God's truth." As a result, an astonishing reversal of what our Lord taught has taken place. Pastors and Christian leaders now promote the very love of self that Paul warned would characterize men in the last days and from which Christ came to deliver us by His Cross! And Satan is laughing in triumph.

Stirring in New Ingredients

Me, Myself & I is typical of many books written to defend Christian psychology. Its author, Archibald D. Hart, is professor of psychology and dean emeritus of Fuller Seminary's School of Psychology. Hart is also a certified biofeedback practitioner and a board-certified diplomate fellow in psychopharmacology. Advertisements for the book called it "a response to Dave Hunt and John MacArthur, Jr." In fact, Hart's quarrel is not with two Christians but with

God's Word, which he (like other "Christian" psychologists) denies is sufficient to provide counsel for every emotional and spiritual need, even though it claims to be.

In keeping with his profession, Hart also believes that along with psychological counseling Christians also need psychoactive drugs and biofeedback to keep themselves emotionally stable. Yet none of these unbiblical remedies that come from the world were ever used by Christians for the first nineteen hundred years of the church's existence. In fact, they have been shown to be harmful and habit-forming. We have quoted psychiatrist Peter R. Breggin, one of the world's foremost psychoactive drug experts, who warns against the use of psychiatric medications. He cautions, however, that those taking them must only come off of them under the supervision of a competent physician. In his book, *Your Drug May Be Your Problem*, Breggin warns:

> Psychiatric medications are, first and foremost, psychoactive or psychotropic drugs. They influence the way a person feels, thinks, and acts. Like cocaine and heroin, they change the emotional response capacity of the brain. If used to solve emotional problems, they end up shoving those problems under the rug of drug intoxication while creating additional drug-induced problems. . . .
>
> The choice is not between psychiatric drugs and some other "therapy" but between psychiatric drugs and all the resources that life can offer us.[1]

Breggin's book is endorsed by numerous medical scientists. Typical of the endorsements are the following: psychiatrist Alberto Fergusson writes, "This book is one of the most important things that has happened to psychiatry. . . Peter Breggin and David Cohen must be praised for the courage they have had to unmask many pseudo-scientific conclusions frequently present in supposedly scientific literature." Another psychiatrist states, "One hundred years from now, people will read current psychiatric textbooks with the same incredulity we have about blood-letting and snake oil. *Your Drug May Be Your Problem* will be remembered as the turning point and as the beacon that showed the way out of these dark days of widespread psychiatric drugging."

Calling God a Liar!

How tragic it is that not only has the secular world been deceived by the propaganda from the drug industry but that the church has fallen into the same pattern of looking to drugs for the solution to emotional problems. What a slap in the face to our Lord Jesus Christ, who promised to be our sufficiency, never to leave or forsake us. He has proved Himself both faithful and true for millions of Christians in every imaginable trial during nineteen hundred years. Yet today's Christians, instead of trusting Him alone, have turned to drugs that even the world warns are delusive and harmful!

How has this happened? It has been through the influence and leadership of Christian psychology and psychiatry, introduced into the church by heretics such as Norman Vincent Peale, that this destruction of the faith once delivered to the saints has been wrought. Even more incredible is the fact that this Pied Piper leading us away from God's Word and trust in Him alone as our sufficiency has at the same time been lionized as the new answer to how to live the Christian life. Christian psychology and psychiatry are looked to as the new Moses, who will lead us through the wilderness of life's trials to the promised land of victory. The truth is, however, they have led us back into Egypt.

How do Christian psychologists and psychiatrists defend the introduction of this deadly delusion among the saints? They say that psychology and psychiatry are perfectly compatible with Scripture and can be integrated with God's Word. Those very words of attempted justification—*compatible and integrated*—reveal the fraud and are self-indicting. To introduce something as being compatible with and suitable for integration into the Bible is to accuse the very Word of God of being insufficient. Indeed, it is to accuse God, who cannot lie, of lying, inasmuch as His Word promises to have given us all that we need for emotional comfort and direction and spiritual authority and power.

Nor is the accusation that the Bible is insufficient and thus that God is a liar made by mere implication, though that would be evil enough. Hart leaves no doubt concerning biblical insufficiency. He states repeatedly, "We desperately need a Christian psychology. . . . [2] The need for 'integrating' psychology and faith is urgent."[3] If such is indeed the case, then four logical conclusions must follow:

1) From its very beginning, the church, including Jesus who founded it and Paul and the other apostles and prophets (to say nothing of Old Testament saints such as Moses and Daniel), desperately needed psychological help that hadn't yet been invented. The heroes and heroines of the faith mentioned in Hebrews 11 would have all lived happier, more fulfilling, fruitful, and godly lives had psychological counseling been available in their day.

2) Because Scripture lacks essential insights into human personality, behavior, and treatment, which are found only in the recently developed field of psychology, the church was incapable of properly

dealing with many emotional and spiritual problems for nearly two thousand years. The Old Testament saints had been similarly handicapped for another four thousand years before that.

3) Essential diagnoses and cures of spiritual and emotional problems, which the Holy Spirit (through lamentable ignorance or oversight) failed to include in Scripture, have at last been supplied by humanists, many of whom (like Freud) were rabidly anti-Christian. Thanks to these godless prophets of psychology, the church can at last deal with the full range of emotional and spiritual problems for which Spirit-filled Christians have desperately needed psychological help for twenty centuries.

4) As a result of these new and essential psychological insights that have been brought into the church by Christian psychologists to supply what is lacking in Scripture, today's Christians live far happier, more fruitful, and victorious lives than believers at any time in the past who trusted in God and His Word alone. Because they knew nothing about psychology, Daniel, Enoch, David Livingstone, Moody, Paul, Peter, Spurgeon, Hudson Taylor, John Wesley, et al., relying only upon the Holy Spirit and God's Word, lived inferior lives to those of today's Christians.

Obviously, all four of these conclusions are blasphemously false.

Failure to Distinguish the Spiritual from the Physical

Christian psychology tries to merge Christ with Freud and a host of godless theorists. Talk about ecumenism! Psychology is the bridge, the ecumenical glue, that deceitfully unites Christian and pagan in a common language and faith. This humanistic religion's priesthood performs rituals known as psychotherapy for the healing of the soul. Whether these priests are atheists, Roman Catholics, or evangelicals, and whether they quote the Bible or deride it, all have studied similar academic courses, had to give the same answers to pass the course exam, boast similar degrees, and are licensed by the same secular authorities. When will the church awaken to the obvious fact that putting the adjective "Christian" in front of the noun "psychology" is meaningless as well as deceptive!

Hart argues, "The study of the psychology of learning, perception, and personality is just as valid as the study of anatomy or surgery. But I have yet to hear Dave Hunt or anyone else clamoring for a 'Christian theory of surgery.'"

Of course not. The Bible is not a surgery textbook. There is a difference between body and soul, flesh and spirit, brain and mind, glands and morals, germs and will, disease and sin—between "tissues and issues," as the Bobgans put it.

Hart should ask himself, "If it makes no sense to call medicine, chemistry, learning/perception theory, etc., 'Christian,' why should psychology be called 'Christian'?" Why indeed! This error stems from psychology's erroneous claim to deal with the soul (*psyche*) and to offer solutions to spiritual, moral, and emotional problems for which God's holy and inerrant Word claims to have the only and sufficient answers. Psychology is, in fact, an illegitimate rival to the promises God makes in His Word.

In spite of Pentecostal and charismatic claims that no Christian need ever be sick, the Bible does not offer total and perpetual physical healing in this life. ("By [His] stripes ye were healed" refers to sin, not sickness; 1 Peter 2:24.) God's Word does, however, offer total and perpetual spiritual healing, and that includes the emotions. The Bible doesn't claim to be a chemistry or physics or auto mechanics handbook. None of these disciplines offers anything that could be called "Christian."

Then what is "Christian" about psychology? Nothing. Remember that what psychology offers was never part of the Christianity of Jesus or Paul! In fact, Hart admits, "Dave Hunt is correct when he says that we have not yet developed a Christian psychology at the therapeutic level."[4] He is admitting that Christian psychology isn't really "Christian."

Should We Believe and Follow God or Man?

Scripture declares that God's "divine power hath given unto us all things that pertain unto life and godliness, through the knowledge of him that hath called us to glory and virtue: whereby are given unto us exceeding great and precious promises: that by these ye might be partakers of the divine nature, having escaped the corruption that is in the world through lust"(2 Peter 1:3–4). In His grace and infinite power, God provides all we need to live holy, happy lives—fruitful lives of service to Him and to others.

The question is whether we believe God, are willing to obey His Word, and are content with what He has given us for "life and godliness." Do we trust His "divine power" as sufficient, or do we think that some psychologist, "Christian" or secular, knows what God doesn't and can do what God can't? Each Christian is a branch in Christ, the true Vine. Is not the life of Christ, the Vine, sufficient to produce a life in us that glorifies God and bears fruit for eternity? Does the "divine nature" of which we are partakers by faith need psychotherapy? Surely not!

Hart argues, "I need all the help I can get in understanding the truth about myself, its sinful nature, how it needs to be regenerated and filled with God's Spirit."[5] Hart goes on to make it clear that God has not provided in His Word and through His Holy Spirit and Christ living in us "all the help" we need—and that the missing "help" God has not provided has been supplied by the atheistic founders of psychology:

> Being a Christian involves growing into the likeness of Christ. True, this is a spiritual process. But it is also an emotional and psychological process. We need God's restorative grace, but we can also benefit from the understanding that psychology can provide. . . .
> [God calls us] to integrate who we are in our minds with what we are in our spirits. . . . We desperately need . . . a vision of how we can be healthy in our whole beings—how spirituality and psychology can work together to make us more complete in Christ.[6]

Hart could not have stated more clearly that the Bible is not sufficient. According to Hart, something vital is missing that every Christian desperately needs and that Christians have lacked from the days of Christ and Paul until Freud and his anti-Christian cohorts came to the rescue. "Spirituality and psychology" must work together—obviously a "solution" to a desperate need that was unavailable until the advent of psychology in the nineteenth century.

The Bible never offers "spirituality" to *anyone* as a help or solution to *anything*. Christ promised the indwelling Holy Spirit as our Comforter (John 14:16–17), who would lead us into all truth (John 16:13). To turn to Christian psychology for help is to turn one's back on the Comforter from heaven and to spurn Christ himself, who wants to live His life in us.

What God Promises in His Word

If we believe the Bible, what Hart proposes is not what we "desperately need" but what he is desperate to persuade us we need lest his training in psychology, psychopharmacology, and biofeedback be exposed as useless—especially for Christians. Psychology had its birth in the secular world because mankind sought a solution to emotional problems without acknowledging the Creator while continuing to live in rebellion to His laws written in every conscience. Christians who couldn't live by faith what the Bible promised turned to psychology to help them to live the Christian life. They believed the lie that integrating psychology with theology would do what theology alone could not. Integration was constructed upon the sandy foundation of the claim that Scripture is inadequate.

But the Bible itself promises that we will have all that we need in this life and the life to come if we will trust God and obediently walk by faith. Christianity differs from every religion in the world. They are all do-it-yourself projects. Buddha, Confucius, Zoroaster, Muhammad, and all the rest are dead in their graves. They can offer no help to those who try to follow their teachings. Christ alone conquered death, left behind an empty grave, and promises to live His very life in those who believe on Him: "Because I live, ye shall live also" (John 14:19).

Paul declared that Christ lives in our hearts by faith (Ephesians 3:17). Christianity is not a do-it-yourself-kit religion for which "we need all the help we can get." Nor is it the imitation of Christ in our own strength, sincerely trying to be like Him. It is *Christ living His life in us* in the power of the indwelling Holy Spirit. Need we look anywhere else than to Him?

Indeed, Christ "is our life" (Colossians 3:4). The Christian simply needs to allow and trust Christ to fully express Himself through him or her. It is blasphemy to suggest that the risen Christ who lives in the Christian needs psychological help! The problem is that Self instead of Christ is in control.

Self is the heart and driving force of all psychotherapy—secular or Christian. The aim is always self-improvement, self-actualization, self-assertion, self-love, self-image, self-esteem, self *ad infinitum*. Therefore, "Christian" psychology is forced to defend the self that Scripture says must be denied. That defense is the theme of Hart's book. His final summation declares, "Christians need help . . . in reclaiming the promised land called 'self' for God" (p. 248)." Incredible! Hart's biblical illiteracy and spiritual blindness (as with other "Christian" psychologists) are staggering.

There is a difference between denying self (Christ's requirement), and self-denial (Hart's gospel). The latter involves Self giving up its desires in order to achieve self-improvement and pat itself on the back. Christ's "deny self," says Hart, really means Self behaving itself by self-control and saying yes to Christ. He tells us that rather than being denied Self must be accepted, affirmed, esteemed, improved—and that in order to develop the self, one must first understand it (p. 71). The truth that *is* Christ and that He spoke in His Word has been turned upside down and inside out!

God's Word Is *The Truth*

The fact that we must derive God's Truth from the Bible itself, and the fact that there is no other source, are both clear from Christ's statement: "If ye continue in my word, then are ye my disciples indeed; and ye shall know *the truth*, and the truth shall make you free" (John 8:31–32). Simple exegesis indicates that the Truth, which alone sets us free from sin and Self, is:

1) Revealed only through His Word

2) Understood only by those who "are of God" (John 8:47) and who obey ("if ye continue") His Word

3) Hidden to all others (see vv 43-47)

Each of these essential points is denied by the "all truth is God's truth" myth. It credits those "not of God" with revelations of "God's truth." These new "revelations" from the mouths and pens of atheists who hate God's Word have been embraced by Christian leaders as essential supplements to supply what the Bible allegedly lacks.

Solomon wrote, "My son, give me thine heart, and let thine eyes observe my ways. For a whore is a deep ditch; and a strange woman is a narrow pit" (Proverbs 23:26–27). Here we have the simple ingredients of a godly life. There must first of all be the *relationship to God as children* ("My son . . . ") born into His family by His Spirit. Then follows *surrender of our hearts* to Him ("give me thine heart"), which involves both love and commitment. Christian psychology is a tempting "strange woman" who wants to lead us away from trust in Christ alone.

Next we *observe His ways, follow His example, obey His Word.* How can we do this? Motivation comes through our love for Him and the wisdom imparted by His Word. No matter how pleasurable for the moment, unfaithfulness to God (as to one's spouse) and disobedience to His Word eventually swallow us up in a deep ditch and a narrow pit bitter as death itself.

Why should husband and wife be faithful to one another? Why not so-called free sex? For one thing, sex is never "free" but always carries obligations and consequences that cannot be escaped. Of course it is possible for a husband or wife to "tire" of each other and to "fall in love" with someone else—but that is not real love. God's Word tells us that "love" is more than sexual passion or pleasure—it is obedience to God's command and requires faithfulness.

The Deadly Effect of Psychological Revisionism

The God-ordained relationship between male and female (like our relationship to Him) involves total commitment. The man who cheats on his wife or divorces her to marry a "more attractive" woman may enjoy what seems to be pleasure and fulfillment for a time. Eventually, however, the remorse for having broken his marriage vows and having dishonored the God who created him will turn illicit pleasure into great pain. Obedience to God's Word gives joy now and eternally. Exchanging that deep and lasting satisfaction for temporary pleasure is a bad bargain indeed.

Christian psychology's new source of "truth" introduces a convenient escape from the clear teaching of the Bible. It allows one to say, "I can't love my wife or husband or parent—and God wouldn't want me to endure this miserable and painful situation." Yet we are *commanded* to love: first of all God, then neighbor as ourselves, and finally even our enemies. True love comes from obedience to God's Word and is thus based upon commitment to sound doctrine.

Nor is there any excuse under any circumstances for not loving spouse or parent, friend or foe, whether they mistreat or even hate us. The same is true of all of the ingredients of a happy, productive, fruitful, victorious life: they come from obedience to sound doctrine. Far from being divisive, as some complain, doctrine is our very life. Those who will not endure it delude themselves with a false "Christianity" that will be severely judged for its fundamental unbelief and disobedience—and may even be found to be false in the end.

Christian psychology, however, derived not from Scripture but from humanistic sources, makes convenient and justifies on "scientific" grounds the "I can't" excuse. It covers all manner of sins as only love is supposed to do (Proverbs 10:12). And in the delusive process, self-esteem is salvaged (isn't that to psychology's credit?). The unfaithful spouse doesn't need to feel guilty after all because the lie of self-love has given her or him convenient justification.

The Bible, however, does not encourage excuses. It does not say, "Rejoice in the Lord . . . unless you are unable to do so because of an unhappy childhood, a bout of 'depression,' or adverse circumstances." It does not say, "Be anxious for nothing . . . unless you have a nervous disposition and the weight of circumstances drives you to anxiety." It does not say, "Forgive . . . unless you are unable to because of abuse, etc."

We are not excused from obeying the command "Be not afraid" because we happen to be timid and fearful. Nor are we excused from the command "Let the peace of God rule in your hearts" because we have been diagnosed as susceptible to stress. Nor are we excused from the command to love because we find certain people unlovable.

Unfortunately, however, the simple obedience to God's Word that sound doctrine compels has been undermined by psychological "counseling" that nourishes self-pity, which leads to unbelief and rebellion. Therapy comes to the rescue. It offers to justify self-pity and unbelieving disobedience, to comfort us in our rebellion, and to provide the peace and joy that only God can give to those who trust and obey Him.

Love, joy, peace, etc., are clearly declared to be the fruit not of psychological counsel but of the Holy Spirit working in our lives (Galatians 5:22–23). How? Through some magic process by which God "zaps" us and we are transformed? No, but as God's Truth grips our hearts, we are fully persuaded to be ruled by His Word, to obey Him, and to trust Him to fulfill in us what He has promised.

This is not to deny the miraculous working of the Holy Spirit powerfully in our hearts and through us in others, in ways beyond human comprehension. It is merely to say that the Bible clearly declares that God works in our lives through our obedience to His Word. As Jesus said and as we often quote because it is so basic to everything else, "If ye continue in my word, then are ye my disciples indeed; and ye shall know the truth, and the truth shall make you free" (John 8:31–32).

A Biblical "Litmus Test" for Truth

The litmus test of truth for victorious Christian living must be: Is it derived from Scripture, or is it the wisdom of this world packaged in Christian terminology in order to make it appear to be compatible with Scripture? This test should be applied not only to the sermons and writings of others but also to ourselves. We should each get on our knees and ask God, "How much of my daily life is rooted in Your Word, and how much is rooted in the world? When I am happiest, is it because I know I have pleased my Heavenly Father, am rejoicing in His grace and love, and 'the joy of the Lord is my strength' (Nehemiah 8:10)? Or am I happy because I have achieved worldly goals that bring the same joy to those who 'know not God and obey not the gospel'?"

Jesus accused the Pharisees of establishing traditions that nullified Scripture. Even the clear command to "Honour thy father and mother" had been turned completely around by the Pharisees (Matthew 15:1–6). Christ indicted them with their having established a system of religion that allowed men seemingly to honor God outwardly while in their hearts they remained committed to Self.

What left men's hearts far from God while their lips seemed to praise Him? Christ summed up His indictment by declaring that Israel's religious leaders had substituted the traditions of men for the true doctrine of God's Word (vv. 7–9). This same "leaven of the Pharisees" is fermenting in today's church. Not only have traditions of men been cloaked in pseudo-scientific language and brought into Christianity as "Christian" psychology but so has the "counsel of the ungodly" (Psalm 1:1), which we are to avoid. May God help us to boldly expose it and to stand uncompromisingly for obedience to His Word.

1. Peter R. Breggin, M.D., David Cohen, Ph.D., *Your Drug May Be Your Problem: How and Why to Stop Taking Psychiatric Medications* (Reading, MA: Perseus Books, 1999), 12-13.

2. Archibald D. Hart, *Me, Myself & I: How Far Should We Go in Our Search for Self-Fulfillment?* (Ann Arbor, MI: Servant Publications, 1992), 11, 21, etc.

3. Ibid., 247.

4. Ibid., 22.

5. Ibid., 27.

6. Ibid., 30-31.

CONTENDING FOR—OR COMPROMISING—THE TRUTH?

— Dave Hunt —

THERE IS AN INTERNATIONAL CRISIS within the church. Christian psychology has undermined faith in God and His Word and corrupted the gospel. The very definition of what it means to be a Christian is being revised. Instead of the needed reproof from pastors and Christians leaders, we have naïve acceptance of the theories and practices of psychology. Children and youth are among the most vulnerable victims, with hardly a church rising to their defense with warnings and sound doctrine to counter the world's influence. The secular world has no thought for God and is swaying Christian youth, while evangelical schools and churches are sinking deeper and deeper into compromise.

One author recalls, "My alienation from Christian values intensified in high school, where my teachers exposed me to fascinating ideas such as the theories of evolution, reincarnation, and extrasensory perception."[1] Thomas Sowell writes, "The media are concerned about a threat to education from the so-called religious right. There was no such outcry when the left began its pervasive brainwashing."[2] A university student from England reports: "At present I'm in a real battle. I'm training to be a Secondary School teacher. The syllabus includes 'stilling' or mystic meditation, introducing children to [power] animals and ancient spirits. The school is a mainstream state school and the [administration] is endorsing these shamanistic techniques."[3]

Tragically, most pulpits say little to counter the sea of faithlessness and immorality in which the church and especially its youth are literally drowning. Youths attending evangelical churches, generally deeply entrenched in the ways of the world, are seldom taught about biblical separation. The solemn command to earnestly contend for the faith once delivered to the saints (Jude 3) has been deliberately set aside by the evangelical church. This fact speaks volumes about the condition of "the faith" today. God's Word is neglected, experience is valued above truth, a psychologized gospel is being preached, a false and selfish "faith" is promoted in order to get what one wants from God, and sound doctrine and correction are despised as "divisive" and "unloving."

A subtle and appealing error is spreading from America (where it usually seems to start) to the rest of the church worldwide. And underneath the surface, often hidden or overlooked, is the pervasive influence of Christian psychology.

Error Must Be Addressed

Who will obey Jude's injunction to "earnestly contend for the faith . . . once delivered to the saints"? Not Rick Warren, who has been writing a column in *Ladies Home Journal* since December 2004, without once providing even a hint of the gospel of God's grace in Christ Jesus. Instead, he has fed readers with a steady diet of pop psychology: learning to love, esteem, and feel good about oneself, reminiscent of the heresies of Norman Vincent Peale and his chief disciple, Robert Schuller. What an opportunity thrown away by a Christian leader who knows the gospel and could have presented millions who desperately need it with God's undiluted way of salvation had he remained true to God's call on his life.

To contend for the true faith, one must not only give the gospel clearly but also speak out against error, especially confronting false gospels and what Peter identified as "damnable heresies" that would be taught in the church in the last days (2 Peter 2:1). Yet obedience to this injunction is carefully avoided by most of the popular evangelists on radio and TV in order to cultivate the largest audience possible. Billy Graham preaches directly from the Bible but has never spoken out against Roman Catholicism's false gospel that has sent billions to hell. In fact, he has repeatedly endorsed it. Billy enthusiastically described a Roman Catholic Mass (where he had preached the sermon), with its prayers for the dead and its false gospel, as "a very beautiful thing and certainly straight and clear in the gospel. . . . "[4] He gratefully quotes a U.S. Catholic newspaper: "Never once, at least in our memory, has Billy Graham attacked the Catholic Church."[5] Apparently, the millions Rome slaughtered and burned at the stake died in vain! Those facts are now suppressed for fear of offending Rome.

As with the psychiatric industry (see below), Billy wimped out on homosexuality: "I have many friends who are gay and I never condemn them from the pulpit."[6] Surely, there could be no more appropriate place than the pulpit for at least warning such "friends" as well as many others of the fact that a gay lifestyle shortens life expectancy by decades and is condemned in the Bible. Although acknowledging that homosexuality is a sin, Billy said it is no worse than many other sins, such as pride.[7] It seems doubtful that God would have destroyed Sodom and Gomorrah for pride, which is universal.

Paul declares that the Bible is to be used for "doctrine . . .

reproof . . . correction . . . instruction in righteousness" (2 Timothy 3:16). Yet Billy Graham, who preaches from the Bible, fails to use it faithfully for its major purpose. Robert Schuller and his son, who is replacing him on *The Hour of Power* (one of the most popular religious TV programs, with an estimated worldwide audience of 20 million[8]), have built and maintained their popularity by tickling listeners' ears with what they want to hear (2 Timothy 4:3–4) instead of giving them the truth they need—a truth that this father and son team apparently have never themselves embraced wholeheartedly. Where are the church leaders who have stood up against the heresies of Peale (who brought psychology into the church) and Schuller? In fact, Billy Graham and many other leaders have repeatedly commended them.

Who will stand boldly and firmly for the undiluted truth of God? Not most Christian publishers. Putting profits ahead of sound doctrine, they have made fortunes cultivating authors who give readers what they want instead of the biblical truth they need. Some have also sold out to the world monetarily as they already had morally. Isn't this the opposite of contending for the faith that we should expect from all Christians, and especially publishers, who play such a key role of leadership? They have been the major means of popularizing psychology in the church.

Deadly Compromise on Every Hand

In 1988, Zondervan and its NIV Bible were purchased for $56.7 million by Harper & Row Publishers (now HarperCollins Publishers), who publish pro-homosexual books such as *Making Out, The Book of Lesbian Sex and Sexuality* ("Beautifully illustrated with full-color photography . . . ") and others. HarperCollins is a subsidiary of Rupert Murdoch's The News Corporation, which owns Twentieth Century Fox and Fox Broadcasting. The latter produces some of the most immoral, anti-family shows on television. Murdoch purchased the Family Channel from Pat Robertson for $1.9 billion. CBN donors had provided the money to buy and operate the Family Channel in order to get the gospel into the secular market. They were not only betrayed but also robbed, having received no refund out of the huge profit.

Murdoch, an alleged born-again Christian,[9] was knighted by the pope after donating $10 million for a new Catholic cathedral in Los Angeles. He built "a media empire on the chests of topless models and edgy, pushing-the-envelope Fox TV network shows [and] recently began building a stable of hard-core porn channels for the BSkyB subsidiary."[10] Yet Billy Graham calls Murdoch a friend and says "he has been very supportive of our work. . . . "[11] Pastor Rick

Warren of Saddleback Church, of which Murdoch has claimed to be a member (and Rick has claimed to be his pastor) has been challenged either to bring Murdoch to repentance or excommunicate him from Saddleback.[12] In fact, Murdoch is not a member and has never even attended Warren's church, so Rick has no authority over him. Why Rick ever said he was Murdoch's pastor remains a mystery. Who could deny that something is seriously wrong in the evangelical church as a whole, from leaders on down?

Now Warren is feeling the heat from Christians who point out that although he has taken a biblical stand against pornography and has said that public sin must be reproved publically, he has not done so in the case of Murdoch, an esteemed friend. Sadly, Warren defends himself by saying that "Some people who only focus on moral purity . . . couldn't care less about the poor, sick, uneducated [and] haven't done zip for those people."[13] What Warren says is generally true. However, pointing to others' lack of concern for "the poor, sick, uneducated" does not excuse Warren for his own failure to openly oppose heresy. Rick Warren's popularity may be catching up with him. He will find it increasingly difficult, in spite of all the social good he has done, to defend himself for his compromise of the biblical faith he believes and at times preaches. Meeting bodily temporal needs is no substitute for meeting eternal spiritual needs with the gospel.

Chuck Colson and J. I. Packer gave their endorsement on the back cover of *Ecumenical Jihad,* which describes Confucius as God's "prophet" on the way to heaven, Buddha and Muhammad already there,[14] suggests a "hidden Christ of Hinduism" and of other pagan religions,[15] says that pagans and even atheists and agnostics may be secret believers in Jesus without knowing it,[16] that the transubstantiation effected by Catholic priests in the Eucharist is inexorably transforming the entire universe into one giant Cosmic Eucharistic Christ,[17] and that ultimately everyone, including even evangelicals, will be united in the Roman Catholic Eucharist and Mary.[18] What is happening in the church of Jesus Christ through its leadership is shocking!

The Billy Graham Evangelistic Association (BGEA) published a special "Crusade Edition" (1962, 1964, 1969) of *Halley's Bible Handbook,* from which they removed Halley's careful documentation of the evil of the popes and the slaughter of true Christians. How else could BGEA maintain the support and friendship with Roman Catholics that Billy has cultivated carefully over the years? Says Billy, "I am very comfortable with the Vatican. I have been to see the Pope [John Paul II] several times. . . . He and I agree on almost everything."[19] Zondervan published a revised edition of *Halley's Bible Handbook* in 2000, which likewise eliminated references to the RCC's heresies and the millions of evangelical Christians slaughtered by Rome. Instead, it says: "The Roman Catholic Church responded to the Protestant Reformation by reforming and renewing itself."

When challenged about such lies, Stan Gundry, Zondervan's Vice President and Editor-in-Chief, responded, "The purpose of the rewriting was . . . to give a more balanced portrayal of the history of Christianity." Whitewashing Roman Catholic doctrine and practice and leaving out the slaughter of millions of Christians gives a "more balanced" history?! And who owns Zondervan, publisher of Rick Warren's *The Purpose-Driven Life*? None other than Rupert Murdoch. Why would a Christian publisher sell out to "one of the world's leading pornographers,"[20] and why would a pornographer want to own a Christian publisher? The motive on both sides is obviously money—to be expected of a pornographer but shameful for Christians. Such hypocrisy, however, which put a profit into the hands of Zondervan's stockholders, is scarcely noticed by church leaders, who are only too pleased to have another wealthy "Christian" on their side.

What Do "Christians" Really Believe?

What is *the faith* (gospel) for which we are to "earnestly contend"? Paul defines it as the death, burial, and resurrection of Christ *according to the Scriptures* (1 Corinthians 15:3–4). Surely that involves who God is, who Christ is, the problem between God and man, the only means of man's forgiveness by God, and the eternal consequences for those who reject the biblical gospel—all according to the Bible, not according to anything or anyone else.

Scripture declares that everyone who believes the gospel of Christ is made "a new creature: old things are passed away; behold, all things are become new" (2 Corinthians 5:17). To suggest that these "new creatures," in whom Christ lives as their very life, should need any help whatsoever from Freud or the other godless originators of psychology or from any of their current followers is to spit in the face of Jesus Christ! Yet this is the universally held position of today's church! Apparently, most Christians don't *really* believe that Christ is indwelling them and that they are in Him like branches in the True Vine (John 15:1–14). They don't *really* believe that we are "more than conquerors through him that loved us" (Romans 8:37) or that God "always causeth us to triumph in Christ, and maketh manifest the savour of his knowledge by us in every place" (2 Corinthians 2:14).

Jesus, who is the truth (John 14:6), said to the Father, "Thy word is truth" (John 17:17). The entire Word of God is foundational to the faith for which we are to earnestly contend against all who deny it. The very foundation of Christian psychology is a denial of the sufficiency of Scripture—a denial that must boldly be maintained in order to support Christian psychology in any respect. Were the church to believe and preach and live what Scripture commands and promises, every Christian psychologist would have to find another job! This statement is irrefutable.

Sadly, the church and world are being robbed of the pure Word of God by professing evangelicals. One of Rick Warren's favorite versions of the Bible, Eugene Peterson's *The Message* (NavPress, 1993), changes God's Word into the "social gospel," downgrading salvation to earthly improvement. Yet it is praised by evangelical leaders! The popular *Renovaré* "Bible" rejects divine inspiration and trashes prophecies about Israel and Christ. DVD "Bibles" are increasingly popular. Slowly but surely, Christians are replacing the pure Word of God with dramatizations thereof that may eventually be the only "Bible" most Christians "read."

Facing Unpleasant Facts

Although America is acknowledged to be the most religious country in the world, with more than 90 percent of its citizens consistently claiming to believe in God, the favorite deities of many bear no relationship to the God of the Bible. That book is in more than 90 percent of America's homes, yet only 20 percent of owners read it daily. Never was a best-selling book ($1 billion in sales annually) read in such tiny fragments, so laboriously, and with such little genuine interest. Biblical illiteracy even among so-called born-again believers has reached scandalous proportions, with little help from pulpits to remedy the situation. We are raising a generation of youth on the spiritual junk food of Bible translations presented in comic book form or as video games. The Bible is being "improved" by script writers, movie directors, and actors, who are replacing the actual "incorruptible . . . word of God" by which we are "born again" (1 Peter 1:23–25), with dramatic misrepresentations. The entire New Testament is now on video and may soon be the only "Bible" young people know.

Failure of the church to speak the truth "as the truth is in Jesus" (Ephesians 4:21) has left the world to flounder in evil, with almost no biblical correction from Christian leaders. This is not surprising. The most popular "gospel" and perspective on life among Christians is that presented by "Christian" psychologists; and psychology in the church is the same as secular psychology in the world, which is its source. This ecumenical bridge has brought the church and the world increasingly closer together. As a result, the influence of the world can be seen almost everywhere in the church.

The old hymns that had depth of meaning and sound doctrine have largely been replaced by shallow, repetitive, jazzy choruses with a beat that appeals to today's youth. Supposed worship of God often seems more like entertainment. The Bible has been mutilated to create new paraphrased versions that dumb Scripture down so far that it would be almost unrecognizable to past generations. America's pulpits preach "loving Jesus" in the place of believing on and obeying Him, forgetful of His declaration, "If a man love me, he will keep my words" (John 14:23). Christianity is metamorphosing into a popular religion to which the ungodly can convert without any noticeable change in the way they live.

Ironically, Christians are repeating in the church the same error that conservatives recognize and oppose in government and education. The American educational system, the world's most costly, is an international disgrace, with our students ranking near the bottom in most academic comparisons. There are about five hundred thousand violent incidents each month in our schools, including serious injuries to a thousand teachers. We have fifteen to twenty times as many students in special education classes as other developed countries. How did we arrive at this current national disgrace?

Psychology's Expanding Ripple

Most of the blame can be laid on the doorstep of the so-called Mental Health Profession, which has literally manufactured victims and cowed the world and the church into submission by claiming an expertise it doesn't have but to which everyone must submit. Psychiatrists and psychologists increase their influence by inventing new "scientific" labels for every aspect of human behavior, including much that used to be called "normal." Old-fashioned laziness, selfishness, and disobedience are now categorized as "mental disorders" with prescribed "professional" treatment, which most likely includes harmful psychotropic drugs. And so it is in the church as well through "Christian" psychology.

The "Bible" of this highly profitable growth industry is the *Diagnostic and Statistical Manual of Mental Disorders*. It has gone through many revisions since it was first conceived and published in 1952 by the American Psychiatric Association, with one hundred twelve "mental disorders" listed by name. By 1987, when *DSM-III-R* was issued, an apparent epidemic of mental illness had struck the United States, and the number of "mental disorders" had more than doubled to two hundred fifty-three. Almost none could be supported scientifically, and many had been included (or excluded) by vote of members.

For example, under pressure from the homosexual community, homosexuality, long listed as abnormal behavior, was declared to be a "sexual preference." Did this result from a scientific study and finding? No. It was by a vote of 5,854 in favor, and 3,810 opposed. And they dare to call this "science"!

Psychology couldn't possibly be a science for many reasons that we have enumerated elsewhere. To this fact the *DSM* itself attests: ". . . there is no satisfactory definition that specifies precise boundaries for the concept 'mental disorder. . . .' For most of the *DSM-III* disorders . . . the etiology is unknown. A variety of theories have been advanced, buttressed by evidence—not always that convincing—to explain how these disorders come about."[21]

Of course, these "disorders" require professional treatment by those who have diagnosed them. This belief assures the psychology and psychiatry industry of growth and almost totalitarian power. Those who accept their authority are firmly in their clutches and in the iron grip of the drug industry with which psychology and psychiatry have a close and profitable relationship. Gradually, the concerned patient becomes convinced that he or she does indeed have a dread "mental disease" and enters a thorny wilderness of treatment accompanied by confusion and warnings. It can be frightening just to read the label on the container listing the possible serious side effects of the psychotropic medication (from increased depression to suicide to brain and nervous disorders, etc.) that the doctor so readily prescribed and the pharmacist dutifully provided.

Pushing the Bible and Its Wisdom Aside

Raising a child, though a difficult responsibility that parents must take seriously, used to be a routine that was successfully completed by millions. Pioneer/frontier families of eight and ten or more children (with nothing except common sense and firm discipline) did quite well under almost impossible conditions far more rigorous than anything experienced by today's families. Children have different personalities and ambitions and can be difficult to understand and to train—but the parents learn to be firm and the children, in spite of initial complaints, actually prefer to have definite rules that are enforced impartially.

The Bible advocates "the rod" as the remedy for disobedience. Solomon declared, "He that spareth his rod hateth his son: but he that loveth him chasteneth him betimes" (Proverbs 13:24). Spanking is now "child abuse" and correction of any kind is avoided as "negative" and harmful to a "positive self-image," which is the key to all "behavior modification." The same delusions of humanistic psychology that have created rebellion in the world have entered the church and now plague it through "Christian" psychology.

The purpose of school is to teach essential skills and knowledge in subjects that prepare students to earn a living. Psychology provides phony excuses for laziness, rebellion, and sin. No one is guilty; everyone is a victim. The heart is not evil, as the Bible repeatedly declares; low self-esteem is the problem, as James Dobson and other "experts" declare—a delusion they have imported from the world. Sin has become "mental illness," requiring not repentance but therapy. Instead of the fundamentals of reading, writing, and math, educators consume vital school time teaching environmentalism, sex education (which has only made matters worse), multiculturalism, self-esteem, and self-importance. The only hope is a return to the old-fashioned fundamentals of teaching the essentials and enforcing discipline.

The church, too, needs to return to biblical fundamentals and God's truth without compromise. The church's purpose is to love and worship God and to call out of this world citizens for heaven—not to reform society. If Christians could persuade everyone on earth to live as uprightly as Nicodemus, they would still be bound for hell—and doubly hard to convince of their need of Christ because of their splendid morality.

Society will not even be reformed when Christ himself rules the world from Jerusalem, with Satan locked up for a thousand years and earth an Edenic paradise once again. For when Satan is later released, he will deceive millions, who will make war to destroy Christ (Revelation 20:1–9). The Millennium is the final proof that a perfect environment without crime or war and a righteous government are neither the solution nor God's goal. Sin is in the human heart. Yes, God will destroy this present universe and create a new one without sin. But its inhabitants will be a new race of repentant sinners transformed through faith in the Lord Jesus Christ as the One who paid the debt for sin.

To be saved, one must only believe the gospel. There is nothing else that anyone or any religious institution can do to save a soul. It is equally unbiblical to teach that salvation can be lost if one fails to live a good enough life, yet this error persists worldwide. Yes, the Scriptures urge us to live holy, fruitful lives for Christ, which is the norm for real Christians. And yes, the warnings to those who do not (if taken in isolation) sometimes seem to teach that one can lose his or her salvation. [We offer a tract titled "Once Saved, Always Saved?" that goes into the relevant Bible verses in detail on this important subject.][22]

Suffice it to say that if salvation may be lost by not living a good enough life, then those in heaven will be able to boast before God's throne: "Christ died to save me, but I kept my salvation by the good life I lived, so I deserve credit, too, for being here." On the contrary, salvation, both in its reception and retention, is all of God and all of grace through Christ, "not of works, lest any man should boast" (Ephesians 2:9). He will share His glory with no one (Isaiah 42:8; 48:11).

Faith in Christ brings liberty, joy, and great peace. Yet many Christians labor under the impossible burden of trying to live up to a standard they can't maintain in order not to lose their salvation. Christianity isn't just difficult, it's impossible! The only one who can live the Christian life is Christ himself. *Stop trying to live it in your own strength and let Christ live it through you by faith in the power of the Holy Spirit.* Rest in Him!

There are those who reject works for their own salvation yet work mightily to save others through fleshly attractions and techniques. They reason that surely sinners would come to Christ if they were invited by a beautiful actress, a top athlete, or popular public figure. And now we have "virtual reality." Satan will use it for the greatest seduction ever of mankind. It will enable anyone to have the wildest adventures and even sex orgies in one's own living room. Paul Crouch is going to be the "*First* to use it for the *Gospel*!" He exults, "What if at the end of the film, Jesus Christ, Himself, could walk up to you and invite you to accept *Him*?!"[23] [Emphasis in original.] Yet in His day, multitudes confronted Jesus Christ in person, not some actor or "virtual reality," and even so they rejected Him. Dramatizations of the gospel are a vain delusion that obscures the truth presented by God in written words in order to bring us to Christ, who is "the Word of God" (Revelation 19:13).

Would Christ have been more effective if only He had used Christian psychology? Wouldn't that have helped Him in counseling the woman at the well? No! Then of what value is psychology today? Would Paul have won more souls if he only he'd had at his disposal virtual reality, or at least a rock band or some brick-smashing musclemen on his tour? In fact, he preached the gospel "in weakness and . . . trembling," and carefully avoided using human wisdom to persuade anyone (1 Corinthians 2:1–5).

People are being persuaded to become "Christians" by fleshly means and for prosperity or healing or the better family life they've been promised rather than by repentance of their sin and faith in Christ. Let us, like Paul, devote ourselves to the pure gospel in reliance upon the Holy Spirit to convince and convict and regenerate through His Word.

1. Will Baron, *Deceived by the New Age* (Nampa, ID: Pacific Press Publishing Association, 1990), 19.

2. *Forbes*, February 1, 1993.

3. Letter from England on file.

4. David Cloud, *Flirting with Rome* (Way of Life Literature, 1993).

5. Billy Graham, *Just As I Am:The Autobiography of Billy Graham* (San Francisco, CA; New York, NY: HarperSanFrancisco/Zondervan, 1997), 368.

6. *Denver Post*, April 19, 1987.

7. *20/20 TV Show*, May 2, 1997; *Christian News*, October 20, 1997, 7.

8. http://videoediting.digitalmedianet.com/articles/viewarticle.jsp?id+10661.

9. http://www.arcamax.com/religiousnews/s-189789-933803.

10. http://www.wnd.com/news/article.asp?ARTICLE_ID=55616.

11. Graham, *Just As I Am*, 334.

12. http://www.arcamax.com/religiousnews/s-189789-933803.

13. http://www.latimes.com/news/nationwide/nation/la-na-orphans13may13,1,1469713.story.

14. Peter Kreeft, *Ecumenical Jihad* (San Francisco: Ignatius Press, 1996), 96-111.

15. Ibid., 156-60.

16. Ibid., 156-61.

17. Ibid., 158.

18. Ibid., 145-55.

19. *Larry King Live*, January 21, 1997, transcript obtainable from Federal Document Clearing House, 1100 Mercantile Lane, Suite 119, Landover, MD 20785.

20. http://www.worldnetdaily.com/news/article.asp?_ID=55616.

21. American Psychiatric Association, *Diagnostic and Statistical Manual of Mental Disorders* (Washington, D.C.: Third Edition, 1980), 1.

22. See "Once Saved, Always Saved," a tract by Dave Hunt, offered by The Berean Call, PO Box 7019, Bend OR 97708.

23. TBN's December 1994 newsletter.

A GOD WHO HIDES HIMSELF

— *Dave Hunt* —

"**Y**OU'VE COME A LONG WAY, BABY!" said the cigarette ad. And so today's woman has. She is free to smoke and destroy her lungs, arteries, and heart like a man. She is also free to turn her womb into an execution chamber with the blessing of America's highest court of justice. Popular TV talk show hosts congratulate her for the "courage" to murder her own offspring to protect her personal "rights." And millions demonstrate in the streets for "the right of choice" not only for abortion but for all manner of "freedoms"—homosexuality, bestiality, incest, pedophilia, and drugs. Those brazenly flaunted perversions would have made past generations blush with shame. Yes, she's come a long way, and so have we all.

The liberal, humanist agenda is clear: to do away with our God-given conscience. Virtue is ridiculed, evil is praised as good and liberating, and biblical moral standards are mocked as the narrow-minded thinking of a past generation out of touch with today's reality. Inevitably, "negative" judgments about homosexuals, the government, women's reproductive rights, and non-Christian religions will be forbidden—and likely much sooner than most Christians suspect.

The seeds of this liberal totalitarianism are sprouting even in evangelical circles, where those who dare to oppose false teachings and sin are accused of division, are denied a voice from pulpits, radio and TV, and their books are refused display in many Christian bookstores. To fail to see the connection between the censoring of biblical reproof in the church and the rejection of corrective teaching as "negative," and the coming government ban upon any criticism of immorality, is to be blind indeed. Once it was the law that ruled, now it is the "minorities" who dictate behavior and attitudes—and woe to those who oppose them.

Who is behind it all? Satan, "the god of this world" (2 Corinthians 4:4). To be called by that title, he must be the leader of all false religions. What does he get out of the hypocrisy, pretentious piety, and religious malevolence he has inspired? A cry of rage in billions of minds swells to a tidal wave of protest against God. He is mocked and blamed for what Satan and his follower, man, have done.

"Where are you God?!" The hollow accusation echoes across the ages. In a still, small voice God whispers through His prophets, "Verily thou art a God that hidest thyself, O God of Israel, the Saviour" (Isaiah 45:15). Where is God hiding?

A Sociologically and Psychologically Rejected but Truthful Diagnosis

What is wrong with America is not complicated nor will expensive government programs cure it. These programs have produced statistics indicating that more than 6 million adults have served time in State or Federal prisons and one of every fifteen persons will serve time in a prison during his or her lifetime. Mankind is in a state of rebellion against God and His standards, having deliberately chosen to go its own way. Psychology, by encouraging the idea that we are all victims of parental abuse, government tyranny, bad luck, or a hundred other reasons, has accelerated the growth of crime in America, a statistic unmatched anywhere in the world. Could that be because we are the most psychologically analyzed, treated, medicated, and coddled of any society today or in history?

From its very beginning, "Christian" psychology also followed secular psychology's rejection of Scripture. Christ declared: "For out of the heart proceed evil thoughts, murders, adulteries, fornications, thefts, false witness, blasphemies: These are the things which defile a man. . . " (Matthew 15:19). Instead, psychology blames rebellious, criminal behavior on everything except the heart of man. This is why psychology fails; therapy tries to deal with the symptoms, but it cannot change the heart. Yet it is in the heart that evil is hatched and out of the heart that it manifests itself in attitudes and actions. Only God can search and change the heart.

It was only after years of working directly with hundreds of criminals that clinical psychologist Stanton E. Samenow and psychiatrist Samuel Yochelson, though not Christians and thus not "Christian psychologists," were forced to admit that Christ, in contrast to modern psychology, had correctly diagnosed humanity. They concluded,

> Crime resides within the person and is "caused" by the way he thinks, not by his environment. . . . We found the conventional psychological and sociological formulations about crime and its causes to be erroneous and counterproductive because they provide excuses.[1]

After closely studying hundreds of criminals firsthand as the assistant to Dr. Yochelson (who pioneered this new approach), Dr. Samenow confessed:

When I began this work, I believed that criminal behavior was a symptom of buried conflicts that had resulted from early traumas and deprivation of one sort or another. I thought that people who turned to crime were victims of a psychological disorder, an oppressive social environment, or both. [For] inner city youths, I saw crime as being almost a normal, if not excusable, reaction to the grinding poverty, instability, and despair that pervaded their lives . . . and that kids who were from more advantaged backgrounds had been scarred by bad parenting and led astray by peer pressure. . . .

When it came to understanding Yochelson's "crooks," as he referred to them, I discovered that I had to unlearn nearly everything I had learned in graduate school. Only reluctantly did I do so, debating many points along the way. But Dr. Yochelson told me that he had had to do exactly the same. . . .

We found the conventional psychological and sociological formulations about crime and its causes to be erroneous and counterproductive because they provide excuses. In short, we did a 180-degree turn in our thinking about crime and its causes. From regarding criminals as victims [of past traumas and deprivations] we saw that instead they were victimizers who had freely chosen their way of life.[2]

But the psychology industry's "experts" continue to convince judges and juries that it isn't really the criminal's fault, even in the case of murder or attempted murder. Consider the following example:

The Durham decision (District of Columbia Court of Appeals, 1954), enunciated by Judge D. L. Bazelon, held that people could be ruled not guilty by reasons of "irresistible impulse." That decision later led to the acquittal of John Hinckley in the attempted assassination of President Ronald Reagan. Bazelon himself has since questioned that decision, but it is still in effect.[3]

A Profession in Conflict with Itself

Even from a secular point of view, clinical psychology is dead wrong on nearly all of its conclusions and therapies. Far from being beneficial, it has proved to be harmful. Increasing numbers of disillusioned psychologists are speaking out against their own profession. As one clinical psychologist, after years of trying desperately to prove that her profession worked by showing demonstrable benefits, wrote:

Psychology presents itself as a concerned and caring profession working for the good of its clients. But in its wake lie damaged people, divided families, distorted justice, destroyed companies, and a weakened nation. Behind the benevolent façade is a voracious self-serving industry that proffers "facts" which are often unfounded, provides "therapy" which can be damaging to its recipients, and exerts influence which is having devastating effects on the social fabric.

The foundation of modern psychology, its questioning and critical thinking, if not an illusion from its inception, has at the very least been largely abandoned in favor of power and profit, leaving only the guise of integrity, a show of arrogance and a well-tuned attention to the bottom line. What seemed once a responsible profession is now a big business whose success is directly related to how many people become "users."

No matter where one turns, one finds the effects of the psychology industry. It's influence extends across all aspects of life, telling us how to work, how to live, how to love and, even, how to play. We are confronted by psychologists expounding their theories on the endless list of TV talk-shows . . . TV news journals and in the supermarket tabloids. . . .

People who are mildly anxious, slightly unhappy or just plain bored are turning more and more to psychology for relief. Some do this through weekly appointments; some do it by frequenting seminars and workshops; some do it by endlessly buying books on "abuse," "adult children," "trauma and stress," "recovery"; all in pursuit of an elusive experience held out, like a carrot or pot of gold, by the Psychology Industry.

It is not news to say that psychology has become an influential force or that society is becoming more and more filled with people who consider themselves victims of one sort or another.

What is news is that psychology is itself manufacturing most of these victims, that it is doing this with motives based on power and profit, and that the industry turns people into dependent "users": with no escape from their problems.[4]

In spite of exposés, the influence of psychology grows ever larger in our society, and the list of its manufactured victims grows ever longer and more tragic. Nor is Christian psychology any different from its secular partner that regulates it. Psychology's lies persist while the Bible, which has the only answers, is neglected or misinterpreted. Typical is the following from the Tompkins County, New York Mental Health Association *Journal*: "The [psychological] healing process cannot be completed until the childhood memories that were stuffed into the subconscious during the abuse are remembered, talked about and openly acknowledged. 'The truth shall set us free' remains the basis for all deep psychotherapy. . . . "

What a perversion of Christ's words! The truth of which He spoke has no relation to psychotherapy. Instead, it sets one free from sin by God's supernatural power working in those who repent, believe on Christ as having paid the penalty for their sins, are, by that faith, "born again" of the Holy Spirit, and obey God's Word. There is no other way. Christian psychology actually hinders the transformation by turning the believer to self and psychological theories and therapies that can only lead one away from total dependence upon God, His Word, and the indwelling Spirit of Christ.

"Christian" Psychology Is Not Christian

Every evil in today's world is a continuation of the rebellion against God that began in the Garden of Eden. "[R]epentance toward God, and faith toward our Lord Jesus Christ," which Paul and the other apostles preached (Acts 20:21), is the only remedy. Yet the church is diluting the gospel and devoting itself to social and political activism in alliance with the ungodly. Saving the world has replaced saving souls. Those "dead in sin" (Ephesians 2:1; Colossians 2:13) are being embalmed, even by Christians, with toxic sociological and psychological formulas instead of being raised to new life in Christ. Through redefining as mental illness what the Bible labels sin, modern man, like Adam and Eve, still hides from God. Consequently, God is hidden from His creature.

For a generation now, the pens and pulpits of prominent evangelicals, following the heretical lead of Norman Vincent Peale and his protégé Robert Schuller, have poured forth an ever-increasing flood of sincere but misguided advice rooted in selfist psychology. Multitudes of Christians have been persuaded thereby that they do not love themselves enough, when, in fact, their real problem is that they do not love God as they ought. Instead of seeking God, they are seeking to know themselves. The gospel of self-love and self-esteem, unknown in the church for more than nineteen hundred years, was not discovered at this late date through diligent Bible study and Spirit-inspired insight into Scripture. In fact, far from being taught in God's Word, this "new truth" is condemned therein. It has another source.

The facts are undeniable. Christian psychology sprang from godless theories foisted upon society as a rival gospel by psychologists determined to destroy Christianity. Typical was Freud, who, as research psychiatrist Thomas Szasz (himself a Jew) reminds us, was motivated by "the desire to inflict vengeance upon Christianity." Many of Jung's key theories and practices, by his own admission, were inspired by the "spirit" world. Inexplicably, the enticing speculations of anti-Christians—though so clearly contradictory to God's Word—have been welcomed by the church as a new source of "God's truth." Christian psychologist Bruce Narramore has unashamedly admitted that the theory (now popularly accepted as evangelical truth) that self-love and self-esteem are desirable originated with "humanistic psychologists like Carl Rogers and Abraham Maslow"[5] and only recently has begun to be embraced by Christians.

The fact that Maslow reversed Christ's "seek ye first the kingdom of God, and his righteousness"(Matthew 6:33) and put spiritual needs last did not deter Christian leaders from proclaiming his "hierarchy of needs" as a newly discovered part of "God's truth." Nor did it concern Christian psychologists, who built upon his theories, that Rogers called Self the "god within" and turned from his dying wife to another woman in order to worship at Self's "altar within," as he advocated—or that after her death Rogers' wife contacted him in a séance and gave her approval of what he'd done, which caused great relief to the psychologist.

Following in the footsteps of godless psychologists, Christian psychology brazenly turned Christ's "deny self" into "love, esteem, accept, develop, assert and highly value self"—and almost no one seemed to notice the switch. It wasn't surprising that Peale's most famous disciple, Robert Schuller, would declare that Christ had endured the cross to sanctify His and our self-esteem. But it was shocking how many evangelical leaders would join Billy Graham in endorsing Schuller's books and ministry and how eagerly his unbiblical humanistic theories were embraced by Bible scholar/shepherds and taught to trusting sheep.

Inspired by anti-Christians, an ever-growing number of today's prominent evangelicals preach sermons and write books glorifying Self—and Christians love it. Leading Christian publishers eagerly use their presses and prestige to proclaim the popular new gospel. Christian psychologists and psychiatrists, the new infallible authorities on spiritual problems affecting individuals and families, follow new extra-biblical sources of "God's truth" (Freud, Jung, Maslow, Rogers, Adler, Milton H. Erickson [founding president, American Society of Clinical Hypnosis], R. D. Laing, Adolph Meyer [past president of APA], Philippe Pinel [father of modern psychiatry], Robert Spitzer [chair of DSM-III, 1980], Viktor Frankl, William James, et al.).

With their new gospel, Christian psychiatrists and psychologists are the most sought-after conference speakers, while the growing budget to advertise their expanding and lucrative empires of clinics and counseling centers has sparked an explosion in Christian radio. One of the top-rated Christian radio programs, airing on two thousand stations, is not hosted by a Bible teacher, but by James Dobson, a psychologist. Known as "America's foremost authority on the family," Dobson is the most trusted advisor in the church. Yet, according to his office, Dobson deliberately avoids an emphasis upon God's Word and bases his counsel upon humanistic psychology, especially the theory of self-esteem.

Moreover, those giving phone counsel in Dobson's ministry are required to be licensed. It is quite clear that he has more confidence in psychology than in Scripture and in psychologists than in biblical prophets and apostles.

The new gospel and its psychologized view of Scripture have become the standard belief in evangelical churches, seminaries, and universities. Those who oppose it as unbiblical are dismissed as ignorant, narrowminded, and unscholarly.

The greatest growth in both the world and the church (other than in drugs, which has been astronomical) has been in the numbers of those dispensing and those receiving psychological counsel. At the same time, the number of Christians involved in immorality, divorce, and the living of frustrated, unhappy lives has kept pace with the rapid growth of the same evils among the ungodly. And why not, since both largely follow the same humanistic theories not only in the creation/evolution debate but in psychology? Like the unsaved, most Christians are convinced of an urgent need to esteem and value themselves more highly—when, in reality, the real problem is that they value themselves too highly and care too little for others and God!

Symptoms of the Last Days

There can be no doubt that we are in the "perilous times" that Paul warned would be characterized by men being "lovers of their own selves" (2 Timothy 3:1–2). Man has always been narcissistic, but for the first time in history self-love is praised and promoted—and selfishly "looking out for Number 1" is a virtue! Even among many evangelicals God commands little reverence and is generally treated as though He exists primarily to fulfill man's desires.

Multitudes of Christians uncritically accept heresy from a Benny Hinn who promises physical healing that doesn't happen, but they refuse correction that would bring desperately needed spiritual healing. Millions seek happiness, but few desire holiness. The gifts are eagerly sought; the Giver is slighted. The pursuit is of blessings rather than the Blesser. Paul's desire "that I may know him" (Philippians 3:10) has been exchanged for "that I might know myself and have my plans blessed by Him." Yet the Bible plainly states that God "is a rewarder of them that diligently seek *him*" (Hebrews 11:6). Those who seek *blessings* from God rather than seeking *Him* are to be pitied no matter how much health or wealth they imagine they receive by positive/possibility thinking. Such self-centered prayers are not "answered" by God but by circumstance or Satan.

Many Christians selfishly imagine that the above verse provides a formula for getting a car, house, good job, and other things from God. Yet what a bad bargain it would be to receive the whole world instead of Him! God wants to reward us with Himself, but most Christians are seeking everything else. Yes, we do have needs in this life and He has promised to meet them. But He has told us to seek first the kingdom of God (which is "not meat and drink" [Romans 14:17] but Himself reigning in our hearts) and His righteousness (Matthew 6:33), and whatever needs we have will be supplied. Those who seek God with the whole heart have no anxieties! This—not psychological therapy—is the antidote for unhappy or fearful souls.

Today's world is rushing headlong to judgment. Many Christians, caught up in the mad pace, find little time for the one worthwhile pursuit both for this life and the next: knowing, loving, and worshiping God. Christianity has been formularized: a few songs, some prayers, a brief, uplifting sermon, hasty parking lot greetings; then, conscience too easily appeased, a hurried departure to the real world of earthly pursuits and pleasures. How paradoxical that the lives of His professed followers leave so little room for God! It is not our natural bent to seek Him but rather to hide from Him. We can only seek God as He first has sought us and draws us to Himself through the wooing of His Holy Spirit in our hearts. This He will do if He is our true and deep desire.

What does it mean to seek God—and, after all, what is the point? Is He not "a God who hides Himself"? Where was God in the Gulag, or Auschwitz? Where has He been hiding in Iraq, Afghanistan, Sudan, Israel, Somalia, or in the earthquakes, hurricanes, tidal waves, tornadoes, floods, and fires that ravage this earth? Where is God when we pray and have no sense that anyone is hearing or even cares? Where and why does He hide when we need Him most? Has He no pity for the weeping widow or orphan?

God is not mocked. He is too loving and wise to jump to the aid of those who, having turned a deaf ear to the witness of creation and conscience, now suddenly cry out in disaster for His help. The very tragedy prolonged may prove to be the only means of causing a stubborn heart to turn to Him at last. Christ didn't rush right back to Bethany to raise Lazarus from a sick bed but waited to raise him from the dead in a far greater demonstration of power. The cry must be deeper than a plea for mere rescue from trouble. One's utter hopelessness without God—the opposite of self-esteem, self-worth, etc.—must be seen and the sin of self-importance and self-will confessed. One's desperate need of Him not only in the present circumstances but for eternity must be confessed if God is to be known.

When the God Who Hides Will Be Revealed

It is not easy for God to reveal Himself. He won't reward mere curiosity. It requires a passion to know Him on our part. How can He help those who, if He worked a miracle in response to their cry, would give credit to Buddha, to Allah, or to some "spirit" or idol or occult force? Reinforcing faith in false gods would not be a kindness but would only grease the road to hell. God hides Himself—not from those who can see but only from those who won't. The ego of man is so inflated that it obscures the God who fills the universe, whose infinite wisdom and power are conspicuous in every leaf and star.

Men are blinded because of their freely chosen false ideas. Most people are not interested in knowing the true God but a "god" who suits their taste, with whom they feel comfortable, and who gives them their desires. Masons, New Agers and members of many of the numerous Twelve-Steps programs such as Alcoholics Anonymous insist that any concept of a "higher power" will do; just believe in "God as you conceive Him to be." God will not reveal Himself to that false faith—but Satan will happily oblige to foster such delusion.

Even many professing Christians have been deceived by popular church-taught formulas for knowing God. One of the most deadly is the belief that God or Christ can be known by visualizing them as one imagines them to be. These visual images conjured up in "inner healing" or "two-way prayer" sometimes even speak, and this is the fastest way to pick up an "inner" or "spirit guide"—literally a demon masquerading as "God," "Christ," "Mary," or whomever one wished to meet and visualized for that occult purpose. The demonization that takes place is not entered into deliberately but is a form of entrapment about which the visualizer cannot complain because he has involved himself in unbiblical techniques that cheapen God and lead in a direction that common sense ought to recognize as deadly.

Nearly thirty years ago, Iran's Ayatollah Khomeini declared, "The purest joy in Islam is to kill and to be killed for Allah!" Since then, hundreds of "suicide bombers" have demonstrated their faith in this Allah of Islam, who promises rewards in "Paradise" for murdering innocent women and children, the more victims the greater the reward—and especially if they are Jews. Such is not the God of the Bible, who *is love* and whose followers He empowers to love in His name even their enemies.

Now God hides Himself from a world determined not to follow Him but to take its own way. As it was in Israel, so today, everyone wants to do whatever he wants. Any gods will be accepted and honored that honor man as he is, call for no repentance, and promise a false peace built upon "the brotherhood of man." The true God is hidden from a world that has sunk to such depths that He can only reveal Himself in the worst judgment ever known.

Yes, "the day of the Lord *will* come" (2 Peter 3:10). When Christ returns, as He left, to the Mount of Olives, the entire world, including the fish, birds, animals, and insects, will tremble at His presence (Ezekiel 38:18–20). God will reveal Himself to the entire world in judgment: "Every eye shall see him . . . and all kindreds of the earth shall wail because of him" (Revelation 1:7), and all flesh will know that He is God!

May our passion be to know and love Him now. May our lives be characterized by a reverent fear of Him. And may we persuade those about us to know, through Jesus Christ, the only true God, whom to know is life eternal.

1. Stanton E. Samenow, Ph.D., *Inside the Criminal Mind* (New York: Times Books, 1984), xiv.

2. Ibid., xii-xiv.

3. Robyn M. Dawes, *House of Cards: Psychology and Psychotherapy Built on Myth* (New York: The Free Press, 1994), 229.

4. Dr. Tana Dineen, *Manufacturing Victims: What the Psychology Industry Is Doing to People* (Westmount, Quebec: Robert Davies Publishing, 1996), 15-16.

5. Bruce Narramore, *You're Someone Special* (Zondervan, 1978), 22.

LOVE IS A COMMAND

— Dave Hunt —

GOD GAVE TEN COMMANDMENTS to Israel at Mount Sinai, which Christ sums up as, "Thou shalt love the Lord thy God with all thy heart, and with all thy soul, and with all thy mind . . . [and] thy neighbor as thyself" (Matthew 22:37–40). These are the essence of the Bible upon which, Christ said, "hang all the law and the prophets." While nothing else can rival these two primary commandments, many others are given. Paul tells us to "rejoice ever more . . . in everything give thanks . . . be anxious for nothing," etc. Christ says, "Come unto me . . . and I will give you rest (Matthew 11:28). . . . Follow me (Matthew 4:19) . . . abide in me" (John 15:4), etc.

Never is there in all of the Bible the slightest suggestion that certain people, saved or unsaved, might not be able to obey these commands. No room for excuses is given. No one is allowed to say, "I can't love God because my natural father abused me and I could never love him; I can't rejoice because I'm of a melancholy disposition for which I'm on medication, and so many things have been going wrong; I can't give thanks in everything because so many bad things have happened to me; it's impossible for me not to be anxious and worried because this is just the way I am and life has dealt me such heavy blows, etc."

We can offer no excuse for disobeying any of God's commands. If this seems harsh, don't blame me! I am only pointing out what the Bible clearly declares. This fact must be faced honestly and with faith in the Lord, who can do for us what we can't do ourselves.

It is right here that psychology appeals to human nature by providing the justification we all seek for our unbelief and disobedience. It comes to our rescue with scientific-sounding terms such as addiction, syndrome, mental disease, behavioral disorder, etc., that psychology says we can hide behind. The church is plagued by the "yes, but" syndrome. *Isn't the Bible God's inerrant Word?* "Yes, but . . . I've tried it, and it doesn't work for me." *Don't we have the leading of the Holy Spirit, and Christ indwelling to guide and empower us?* "Yes, but . . ." and silence. *Was not the Word of God, the comfort and guidance of the Holy Spirit, and the indwelling Christ sufficient for suffering and martyred Christians during the first eighteen centuries of the church?* "Yes, but . . . the world is more complex today and we need additional help." *The heroes and heroines of the faith mentioned in Hebrews 11 triumphed amidst fierce persecution without psychology.* "Yes, but . . . you don't understand my situation . . . my children, my husband [or wife], my boss, the abuse I suffered as a child . . . and they say it could affect me for life."

Just remember, there is no allowance for such excuses in Scripture.

The Illness Excuse

Many of psychology's most appealing "escape hatches" from responsibility incorporate the words "illness" or "disease." Here is how the argument goes: "No one is blamed for coming down with a physical illness, so why should I feel guilty for having a mental illness?" The analogy, however, fails miserably. Physical bodies are afflicted with illness—but not souls, spirits, or minds, which are nonphysical. As the Bobgans often say, "There is a difference between tissues and issues." World-renowned psychiatrist, Thomas Szasz, titled one of his books, *The Myth of Mental Illness.* Although we often speak of thieves and murderers as "sick," Szasz proves that there is no such thing as a "mental illness."

Another of Szasz's books was titled, *The Myth of Psychotherapy.* Nor is Szasz alone in his withering criticism. Many more secular psychiatrists and psychologists than we can name here are exposing their own profession. In a book subtitled *Overcoming the Illness Excuse*, British psychiatrist Garth Wood bluntly charges that "what has become big business is in fact fraud. The evidence does not support the claims of psychoanalysis and psychotherapy."[1] Psychiatrist Lee Coleman titled his exposé of psychiatry *The Reign of Error.* Having testified in more than one hundred thirty criminal and civil trials, Coleman explains that his task is "to educate the judge or jury about why the opinions produced by professionals [psychiatrists/psychologists] have no scientific merit."[2] "Not guilty by reason of insanity" has been a favorite escape route for the guilty, but it is almost always a ploy.

Yet Christian psychologists have embraced and imported into the church the very same myths that so many secular psychologists and psychiatrists continue to expose as unscientific and fraudulent. Incredibly, an anti-Christian religion, propped up by discredited theories, has become the mainstay of an entire industry called "Christian psychology" and it is eating at the heart of the church. Even more astonishing is the fact that many Christian leaders have warmly welcomed psychology as something that has been missing for nineteen hundred years and for lack of which the church has been handicapped in healing hurting people.

The Tragic Gullibility of Evangelical Leaders

The shepherds of the flock have fallen asleep while "grievous wolves" have entered in to ravage the sheep (Acts 20:28–29), with Christian academia leading the pack. Wanting to keep up with the world and to attract more students to support growing budgets, Christian universities and seminaries jumped on the psychology bandwagon because it is one of the most popular subjects and thus has proved to be one of the most profitable. Of course, part of the game was promoting this delusion in the church. A George Fox University ad was headlined, "Our Psychology Doctorate Comes With Something Special—A Christian Worldview."[3]

Now that says a lot. One would never advertise, "Our Bible courses come with something special—A Christian Worldview." Then why should it be "special" for something called "Christian psychology" to have a Christian worldview? How can Christians be so blind! In fact, as we have seen, psychology, far from being found in the Bible, is irretrievably *anti*-biblical. Fitting it into a "Christian worldview" would really take some sleight of hand—but the audience *wants* to be deceived by "experts" with academic degrees.

Christian academia saw an unprecedented opportunity and quickly began to promote psychology as the new Savior. A Fuller Theological Seminary brochure boasted, "As a profession, Christian psychology isn't just new. It's Fuller. . . . Fuller's School of Psychology has it all . . . from an M.S. in Marital and Family Therapy to a Ph.D. in Clinical Psychology."[4] Would such a degree have helped Paul or Apollos or have fit *anywhere* in the early church? That's a ridiculous question, which only shows how wrong such degrees still are today. Then why are they so highly prized? We've forsaken the Lord and wandered from His Word. Early church leaders and Christians probably wouldn't even recognize most of us as Christians.

The following excerpt from a full-page advertisement in *Christianity Today* by Wheaton College Graduate School accurately presents the delusion that is sweeping the church: "Symbols for a new Century in Psychology—Psy. D. and M.A. in Clinical Psychology . . . commitment to Scripture and the integration of psychological theory with Christian faith. . . . " The Wheaton ad fails to explain why *theories* of anti-Christians are being *integrated* into Christianity. There *is* no explanation, though it has been sought for decades. Nor is it explained why such an incongruous mixture as *theory* (psychological or any other) with *faith* would be desirable. One is reminded of the closing lines of a poem:

Who would leave the noonday bright to grope mid shadows dim?
And who would leave the fountainhead to drink the muddy stream,
Where men have mixed what God has said with every dreamer's dream?

Pastors, evangelists, and church leaders swallowed the bait, hook, line, and sinker. They believed the lie that psychology was both biblical and scientific without taking time to check. And why should they check, when it was all endorsed by "experts" who had degrees in a profession in which their followers had little knowledge but implicit (and misplaced) faith? Jerry Falwell was one of the gullible many who fell into this trap. Tragically, these "victims" of delusion led multitudes of others into the same departure from the faith. Several years ago, Jerry enthusiastically and naïvely notified his mailing list:

> Next Sunday I will announce on National Television an historical breakthrough to the Body of Christ. The impact . . . will excite the
> · Christian world, and launch a new era of ministry. . . .
>
> There are simply not enough trained Christian Psychologists, Psychiatrists and Pastors to meet the counseling needs of the teeming masses who are crying out for help.
>
> Liberty Institute for Lay Counseling will provide the necessary training. . . . You can be one of these. . . !
>
> Picture this. . . ! Dr. Gary Collins and his staff . . . are there [in your home] with you via audiocassette. . . . [5]

Like so many other Christian leaders who credulously fell for the same propaganda, Falwell (since deceased) obviously hadn't thought this through carefully. *Historical breakthrough to the Body of Christ . . . a new era of ministry?* Well, "new" was right. The apostles and early church never heard of psychology, nor was it known at all in the evangelical church for nineteen hundred years until Norman Vincent Peale brought it in. But what made it *new*? There was a question to ponder, but few did.

The obvious implication of this newness should have been plain enough. "New" meant that it wasn't biblical at all or some preacher or evangelist would have discovered this teaching in the Bible centuries ago. That fact should have caused Falwell to ask himself, "If it didn't come from the Bible, where did it come from? And how could anything not in the Bible be of any spiritual value to the church at all?" He apparently never asked those questions. It was enough that this "new ministry" would be a boon to Liberty University and its extension program. That welcome fact may have made it difficult to see how unbiblical and anti-Christian "Christian" psychology is.

"Christian" Psychology Is Anti-Christian

The very term "Christian Psychology" is misleading and has deceived a majority of Christians into imagining that there is such a discipline, when the truth is that it doesn't exist. Go to any university or public library and look through the index in every volume dealing with psychology. One will find literally hundreds of different psychologies listed (Freudian, Jungian, Adlerian, Humanistic, Behavioristic, Transpersonal, etc.) but no listing for "Christian" psychology as distinct from any other psychology. Why not? The reason is simple: it does not now, nor did it ever, exist. There is no school of psychology founded by a Christian or taught in the Bible that one could accurately refer to as "Christian."

Psychology was the invention of atheists in the secular world. Christians have adopted its theories and then attached the deceitful label "Christian" to the very same beliefs and practices that the founders intended to be anti-Christian. Psychiatrist Carl Jung, one of the founders most admired by Christian psychologists, claimed to have had a dream of God defecating on the church, a dream that pretty much expressed Jung's own opinion. Taught to him mostly by demonic spirit entities, psychology/psychiatry became Jung's Antichrist religion. It has been warmly received into the church and is taught there with great enthusiasm and authority today.

Professor emeritus of psychiatry, Thomas Szasz, a Jewish atheist, calls psychiatry a "secular state religion . . . a social control system, which disguises itself under the claims of scientificity . . . a pseudoscience that parodies medicine by using medical sounding words . . . heartbreak and heart attack belong to two completely different categories."[6]

Is psychology really anti-Christian? Indeed it is, and it is outright fraud to attach the label "Christian" to any part of it.

Szasz explains that "One of Freud's most powerful motives in life was. . . to inflict vengeance on Christianity. . . ."[7] Szasz called psychotherapy "not merely a religion that pretends to be a science . . . [but] a fake religion that seeks to destroy true religion."[8] E. Fuller Torrey, another internationally respected psychiatrist, whom the *Washington Post* has called "the most famous psychiatrist in America," says, "Psychiatry has been willing to sanctify its values with the holy water of medicine and offer them up as the true faith of 'Mental Health.' It is a false Messiah."[9]

The Latest Attempt at Justification

Embarrassed by much criticism for having attached the label "Christian" to atheistic theories, psychologists who claim to be Christians have spent many years attempting to "integrate" psychology and theology. All such efforts have failed. Finally, some enterprising members of the American Association of Christian Counselors (AACC) took a bold approach that no one had ever thought of before—bold because it was so preposterous. They declared that psychology had, after all, come from Scripture itself, though no one had ever noticed it there. Here is what they are now trying to say:

> Christian psychology began in the Scriptures of the Hebrews and early Christians. Later, Christian thinkers and ministers throughout the ensuing centuries developed many understandings of human beings, using the Bible as a canon or standard for reflection. As a result, the history of Christian thought contains countless works of psychological import that offer the Christian community a rich treasure of insights, themes, and foundational assumptions upon which to ground the project of a Christian psychology. . . . [10]
>
> To develop what we believe will be a more valid psychology, Christian psychologists will look to the Bible and the Christian tradition as orienting guides for our investigations. . . .
>
> We also seek to produce distinctively Christian theories, research programs, and soul-care practice, where appropriate. . . . [11]

That's a nice attempt, but it won't fly. That brief statement is filled with contradictions and misinformation. There is no reference to "psychology" in the writings of early Christians. Nor is it true that "Christian psychology began in the Scriptures. . . . " If that were the case and actual verses could be quoted to show that psychology is *taught* in the Bible, why the decades spent trying to show that psychology is *compatible* with Scripture? How is it that, after so many years of wasted effort, Christian psychologists have suddenly "discovered" that psychology has been right there in the Bible all along but no one noticed it? If psychology is truly in the Bible, why has this alleged fact only now come to light?

The truth is that neither the word nor the concept is found even *once* in the Bible. "Christian" psychologists never got one of the psychological ideas they promote from studying the Bible. No one would ever have thought of "Christian psychology" had it not been for the atheists who invented the various schools of psychology that Christians adopted and follow today. We have elsewhere quoted Bruce Narramore declaring that it was humanistic psychologists Maslow and Rogers, not the Bible, from whom Christian psychologists learned about self-love and self-esteem. We have also quoted James Dobson saying that psychology is a worthy profession for a Christian young person to train for, provided his faith is strong enough to withstand the humanism to which he will be exposed. That doesn't sound like it is learned from the Bible but rather from humanists, which is indeed the case!

The Bible is God's revelation to man. It does not provide a base for what the AACC calls "many understandings of human beings"—nor did the prophets and apostles and early church ever "look to the Bible and the Christian tradition as orienting guides . . . " for developing a "Christian psychology." The "diagnosis" of man's condition is simple and to the point: the sin of unbelief and rebellion brings separation from God and eternal doom for those who refuse to accept Christ as Lord and Savior, the One who on the Cross paid the full penalty for the sins of the world. The remedy is equally simple: "repentance toward God, and faith toward our Lord Jesus Christ" (Acts 20:21). The Bible does not provide any basis for "many understandings." There is only one understanding; all the rest (supplied by psychology) are truth-denying, worthless attempts to supply excuses.

The Greatest Commandment Defines the Greatest Sin

According to our Lord, "Thou shalt love the LORD thy God with all thine heart, and with all thy soul, and with all thy might" (Deuteronomy 6:5) defines the relationship that God intended to have with all mankind and desired to demonstrate in His calling and love for Israel. Though not explicitly stated in the Ten Commandments (Exodus 20; Deuteronomy 5), according to our Lord Jesus Christ this first commandment is the greatest one ever given by God to man (Matthew 22:37–38; Mark 12:29–30).

Since Christ called this the greatest commandment, failure to love God with one's entire heart, soul, and might must be the greatest sin of which one could be guilty. Indeed, not loving God is the root of all sin. Nor is our Lord's explanation of the Ten Commandments a condemnation only of atheists and pagans. It is also a terrible indictment of most Christians. How shamefully little love we give to God! "With *all* thine heart, with *all* thy soul, with *all* thy might!" said Jesus. My own conscience has been deeply convicted by that word *all*.

God is not demanding that we "fall in love" with Him. This is a concept popular in novels and movies that depict a man and a woman "falling in love," then "falling out of love," ending their relationship and "falling in love" with someone else. Whether those involved in this fiasco are Christians or not (sadly, the divorce rate is the same for both), divorce does not express biblical love! If it were, how could we be sure that Christ would continue to love us? The fact that "God *is* love" tells us of love's unwavering faithfulness. A beautiful hymn begins, "O love that will not let me go. . . . " Such is the nature of God's love—and that love is to flow through us to others.

Love is a command that all are expected to obey, first toward God and then toward one's neighbor. Its foundation is not emotion but commitment and integrity. The marriage ceremony recognizes this fact. It calls for a promise from both parties, a commitment until death parts them. It is astonishing how many supposed born-again Christians can break their marriage vows, then repeat to a second or third or fourth person the same vows they have already broken. Why has the incidence of divorce both within the church and outside risen steadily until more than half of marriages entered into today will end in divorce?

Hollywood could rightly be blamed for much of this avalanche of immorality and lack of commitment that has overtaken us; but both within and without the church a large share of the blame must go to psychology. It provides a host of excuses, from alleged incompatibility to mental cruelty—excuses that no one even thought of a hundred years ago when divorce was hardly known (certainly not among Christians). In fact, much of the deterioration in society and the church from then until now—especially its acceleration in the last fifty years—has come about through the advent of psychology and its justification of divorce and the excuses it provides.

The Impossible Command

The second commandment, according to our Lord, is "Thou shalt love thy neighbor as thyself." Obedience to this command is the essential evidence of truly loving God. John reminds us, "He that loveth not his brother whom he hath seen, how can he love God whom he hath not seen?" (1 John 4:20). Love of neighbor (i.e., all others) is the inevitable result of loving God. These two commandments (to love God, then neighbor), like blossom and fruit, are inseparable. There cannot be one without the other. Moreover, "On these two commandments," said Jesus, "hang all the law and the prophets" (Matthew 22:40, etc.). Here is the essence of all Scripture and of God's requirements for mankind.

Love your neighbor as yourself! Who could possibly keep that command?! Were it not for God's grace and the redemptive work of Christ, this clear teaching from Scripture would hang over us like a death sentence. We have disobeyed the first and greatest commandment and as a result could not keep the second. The penalty for sin is death—eternal separation from God and from the life and love that is in Him alone. How desperately we need the Savior our heavenly Father has given to us! And, oh, how God's gracious and complete provision in Christ should create in our hearts the very love for Him that He longs for from us!

The church is busy with conferences, conventions, seminars, and workshops, where numerous subjects, from healing to holiness, from prosperity to prophecy, from miracles to marriage counseling, are taught and discussed. Yet biblical teaching on loving God is conspicuous by its absence. No seminary offers a major in this subject, much less a degree. Instead, there is much emphasis upon loving, esteeming, and developing *self*—a teaching unknown in the church until recently imported from humanists by Christian psychologists.

Inasmuch as these two commandments—love for God and for neighbor—are the essence of Scripture, nothing further need be nor can be added. Yet to these two has lately been added a third: the love of self. Moreover, this newly introduced "law" is declared to be the *first* commandment and key to all else. It is now widely taught that self-love is the great need— that we cannot fully love either God or neighbor until we first of all learn to love ourselves.

The command to "love thy neighbor as thyself" is pointed to by Christian psychologists as proof that the Bible agrees with humanistic psychology. On the contrary, as we have already shown, far from teaching self-love, Christ was rebuking it. He was saying, "You feed and clothe and care for yourselves day and night. Now give to your neighbors some of the attention that you lavish upon yourselves. Love your neighbor as you excessively love yourselves." Christ would hardly tell us to love our neighbors as we love ourselves if we did not already love ourselves enough. But what person can keep this impossible commandment? What can we do?

Setting the Record Straight

During the nineteen hundred years before the advent of psychology, no one had found either self-love or self-esteem taught in the Bible. Calvin, Luther, Wesley, Spurgeon, Moody, et al., found just the opposite there. As Bruce Narramore admits, it was the humanists who discovered this new "truth"—and now even pastors and Christian leaders find the lie appealing and pass it on to their flocks in books and sermons.

The major support for the self-love lie to which Christian psychologists point is Christ's command to "love your neighbour as yourself." Tragically, love for God is not only neglected, it is given a secondary position, and self-love is made preeminent. Instead of being convicted of our failure to love God with our whole heart, soul, and might as the gravest of sins and the root of all personal problems, we are being urged to focus upon loving and esteeming and valuing ourselves. What a perversion of Scripture!

There is a growing emphasis today upon world evangelism, and surely that is needful and commendable. We ought to obey the Great Commission given to us by Christ. There is also an awakening social conscience, a concern to demonstrate practical Christianity in caring for those around us, from the unborn threatened with abortion to the homeless and deprived and to orphans needing adoption. Yet that which must come first—deep love of God—is largely forgotten. Christ's words to the rabbis of His day are addressed to us as well: "These ought ye to have done, and not to leave the other undone" (Matthew 23:23).

Charitable deeds can be done in order to call attention to oneself rather than out of love for God and those in need. Paul explained, "Though I bestow all my goods to feed the poor, and though I give my body to be burned, and have not love, it profiteth me nothing [i.e., there will be no reward from God]" (1 Corinthians 13:3). No matter how kind and generous, no matter how many charitable deeds are done, if they are not motivated and sanctified by an all-consuming love for God, they are of no value at all in His eyes. Have we really faced this truth? How amazing and sad that the love we ought to have for God can be buried in the flurry of activity of serving Him! Indeed, the average Christian, while he may love much else, including even the world that he is forbidden to love, gives little serious thought to loving God. But it's a command! When did you last, with a fervent heart overflowing with gratitude, tell God you love Him with all your heart? It should be our constant theme.

Getting Our Priorities Straight

Many issues of great concern legitimately occupy the attention of church leaders and their flocks. Yet the greatest commandment, and that which God desires from us above all, is scarcely mentioned, much less given the prominence it ought to have in church fellowship and individual lives. How tragic! And what an indictment of Christianity today! None of us is innocent of this great sin of failing to love God as we ought. My own heart has been broken as I've been convicted anew of how far I fall short of keeping the essence of God's commandments. I have cried out to Him with new sorrow and longing that He would help me to love Him with my whole heart and my neighbor as myself.

The Bible is filled with injunctions to love God, with explanations of why we ought to, and of the benefits to be derived thereby. Here are a few examples. Look up others for yourself and meditate upon them. "And now, Israel, what doth the LORD thy God require of thee, but to fear the LORD thy God, to walk in all his ways, and to *love him,* and to serve the LORD thy God with all thy heart and with all thy soul" (Deuteronomy 10:12) "that thou mayest live" (30:6), "for he is thy life, and the length of thy days" (30:20).

"O LORD God of heaven, the great and terrible God, that keepeth covenant and mercy for them that *love him* and observe his commandments" (Nehemiah 1:5); "All things work together for good to them that love God"(Romans 8:28); "Eye hath not seen, nor ear heard, neither have entered into the heart of man, the things which God hath prepared for them that *love him*" (1 Corinthians 2:9). God even tells us in Deuteronomy 13:1–3 that He allows false prophets to work signs and wonders as a test to see "*whether ye love the LORD* your God with all your heart and with all your soul." We live in a time of such testing. Loving God fervently will keep us from apostasy.

Falling in Love?

Yes, love is commanded. True love begins in and is sustained by the will, not by the emotions. The fact that love is commanded seems incomprehensible even to many Christians. The world has conditioned us to believe that one "falls in love" and that love is a romantic attraction between the sexes. "Boy meets girl and falls in love" is the most popular theme of novels and movies. Yet "love" without God eventually brings sorrow.

"Falling in love" is perceived as being helplessly swept up in a mysterious, euphoric, overpowering feeling over which one has no control. Inevitably, however, such "love" loses its magic. One is thus equally helpless in "falling out of love" and thereafter "falling in love" with someone else. A commitment of the will is missing. We are commanded to love with purity—God first of all, with our whole being, and then our neighbor as we, by nature, excessively love ourselves. Love is a commitment to God that demonstrates itself in human relationships.

Yes, "falling in love" transforms for a time those who experience it. They suddenly become different persons. Someone else becomes more important than oneself, bringing deliverance from the slavery to self that ordinarily imprisons us all. Self no longer receives priority, but another has become the primary focus. The love and attention that once was lavished upon oneself now is given to the one who has become the object of one's love—and that brings tremendous freedom and joy. This temporary release from self-centeredness explains more than anything else the ecstasy of love—a fact that those "in love" generally fail to realize.

If loving others is so transforming, how much more so to genuinely and deeply love God. How can this come about? God is so great, so far beyond our finite ability to comprehend, that it seems impossible to know Him. And it is impossible to love a person (except with God's love) whom one doesn't know. Love is above all personal. Those who truly know God cannot help but love Him.

No Excuse Allowed for Disobedience

God's standard is perfection. We can't attain to it. So what are we to do if taking an honest look at ourselves reveals that we can't truthfully tell God that we love Him with all of our heart, mind, soul, and strength? Shall we look to Christian psychology to help us? What are we to do when we realize that we just don't have it in us to love our neighbor as ourselves? And suppose we also realize that it just isn't possible for us always to be joyful and rejoicing no matter what befalls? Is it psychotherapy that we need? No, that is not the solution.

Paul didn't tell the Galatians that "love, joy, peace," et al., were the fruit of *therapy* but the fruit of the *Spirit* (Galatians 5:22–23). The first step toward wisdom is realizing that we can't obey the commands of God in our own strength. The old hymn says, "I tried the broken cisterns, Lord, but ah, the waters failed. Each time I stooped to drink they fled, and mocked me as I wailed." That's because these "broken cisterns, that can hold no water" (Jeremiah 2:13) represent our own efforts instead of reliance in faith upon God.

Love is not primarily a feeling. It is a commitment. This is the missing ingredient in much that is called love today. A genuine and lasting commitment to one another is often lacking even in Christian marriages, due to worldly influence and the promotion by church leaders of loving, esteeming, accepting, and valuing Self. If even *one* marriage partner believes psychology's lie that loving oneself must come first, the marriage is doomed.

Purposeful commitment is not only missing in many marriages but is also the missing ingredient in many a Christian's relationship with God. Rather than working up a *feeling* that you love God, make a commitment to Him to love and obey Him. Jesus promised, "He that hath my commandments, and keepeth them, he it is that loveth me . . . and I will love him, and will manifest myself to him . . . and my Father will love him, and we will come unto him, and make our abode with him" (John 14:21–23).

We need to know God and His love in our hearts. As we seek Him in His Word and in prayer, He will reveal Himself by His Spirit. We can indeed love Him with our whole heart, soul, and might as we trust Him to reveal His love to us. Then we can truly say with our whole heart, "We love him, because he first loved us" (1 John 4:19). May He grant us a fresh conviction of the sin of not loving Him as we ought, and may the desire to obey this first and greatest commandment become our passion. Only then will we begin to manifest that love for one another that Christ said would be the mark whereby the world would be able to recognize His true disciples—those to whom He said, "If ye love me, keep my commandments."

1. Garth Wood, *The Myth of Neurosis: Overcoming the Illness Excuse* (Harper & Row, 1987), 265.

2. Lee Coleman, *The Reign of Error* (Beacon Press, 1984), xii-xv.

3. *Christianity Today*, October 2, 1995, 80.

4. Brochure on file.

5. Undated letter and brochure on file.

6. http://en.wikipedia.org/wiki/Thomas_Szasz.

7. Thomas Szasz, *The Myth of Psychotherapy* (New York: Dooubleday, 1978), 14, 139.

8. Szasz, *Myth*, 28.

9. E. Fuller Torrey, *The Death of Psychiatry* (New York: Penguin, 1974), 107.

10. http://www.christianpsych.org/.

11. Society for Christian Psychology. A Division of the American Association of Christian Counselors, http://christianpsych.org.

KNOWING AND LOVING GOD

— *Dave Hunt* —

Hear, O Israel: . . . thou shalt love the LORD thy God with all thine heart, and with all thy soul, and with all thy might. —DEUTERONOMY 6:4,5

This is the first and great commandment. —MATTHEW 22:38

If a man love Me, he will keep My words: and My Father will love him, and we will come unto him, and make our abode with him. —JOHN 14:23

BOTH THE TEN COMMANDMENTS (Exodus 20:1–17) given to Israel and the moral law that God has written in every conscience (Romans 2:14–15) require each of us to love God with our entire being. Such a demand is laid upon us not because God needs our love, for He is infinite and lacks nothing. Nor is it because God is self-centered or proud and thus demands that we love Him above all else for His own self-gratification. He commands us to love Him with our whole heart because He is worthy, because He can thereby bestow His love upon us, and because nothing else could save us from our own egotistic Self, which is our incorrigible and worst enemy.

This first and greatest commandment is given for our own good. God loves each of us so much that He wants to give us the greatest possible blessing: Himself. He does not, however, force Himself upon anyone, for that would not be love. We must genuinely and earnestly desire Him. "And ye shall seek me, and find me, when ye shall search for me with all your heart" (Jeremiah 29:13) is the promise of God, who otherwise hides Himself (Isaiah 45:15). And again, "He is a rewarder of them that diligently seek him" (Hebrews 11:6).

This fervent seeking after God with the whole heart, without which no one can know Him, has always been the mark of His true followers. One of the psalmists likened his passion for God to the thirst of a deer panting for water (Psalm 42:1–2). David expressed it the same way: "O God . . . I seek thee: my soul thirsteth for thee. . . ." (Psalm 63:1). What greater desire could one have than knowing the infinite, loving God who created us?

Thirsting for Self Rather Than for God

Sadly, instead of seeking God, both today's secular and Christian worlds, deluded by psychology, are searching for Self. Who can ever forget the pitiful words from most hippies' mouths? When asked about their purpose in life, the response was almost like a recording, "I'm trying to find myself." Traveling through many countries in Europe and North Africa in the sixties, our family often picked up youthful hitchhikers. As a prelude to presenting the gospel, I would always ask them why they were traveling and where they were going. It was a struggle for our four young children (ages 8–15) to hold back their laughter each time they heard this same ridiculous response. These dear hippies were indeed lost, but it was God they needed to find, not something within themselves.

Not only the world but the evangelical church as well, poisoned by the venom of the deadly viper, has taken up the pursuit of Self in spite of the biblical injunction to seek God. In his book *Me, Myself & I*, Archibald D. Hart, Dean of Fuller Theological Seminary's Graduate School of Psychology, sounds like he is still on that pitiful hippie search:

> Ever since I started studying psychology more than thirty years ago, I have been vexed by what appeared to be a conflict between how psychology views the "self" and how theology (at least the particular brand of Christian teaching I had learned) views the self. . . . Ambiguity between the help I tried to give hurting people from a spiritual point of view and the skills that were emerging in my formation as a Christian clinical psychologist tore me up for many years.[1]

What a tragedy that he continued to pursue training in psychotherapy in spite of its many obvious conflicts with God's Word. How did Hart resolve his inner struggle? He was troubled by the teaching of "'dying to self' (Matthew 16:24) . . . 'crucifying the self' (Galatians 2:20) . . . 'sacrificing the self' (Romans 12:1) . . . and being 'delivered from one's self' (Luke 4:18)." He complained against what he knew Christ himself taught: "Must it always be self-hatred . . . or can we even dare to 'love' ourselves?"[2]

He continues, "Almost every week or two, I sit with a pastor or devout Christian who struggles to make sense out of this same confusion. . . . 'Know thyself' has been variously attributed to Plato, Pythagoras, Thales, and Socrates. Modern psychotherapists continue to preach the same message. . . . Knowing ourselves is the very foundation upon which any healthy self-esteem must be built. . . . How and what sort of value are we to place on ourselves?"[3]

Hart is confused. He is so obsessed with self-analysis that he doesn't realize that he has switched horses in the middle of the stream, jumping from "dying to . . . crucifying . . . sacrificing . . . self" to knowing and esteeming ourselves. The Bible never advocates knowing ourselves (the goal of psychology) but knowing God. It never calls us to esteem ourselves but exhorts, "In lowliness of mind let each esteem other better than himself" (Philippians 2:3). Of course, that wisdom contradicts the psychological theory in defense of which Hart has devoted his life. It isn't easy to justify himself in face of God's Word, but Hart is determined. Undaunted, he lists sixteen Bible verses to support his thesis.[4] To show his confusion, here are his paraphrases of four of the verses that he uses and my simple commentary:

1) Ignorance of the self misleads and deceives (Isaiah 44:20).

But this verse has nothing to do with "ignorance of the self." It condemns idol worship and says of the idolater, "a deceived heart hath turned him aside." Has Hart become a worshipper of Self?

2) The Christian doesn't judge the self (1 Corinthians 4:3).

How does this justify knowing the self? It is the opposite. One cannot judge what one doesn't already know.

3) The self is to walk as Jesus walked (1 John 2:6).

This is referring to a person, not to the mysterious "self" that still has Hart so confused.

4) We are never to forget ourselves (James 1:24).

On the contrary, this is not an injunction to never forget ourselves but not to forget God's Word. It is an exhortation against being only "a hearer of the word [of God], and not a doer."

Pardon Me, Your Ego Is Showing!

Amazing though it seems, there have also been those within the church—and not only Norman Vincent Peale and Robert Schuller but evangelical leaders— who, following the lead of Christian psychologists, openly promote the love and even divinization of Self. Sadly, this delusion (which inevitably breeds an entire herd of other heresies) has received support from many Christian leaders who would never teach such lies themselves but have endorsed the writings of those who do.

Sir John Marks Templeton, wealthy originator and funder of the "Templeton Prize for Progress in Religion," though probably well-meaning, is one of the most deluded men in the world. He has managed to deceive multitudes of others, among them even evangelical leaders. His occult and anti-God views have been clearly proclaimed for decades in the many books he has written. Yet his writings have been endorsed not only by Norman Vincent Peale and Robert Schuller, as we would expect, but by *Christianity Today*, Chuck Colson, Billy Graham, and Bill Bright, to name a few. It is not surprising, then, that having rejected the true God, Templeton promotes psychology's love of Self—the Self that he says is "God within all mankind." In his book, *Discovering the Laws of Life*, Templeton writes:

> Through our choices and attitudes we create our own heaven or hell right here on earth . . . the only place we can find heaven is in our own hearts. . . .
>
> Our innate goodness is an essential fact of our existence. . . . When we perceive this truth, we will experience heaven on earth . . . peace and the presence of God within us.
>
> Be honest. Be true. Love all parts of yourself. . . the godhood within you . . . is in a state of becoming perfect.[5]

The above is only a small sample of the Antichrist teachings in this abominable book. More of the same is to be found in his other writings. Yet the entire back cover of at least one issue of *Christianity Today* was devoted to an ad promoting *Discovering the Laws of Life*.[6] Headlined "WILL INSPIRE MILLIONS OF READERS," the ad contained the endorsements of five prominent religious leaders who also praised the book on its jacket cover: Norman Vincent Peale (who also wrote the foreword), Robert Schuller, Billy Graham, and two prominent Catholic New Age leaders. One thing that all of these endorsers (along with the editors of the magazine that carried the ad) have in common is their respect for psychology and psychiatry.

"Lovers of their own selves"

In fulfillment of Paul's prophecy that in the last days men would be "lovers of their own selves" (2 Timothy 3:2), as we document elsewhere, self-love and its twin, self-esteem, are widely taught in the church as part of Christian psychology. Psychologist James Dobson is doing his best to counter what he calls a raging epidemic of low self-esteem afflicting people everywhere. As we have already noted, he says that if he could give a prescription to all the women of the world, it would be a heavy dose of self-esteem administered three times daily until the symptoms disappeared.[7] In his great (and we are sure) genuine concern for youth, Dobson warns of the danger of "irreparable damage" to a child's self-esteem, using terms such as "there is no escape"[8] and "damaged child"[9] —enough to frighten any parent into the arms of the nearest available Christian psychologist instead of into the arms of the Lord!

Dobson deserves the honorary title, "Apostle of Self-Esteem," having done more to make the church comfortable with psychology in general and the gospel of self-esteem in particular than anyone else—even than Robert Schuller. More than three thousand broadcast facilities, including some secular stations, carry *Focus on the Family*.[10] According to his ministry, Dobson deliberately doesn't teach from the Bible because he is not a pastor or Bible teacher. His council is based upon the theories of various schools of psychology.

Dobson could also be called the "self-esteem missionary." He has even taken his message to China where, with the blessing of that government, he expects to contact 200 million Chinese families. Is he bringing the gospel of Jesus Christ to China as Hudson Taylor and other missionaries (many of whom were martyred there) have done? No, the Chinese government with whom Dobson has entered into unholy partnership would not allow it. He is going to teach the Chinese "family principles"—from psychology, of course, not from the Bible.

The extent of Dobson's faith in psychology (apparently greater than in *sola scriptura* of the Reformers) can be seen in the astonishing fact that all telephone counselors at the Focus on the Family facility in Colorado Springs are and must be "licensed mental health professionals." Does their counsel include recommending a good evangelical pastor near the caller's home? No. The only pastors on the referral list must also be "licensed mental health professionals." Clearly, Dobson has more confidence in psychology than in God's Word—at least in God's Word alone, without the added wisdom of the theories invented by atheistic anti-Christians.

Not having been a "mental health professional," Paul would not have made the approved list in his day. Nor would Peter, or James, or John—or any of the Reformers, or Moody, Spurgeon, C. T. Studd, Hudson Taylor, or a host of other men and women of God down through the ages. That simple fact is enough to reveal what psychology has done inside the church in turning believers from faith in God and His Word alone to faith in psychology. It is a shameful development!

How astonishing that the infinite Creator of the universe offers Himself to such degraded yet egotistical creatures as ourselves! Nor is His love an impersonal cosmic force; it is intimately personal. Think of that! Such love should awaken a fervent response within us. Yet how many of us express our love to God even once a day, let alone love Him with our entire being? Sadly, even Christians are caught up instead in the forbidden love of Self, which inevitably leads to the equally forbidden love of the world (1 John 2:15) and the pursuit of its deceitful rewards.

Confronted by the Greatest Commandment

Loving God is the first and greatest commandment because our obedience to all of His other commandments must be motivated by love for Him. Moreover, since God commands us to love Him with our whole being, then our entire life—yes, everything we think and say and do—must flow from that love. Paul reminds us that even giving everything one possesses to the poor and being martyred in the flames is in vain unless motivated by love for God. Nor is there true love without complete trust—and that trust is lacking in those who cannot believe God's promises of life, godliness, joy, and victory over self, without supplementary help from His enemies, who invented every foundational theory of psychology!

If loving God with one's whole being is the greatest commandment, then not to do so must be the greatest sin—indeed, the root of all sin. How is it, then, that loving God, without which all else is but "sounding brass, or a tinkling cymbal" (1 Corinthians 13:1), is not even found in the course lists of our theological seminaries? How can it be that this "first and great[est] commandment" is so neglected in the church? The sad truth is that among today's evangelicals, *because of Christian psychology*, it is not loving and esteeming God but self-love and self-esteem that are presented as the pressing need!

I speak to my own heart. At times I weep that, like Martha (Luke 10:38–42), in the busy-ness of *serving* Christ, I give so little thought or time to loving Him. Oh, to be more like Mary!

How does one learn to love God without ever having seen Him (John 1:18; 1 Timothy 6:16; 1 John 4:12, 20)? Obviously, there must be a reason for loving God—or for loving anyone. Yes, reason and love do go together. Love must result from more than a physical attraction, which, in itself, can only arouse a fleshly response. In addition to the outward appeal, there are the inner beauties of personality, character, integrity, and, of course, the other's love response. God loves without such reasons, because we could never provide a reason for Him to love us. Our love, however, even for Him, requires reason. "We love him, because he first loved us" (1 John 4:19).

Our heavenly Father loves even those who make themselves His enemies, those who defy Him, reject His laws, deny His existence, and would tear Him from His throne if they could. Christ proved the infinitude of His love by going to the Cross to pay the penalty for the sins of the entire world (John 1:29), and even asking the Father to forgive those who nailed Him there (Luke 23:34). Such is the love that the Christian, having experienced it for himself, is to manifest to all others through Christ living in him: "Love your enemies, bless them that curse you, do good to them that hate you, and pray for them which despitefully use you, and persecute you" (Matthew 5:44).

How Can We Keep His Commandments?

To love God with our whole heart and our neighbors as ourselves is not something we can produce by self-effort—much less through any help from psychology. Love for our fellows must be the expression of God's love in our hearts. Nor can we love God except by coming to know Him as He is. A false god won't do. Yet at the 1993 National Prayer Breakfast in Washington, D.C., some Christians present were encouraged when then-Vice President Al Gore said, "Faith in God, reliance upon a Higher Power, by whatever name, is in my view essential." No one can love Al Gore's "God" any more than they could love the 12-Steps "God as you conceive Him to be." That would be like loving some imaginary person. To know the true God is to love Him; and to know Him better is to love Him all the more. On the other hand, not to know Him is to reject the revelation He desires to give each person of Himself—and that means being lost forever (John 17:3)!

Most of us have an all-too-shallow knowledge of God. Nor can our love for God grow except from a deepening appreciation of His love for us—an appreciation that must include two extremes: 1) God's infinite greatness; and 2) our sinful, wretched unworthiness—a truth that Hart struggled with and Christian psychology rebels against. That He, who is so high and holy, would stoop so low to redeem unworthy sinners supremely reveals and demonstrates His love. Such an understanding is the basis of our love and gratitude in return and will be the unchanging theme of our praise throughout all eternity in His glorious presence (Revelation 5:8–14).

There can be no doubt that the clearer one's vision of God becomes, the more unworthy one feels and thus the more grateful for His grace and love. Such has always been the testimony of men and women of God. Job cried out to God, "I have heard of thee by the hearing of the ear: but now mine eye seeth thee. Wherefore I abhor [hate] myself, and repent in dust and ashes" (Job 42:5–6). Isaiah likewise lamented, "Woe is me! for I am undone; because I am a man of unclean lips, and I dwell in the midst of a people of unclean lips: for mine eyes have seen the King, the LORD of hosts" (Isaiah 6:5). We need a fresh vision of God!

Such recognition of their sin and unworthiness did not decrease but enhanced the saints' love for God and appreciation of His grace. The more clearly we see the infinite chasm between God's glory and our sinful falling short thereof (Romans 3:23), the greater will be our appreciation of His grace and love in bridging that gulf to redeem us, and the greater our appreciation of His love for us, the greater will be our love for Him.

There is no joy that can compare to that of love exchanged. Nor is there any sorrow so deep as that of love spurned or ignored. How it must grieve our Lord that His redeemed ones love Him so little in return! That grief comes through in scripture passages such as these: "I have nourished and brought up children, and they have rebelled against me" (Isaiah 1:2); "Can a maid forget her ornaments, or a bride her attire? Yet my people have forgotten me days without number" (Jeremiah 2:32).

Amazing Spiritual Blindness

Even more reprehensible, if possible, than forgetfulness and neglect is the teaching of Christian psychology that God loves us because we are lovable and worth it. Richard Dobbins, best known Assemblies of God psychologist, suggests that one repeat, "I am a lovable, forgivable person." Bruce Narramore boasts, "The Son of God considers us of such value that He gave His life for us." If that were true, it would only increase our self-esteem (which, indeed, Narramore teaches) but decrease our love for Him and our appreciation of His grace. The Bible teaches that our love for God and our appreciation of His love and forgiveness will be in proportion to the recognition of our sin and unworthiness. That truth, found over and over throughout God's Word, is vigorously opposed by Christian psychology to the detriment of the Christian faith!

Such was the lesson Christ taught Simon the Pharisee when He was a guest in his house. Jesus told of a creditor who forgave two debtors, one who owed a vast sum and another who owed almost nothing. Then He asked Simon, "Which of them will love him [the creditor] most?" Said Simon, "I suppose . . . he, to whom he forgave most." "Thou hast rightly judged," replied Jesus. Then, rebuking Simon for failing even to give him water and a towel and commending the woman who had been washing His feet with her tears and wiping them with her hair, Christ declared pointedly, "Her sins, which are many, are forgiven; for she loved much: but to whom little is forgiven, the same loveth little" (Luke 7:36–47).

It is both logical and biblical that the more sinful and worthless we realize we are in God's eyes, the greater our gratitude and love that Christ would die for us. Clearly the emphasis of Christian psychology in trying to build up our self-esteem and self-image undermines the very basis for gratitude to Christ for dying to redeem us. When some years ago the Biola University choir was going to sing at Schuller's Crystal Cathedral, they had to change the words of a well-known hymn from "that He would die for such a wretch as I" to "for such a one as I." The flesh fights the awful truth about self, which is a major reason that so many turn to psychology for the unbiblical comfort it offers.

One would think that Christian psychologists promoting self-esteem, self-image, self-worth, and the other selfisms would be ashamed that they are simply echoing the world. Los Angeles psychotherapist, Nathaniel Branden, is credited with pioneering the psychology of self-esteem in the secular world,[11] from whence Christians learned this gross error. Branden (whom Dobson echoes) says, "The reputation you have within yourself, your self-esteem, is the single most important factor for a fulfilling life."[12] He is not echoing what Christian psychologists say on this subject—they are echoing him.

Let the world believe this; they have no other hope, nowhere else to turn except to self. But this is contrary to what the Bible teaches. Not one of the heroes of the faith had high self-esteem but, like Paul, considered themselves to be "less than the least of all saints" (Ephesians 3:8).

Jesus told of two men who "went up into the temple to pray" (Luke 18:9–14). The one, a Pharisee, had a very exalted view of himself; the other such "low self-esteem" that he "would not lift up so much as his eyes unto heaven, but smote upon his breast, saying, God be merciful to me a sinner." Jesus said that God didn't even hear the first man's prayer but that "he prayed . . . with himself." Of the other man, with such a miserable view of himself, Christ declared, "This man went down to his house justified." This is God's view of high and low self-esteem—don't be deceived by any other!

Losing Christ to Salvage Self

Christian psychology and psychiatry have embraced psychotropic drugs as mood enhancers for those who, according to psychological theories, are depressed or have too low an opinion of themselves. Prozac, for example, is not prescribed on the basis of a scientific examination of the brain but on a behavioral profile—not to balance some alleged "chemical imbalance" in the brain but to artificially elevate one's feelings about oneself. Pursuing a supposed chemical solution ignores getting right with God through Jesus Christ. And in doing so, one misses the real miracle and blessing of the life Christ gives to those who love and trust Him.

Paul said, "But when it pleased God . . . to reveal his Son in me . . . " (Galatians 1:15–16). Christianity is the revelation of Christ in the believer's life through the power of God—and those who look to chemical solutions have turned their backs upon the real solution that God wants them to receive obediently in faith.

To whatever extent and by whatever means we imagine that we are lovable or worth Christ's sacrifice, we lessen our appreciation of His love. The Bible teaches that God loves us not because of who we are but because of who He is. "God is love" (1 John 4:16). If God loved us because something attractive or worthwhile within us elicited that love, then, changeable creatures that we are, we could lose that appeal and, with it, God's love. But, praise His holy name, He loves us because He "is love," and He never changes. Love is the very essence of His character. That fact gives us confidence that "neither death, nor life, nor angels, nor principalities, nor powers, nor things present, nor things to come, nor height, nor depth, nor any other creature, shall be able to separate us from the love of God, which is in Christ Jesus our Lord" (Romans 8:38–39). We are secure—and all the glory is His!

We often find it difficult, especially in trying circumstances, to rest in God's great love for us—no doubt because deep within our hearts we know how unworthy we are. Christian psychology tries mistakenly to cure this sense of unworthiness by persuading us that we are worth it after all. Robert Schuller declares, "The death of Christ on the cross is God's price tag on a human soul. . . . [It means] we really are Somebodies!"[13] Not so. Christ did not die for Somebodies but for sinners.

Dobbins agrees with Schuller at least on this point: "If we hadn't been worth it, He wouldn't have paid the price." On the contrary, the greater the price, the costlier our sin, not our worth. That the sinless Son of God must die upon the Cross to redeem us shouldn't make us feel good about ourselves but ashamed, for it was our sins that nailed Him there. Yet Bruce Narramore calls the Cross "a foundation for self-esteem!"

Attempting to Support a Lie with Scripture

Of course those who brought humanistic psychology's selfisms into the church attempt to find support in Scripture. Bruce Narramore quotes Psalm 139 and suggests that the "wonderful pattern for growth, fulfillment and development" that "God built into our genes . . . is the ultimate basis for self-esteem." Sound reason has forsaken him. Surely the genius of the genetic code should cause me to bow in wonder and worship at the wisdom and power of God—but self-esteem? Seeing the marvels of God's creative power in my genes is no more cause for self-exaltation than seeing God's creative power in another's genes or in any other part of the cosmos—I didn't create any of God's marvels.

Psychology's humanistic, self-inflating false gospel is being increasingly embraced by evangelicals. Establishing the counselee's self-worth is a key concept utilized at Rapha counseling centers founded by Robert S. McGee. He dares to say that Christ's declaration, "the truth shall make you free" (John 8:32), referred in part to "our sense of self-worth."[14] Rapha was founded upon the belief that "The need to believe we are significant is the driving element within the human spirit."[15] Is the "driving element" in sinners good? McGee speaks much truth concerning the Cross and salvation, but all he writes is clouded by his unbiblical and foundational view of the sinner's "search for significance." It is a false gospel!

McGee goes to great lengths to find this belief in the Bible. One would think that the concepts that he claims are so important would appear again and again in Scripture, but they never appear except in his forced interpretations. He begins his book by telling us things about Adam and Eve that are completely foreign to the Bible but that he reads into the text for support. We commend him for trying to be biblical, but, sadly, he has begun with psychology's false ideas of self-worth and self-esteem and then interpreted Scripture to support them, finding meanings in the writings of the prophets and apostles that would startle them.

Anthony A. Hoekema writes, "Surely God would not give His Son for creatures He considered to be of little worth!" Thus the love and gratitude toward God that the Cross ought to arouse in us is stifled by the perverted new belief that He did it because we are worth it. Jay Adams points out the horrible error of teaching that what God does for us is "a response on His part to our significance rather than an act of His love, free mercy, goodness and grace!"

"Turn Your Eyes upon Jesus"

Our song for eternity will be, "Worthy is the Lamb" (Revelation 5:12). Heaven has no place for the erroneous belief that Christ died because we are worth it. Then *we* get part of the glory. This teaching is a heretical attempt by Christian psychologists to share God's glory, which He declares He will share with no man. Christ's death in our place had nothing to do with our worth but with the depths of our sin, the demands made by God's justice, His infinite love without any corresponding worth on our part, and His eternal glory.

Paul declared, "By the grace of God I am what I am" (1 Corinthians 15:10). No basis for self-esteem there! Dare we think that we will ever be able to erase from our memories the fact that we are unworthy sinners saved by grace? It is true that God in His grace will give us crowns and rewards, and we will even hear from our Lord's lips, "Well done, thou good and faithful servant: . . . enter thou into the joy of thy lord" (Matthew 25:21; 1 Corinthians 4:5).

Will that give us a positive self-image, a sense of self-worth and self-esteem? C. S. Lewis answers: "The child who is patted on the back for doing a lesson well . . . the saved soul to whom Christ says, 'Well done,' are pleased and ought to be. For here the pleasure lies not in what you are but in the fact that you have pleased someone you rightly wanted to please. The trouble begins when you pass from thinking, 'I have pleased him,' to thinking, 'What a fine person I must be to have done it.'" Sadly, that self-centered error is the foundation of all that Christian psychology stands for and has brought into the church.

The Lamb Is All the Glory

Our love for God even influences whether we yield to temptation. Lust is called both "deceitful" (Ephesians 4:22) and "hurtful" (1 Timothy 6:9) because it entices us with pleasure that is brief and involves disobedience to God and thus leads to pain and ruin in the end. Those whose focus is upon themselves think of God's commandments in terms of pleasures denied. But those who are enraptured by God's love have been delivered from self and find true and lasting pleasure and joy in obeying and thus pleasing Him. There is a joy that comes from loving and pleasing God that is so far beyond any pleasure of this world that temptation loses its power by comparison.

Christian psychology's new theology denies us this path of victory. Its joy is selfish, a child of our self-worth, self-love, self-image, and self-esteem. But to obey the first and great commandment is necessarily to deny self, as Christ commanded (Matthew 16:24). Nor can one deny self and at the same time love, esteem, and value self.

Seeing God's love as a response to my significance and worth salvages just enough value and glory for Self to rob God of the full love and praise he deserves. Let us forget ourselves, our needs, and our hurts and seek to know and love God (Father, Son, and Holy Spirit) because of who He is and His love and grace to us. His love will then flow through us to others, whom we will then esteem better than ourselves (Philippians 2:3).

Heaven will be the ecstatic joy of eternal and infinite love: God's love to us and our love to Him in glorious response. Self will be forgotten in the wonder of our Lord's person, which is the glory of heaven. What a taste of heaven we could have now—and at the same time bring satisfaction to our Lord. Herein is true joy, now and eternally (Hebrews 12:2)!

An old hymn[16] gives us a glimpse of what it will be like for the redeemed Bride of Christ to awaken in His image in heaven:

> *The bride eyes not her garment, but her dear bridegroom's face.*
> *I will not gaze at glory, but on my King of grace.*
> *Not at the crown He giveth, but on His pierced hand*
> *The Lamb is all the glory in Emmanuel's land!*

1. Archibald D. Hart, *Me, Myself & I* (Ann Arbor, MI: Servant Publications, 1992), 35-36.

2. Ibid., 40.

3. Ibid., 36.

4. Ibid., 41-42.

5. John Marks Templeton, *Discovering the Laws of Life* (The Continuum Publishing Company, 1994), 6, 7, 208, etc.

6 *Christianity Today*, April 24, 1994.

7. James Dobson, *What Wives Wish Their Husbands Knew About Women* (Tyndale, 1975), 35.

8. James Dobson, *Hide or Seek*, Revised Edition (Old Tappan, NJ: Fleming H. Revell Company, 1979), 32.

9. Ibid., 59.

10. http:findarticles.com/p/articles/mi_m1589/is_2000_Feb_15/ai_59410458.

11. http://www.selfgrowth.com/experts/nathaniel_branden.html.

12. Nathaniel Branden, quoted by Ken Ogden, "Author's Corner," *Esteem*, vol. 2, No. 1, February 1988, 11.

13. Robert Schuller, *Self-Esteem: The New Reformation* (Word, 1982), 7, 104.

14. Robert S. McGee, *The Search for Significance* (Pasadena, TX: Robert S. McGee, 1985), Introduction.

15. Ibid., 13.

16. Anne R. Cousin, "The Sands of Time are Sinking" or "Emmanuel's Land," 1857, inspired by the letters of Scottish theologian Samuel Rutherford (1600?–1661).

GREAT IS THE MYSTERY!

— Dave Hunt —

IN SPITE OF THOUSANDS OF YEARS of inquiry into the universe, and the exploding information through the super technology of today's computer-aided science, we still know almost nothing in comparison to what remains unknown. We don't know what energy is, or what an electron, gravity, light, time or space are. Science can neither tell us *how* everything came into existence nor *why*. The latter two questions (how and why) are of immense importance, but science avoids them because it has no answer.

Though not idol worshipers in the primitive sense, scientists, university professors, business executives, and political leaders—no matter how brilliant but who do not know Christ—fit the description in Romans 1 of those who reject the witness of the universe and worship the creation instead of the Creator. Carl Sagan spoke with great reverence of the *cosmos* as though it were God. He believed that it had brought us into existence. Is it possible for Christians also to be caught up in this same materialistic mind set and to miss what God offers us in Himself?

Scientific analysis of the universe can lead man only to a dead end. Referring to the physical universe, British astronomer Sir James Jeans declared that our growing knowledge has only revealed this astonishing truth: "We are not yet in touch with ultimate reality."[1] The ultimate knowledge of everything can be found only in the God who brought all into existence. Yet, incredibly, while seeking to unravel the secrets of the universe, science neglects its Creator. In fact, the scientific and academic worlds are mostly dominated by those who reject the biblical revelation of God.

Science's inability to comprehend what is most important is most glaringly seen in its ignorance of physical life. We don't know what *life* is, yet our planet is teeming with it. Living things are composed of chemical machines. The secret of life, however, lies not in the chemicals of which living things are built nor in the correct combination thereof. The right conglomeration of chemicals that moments before was alive is still intact, but no scientific process can restore the life that has left a corpse.

Science seeks to discover how life is imparted to otherwise dead matter, hoping to reverse the death process and thereby create eternal life. But that secret will never be found by examining living creatures because the life they have is not their own. Life has nothing to do with chemicals, though it manifests itself through them. Nor can life exist, whether in an individual cell or the entire body, except in the form God intended.

One of the many things we know today that Darwin never imagined is the fact that every kind of life, from microbes to plants to birds and animals to mankind, is defined by precise words and language. Nearly two thousand years ago, the Bible said, "Through faith we understand that the worlds were framed by the *word* of God" (Hebrews 11:3). In explaining who Jesus Christ is, the Bible declared, "In the beginning was the *Word*, and the *Word* . . . was God. . . . All things were made by him. . . " (John 1:1–3). The key role of words was stated fifteen hundred years earlier. In the very first chapter in the Bible we find the expression "God *said*" eight times, from "And God *said*, Let there be light: and there was light . . . " to "And God *said*, Let us make man in our image. . ." (Genesis 1:3, 6, 9, 11, 14, 20, 24, 26).

What About Life?

The importance of *words* at the foundation of everything that was created is seen most powerfully in the case of life. Life is based not only upon but indeed cannot exist without the information encoded on DNA. This instruction manual for life is written in an ingeniously simple yet at the same time complex language of only four letters divided into three-letter words. The alphabet is identical for every living thing from a single cell to the human brain. The fact that the DNA for plants and animals is identical to man's is no more evidence that man descended from apes than that he descended from a tulip or garden slug.

Indisputably, no information was ever originated by the medium through which it is communicated. The ink and paper do not originate the information on a printed page, nor does the audio or video tape originate the information it contains and automatically communicates each time it is played. This fact is elementary, understood, and admitted by all. Even the most dedicated of atheists must confess this truth.

Intelligence is nonphysical because it conceives of and uses nonphysical constructs that clearly do not originate with the material of the brain or body. This fact takes us beyond the physical universe into the realm of spirit. We do not know what a soul or a spirit is, or what it means that God "is a Spirit" (John 4:24) who "created man in his own image" (Genesis 1:27).

Information can originate only from a conscious intelligence, a quality found only in personal beings. Whenever one encounters information of any kind through any medium, one is receiving an intelligent message from a personal being. We all know that a single cell, the smallest unit of life, is more complex than New York City. Clearly, the information that provides the directions for constructing and operating the incredibly small and complex machines that make up the 100+ trillion individual cells of many diverse kinds in the human body, and the untold numbers and varieties of cells in other living things, could originate only with an Intelligence infinitely beyond our capacity to comprehend. Without this information on the DNA, there can be no life of any kind. Whoever (it can't be *whatever*) originated that information is the source of all life.

Moreover, DNA not only defines all physical life, but it distinguishes between *kinds* of living things. Exactly as God said that every living thing would reproduce "after his kind . . . " (Genesis 1:21, 24, 25), DNA defines each species and will not allow one kind of living creature to evolve into another kind. *It simply cannot happen.* There can be modifications of size, color, strength, etc., within a given species, but those come either through combinations of what is already present in the genes or through copying errors. Errors in transmission from one generation to another, however, can only cause deterioration, not improvement. A new kind of creature would require infusion of new information from the Intelligence that created all life. This cannot occur by natural selection or by any evolutionary process.

The Mystery of Life

The proven and universally accepted law of biogenesis declares: "Life comes only from life." Therefore, the First Life could not have evolved from non-life; it must be eternal, without beginning or end. Life is not innate in matter. The chemicals of which every living thing is composed are lifeless in themselves; therefore life must be imparted from an outside source. The only possible source of life would be the eternal Creator, who alone has life in Himself and whose name is "I AM" (Exodus 3:14), the self-existent One. Clearly claiming to be that One, Jesus told the Jews, "If ye believe not that I AM *he* [*he* is in italics, added later by the translators], ye shall die in your sins. . . " (John 8:24).

Scripture tells us, "And the LORD God formed man of the dust of the ground [that contains all of the chemicals of which our bodies are made], and breathed into his nostrils the breath of life; and man became a living soul [a nonphysical being living in a physical body]" (Genesis 2:7). So man has two kinds of life, physical and nonphysical. The first is temporal, the second, man's nonphysical being, will never cease to exist inasmuch as it is not subject to temporal laws. Both components of life were given to man by God.

Jesus, who said, "I and my Father are one" (John 10:30), claimed to be that Source of life: "I am the resurrection, and the life" (John 11:25)—and He proved it by laying down His life and rising from the dead. He said, "No man taketh [my life] from me, but I lay it down of myself . . . and I have power to take it again. . . " (John 10:17–18). And so He did.

Of Christ it is written, "All things were made by him; and without him was not anything made that was made. In him was life; and the life was the light of men" (John 1:3–4). That statement, "the light of men," is a further indication that the life the Creator gave to man is more than physical; it involves the "light" of reason and separates man from all other living creatures. This inescapable conclusion, after years of investigation, turned Mortimer J. Adler (long-time Chairman of the Board of Editors of the *Encyclopedia Britannica*) from atheist to professing Christian.

In the preface to his *Encyclopaedia Britannica Lectures* at the University of Chicago, Adler declared: "Man differs radically in kind by virtue of an intellectual power possessed by no other animal and *not seated in the human brain*" [emphasis added]. In other words, there is a nonphysical life that has the "light" of intelligence and reason that does not originate with the brain and is not part of it. This obvious fact has a simple proof, which I have often presented.

Words communicate conceptual ideas. Neither ideas nor the words by which they are communicated are made of matter nor do they occupy space. Thoughts, which are nonphysical, cannot be produced by the physical human brain (best described as "an information processing system") for two additional obvious reasons: 1) If thoughts originated with the brain (who identifies oneself with one's brain!), we could make no decisions but would, in fact, be prisoners of our brains, wondering what the brain would think of next and what duties it would require of us; and 2) Conceptual ideas such as justice, truth, goodness, evil, etc., could only have a nonphysical source independent of the brain because they have no physical quality: they can neither be physically seen, felt, heard, smelled, or tasted but are separate and distinct from our five senses and the physical universe in which our bodies exist and of which they are a part.

Even Physical Life Depends upon Something Nonphysical

Clearly, there is much more to life than is physically manifested through our bodies. There is, unquestionably, a nonphysical side to man. Words and the conceptual ideas they express (including those imprinted on DNA), though physically communicated, are not part of the dimensional, physical universe.

The idea of "justice," for example, is immaterial and non-spatial. It has nothing to do with and cannot be described in terms of any of the five senses but lies in another realm that can only be comprehended as nonphysical, or spiritual. Conceptual ideas, as Adler said, present an impassable gulf between man, who can understand them, and all other creatures, which cannot.

Unquestionably, the DNA of every living thing contains rational instructions that had to be conceived ahead of time before they were put down in writing and encoded into the genome. The *idea* (Architect's plans) of the living creature, together with every cell that would make up its body, is an intelligent (and therefore nonphysical) concept that had to exist in the mind of an Intelligence *before* it was communicated in physical form and executed. The *concept* expressed in DNA could not possibly have developed by any evolutionary process. It is clear that any *idea* expressed in words (no matter in what physical form presented) must have existed in nonphysical form prior to its physical expression.

DNA is the physical medium through which intelligent instructions are expressed in words—but DNA neither originated the words or ideas they express nor encoded them into itself. The completed cell or body that would result from fulfilling the instructions could have existed only in the mind of the One whom even Richard Dawkins (who hates the very concept of God) is forced to describe as the *architect*![2] Thus, even physical life depends upon nonphysical and non-spatial concepts.

The DNA, the genome, the cell, the body—none of these either understands the written instructions or can reason about the incredibly complex processes this intelligent language describes. Nor can any living creature *except man* understand or reason about anything. Only man could crack the DNA code, understand, and intelligently discuss it. This fact places man and all other creatures on separate sides of an impassable gulf that evolution can not possibly bridge.

The Death of Psychology

The facts we have just presented should spell the death of psychology. Why? Because, following the lead of Darwin and Freud, it is atheistic, materialistic, and evolutionistic. In other words, it denies the nonphysical element of man and cannot deal with the real essence of humanity. Darwinian evolution became the rationale for psychologists to study the behavior of lower creatures in order to learn about human behavior—a foolish pursuit. Behavioristic psychologist B. F. Skinner's favorite experimental creature was the pigeon. He trained some of these birds to adopt various patterns of strange behavior in order to coax a random, automatic mechanism to deliver food. Incredibly, he theorized that the pigeons "thought" that their "ritual" behavior was causing the food to be delivered—and from that insupportable theory he suggested that the pigeons had developed a kind of "superstition." He imagined that by studying these pigeons he could learn how human superstitions developed.

Common sense rejects such nonsense, but this Harvard University psychologist spent much time and effort studying, analyzing, and speculating about his pigeons, rats, etc. In the process he developed a special cage that is to this day known as a "Skinner box" and is still used for such experiments. The pigeons' behavior was, in fact, no more than a conditioned response driven by hunger similar to the salivating of Pavlov's dog. Human superstitions, on the other hand, though irrational, result from ideas that require thought. The person "knocking on wood" or avoiding the number thirteen, for example, knows that these are irrational actions but will persist in them anyway, "just in case."

A reasoned idea, however, could not be created by a "stimulus-response mechanism." In fact, it couldn't be a conditioned response because no consistent results have been observed often enough for any human superstition to produce "reinforcement." Even a rat would give up in discouragement if it tried to make astrology work, but humans persist. Incidentally, "Almost all psychiatric drug research is done on . . . brains of animals, usually rats."[3] Darwin's reinforcement of Freud, and the influence of both together, is still the dominant force in secular psychology—and that carries into Christian psychology, which is derived from it.

Man's ability to form conceptual ideas and express them in speech cannot be explained in terms either of natural selection or stimulus/response reactions. There is an impassable chasm between man and animals. This fact turns into nonsense most of the experiments on animals in the attempt to learn about man. It is folly to attempt to deduce from the conditioned or instinctive behavior of animals an understanding of rational human behavior. Yet much psychology that Christian psychologists have borrowed from the secular world and brought into the church rests upon such assumed relationships.

Psychology is based upon a Freudian-Darwinian model of man that is irreconcilable with the biblical model. Of course, Christian psychology stands upon the same false foundation because secular psychology was the inspiration for "Christian" psychology. The adjective was added in order to make this godless religion acceptable in the church. As we have already noted, the founders of today's psychology were atheists and anti-Christians. God created man in His image. The rebellion that marred that image separated man from God and brought the penalty of eternal punishment from a Holy God. This biblical truth has no place at all in psychology, Christian or secular. In Scripture alone we have the reason for man's selfish (sinful) behavior. Only on that accurate diagnosis can any hope for a cure be founded.

Building upon a false foundation that rejects the biblical truth about man can only lead to false conclusions concerning man's behavioral problems. And from there, of course, the solution will also be wrong. Yet this secular misdiagnosis (in fact, outright rejection of the biblical one) is the foundation of Christian psychology. That fact nullifies the claim that "Christian" psychology is biblical, in spite of all attempts to purge out the humanism in the process of "integration" with Scripture. Satan's lies cannot be integrated with God's truth. No wonder Christian psychologists acknowledge that they haven't been able to accomplish this feat.

The Place of Truth

As quoted above, the Bible says of Jesus, "In him was life; and the life was the light of men" (John 1:4). Christ declared, "I am the light of the world: he that followeth me shall not walk in darkness, but shall have the light of life" (John 8:12). The reference is not to physical light but to the spiritual light of truth, which, when believed through the gospel and the receiving of Christ as Lord and Savior, brings life to the sinner out of the spiritual death that Adam suffered and we all inherited from him.

Truth, as we have seen, is not physical but spiritual. As such, it could only be understood by a spiritual being. Christ, who is called the "living Word of God" and who declared, "I am the truth" (John 14:6), is the very embodiment of truth. Truth has no meaning for animals. Their limited "intelligence" knows nothing of righteousness and evil, right and wrong, morals and ethics, love, compassion, mercy, or understanding. Animals act only by instinct and conditioned responses to physical stimuli.

The solution to man's behavioral problems is neither to establish conditioned responses nor to dull the brain with drugs, but these are all psychology can offer. What all mankind needs is to be restored to fellowship with God through receiving Jesus Christ as Lord and Savior, the One who *is* the truth, and who declared, "No man cometh unto the Father, but by me."

Psychology knows nothing of the spiritual side of man that comes from God and bears the imprint of His image. Psychology, in fact, denies this essential truth about man. Yes, there is some use of the word "spiritual," but it is far from the teaching of God's Word. Furthermore, a huge part of psychology and psychiatry depends upon drugs that can only affect the physical brain, and are, in fact, a doorway into the occult. To attempt to improve the behavior of man (a nonphysical being made in the image of God and living in a physical body) through a chemical adjustment of the brain is obviously a wrong approach.

A "biochemical imbalance" is a popular diagnosis by Christian psychologists. Yet the truth is that no examination was made of the brain to determine what chemical was out of balance and where this problem exists in the brain. In fact, no such examination is possible. It is a fraud to make such a "diagnosis" and then to prescribe drugs that, far from curing the mysterious and unidentified "imbalance," can actually cause it.

The three-pound human brain is the most complex organism in the universe. It has, by various estimates, from 10 to 100 billion neurons, each connected to other neurons by about 10,000 synapses, of which there are about 200 trillion. The brain has 100,000 miles of myelinated nerve fibers plus more electrical connections than all of the electrical appliances in the world. Medical science has a long, long way to go to gain a full understanding of the brain.

A team of thousands of medical doctors, neurologists, geneticists, and computer geniuses could not put the human brain together, with all of its connections through the nervous system to the rest of the body. To imagine that random errors in copying DNA plus billions or even trillions of years created the human brain and nervous system plus eyes, kidneys, heart, lungs, etc., is beyond the pale of reason.

Though it is common practice for both secular and Christian psychiatrists and psychologists to prescribe psychotropic drugs to "adjust" the brain, it is almost criminal to do so.

The Irresponsibility of Prescribing Drugs to "Fix" the Brain

Although there could be chemical or neurological problems, which have a physical origin, most of the "psychological problems" that clinical psychology or psychotherapy, Christian or secular, seeks to treat are not the result of a "broken or malfunctioning brain." These problems are the result of wrong ideas, thoughts, attitudes, and decisions. These are not physical phenomena and are independent of the brain, so "adjusting" the brain will not help. Psychiatrist and leading drug expert Peter R. Breggin unmasks the misinformation driving the psychology/psychiatry/drug industry, of which "Christian" psychology is a part:

> Psychiatric drugs . . . produce numerous serious and potentially fatal adverse reactions. . . . Depression, guilt, anxiety, shame, chronic anger, emotional numbing . . . signal that something is amiss and requires special attention. . . . Should we immediately focus on relief of the pain? On the contrary. . . .

Many educated and informed people have come to believe that psychiatry and psychiatric drugs provide the best last resort [for] psychological distress. Indeed, such drugs are increasingly the *first* resort. It appears that we have replaced reliance on God, other people, and ourselves with reliance on medical doctors and psychiatric drugs. . . .

Our emotional and spiritual problems . . . are declared to be biological and genetic in origin. . . . Many educated Americans take for granted that "science" and "research" have shown that emotional upsets or "behavior problems". . . require psychiatric drugs. . . . Few . . . realize that they are being subjected to one of the most successful public relations campaigns in history. . . .

Feeling fatigued? Take Prozac. Feeling as though you've lost your enthusiasm or direction? Take Paxil or Zoloft. . . . Feeling trapped in an abusive relationship? Take Effexor, Luvox, or lithium. Feeling a little nervous? Take Xanax, Klonopin, or Ativan. Having trouble disciplining your child? Give the child Ritalin, or Dexedrine, or Adderall. Having trouble focusing on work that bores you? Try Ritalin yourself. Having ups and downs of any kind? Take any number of psychiatric drugs. . . .

[To] focus on the molecular level by looking for biochemical imbalances [is] sheer speculation.

Why would a biochemical imbalance be at the root of feeling very depressed any more than it would be at the root of feeling very happy? The idea of individual biochemical imbalances is wholly at odds with the complexity of the brain. . . .

We have no techniques for measuring the actual levels of neurotransmitters in the synapses between the [brain] cells. Thus all the talk about biochemical imbalances is pure guesswork. . . . Research in no way [shows] that psychiatric drugs correct imbalances. Rather, it shows that psychiatric drugs create imbalances. . . .

The notion that Prozac corrects biochemical imbalances is sheer . . . propaganda from the biological psychiatric industry. But disruption of biochemical reactions in the brain, causing severe biochemical imbalances and abnormal rates of firing among brain cells, is a proven fact about Prozac that cannot honestly be disputed. . . .

The approach taken by psychiatrists and other medical doctors . . . is both simple-minded and destructive . . . the doctor almost always assumes that the problem lies in the "hardware" of the brain (i.e., in "biochemical imbalances"). . . .

It is impossible to reduce a person's emotional suffering to biochemical aberrations without doing something psychologically and morally destructive to that person. [Emphasis added][4]

Yet reliance upon drugs to do what Breggin says they cannot do is prevalent among Christian psychologists and psychiatrists just as it is among non-Christian practitioners. As Breggin says, drugs cannot treat the real cause: they only ease the symptoms by dulling the brain, a process that, far from helping, can hinder the healing of the underlying spiritual problem. Drugs certainly do not illuminate the truth that mankind needs to believe, understand, and obey.

The Mystery of Iniquity

Two of the great mysteries the Bible reveals are "the mystery of godliness" and "the mystery of iniquity." How evil could arise in God's "good" universe (Genesis 1:31) is a mystery we have discussed in detail elsewhere—"the mystery of iniquity" (2 Thessalonians 2:7). It will reach its fullness in Antichrist, through whom Satan will rule the world. In Antichrist, Satan will be manifest in the flesh, as God was, and is, in our Lord Jesus Christ.

Satan must be brilliant beyond our comprehension, apparently second only to God in power and intelligence, yet he is blinded by his own egomania to the wisdom and understanding that man is to seek and can obtain from God alone. It is a mystery that Satan, having known intimately the holy and glorious presence and power of God on His throne, could ever have desired, much less dared, to rebel. How could he have imagined that he could ever defeat God?

Surely this is a great mystery, the mystery of iniquity! How could it be that in the heart of the cherub closest to God, who dwelt continually in His presence, the ultimate evil was conceived? By one fateful choice, the most beautiful, powerful, and intelligent angelic being ever created became for all time the ultimate in evil: the arch enemy of God and man, the "great dragon . . . that old serpent, called the Devil, and Satan, which deceiveth the whole world" (Revelation 12:9; 20:2)!

None of the explanations/excuses psychology offers for inappropriate behavior or attitudes on the part of mankind fit Satan. He was not raised in a "dysfunctional family" or in a ghetto, nor was he "abused as a child." Certainly, today's popular diagnosis of "low self-esteem" or a "poor self-image" was not Satan's problem! Scripture says he was lifted up with pride: "O covering cherub. . . . Thine heart was lifted up because of thy beauty" (Ezekiel 28:16–17). He is apparently a self-deceived ego-maniac. The root of Satan's rebellion against God was not low self-esteem, but pride—and it is the same for every person who follows him.

Nor do any of the standard excuses for rebellious and selfish behavior promoted by today's Christian psychologists apply to Adam and Eve. Neither was raised in a dysfunctional family, abused as a child, belonged to a despised and mistreated minority, had a chemical imbalance, bad self-image, or felt inferior. To accept any explanation for evil in the human heart and life that doesn't fit Adam and Eve is to be deceived—Christian psychology, like its secular father, rests upon this false foundation.

The Mystery of Iniquity Today

Paul warns that a man should not become an elder until he is mature in the faith, "Not a novice, lest being lifted up with pride he fall into the condemnation of the devil" (1 Timothy 3:6). This tells us again that pride was Satan's downfall—and is man's besetting sin as well. "Pride goeth before destruction, and an haughty spirit before a fall" (Proverbs 16:18).

It is a great mystery that Eve would believe the serpent's lie contradicting what her gracious Creator had said. The serpent, however, knew the bait to use. He tempted Eve with the pride that had been his own downfall. If she ate of the forbidden fruit she would become wise like God. In fact, she would become one of the gods and would never die. It was a promise from the father of lies (John 8:44)—a poor foundation upon which to build one's life.

Adam was not deceived (1 Timothy 2:14), which may have made his sin even worse than Eve's. No doubt, out of love for Eve and not wanting to be separated from her, he joined her in disobedience, knowing full-well the consequences. It remains a mystery, however, that anyone under any circumstances would rebel against God—that anyone would choose the pleasures of the moment in exchange for eternal separation from the Source of love and life.

The heart of this mystery is the autonomy of intelligent created beings who clearly have not only the power of choice but something called self-will. At least some angels (Satan and those who joined his rebellion) and all men have the power to decide whether to serve God and Christ or their own selves. In deciding upon beliefs or actions, though evidence may be weighed, ultimately reason is set aside in order to bow before the throne of Self. We are our own worst enemies. To the oft-asked and very puzzling question, "Why do some believe on Christ, and others don't?", we can only reply, "Ask them. They made the choice and must know why."

Self entered the world when Eve made the choice of disobedience for all of her descendants. This is why Christ said there is no hope except we deny self (Matthew 16:24). And the only way that can be done effectively is to embrace the Cross of Christ as our own so that we can say with Paul, "I am crucified with Christ: nevertheless I live; yet not I, but Christ liveth in me. . . ." (Galatians 2:20).

Christian psychology has no solution to self. In fact, following secular psychology, instead of the denial of self, it promotes (in direct disobedience of Christ) Satanic selfisms of every kind, from raising self-esteem to improving one's self-image. This, however, only exacerbates the problem. Man was made "in the image of God" to reflect God's glory. Sin marred that image and caused man to "come short of the glory of God" (Romans 3:23). The most perfect image is found in a mirror. The mirror has only one purpose: to reflect a reality other than its own. Should a mirror try to develop a positive "self-image"? In fact, to do so would be the height of rebellion against its maker.

If there is something wrong with the image in the mirror, the only solution is for it to get back into a right relationship with the one whose image it was designed to reflect. So it is with man—he needs to get back into a right relationship with God through Jesus Christ. The worst thing he could do would be to develop a "positive self-image." That would be pride and a continuation of the rebellion that separated Adam and Eve from God at the beginning. Yet Christian psychologists and pastors by the thousands, following James Dobson and atheistic psychology, teach that the greatest need among Christians is to raise self-esteem and self-image.

The Great Mystery of Godliness

Neither godliness nor iniquity has a physical source; and neither secular nor Christian psychology is able to deal with these mysteries. Yet an understanding of these mysteries reveals the secret to sinful behavior and its cure.

Paul's earnest desire was that all believers might attain unto "the full assurance of understanding, to the acknowledgement of the mystery of God, and of the Father, and of Christ; in whom are hid all the treasures of wisdom and knowledge" (Colossians 2:2–3). Secular knowledge pursued in our universities can never provide the treasures of wisdom and knowledge that are hidden in Christ. Christ can never be discovered by scientific inquiry. He can only be revealed by His Spirit through His Word to those who believe on Him.

The solution to evil through the incarnation is a great mystery: "Great is the mystery of godliness: God was manifest in the flesh, justified in the Spirit, seen of angels, preached unto the Gentiles, believed on in the world, received up into glory" (1 Timothy 3:16).

"God was manifest in the flesh." What a mystery! God could become a fetus in Mary's womb? John the Baptist as a six-month-old fetus leaped in the womb of Elizabeth in recognition that Mary was pregnant with the Messiah. Amazing! Incomprehensible! Yet we know this is the only way it could be.

"Seen of angels." These heavenly beings must have watched in astonishment. The One whom they had known as God the Son and one with the Father for at least four thousand years by earth time (we know not how much earlier angels were created), was growing in the virgin Mary's womb, soon to be born a babe needing a mother's milk and care—truly man, yet at the same time truly God. Mystery of mysteries!

"Believed on in the world." The Apostle John speaks in awe of this One whom "we have heard . . . seen with our eyes . . . looked upon, and our hands have handled, of the Word of life. (For the life was manifested, and we have seen it, and bear witness, and show unto you that eternal life, which was with the Father, and was manifested unto us)" (1 John 1:1–2). In his Gospel, John says, "The Word was made flesh, and dwelt among us, (and we beheld his glory, the glory as of the only begotten of the Father,) full of grace and truth" (John 1:14).

Yes, "Believed on in the world." Certainly John believed, as did Paul, that Jesus the Messiah of Israel was truly "God manifest in the flesh." To be a Christian, one must believe that Jesus Christ is God come as a man to redeem us. What love it was to come from heaven's glory to stoop so low—to be rejected, hated, misunderstood, mocked, maligned, stripped, scourged, and crucified by those He came to redeem! And yet from the Cross, speaking of those who heaped this abuse upon Him, Christ cried, "Father, forgive them; for they know not what they do" (Luke 23:34). To answer that prayer, the Father had to put upon His Son the sins of the world, and Christ had to bear the full penalty those sins deserved as though they were His own.

"Received up into glory." His sacrifice accepted by the Father, He is glorified at the "Father's right hand" and interceding there for us (Romans 8:34). But even before that great meeting in His presence in the Father's house, "beholding as in a glass the glory of the Lord, [we] are changed into the same image . . . by the Spirit of the Lord" (2 Corinthians 3:18).

Christ Living in Christians

Surely, if the incarnation is the great mystery of godliness, then for us to live godly lives we must have Christ dwelling within us and living His life through us: "Christ in you, the hope of glory, whom we preach. . . " (Colossians 1:27–28). This is the "hope of his calling," which Paul prayed that the Ephesian saints would understand (Ephesians 1:18). Peter explains that God "hath called us unto his eternal glory" (1 Peter 5:10). We are going to be like Christ. The glory that the disciples beheld in Christ will be manifested in us!

All of the reasons why Christians seek psychological help would vanish if the life of Christ were manifested in them. This is the only solution, and psychology, whether secular or Christian, has nothing to offer in this regard. We need to feed upon Christ in His Word and to set our affection upon Him rather than upon the things of the world.

Our knowledge of both the physical and spiritual is limited at best, but one day we will fully know when we are with Christ in our glorified bodies: "For now we see through a glass, darkly; but then face to face: now I know in part; but then shall I know even as also I am known" (1 Corinthians 13:12). When in His presence we fully know Christ as He truly is, all limitations will have vanished—even our lack of power to finally overcome sin. When we see him, "we shall be like him; for we shall see him as he is" (1 John 3:2). Knowing Christ is everything!

We are transformed by His Word, the Word of Truth upon which we feed for spiritual nourishment. The written instructions that God spoke into DNA and that are essential for physical life present a powerful picture of the "words that . . . are spirit, and . . . life" (John 6:63), which He speaks into our hearts and lives when we trust and obey Him. This is the living Word of God, which, when believed (1 Peter 1:23–25), creates and nourishes spiritual life.

The very life of Christ manifest in our mortal bodies through His indwelling Holy Spirit is God's desire for every redeemed son or daughter of Adam and Eve. Knowing that fact, and with this desire and hope in one's heart, who would leave the fountainhead of all wisdom to seek assistance in the "foolishness" that God has labeled "the wisdom of this world" (1 Corinthians 3:19)?

---

1. Sir James Jeans, *The Mysterious Universe* (Cambridge University Press, 1931), 111.

2. Richard Dawkins, *The Selfish Gene* (Oxford, England: Oxford University Press, 30th Anniversary Edition, 2006), 23.

3. Peter Breggin, M.D., David Cohen, Ph.D., *Your Drug May Be Your Problem: How and Why to Stop Taking Psychiatric Medications* (Reading, MA: Perseus Books, 1999), 7.

4. Ibid., ix, 3-10.

GOD AND SELF

— *Dave Hunt* —

THERE WAS NO PLACE FOR GOD in the beliefs of the founders of psychology. How, then, could there be any possible way to fit God into this ungodly system? It was atheistic from the very beginning and still is. How could Christians have imagined that this religion of self-deification invented by atheists and humanists could be integrated with the Bible? Yet for decades this has been the dream of psychologists who call themselves Christians. In their book, *The Integration of Psychology and Theology*, Christian psychologists John D. Carter and Bruce Narramore happily announce that "psychology is making inroads into areas traditionally considered the domain of Christianity . . . the whole process of 'curing sick souls' is rapidly moving from the church to the doorsteps of psychologists and other mental health professionals."[1] And that's supposed to be good?

Thomas Szasz, a non-Christian psychiatrist, considers it a step downward that the salvation of sinful souls has been turned into the cure of sick minds. The problem with man is sin, a condition denied by psychology and for which it has no cure. Szasz says that the entire problem of human behavior ought to be taken back into the church because psychology and psychiatry have nothing to offer. Yet Carter and Narramore tout the invasion of psychology into the church as a blessing from God.

If this addition of psychology to Christianity is indeed beneficial, then Christians have been deceived for nineteen hundred years into believing that Christ's "divine power hath given unto us *all* things that pertain unto life and godliness, through the knowledge of him that hath called us to glory and virtue. . . " (2 Peter 1:3). Furthermore, if the promises pertaining to a life of virtue and fruitfulness are not true, then neither could the promises of reaching the glory in heaven above be true. Obviously, this is a serious charge that undermines the entirety of Scripture.

If the integration of psychology and theology is a good thing, then biblical Christianity, as expressed through true believers by Christ living within in the power of the Holy Spirit, must be deficient in some essentials that psychology supplies and that Christians were without until Freud, Jung, et al., came to the rescue. How could that possibly be true? That idea contradicts the Bible and is a slap in the face of the resurrected and indwelling Christ, who surely needs no psychological help in order to express His new life triumphantly in and through His own.

Paul said that the Word of God is given to us so that "the man of God may be perfect (i.e., mature, complete, all that God intended), thoroughly furnished unto all good works" (2 Timothy 3:17)—having all that is needed to accomplish anything the Lord asks us to do! What more could a Christian need? Yet Carter and Narramore go on to say:

> Most Christians . . . see much potential in a *scientific* study of the human being. They know that objective data and well-constructed *theories* will *expand our understanding* of God's most complex creation. And they believe that the *insights of psychology* can help the church to minister *more effectively* to the total needs of humanity.
>
> They hope that psychology will provide *answers* to problems *not specifically addressed in Christianity*. . . .
>
> Christian psychologists . . . believe that their discipline contains a *great body of truth* and they seek to *apply this truth within the framework of the Christian faith*. . . . We assume that *both psychology and theology* offer a great deal toward an *understanding of the human race*. . . .
>
> Christian *behavioral scientists* have increasingly used the word *integration* to refer to the interaction between . . . their discipline and . . . theology . . . based upon one essential philosophical underpinning—the belief that *all truth is God's truth, wherever it is found*.[2]

This entire statement exudes pride and is an insult to God. It declares that the Bible's promise of having provided for believers "*all* things that pertain unto life and godliness" is a lie—that the church, for nineteen hundred years, suffered from inadequacy due to a lack of scientific knowledge and expertise at last supplied by psychology. The blasphemy could not be plainer: science is superior to God and His holy, inspired Word.

A Rat's Nest of Destructive Errors and Hopeless Confusion

The numerous fundamental fallacies in the above quote should be obvious to any thinking Christian. There can be a "scientific study" of the physical human body and its components, but not of the soul and spirit—yet psychology (especially "Christian" psychology) pretends to deal scientifically with the latter. "Medical science" is a legitimate term but not "spiritual science," much less "Christian science." Turning Jesus into a "scientist" and His teachings into "scientific" statements was the basic blunder of Mary Baker Eddy, founder of the Christian Science cult. By its claim to be following a science of the soul and spirit, Christian psychology partakes of the same egregious errors.

"Behavioral scientists" is likewise an illegitimate term because there can be no science of human behavior. Science must be predictable and repeatable every time, without fail—which is clearly not the case with human behavior. There can be no science when the subject of the experiment is hopping about capriciously with a free will that produces unpredictable behavior. If the behavior of every individual human could be predicted unfailingly, then man is not made in God's image and free to choose to love or to hate, to obey or to disobey, but has been reduced to a stimulus-response mechanism—a robot that can only do what it is programmed to do.

If there could be a "science of human behavior," then for a man to say to his wife or child, "I love you," would be no more significant than to say he had an itch or a gastrointestinal pain. Love, an appreciation of beauty, a sense of justice or injustice, and all other uniquely human emotions and understanding would simply be physical reactions within nerves, glands, and brain cells totally explicable by physical laws and thus as meaningless as a reaction between chemicals in a test tube.

Science can *expand our understanding* of man's physical components but not of his soul and spirit or of his mind and will. These are outside the realm of science and thus beyond the comprehension of psychology, even if it *were* a science. Furthermore, the Bible is the Creator's complete instruction manual for mankind to follow, a fact that is denied if psychology can in any way expand our understanding of moral and spiritual behavior. Consequently, psychology cannot help the church to minister more effectively to the spiritual needs of humanity.

Moreover, if Christianity works according to scientific laws, grace has no part, nor does faith. If Christianity is a "science," then one no more needs to be born again to live the Christian life than to fly an airplane—one only needs to follow the "spiritual laws." Nor could psychology offer any scientific help because (as proved irrefutably) it is not scientific nor can it be.[3] As for psychology containing *a great body of truth* that can be applied *within the framework of the Christian faith*, such a claim could be true only if the Bible were insufficient for life and godliness.

Obviously, neither Abraham, Moses, Joshua, Samuel, David, Isaiah, Jeremiah, Daniel, John, Paul, nor any other biblical saints needed nor would have benefited from psychology. Then why should today's Christians, who face far less challenges and deprivations, need any help from psychology? In fact, they don't. It has nothing to offer.

What Is "God's Truth"?

The Bible is not a compilation of theories but the revelation of all truth, inspired of the Holy Spirit, and thus both inerrant and sufficient. Whatever problems man may have that are *not specifically addressed in Christianity* (quoting Carter and Narramore) cannot be moral or spiritual in nature because the Bible claims to instruct and empower us fully in those areas. Thus the claim that psychology provides anything of any value concerning man's moral and spiritual behavior is a blasphemous denial of the sufficiency and inerrancy of Scripture.

To say that both psychology and theology offer a great deal toward *an understanding of the human race* is to charge the Bible with inadequacy and to elevate psychology at the very least to equality with God's Word. The specious statement that *all truth is God's truth, wherever found* reflects a fundamental ignorance of truth as Christ and Scripture use the term. We have dealt with this fallacy in depth elsewhere and will touch it only briefly here.

Clearly, Christ's statements "I am the truth . . . thy word is truth" declare conclusively that there is no other source of truth than Christ himself and His Word, thus exposing the concept of "wherever found" as a lie. Christ's declaration, "And because I tell you the truth, ye believe me not" (John 8:45) does the same. By revealing *the truth* as something that mankind does not want to believe, Christ eliminated any idea that God's truth is merely factual or scientific. Men are not by nature opposed to mere facts. In its context (John 8:32), Christ's statement, "The truth shall make you free," refers to being set free from sin and self, which once again is outside the realm of earthly facts and science.

Further proving that *the truth* cannot be found anywhere except in Christ and His Word is His statement to Pilate, "Everyone that is of *the truth* heareth my voice" (John 18:37). One could be the most brilliant scientific genius and a veritable encyclopedia of earthly knowledge and still be deaf to the voice of Christ. Why do Christian psychologists insist on promoting this obvious blasphemy? There can be only one reason: in order to cling to and expand their position, power, and income.

Our Lord told His disciples that He would send as their Comforter "the Spirit of truth, whom the world cannot receive, because it seeth him not, neither knoweth him" (John 14:17). He also said that "When he, the Spirit of truth, is come, he will guide you into all truth" (John 16:13).

By these two statements alone, Christ utterly destroys the wishful thinking by which Christian psychologists hope to justify their looking to psychology and its godless founders and practitioners as a source of "God's truth." No, it is "the Spirit of truth" who alone leads into *all truth*. God's truth is revealed to mankind only through the Spirit of truth—and He is totally unknown to the world. Therefore Christian psychologists are guilty of grievous heresy in their claim that "God's truth" can be found outside of Christ himself and His Word.

Honoring Self

Because of its denial of God's existence from its very beginning, psychology has nothing to deal with but man himself. The humanist declares, "But we can discover no divine purpose or providence for the human species. . . . No deity will save us; we must save ourselves."[4] Although it rejects the true God revealed in Scripture, Humanistic Psychology delves into the spirit realm, even engaging mediums for séances, dabbling into Eastern mysticism, shamanism, and occultism of any and every variety. In the process, Self is deified as having infinite potential—which would be essential if it is to be elevated to the status of a god. Carl Rogers, one of the founders of Humanistic Psychology and highly honored by Christian psychologists (though he claimed to have contacted his dead wife in a séance and ended his own life in assisted suicide), called Self "the god within" and advocated worshiping at its altar.

Christian psychology, taking its cue from its secular creator, fell madly in love with Self. In attempting to understand the self, however, Archibald D. Hart, senior professor of psychology and dean emeritus at Fuller Theological Seminary, becomes bogged down in a hopeless swamp of contradictory statements. For example: "The self is the totality of what and who I am as a person."[5] Yet he also declares, "Deep within each of us is a place we call the self. . . . All the skeletons of shame and embarrassment are kept hidden there."[6] How can the self be a place deep within me and yet be the totality of what and who I am?

Contradictions follow one another in confusing procession: "I have the ability to transcend my self."[7] How can I be something different from and even transcend self if self is the totality of what I am? "I can 'know' myself. . . . The self . . . can be known fully only by God."[8] Which is it? "No issue is more important for Christian psychology than the proper understanding of the self. . . . The more I probe and search the self, the more elusive and perplexing it becomes."[9] So pursuing the most important issue leads only to increasing perplexity. What an admission of Christian psychology's bankruptcy!

Similar contradictions are found on nearly every page, along with even more serious errors. For example, "As we learn to graft ourselves onto the true vine [Christ] . . . self-fulfillment becomes Christ-fulfillment."[10] In fact, the Bible never uses such a term. We do not "graft ourselves" onto Christ. The relationship is much more intimate and supernatural than that. We are *in Christ* and

He is in us as our very life; and this happens by God's power the moment we are born of the Spirit through faith in Christ as our Savior. As for self-fulfillment being Christ-fulfillment, John the Baptist's declaration that "He must increase, but I must decrease" (John 3:30) and Paul's "Yet not I, but Christ" (Galatians 2:20) conclusively unmasks Hart's mutilation of Christianity.

Hart seems torn between his loyalty to his profession and his desire to be biblical. Unfortunately, he does not exegete the Bible but reasons from his psychological training and then imposes that view on Scripture, citing verses for alleged support that fail to do so because that isn't what they mean. Numerous examples could be given. As we showed in the chaper titled "Knowing and Loving God," Hart lists sixteen self-concepts under the heading "The Self in Scripture," with a supporting verse for each. In twelve of the sixteen, he totally misrepresents God's Word. Let us take another look at the first and last as examples:

Ignorance of the self misleads and deceives. (Isaiah 44:20)

The verse he cites speaks of an idolater: "He feedeth on ashes: a deceived heart hath turned him aside. . . . " Clearly the deception does not pertain to "ignorance of the self" but to superstitious trust in the alleged power of an idol. Isaiah is not decrying a lack of the self-knowledge Hart advocates but, as the context shows, the folly of trusting an idol to provide help it cannot give.

We are never to forget ourselves. (James 1:24)[11]

Not so. James writes that those who hear God's Word but don't practice what it says are like a man "beholding his natural face in a glass: for he beholdeth himself, and goeth his way, and straightway forgetteth what manner of man he was" (James 1:23–24). James is not telling us "never to forget ourselves" but to bring our lives into line with God's Word.

Scripture Twisting

Psychology seeks to "understand" how and why we think and act as we do. Such an approach would help repair an engine but not a person. We are not programmed robots. Trying to "understand" why a young woman raised in a Christian home becomes a prostitute, why a pastor with a beautiful wife and a fruitful ministry commits adultery, etc., assumes some reason other than self-will and thus offers an excuse for sin. Christian psychology's growing popularity is easy to understand: it protects Self from the accusing finger of conscience and God's Word.

One diagnosis fits all cases: SIN. At the root of sin is SELF. Jesus said that we are all the slaves of sin and self until He sets us free (John 8:34–36). Unbelief is the root of all sin. There is no greater sin than refusing to believe the promises of God and not allowing Him to mold us to His will. The just live by faith.

"Too harsh!" cries the Christian psychologist. "What about the person who was abused as a child or who has been traumatized in a hundred other ways?" Could there be a safer refuge for the wounded and fearful than Christ himself? Is God not able to bring comfort, courage, and deliverance? He promises to do so! Doesn't He keep His Word?

The Bible is all about those who were hated, abused, cast out, falsely accused and imprisoned, tortured, slain, and yet triumphed through faith in God. He has not changed. He will work the same deliverance today for those who trust and obey Him.

Yes, but what about children whose fathers repeatedly lied, cheated, and abused their trust? How can they believe in God as a loving Father when they had no earthly example? Away with such folly that props up foundationless psychology's "house of cards"! Since when was any earthly father a model of the heavenly Father? David said, "When my father and my mother forsake me, then the LORD will take me up" (Psalm 27:10). David's confidence was in God in spite of his parents' failings!

A husband would be hurt and frustrated if his wife refused to believe him. What about disbelieving God! He has promised never to leave us or forsake us. Some husbands, of course, have lied and broken promises so often that their wives would be fools to trust them until such men have allowed God to do in them what David prayed for: "Create in me a clean heart, O God; and renew a right spirit within me" (Psalm 51:10). God can do that, but therapy cannot. Psychological counseling attempts to *develop* rather than to *deny* self. Instead of self-confidence fostered by psychological techniques, what we need is trust and confidence in God and obedience to His will.

Some Commonsense Distinctions

Christ never promised to keep our cars running or to prosper our businesses or to make Christians greater athletes or scholars than non-Christians. He promised eternal life—not just life that never ends, but a divine quality of life here and now: "He that believeth on me . . . out of his belly [innermost being] shall flow rivers of living water" (John 7:38). Every Christian is indwelt by and led of the Holy Spirit (Romans 8:14; 1 Corinthians 3:16). "The fruit of the Spirit is love, joy, peace, longsuffering, gentleness, goodness, faith, meekness, temperance. . . " (Galatians 5:22–23). No therapy can improve upon that! Ask and believe God to fill you with His Spirit.

God made man in His image. This does not refer to a physical image, for "God is a Spirit" (John 4:24). Man was intended, in all he said and did, to reflect God's love, patience, holiness, grace, mercy, truth—the very character of God. Of course that was impossible for man on his own. Man could only be what God had intended for him if God, who had made man in His image (Genesis 1:26–27), expressed Himself through man. God had to be his very life.

Self took control when Adam and Eve willfully acted independently of God. That selfish and evil Self, said Christ, must be denied (Matthew 16:24–26). It is not that man must cease to exist as an individual with emotions, intellect, and will. No, he must willingly allow God to fulfill through him the purpose for which he was created and, after sin, redeemed.

Secular psychology knows nothing of Christ living His life in the believer and neither does Christian psychology—or it would renounce psychology altogether. Our Lord Jesus Christ certainly does not need any psychological help. Then why should the Christian in whom Christ is living as his very life need therapy? Theology does not need to be integrated with psychology—it needs to be separated and delivered from this viper it has mistakenly clutched to its breast. What the believer needs is simply to allow Christ in the power of His Holy Spirit to truly become his life. "Trust and obey, there is no other way."

Jesus, the perfect Man, said, "I can of mine own self do nothing . . . I seek not mine own will, but the will of the Father which hath sent me" (John 5:30). Only through denying self can we enter into this relationship with the Father that Christ enjoyed and begin to experience the life He has for us. May this be our passion and joy.

1. John D. Carter, Bruce Narramore, *The Integration of Psychology and Theology* (Grand Rapids, MI: Zondervan Publishing House, 1979), 9-10.

2. Ibid., 11-13.

3. Sigmund Koch, "Psychology Cannot Be a Coherent Science," *Psychology Today*, September 1969, 66.

4. *Humanist Manifesto II*, The American Humanist Association, 1973.

5. Archibald D. Hart, *Me, Myself & I: How Far Should We Go in Our Search for Self-Fulfillment?* (Ann Arbor, MI: Servant Publications, 1992), 42.

6. Ibid., 69.

7. Ibid., 46.

8. Ibid., 27.

9. Ibid., 73.

10. Ibid., 71-72.

11. Ibid., 41-42.

DÉJÀ VU!

— Dave Hunt —

IT IS STAGGERING TO SEE that in the so-called Protestant church of today there are many parallels to what the Reformers complained about in the Roman Catholic Church of their day. Moreover, many of those who promote these false teachings have been elevated to pedestals of Protestant infallibility as lofty as those of the pope and the Catholic priesthood. Christian psychologists comprise a new Protestant priesthood, which has its own therapeutic "confessional" and cannot be corrected by Scripture. To be a simple Berean and check against the Bible the doctrines of Christian leaders who are parroting the theories of secular psychology masquerading under a "Christian" label is condemned as strongly as daring to question the Pope and Catholic dogma was in Luther's day.

It is the pope's great authority, the huge Church he heads, its antiquity, and, as some insist, "the great good [in spite of overwhelming evil] it has accomplished," which are used to brush aside any questions of doctrinal purity concerning salvation that are raised. In this manner, any actual discussion of the issues and the merits of the arguments for or against Catholicism *vis à vis* biblical Truth are avoided.

The same is now true among evangelicals. The popularity of a certain leader, the size of his church or ministry, how long it has been established, and the great good he or she may have done become the basis for deciding issues rather than the Bible. Needless to say, this practice is very dangerous to the health of the evangelical church.

Two major foundation stones of the Reformation were the sole authority of the Bible and the priesthood of all believers. The Bible teaches that neither man nor organization can add to or take from Scripture or interpret it for others. The response of the Council of Trent (1545–1563) was to reject the Reformers' cry of *sola scriptura!* and to declare that the Bible was not enough for life and doctrine. In addition there were the pronouncements of the popes, of the Councils, and the traditions of the Roman Catholic Church, which were as authoritative as Scripture and more persuasive.

Clearly, the situation is very similar among Protestants today. There are, of course, the various new "prophets" who claim to have "new revelations" that must not be judged and who even deny the right and the responsibility of each believer to check what he has been taught against the Bible. The once very influential but now thoroughly discredited Earl Paulk said, "When we take our Bibles home, get on our knees and make our own decisions concerning the preacher's sermon, we decide the truth of God's anointing [upon a preacher or ministry] according to our own private interpretations."[1] He condemned this Berean activity, although the Bible calls it "noble" (Acts 17:10–11).

History Is Repeating Itself, with a New Twist

Similarly, today's "Christian psychologists," a new infallible priesthood unknown at the Reformation but now highly honored among both Protestants and Catholics, also reject the cry of *sola scriptura!* They respond with their own slogan, "All truth is God's truth!" One can no longer be a simple Berean and "search the scriptures daily" to see whether what is being taught is biblical. No longer is all of "God's truth" pertaining to "life and godliness" (2 Peter 1:3) to be found alone in Scripture, where the Bereans looked to check Paul's teachings.

Christian psychologists claim new sources of "truth" unknown not only to the Bereans and early church but all through history until this century. New "revelations" have been given to the church, and not through men and women of God (as is true of the Bible) but through the godless, antichristian apostles and prophets of psychology (Freud, Jung, et al.). Incredibly, this infusion of humanism and atheism into the church has met with the approval of most pastors and Bible teachers and has been accepted by most of the church as of equal authority with God's infallible holy Word!

Jesus said, "I am the truth" (John 14:6). How could the godless founders of psychology—who surely did not know Jesus but rejected Him—be a source of *the truth* that Christ so clearly declared that He is? He did not say, "I am part of the truth," or "I am one source of the truth." His language excludes anything that claims to be "God's truth" (to use the term of Christian psychologists) that does not come from Christ and in which He does not have preeminence. Right there, psychology is eliminated.

Christ said to the Father, "Thy word is truth." He is not saying that God's Word is *true* but that it is *the truth*. How could there be any part of "God's truth" that is not *the truth*? Behold the basic error of Christian psychology's slogan, "All truth is God's truth." By "God's truth" they mean facts of nature or science. But that is not what Jesus meant when He said, "*The truth* shall set you free." Knowing facts of science or nature cannot set anyone free from sin and its consequences!

Christian psychologists, in their attempt to pass off what is not in God's Word as part of "God's truth," have broadened "the truth," which Christ said that He *is,* to include inventions of atheists. This is not only dishonest but it is the cover under which grievous error has entered the church. In its rejection of *sola scriptura,* Rome unapologetically admitted that it was in rebellion against God's Word. The same must be said of Christian psychologists today: they are in rebellion against God and His Word because they have rejected *sola scriptura!*

A Skewed Battle

In response to the Reformers, the Roman Catholic Church supposedly reformed by attacking the immorality of its clergy. Many evangelicals are on a crusade against immorality in the world. Sadly, and significantly, Christians who are leading the fight against pornography, abortion, homosexuality, child abuse, and other forms of corruption in society rarely oppose false doctrine in the church. In contrast, Christ and His apostles gave no time to crusading against the evils outside in the world, but concentrated upon correction of error within the church. We need a renewal of that biblical ministry today!

Ironically, the one culprit that has been the major cause of the rapid and deep slide into sin in the last forty years is generally promoted rather than opposed by those leading the crusade against immorality in society. That culprit is psychology. The explosion of crime, rebellion, and depravity has coincided with the exponential growth of psychology since the early 1950s, a growth that is still accelerating. Whatever did we do without psychology? Indisputably, both the world and the church were far better off before psychology took over.

Psychology's redefining of sin as sickness has excused wickedness and thus encouraged it. Instead of being held accountable and called upon to repent, the sinner is diagnosed as in need of "therapy." Everything from disobedience to murder is excused these days as some kind of syndrome or addiction. Fornicators and adulterers are now "sex addicts" whose insurance covers lengthy "treatment" at Christian psychiatric hospitals. Christ's command to "Go, and sin no more" (John 8:11) is "too simplistic" these days.

Inventing new kinds of "mental illness" has increased the power of psychiatrists and psychologists over society and boosted profits of drug companies. Rather than upholding essential discipline, schools excuse the culprits as "mentally ill" and intimidate parents into medicating their children. Americans now suffer by the millions from alleged maladies that were unknown a few years ago. These are defined in the "bible of mental illness," the American

Psychiatric Association's *Diagnostic and Statistical Manual for Mental Disorders* (*DSM*). The increasing number of "mental disorders" being listed in added editions without any scientific basis raises a serious question: "Whence this raging epidemic of new mental illnesses—or are we being duped?!

These newly defined "disabilities" are creating a host of new "rights." George Will points out, "You have a right to be a colossally obnoxious jerk on the job. If you are just slightly offensive, your right will not kick in. But if you are seriously insufferable to colleagues at work, you have a right not to be fired, and you are entitled to have your employer make reasonable accommodations for your 'disability.'" In a word, the Americans with Disabilities Act of 1990 (ADA) encourages irresponsible and obnoxious behavior. The authority behind ADA is *DSM-IV*'s nearly nine hundred pages of folly.

Selfish and sinful behavior is no longer wrong but simply a sign that one is "special" and even entitled to "rights" denied to the rest of us! Is it because so many of those Christians leading the crusade against immorality in society are committed to "Christian" psychology that they fail to sound the alarm that psychology itself is the major contributor to today's growing immorality? The gospel is the power of God unto salvation not only from the penalty of sin but from its power in our lives. The church has lost confidence in God and His Word to meet our needs. We must return to *sola scriptura!*

Pharmacology: the New Savior?

The firm discipline children need and the Bible commends (Proverbs 13:24; 22:15; Hebrews 12:6, etc.) is now called "child abuse," and children have even been taken by government agencies from Christian parents who lovingly "applied the rod." Even more frightening, if possible, parents are being threatened with loss of their children for failure to "medicate" them as demanded by schools and government social agencies. What once was recognized as laziness, disinterest, stubbornness, or rebellion is now excused as some new "syndrome" to be treated with drugs. The number of children diagnosed as having "learning disabilities" nearly tripled from 1977 to 1992!

Children with discipline problems and diagnosed as suffering from ADHD (Attention Deficit Hyperactivity Disorder) are placed on Ritalin (methylphenidate) after they and their parents have been convinced by some therapist of their abnormality—a stigma (and excuse) that will probably be with them for life. Yet the National Institutes of Health Consensus Conference declared: "We do not have an independent, valid test for ADHD, and there is no data to indicate that ADHD is due to a brain malfunction."

Anyone who has taken Ritalin in teen years is rejected by the military, even though they no longer use it. Prescriptions for this drug (a central nervous system stimulant similar to amphetamines or cocaine) increased 600 percent from 1990 to 1995. In spite of its addictive nature, disputable evidence of its helpfulness, and many reported incidents of violence and suicide brought on by withdrawal from it, Ritalin is currently being given to more than 2 million American children. There are thousands of drug addicts hooked on illegally obtained Ritalin in cities across the country. The use and abuse in other countries is small by comparison.

Consciousness-altering drugs have for thousands of years been used in primitive societies to contact the spirit realm as part of their religious ceremonies. The New Testament warns that in the last days "sorcery" will be prevalent and the world will refuse to repent of it (Revelation 9:21; 18:23; 21:8; 22:15). The Greek word that is translated as "sorcery" in the New Testament is *pharmakeia/pharmakeus*. Americans live in a drugged society. Not only has the use of illegal drugs exploded, but so has the use of prescribed drugs, especially psychotropic drugs, most of which are harmful, habit forming, and consciousness altering.

An equally powerful method of reaching an altered state of consciousness and entering the spirit world to make contact with "guides" is the simple technique of visualization. This has been the common practice of shamans (witchdoctors, medicine men, etc.) for thousands of years all over the world. It has more recently been adopted by medical doctors and psychologists in their healing practice—and through Christian psychology has entered the church.

A Deadly Development

The Reformers objected to the images of the Catholic Church, which they considered to be a form of idolatry. In its rejection of the reforms that were so desperately needed, the Council of Trent justified the retention of images, which remain an important part of Catholicism today. The fact that so many of the "saints" had used this method and that so many had found images helpful for prayer and worship was considered to be sufficient justification to override biblical prohibition. That was bad enough then. But now, largely through the influence of Jungian psychology, both Protestants and Catholics have lately embraced an even deadlier form of idolatry: visualized images that come alive and even speak!

Richard Foster promises that through visualizing Christ in some biblical setting from His life, as recorded in the Gospels, you can have Him actually come to you and speak to you: "You can actually encounter the living Christ in the event, be addressed by His voice . . . touched by His healing power . . . . Jesus Christ will actually come to you."[2] Contact has clearly been made with the spirit world—but not with God or Christ. You cannot call Jesus Christ from the right hand of the Father to come to you—but any demon will be happy to pretend to be Jesus, and they do.

Carl Jung, one of the founders of psychology who is most highly admired in the evangelical church today, was in touch with demonic spirit entities. At first in dreams, then in visions, and finally in fully wakened consciousness (when he became so psychotic that the distinction between reality and delusion blurred almost completely), Jung had repeated "visitations and revelations" from the spirit world, even including experiences with "God" and the "Holy Ghost" descending upon him "in the shape of a dove."[3]

Christian psychologists and inner healers teaching visualization for pulling memories out of the past as an aid to therapy are too numerous to identify. One more example will have to suffice. Calvin Miller, best-selling author of many Christian books and a highly regarded evangelical Bible teacher, is a leader in opening thousands of Christians to the occult. He writes:

> One door opens to the world of the spirit: imagination. . . . To follow Christ we must create in our minds God's unseen world, or never confront it at all. Thus we create in our minds the Christ. [4]

What "Christ" could that be! He goes on to say,

> Still, imagination stands at the front of our relationship with Christ . . . in my conversation with Christ . . . I drink the glory of his hazel eyes . . . his auburn hair. . . .
> What? Do you disagree? His hair is black? Eyes brown? Then have it your way. . . . His image must be real to you as to me, even if our images differ. The key to [spiritual] vitality, however, is the [visualized] image.[5]

So which is the real Christ that Richard Foster promises will actually appear and speak—the one with the hazel eyes and auburn hair, or the one with the black hair and brown eyes? Obviously, neither. This is a delusion that any rational person ought to recognize as such. The only possible explanation for thousands (even millions) of seemingly sincere and intelligent Christians falling for such gross error is what Paul prophesied for the last days: "For this cause God shall send them strong delusion, that they should believe a lie . . . because they received not the love of the truth. . . " (2 Thessalonians 2:10–11).

169

The Demonization of the Church

Jung was so heavily demonized, as we have documented elsewhere, that he didn't even have to use visualization, the entities appeared to him spontaneously and as real as life. At first he tried to explain away these beings as products of his imagination, but eventually had to acknowledge their objective reality. Jung's wide variety of occult experiences[6] included alleged conversations and even travel with the dead.[7] It was the "revelations" he received out of this milieu of spiritism and near-insane occultism, especially from his spirit guide, Philemon, that became the basis for the psychological theories Jung developed over the remainder of his life[8] and that have so heavily influenced the church through Christian psychology in which Jung is a special hero.

Nick Cavnar, executive editor of the Catholic Charismatic magazine, *New Covenant*, pointed out, "Those who felt that the modern church had become too rationalistic found in Jung support for a more mystical, experiential religion. The charismatic renewal, with its emphasis on spiritual experience and inner healing, has been a natural field for interest in Jung. . . whatever is true in Jungian psychology can be adapted and used by Christians."[9] That is a naïve and dangerous statement but one that Christian psychologists widely accept because they either don't know the truth or suppress it. In fact, nothing is true in Jungian psychology. Psychologist and attorney Nandor Fodor wrote:

> The discussion of [C. G.] Jung's psychic participation must begin with taking a deep breath. It is a story so unbelievable . . . that— ever since it was fully revealed—analytic psychologists have been staggering under the impact, psychoanalysts have ignored it as a fairy tale, and parapsychologists have found it a diet so rich that up to now they have not been able to digest it. . . .
> Jung's . . . doctoral theses of 1899 [was] on "The Psychology and Pathology of So-Called Occult Phenomena. . . . "[10]

Visualization in order to contact the spirit world was taught to Jung by spirit entities that appeared to him, the same source from which Napoleon Hill, Jose Silva, and many other modern and influential occultists learned that imagination/visualization is the most direct and most easily opened door to the occult. Christian psychology brought this shamanic practice into the church. We are back to the practices of witchdoctors (since the beginning) and the Catholic mystics of the Middle Ages, who were the apostles of the denial of the Bible as sufficient for life and doctrine. What happened then is happening again.

Norman Vincent Peale (perhaps the most destructive influential heretic in the history of the church) declared that visualization had always been part of what he had taught and practiced.[11] He wrote an entire book in which he described the amazing results he had achieved through this occult practice, believing it was either from God or simply a power of the mind. Yonggi Cho, pastor of the largest church in the world, claimed that he had been taught by the Holy Spirit that in order to receive answers to prayer one had to visualize what one was seeking. He, too, wrote a book to teach this occult practice to others.[12] Robert Schuller wrote the foreword to that book, in which he said he had tried it and it worked: "I have practiced and harnessed the power of the inner eye and it works. . . . Thirty years ago we started with a vision of a church. It's all come true."[13]

Masquerading Demons

Christian psychologists justify visualizing "Jesus" as a necessary "inner healing" therapeutic technique for dealing with "traumas" allegedly buried deep in the unconscious. This practice, they say, is a helpful tool for Christians because it uncovers and deals with problems that biblical methods such as prayer, repentance, obedience, faith, and the filling of the Spirit, etc., supposedly cannot reach.

We thus have diagnoses and cures that cannot be found in Scripture and that the true church did not need for nineteen hundred years, but which we are now told are essential. This is all justified because it "works" so well for so many, and because it is taught as a part of "God's truth" that somehow was left out of the Bible, although that Holy Book claims to have given all that is needed for the man or woman of God to be "thoroughly furnished unto all good works" (2 Timothy 3:16–17).

It is astonishing enough that the secular world has embraced shamanism (witchcraft) in modern form and is training itself to be demonized by visualizing "inner guides" as part of the new transpersonal psychological, medical, and self-improvement techniques that have recently become so popular. It is more than astonishing, however, that not just Roman Catholics, liberals, and modernists, but the evangelical church itself has accepted and is promoting the same delusional and spiritually destructive techniques among the unsuspecting sheep of our Lord's flock.

Visualization has proved to be the most effective ecumenical tool in Satan's arsenal. Today's Protestants and Catholics have joined together in this same unbiblical practice, which is far more dangerous than the images of wood and stone that the Reformers rejected. Those Protestant "inner healers" who justify their practice because the visualized "Jesus" performs so well must explain how it is that the "Mary" being visualized by the Catholics is no less real and can also "heal." And of course both must explain how it is that all manner of "guides" visualized by occultists (from "space brothers" and Ascended Masters to coyotes and jaguars) perform just as well as "Jesus" or "Mary."

Christian psychology's visualization picked up from Carl Jung, who learned it from his personal spirit guides, has spread widely throughout the professing evangelical church. This is one of Richard Foster's, Calvin Miller's, Cho's, Peale's, and others' major teachings. Christianity has been redefined. We have to agree with A. W. Tozer that a revival of today's "Christianity" would set the cause of Christ back at least a hundred years. We don't need revival; we need a new Reformation that will turn the church back to *sola scriptura*. Let us return to the Lord and to His Word alone.

1. Earl Paulk, *That the World May Know* (K. Dimension Publishers, 1987), 144.

2. Richard Foster, *The Celebration of Discipline* (San Francisco: Harper, 1978), 26.

3. Carl Jung, *Memories, Adventures, and Reflections* (Pantheon, 1963), 10-11, 48, 171-72.

4. Calvin Miller, *The Table of Inwardness* (InterVarsity Press, 1984), 93.

5. Ibid., 94.

6. See, for example, Jung's letter to Professor Fritz Blank published in *Neue Wissenschaft*, Vol. VII, 1951, 14; *Psychology and the Occult* (Princeton Press, 1977), 143-52; *Memories*, 98, 189-92, etc.

7. Jung, *Memories*, 312.

8. Ibid.

9. Nick Cavnar, "Dreaming with Jung," in *PRRM Renewal News*, March-April 1986, 13.

10. Nandor Fodor, *Freud, Jung and Occultism* (University Books, 1971), 86.

11. Norman Vincent Peale, *Positive Imaging* (Fawcett Crest, 1982), Introduction.

12. Paul Yongghi Cho, *The Fourth Dimension* (Logos International, 1979).

13. Robert Schuller booklet, *The Power of the Inner Eye*.

WHAT IS THE TRUTH
OF WHICH CHRIST SPEAKS?

— Dave Hunt —

IT IS AN INDISPUTABLE FACT that *Christian* psychology, so-called, is founded upon the theories of atheists and humanists. No "Christian psychologist" would, much less could, deny this fact—nor are its proponents embarrassed to admit it. How is this atheistic foundation justified for something that is called Christian? That contradiction is allegedly removed by reciting the mantra, "All truth is God's truth." Presumably *the truth* can be found anywhere. Yet what is meant by *the truth* is seldom considered.

By "truth," did Jesus mean historical facts? Was He talking about scientific discoveries concerning the brain and the body during its temporary existence on earth? Or did He mean the truth that saves and enlightens the soul and spirit for eternity? Of course, Christ must have meant the latter. Nor would He have included the former in the same package, because it doesn't meet the criteria He sets for *the truth.*

Clearly, Jesus was referring to something very special. He told Pilate that His mission on earth was to "bear witness unto the truth. Everyone that is of *the truth* heareth my voice" (John 18:37). He surely didn't come from heaven to testify of earthly facts—nor did He mean that everyone who is willing to acknowledge mathematical or scientific facts was His follower.

Jesus told a multitude of Jews who aspired to be His disciples, "Because I tell you the truth, ye believe me not" (John 8:45). He couldn't have meant, "Because I give you the facts about Caesar's date of birth or about the earth revolving around the sun you won't believe me." The truth to which Christ refers could only be something outside the realm of earthly existence and experience—otherwise it would be acceptable to any reasonable and knowledgeable person. What could He have meant?

Jesus said, "Thy Word *is truth*" (John 17:17). He certainly didn't only mean that God's Word is factual or that it contains *part* of the truth. That it *is* truth means far more than that. Jesus, who is called "the Word of God" (Revelation 19:13), also said, "I am the truth." In fact, He said it like this: "I am the way, the truth, and the life: no man cometh unto the Father but by me" (John 14:6).

Surely no one, even a non-Christian, would imagine that Jesus was saying that He is *one of the ways* to the Father. Nor would any reasonable person imagine that when He said, "I am the life," He merely meant that He was one source of eternal life, but there could be others.

Then how is it that when it comes to the second of the three attributes He mentioned (way, truth, life), Christian psychologists argue that Jesus wasn't claiming that He and His Word are the *only* truth but that He left the door open for other sources of truth? This is not honest exegesis but scripture twisting to support one's cause. Way, truth, and life are put in sequence together. The one in the middle is the truth. Isn't it dishonest to claim a different understanding for *the truth* than for *the way* and *the life*, one immediately before and one immediately after?

There is a vast difference between temporal "truths" of history or science and "*the* truth" of God to which Christ refers and that sets souls free for eternity. Neither could our Lord have been referring to *the* truth in the sense of the oath, "I solemnly swear to tell the truth, the whole truth, and nothing but the truth, so help me God." That "truth" could just as well send someone to prison as set someone free—and certainly has nothing to do with eternal life. But *the truth* to which Christ referred sets free for eternity.

How Did This Mantra Become So Popular?

All that we've just said was clearly understood by Christians for nineteen hundred years. Then along came psychology. Its godless inventors never imagined that their theories would ever be considered part of "God's truth." But that day came, and we are living in it now. How did the claim of divine status for psychology arise? It was certainly never suggested by the world. Christians needed to justify themselves when they entered the field of psychology seeking degrees and respect from the ungodly that would gain the ear of the unsaved. Instead, they became willing partners in a fraud.

How could the Peales, Narramores, Dobsons, and others bring humanistic theories of anti-Christians into the church and get Christians to accept them? How else than to claim that "all truth is God's truth" and that psychology was simply one part of the divine wisdom God had given to mankind. Surely, Christian psychologists reasoned, there must be applications and even interpretations of at least *some* Bible verses that had been overlooked by believers since the beginning but could at last be revealed as psychological principles that had been there all the time without ever being recognized as such. And so the mantra "All truth is God's truth" was born. Let us put it to the test of God's Word.

When we speak of psychology within the church, we mainly refer to psychotherapy, sometimes called "the talking cure" (i.e., psychological counseling), also generally known as clinical psychology. Psychotherapy deals with problems of living: happiness, unhappiness, contentment, dissatisfaction, getting along with others, a sense of purpose and meaning that gives value to one's life, how to overcome depression, frustration, irritability, anger, etc. These are subjects upon which God has spoken to believers with finality in His Word. For the first nineteen hundred years of the church's history, no Christian would have imagined that any counsel on such matters was needed outside of Scripture or that any moral or spiritual power for living one's life was required except the indwelling Christ and His Holy Spirit.

This basic understanding, however, if it had continued until today, would have left Christian psychologists with nothing to offer except the Bible. How then could they justify their degrees and claim to have some expertise that any pastor, Bible teacher, preacher—and in fact, ordinary Christian—couldn't equally access from Scripture? Christian psychologists would be out of business with no means of earning a living by charging a fee justified by their boasted psychological credentials!

Psychological counseling—though the psychologist may be a Christian—cannot confine itself to the remedies that God's people (in both Old and New Testament) had relied upon and found sufficient for thousands of years before the advent of psychology. After all, one doesn't need a degree in humanistic psychology in order to understand and apply the Bible. What would be the point of having taken this hard-earned and time-consuming training unless it were used during the counseling for which it had allowed one to be licensed by the world?

Carl Jung said that psychology is the study of the soul but that we don't know what the soul is. Clearly, there is a rivalry between psychology and the Bible because the former attempts to solve, without God and Scripture, the very spiritual problems the Bible claims are the sole province of God and upon which He has spoken with finality.

In His Word, God not only claims to have communicated the truth but that His Word *is* the truth. There are no parts of *the truth* missing from the Bible and left to be discovered among the theories of the ungodly. To suggest that there is such a lack contradicts the clear testimony of Scripture and the consistent teaching of the church for nineteen centuries. That church withstood the Roman arena and the Inquisition and left the stamp of victorious Christian living and the blood of her martyrs upon the pages of history long before Freud or his successors came upon the scene to muddy the clear water of life.

It is a mockery to say that God inspired Freud (whose major motive in life was "revenge against Christianity"[1]) with insight into biblical methods of diagnosing and treating the soul and spirit of man. It is blasphemy to suggest that anti-Christians have been inspired to fill in a portion of *the truth* missing from the Bible, when God himself declares He has revealed all truth in its fullness in His holy Word. But this is the claim of "Christian psychology." Its very foundation rejects basic biblical doctrine. Increasing numbers of those once involved are beginning to see this fact and to openly oppose this false religion.

The Testimony of Scripture

We need only consider a few Bible passages to see the folly of the "all truth is God's truth" excuse for turning from the Word of God to find elsewhere a missing part of the truth that Christ declares and, in fact, *is*. When Christ saddened His disciples with the announcement that He was leaving them, He promised to send to them from the Father a personal comforter and guide:

> I will pray the Father, and he shall give you another Comforter, that he may abide with you for ever; even the Spirit of truth; whom the world cannot receive, because it seeth him not, neither knoweth him: but ye know him; for he dwelleth with you, and shall be in you." (John 14:16–17)

To further assure their troubled hearts, later that same evening Christ explained more about the Comforter, whom He further described as the Spirit of truth: "When he, the Spirit of truth, is come, he will guide you into all truth . . . and he will show you things to come" (John 16:13).

Paul wrote, "the things of God knoweth no man, but [by] the Spirit of God" (1 Corinthians 2:11). It is clear in the context that he is not talking about scientific discoveries made by atheists that provide deeper insight into nature or the witness of a moral conscience, which God gives to all men. Paul is referring not to natural but to spiritual truths, which he specifically states are revealed by God alone and only to true believers.

How could, and why would, God reveal a part of His truth to atheists that He didn't reveal to those He inspired to write the Bible? And why would some of "God's truth" be communicated to humanists who have rejected even the witness of creation and conscience? Were such persons really God's chosen vessels to reveal, at last, in the nineteenth century, previously undiscovered spiritual truths to the body of Christ? Is that either biblical or reasonable?

According to the Bible, the only "truth" from God that the unsaved person can understand is that he is a sinner and needs a Savior. Until he is born again of the Spirit of God through faith in Christ, he cannot understand the "things of God" that are "spiritually discerned." God's truth, says Paul, is only understood by the "spiritual man" who has been born of God's Spirit into the family of God. It is only those, Paul declares, who "have the mind of Christ" (1 Corinthians 2:16). To the unsaved, Jesus said, "He that is of God heareth God's words: ye therefore hear them not, because ye are not of God" (John 8:47).

Yet we are asked to believe that a part of God's truth—heretofore unknown for four thousand years to those who are of God, have studied the Scriptures, have walked in obedience to Him, and who have the mind of Christ—has lately been revealed to those who are *not* of God. Moreover, we are being persuaded that this new humanistic insight ought to be incorporated by the church into its understanding of the Word of God.

Before we accept such an unbiblical and irrational thesis, we need better justification than the specious plea that "All truth is God's truth"!

The Christian life is not a grit-your-teeth-and-hold-your-breath roller-coaster ride. It is Christ living His resurrection life in those who have opened their hearts to Him. To suggest that psychotherapeutic techniques lately discovered by the ungodly are now necessary (or even a helpful option) in order for today's Christian to experience the abundant life in Christ is clearly a modern heresy that denies the sufficiency of Christ and God's Word.

Tragically, the entire Bible is being reinterpreted on the basis of godless psychological theories. This new authority has undermined the confidence Christians once had in Christ's power to save, to keep, and to satisfy. This tragic fact is recognized even by secular psychologists. Bernie Zilbergeld, a clinical psychologist, is certainly not a Christian. After closely observing his own profession for fifteen years, he became badly disillusioned and began to expose it. What he writes is an indictment of "Christian psychology" and ought to open the eyes of church leaders who have embraced this anti-biblical system:

> Psychology has become something of a substitute for our old belief systems. Different schools of therapy offer visions of the good life and how to live it, and those whose ancestors took comfort from the words of God and worshipped at the altars of Christ and Yahweh now take solace from and worship at the altars of Freud, Jung, Carl Rogers, Albert Ellis, Werner Erhard, and a host of similar authorities.[2]

The New Priestly Class

By accepting a "new interpretation" of the Bible in order to conform to the theories of the ungodly founders of psychology, Christian psychologists have embraced an alien gospel. In turn, the church has accepted and highly honored them as a new class of priests supported by humanistic authority. With its own vocabulary, rituals, and academic credentials, this new clergy has gained authority over those who know only God and His Word. The latter are no longer considered to be qualified to counsel from Scripture.

The long-established responsibility of biblical counseling placed by God upon all believers has taken on new meaning: it now involves the diagnosis of psychological problems and the prescription of psychological solutions and must therefore be under the direction of those trained in this art. Nor can appeal be made to the Scriptures as a means of evaluating the doctrines of this new priestly class. They have another source of a vital part of "God's truth" that supplements the Bible and that those without the same academic training fail to understand and cannot dispute from Scripture. The new priests of psychology are thus beyond reach of any correction from God's Word.

In fairness to Christian psychologists, many of them have been motivated by a genuine desire to help the multitudes of hurting people who are not receiving the care and guidance they ought to have from their brothers and sisters in the body of Christ. One of the most desperate needs within the church is for personal, family, and marriage counseling—but it must be biblical and not psychological. For this need to be supplied, the church must be willing to support biblical counselors who can thereby provide the necessary help without charging for it.

Many young people (and older ones as well) sense a call from God upon their lives to work in this vital area, but the church will not support them in such full-time work. The only possibility they can see of being able to support themselves and their families through biblical counseling is to charge a fee. Although they realize that to do so destroys the loving concern at the foundation of biblical counseling, they feel they have no alternative. They still believe they are called of God to help the hurting, but in order to do so without support from the church, they must be licensed by the state. That means they must conform to its ungodly standards of education and competency in order to charge a fee and thereby support themselves and loved ones.

Remember, that every licensed Christian psychologist or psychiatrist has taken the same courses, been subjected to the same brainwashing, been required to give the same answers in order to pass the same tests, and has been licensed on the same basis as the most ungodly members of the same profession. Nevertheless, as we've mentioned several times, but it bears repeating, James Dobson encourages entering the field of psychology with these words:

> Psychology offers a unique opportunity for a person to be of service as a disciple of Christ. . . . I have found it rewarding in my practice to represent the Christian view of marriage, morality, parenting, and honesty, while respecting the right of the individual to make his own choice. What I'm saying is that Christian psychology is a worthy profession for a young believer to pursue, *provided his faith is strong enough to withstand the humanistic concepts to which he will be exposed.* . . . [Emphasis his][3]

What about Christian colleges, universities, and seminaries? Can't one obtain biblical teaching and training there? To give such training was their original purpose. But one cannot pass the state exams for a license by giving answers from Scripture. No aspiring psychological counselor would attend a strictly biblical school because be would not have received the education and training that would enable him to give the answers required for licensing. Thus, the Christian institution is caught in the licensing/acccreditation trap. It takes money to pay teachers and keep the doors open. To do so, psychology courses accredited by the ungodly must be offered or else they will lose large numbers of students because psychology is one of the most popular majors in Christian universities.

To avoid financial bankruptcy, Christian colleges and seminaries have been forced into *spiritual* bankruptcy. Almost all have succumbed to the pressure to be accredited by secular agencies. As a result, courses even in "pastoral counseling" are generally heavily weighted with psychology in order to meet the humanistic standards. Psychology as it is taught at most Christian universities and seminaries is scarcely discernible from what one would study in a secular school. It is one of the largest departments at Wheaton, Westmont, Liberty, Biola, where it is praised as supplying worthwhile and even essential expertise in counseling from Scripture. Such is the state of the apostate church today!

Failure of the church to support biblical counseling and to encourage all Christians to be involved turns counselors with the required degrees in psychology into humanistically trained "professionals." The counselor has to make a living, and the counselee becomes one of many clients in a busy day who come in and out on a strict schedule. But the healing of broken lives is not likely to be accomplished by an hour of counseling once or even several times a week in a professional-to-client relationship. It is far more likely to take place in the context of the caring and loving family of God, the body of Christ, the local church, concerned for the welfare of each member.

There ought to be older couples, mature in the Lord and leading exemplary, Spirit-filled lives of leadership, who give the time and expend the effort to take under their wing younger couples who may be having marital, financial, or other personal problems. Many youth are floundering under the ungodly peer pressures and temptations of today's world, and yes, under the entertainment-centered programs of the average youth group. The young need loving counsel from respected believers who are setting a godly example. The church must return to God's Word as the only and sufficient guide for "life and godliness" (2 Peter 1:3–4)—and everyone must be involved in bearing one another's burdens (Galatians 6:2).

The restoration of true Christianity is an individual matter. Revival begins with each of us. We dare not wait for someone else to say or do what is needed, but each of us, before the Lord, must step out in the leading and power of the Holy Spirit to fulfill that ministry to which God has called us. God's Word enjoins us: "Warn them that are unruly, comfort the feebleminded, support the weak, be patient toward all men" (1 Thessalonians 5:14).

It is very clear from God's Word that the local church was intended to be the place where counsel was given by loving brothers and sisters to those needing help. The following scriptures are a few of the many that make this fact abundantly clear: "Blessed be God, even the Father of our Lord Jesus Christ, the Father of mercies, and the God of all comfort; who comforteth us in all our tribulation, that we may be able to comfort them which are in any trouble, by the comfort wherewith we ourselves are comforted of God" (2 Corinthians 1:3–4); "Bear ye one another's burdens, and so fulfill the law of Christ" (Galatians 6:2), etc. Many more scriptures carry the same exhortation.

The Truth of God vs. the Facts of Nature

Christians who earn degrees in psychology (or those who turn to it for help) generally do so under the mistaken belief that it is a science—which it neither is nor can be. As we have often pointed out, a lengthy study appointed by the American Psychological Association (subsidized by the National Science Foundation and involving eighty eminent scholars) concluded that psychology is not and cannot be a science. This is the case in spite of decades spent in "ritualistic endeavor to emulate the forms of science in order to sustain the delusion that it already is a science."[4] Karl Popper, one of the greatest philosophers of science, concluded that psychological theories have "more in common with primitive myths than with science. . . . "[5]

However, even if psychology *were* a science, this would be the wrong place to turn for help with moral and spiritual problems. Erwin Schrödinger, Nobel prize winner in physics, pointed out that science "knows nothing of . . . good or bad, God and eternity. . . . Whence came I and whither go I? That is the great unfathomable question. . . . Science has no answer to it."[6] If human behavior could be reduced to a science of laws and predictability and repeatability, man would be destroyed as God made him.

Man's problem is that he is willfully separated from God by sin. The only solution is reconciliation through the death, burial, and resurrection of Christ, who thereby paid the full penalty for our sins. When man is right with God and lives in obedience to God's Word, there is peace in his own heart and his relationships with others are right. This is not obtainable through psychology; no biblical help will be found there. Psychology is a "do-it-yourself" kit that God will not honor. He will not consent to being a partner with "Christian" psychotherapy.

Those who proclaim that "All truth is God's truth" confuse the truth with mere facts of nature. Because "all truth" is revealed only by the Spirit of God, "whom the world cannot receive" (John 16:13; 14:17), if science were part of "the truth" to which Christ refers, all scientific discoveries would have to be made only by Christians. Yet many non-Christians are great scientists. Thus, even if psychology were a science, it would still not be part of "God's truth," which is revealed by God only to His own.

The Bible repeatedly claims to be written to those who belong to the Lord, and the truth it communicates is referred to as "the things of the Spirit of God." We are told unequivocally, "the natural [unsaved] man receiveth not the things of the Spirit of God: for they are foolishness unto him: neither can he know them, because they are spiritually discerned" (1 Corinthians. 2:9–14). But the Spirit of God is also called "the Spirit of truth," who reveals all truth (John 16:13). Consequently, no unsaved person knows anything of "God's truth."

Let us rely wholly upon God and His Word and trust and obey His promises fully. Only in that faith and by God's grace and power will anyone ever live the abundant life promised to all those in whom Christ dwells. What more could any trusting Christian need or ask? It is not psychology but God himself who "is able to do exceeding abundantly above all that we ask or think, according to the power that worketh in us, unto him be glory in the church by Christ Jesus. . . . Amen" (Ephesians 3:20–21).

1. Thomas Szasz, *The Myth of Psychotherapy: Mental Healing as Religion, Rhetoric, and Repression* (New York: Anchor Press/Doubleday, 1978), 149.

2. Bernie Zilbergeld, *The Shrinking of America: Myths of Psychological Change* (Little, Brown, 1983), 5.

3. James Dobson, *Dr. Dobson Answers Your Questions* (Wheaton, IL: Tyndale House Publishers, Inc., 1989), 498.

4. Sigmund Koch, "Psychology Cannot Be a Coherent Science," *Psychology Today*, September 1969, 66.

5. Karl Popper, "Scientific Theory and Falsifiability," *Perspectives in Philosophy*, Robert N. Beck, ed. (Holt, Rinehart, Winston, 1975), 343.

6. Erwin Schrödinger, quoted in *Quantum Questions*, ed. Ken Wilbur (Boston, MA: New Science Library, Shambhala,1984), 81.

I WILL BE WITH YOU!

— Dave Hunt —

A VARIETY OF PSYCHOTHERAPIES masquerading under Christian terminology are devastating the church by turning Christians from God to Self. Among the most deadly are regressive therapies designed to probe the unconscious for buried memories, which are allegedly causing everything from depression to fits of anger to sexual misconduct—traumatic memories that must be uncovered and "healed." These offshoots of Freudian and Jungian theories, rooted in the occult, which have destructively impacted society for decades, are taking their toll within the church.

One popular variety of regression therapy is called "inner healing" and was brought into the church by occultist Agnes Sanford (see *The Seduction of Christianity* by this author and T. A. McMahon). It was carried on after her death by those she influenced, such as lay therapists Ruth Carter Stapleton, Rosalind Rinker, John and Paula Sandford, William Vaswig, Rita Bennett, and others. At first most prevalent among charismatics and liberal churches, inner healing has spread widely in evangelical circles. There it is practiced in a more sophisticated form by psychologists such as David Seamands, H. Norman Wright, and James G. Friesen as well as a number of lay therapists like Fred and Florence Littauer. The Littauers' extreme insistence that rare is the person "who can say he truly had a happy childhood" would seem to condition their counselees to recover unhappy and traumatic memories.

Even if it were safely and accurately possible (which it is not), should one probe into the past in order to dredge up forgotten memories? Memory is notoriously deceitful and self-serving. One is easily talked into "remembering" something that may never have happened. Inner healing, like other forms of psychotherapy, creates, by its very nature, false memories. Furthermore, why must one uncover memories of past abuse in order to have a right relationship with God? Where does the Bible say this? And if parts of the past must be "remembered," why not every detail? That task would be hopeless. Yet once the theory is accepted, one can never be certain that some trauma is not still hidden in the unconscious—a trauma holding the key to emotional and spiritual well-being!

In contrast, Paul declared,

> This one thing I do, forgetting those things which are behind, and reaching forth unto those things which are before, I press toward the mark for the prize of the high calling of God in Christ Jesus. Let us therefore [i.e., in view of the prize], as many as be perfect [i.e., mature, trusting in God alone], be thus minded: and if in any thing ye be otherwise minded, God shall reveal even this unto you. (Philippians 3:13–15)

Forgetting the Past and Pressing on to the Joy of His "Well Done!"

Paul was heading for the finish line, as we all are, whether we realize it or not. He said to follow him as he followed Christ toward the prize for overcomers and the crown promised to all those who love Christ's appearing (2 Timothy 4:7–8). The past is gone and to be forgotten if, as Scripture promises, Christians truly are new creations for whom "old things are passed away [and] all things are become new" (2 Corinthians 5:17). Searching the past in order to find an "explanation" for one's present behavior conflicts with the entire teaching of Scripture as well as with common sense. Though it may seem to help for a time, it actually robs one of the biblical solution obtainable through Jesus Christ. What matters is not the past but one's personal relationship with Christ right now.

Yet many people claim to have been helped by regressive therapy. Finding the "reason" in a past trauma (whether real or a "memory" implanted by suggestion in the therapy process) can bring a change in attitude and behavior for a time. Sooner or later, however, depression or anger or frustration or temptation returns, leaving one to renew the search into the past to find that "key" trauma, the memory of which has not yet been uncovered. And on and on it goes—and where it stops, nobody knows.

In keeping with the Freudian foundation of all "inner healing," Fred and Florence Littauer's book, *Freeing Your Mind from Memories that Bind*, presents the thesis that uncovering hidden memories is the key to emotional and spiritual well-being. They suggest that any "memory gaps" from childhood indicate that one has probably been abused (and very likely, sexually). By that definition, we've all been abused. Most of us can't remember every house we've lived in, every school attended, every teacher and classmate, every incident that ever occurred—good or bad—every family vacation when we were children, etc. To teach, as the Littauers do, that these "memory gaps" indicate periods of abuse that have been covered up by the mind is contrary to common sense and is without scientific verification or biblical support.

The "Four Temperaments/Astrology" Delusion

The Littauers, like so many others in this field, base their approach upon the so-called four temperaments. This long-discredited personality theory evolved from the ancient Greek belief that the physical realm was composed of four elements: earth, air, fire, and water. Empedocles related these to four pagan deities while Hippocrates tied them to what were considered at that time to be the four bodily humors: blood (sanguine), phlegm (phlegmatic), yellow bile (choleric), and black bile (melancholy). These characteristics were connected to the signs of the zodiac.

There was never any scientific basis for the four temperaments, yet many Christian psychologists and lay "healers" swear by them today, making them the basis of "personality classification" and the key to behavioral insights. As the Bobgans point out, however, in their excellent book, *Four Temperaments, Astrology & Personality Testing*:

> The medieval view of personality was that the arrangement of stars and planets in the zodiac determined each person's personality both at birth and throughout his life. In spite of the lack of scientific evidence or biblical support, books about identifying and transforming temperaments often sound authoritative. They include both plausible information and wild speculation presented as proven fact. . . .
>
> A person's temperament was believed to have been set according to the configurations of the sun, moon and planets. If a person was born under a particular sun sign, he would have a predetermined temperament.
>
> The four temperaments had virtually been discarded after the Middle Ages . . . until a few lone souls discovered them among relics of the past and marketed them in twentieth-century language. . . . The four temperaments, which had largely gone out of vogue since medieval times, have become popular among evangelical Christians in the same way that astrology has risen in popularity among nonChristians. . . . The four temperaments are that feature of astrology made palatable to Christians.[1]

Like other Christian psychologists and lay inner healers, the Littauers do not derive their theory and practice from a careful exegesis of Scripture but quote an isolated verse now and then in an attempt to give the appearance of biblical support. For example, beneath their second chapter title, "Searching Ourselves," they quote part of a verse, "I, the LORD, search the minds and test the hearts of men" (Jeremiah 17:10, TEV). In fact, this scripture opposes the idea of searching ourselves. It declares that only God can search and understand our hearts: "The heart is deceitful above all things, and desperately wicked: who can know it? I the LORD search the heart . . . to give every man according to . . . the fruit of his doings" (17:9–10, KJV).

The context exposes the lie of the application made not only by the Littauers but by other well-meaning "inner healers." God blesses those who trust only in Him and curses those who trust in anything else—even if they trust *mostly* in Him but also in something else. He promises that those who trust in Him "shall be as a tree planted by the waters, and that [never shall] cease from yielding fruit" (Jeremiah 17:8). A fruitful life (of love, joy, peace, etc.) is produced by the working of the Spirit of God in those who surrender their otherwise deceitful hearts to Him! Nowhere does the Bible say that taking personality tests and learning one's "temperament" aids His work in us. What God promises and performs is not aided but hindered by looking to anything else to make up some imagined deficiency in God's work.

The Littauers have extreme difficulty finding scriptures even remotely appropriate and are thus forced to misapply the Bible. As a further example, the chapter titled "Earliest Memories" (p. 141) is headed by the verse, "My heart breaks when I remember the past" (Psalm 42:4, TEV). In fact, David is not referring at all to "earliest memories" but to the current ridicule and criticism he is receiving from those who "say daily [i.e., presently] unto me, Where is thy God?" The verse, "Write down in a book everything that I have told you" (Jeremiah 30:2, TEV), is quoted directly under the chapter heading "Ready, Aim, Write." That chapter is about taking a "thorough look into your past" and "writing down one's feelings"—about as far from Jeremiah recording Scripture under the inspiration of the Holy Spirit as one could get!

A Spreading Delusion Among Evangelicals

The Littauers are only one example among a host of inner healers, whether licensed Christian psychologists or lay persons, who, though they may be sincere, are leading Christians astray by the millions. Best-selling pop-psychology authors Gary Smalley and John Trent, heavily promoted by James Dobson, came up with their own four temperaments based upon animal types: lion, beaver, otter, and golden retriever! Is that supposed to provide help to

Spirit-filled Christians whose trust is in the Lord God, creator of heaven and earth? Only gross unbelief would turn to this foolishness!

So-called "Personality Profile Tests" are a related delusion that is sweeping the church. They are even being given to missionaries to see whether they will be successful and to Christian teachers, pastors and church staff, etc. Such tests supposedly identify one's "personality type," or "temperament." New ones continue to be invented. The more popular ones are the Myers-Briggs Type Indicator (MBTI), Taylor-Johnson Temperament Analysis (TJTA), Personal Profile System (PPS), Personality Profile Test (PPT), Biblical Personal Profiles (BPP), etc. Though popular, personality tests are unreliable. Human personalities, with the power to choose, and hearts that God says are "deceitful above all things," defy predictive formulas and are far too complex to neatly categorize. Even the once-promising classifications of persons as Type A Personalities (susceptible to heart attack), Type B (less susceptible), and Cancer Personalities, etc., are being discarded because no scientific correlation can be found between disease and "personality type."

These inaccurate and destructive tests have been promoted by a host of popular Christian authors and speakers such as psychologist H. Norman Wright and financial analyst Larry Burkett, now deceased. Four-temperament and personality-classification theories trivialize the human soul and spirit and provide excuses for un-Christian behavior. The focus is on Self, analyzing one's feelings, personality, childhood, and trying to find out why one thinks and does what one does. The choice is ours, and even Christians sometimes make wrong choices in direct disobedience to God's Word. Choice is a matter of the will and can neither be explained nor excused by alleged "personality type." Jesus stated it plainly:

> But those things which proceed out of the mouth come forth from the heart; and they defile the man. For out of the heart proceed evil thoughts, murders, adulteries, fornications, thefts, false witness, blasphemies. . . ." (Matthew 15:18–19)

But the Bible Says. . .

In contrast to inner healing, personality types, and other errors supported by many Christian psychologists, the focus in the Bible is upon God and Christ and His Word, turning us from ourselves to Him, turning us from the past to present obedient service and the hope of His return to take us out of this evil world into the Father's house of many mansions. Instead of seeking to identify one's personality and temperament by reference to speculative systems related to psychology, astrology, and the occult, one's thoughts and actions need to be governed by God's inerrant and sufficient Word.

God promises that if we heed the doctrine in His Word, He will by "reproof . . . correction [and] instruction in righteousness" direct our lives (2 Timothy 3:16). As a result, men and women of God become mature, perfected and prepared "unto all good works" (v. 17). Peter assures us that God "hath given unto us all things that pertain unto life and godliness, through the knowledge of him that hath called us to glory and virtue" (2 Peter 1:3). Jesus declared that those who continue in obedience to His Word are His true disciples who "know the truth" and whom the truth makes free (John 8:31–32). Only those who doubt such promises or are unwilling to take the way of the Cross turn for help to manmade theories and therapies.

The Bible never even hints at "personality types" nor does it categorize individuals by their strengths and weaknesses as a means of identifying their abilities and predicting their success or failure in God's service. Rejecting Saul's armor, with a sling and five stones David conquered the heavily armed giant, Goliath, who had terrorized the entire army of Israel.

What was David's secret? His confidence was not in his personality type or abilities but in the Creator of heaven and earth! Defying Goliath, David shouted as he ran toward him, "I come to thee in the name of the LORD of hosts. . . . This day will the LORD deliver thee into mine hand" (1 Samuel 17:45–46). David's confidence was in the Lord, not in Saul's armor or in himself.

Even had David not been an expert with the sling, God would have enabled him to hit the mark. Paul went so far as to state that God told him that His strength was perfected in man's weakness. Thus Paul declared, "When I am weak, then am I strong" (2 Corinthians 12:10). Such statements refute the entire rationale of personality testing, temperament identification, and self-esteem and self-worth enhancement. Our trust is in the Lord!

The Man or Woman God Uses

The Bible is filled with examples of men and women who were hated, abused, and cast out by their own families—men and women who were friendless, lacking in talents or abilities, yet who triumphed over every adversity, no matter how great, because of their trust in God. The lives and deaths of these heroes and heroines of the faith testify against the unbiblical and humanistic focus upon self that underlies all of the pop psychologies brought into the church from the world and that masquerade as "Christian" psychology.

Moses is but one example among many. When God called Moses to go to Egypt to deliver His people, Moses pleaded that he was incapable of such a mission and asked God to choose someone else (Exodus 3:11, 4:10–13). Did God administer a personality test to show Moses that he was well suited? Did He cure Moses' poor self-image or abysmal sense of self-worth? Did He prescribe inner healing to deliver Moses from those buried memories of being abandoned by his parents and raised in a foster home and the lack of self-identity that resulted? Did He give him a course in self-improvement, self-confidence, and success? On the contrary, God made this promise: "I will be with you!"

The well-meaning "counsel" of those who attempt to help Christians understand themselves by focusing upon self actually robs counselees of the divine presence and power that Moses knew. Human strengths and weaknesses are beside the point. What matters is whether or not the power of God's Holy Spirit is manifest in one's life. Many if not most of the great Bible characters, as well as the more recent heroes of the faith, from the early martyrs to the great missionary pioneers of the nineteenth century, would probably fail today's personality profile tests.

In fact, God did not choose Moses because he was highly qualified. He was chosen because he was the meekest man on the face of the earth (Numbers 12:3). Why would God choose such a person to confront the mightiest emperor of the day on his turf, in his palace, to deliver Israel from his grip? He did so to teach the Israelites to trust in *Him* rather than man for their deliverance! He did so to keep the glory Himself, which He will not share with anyone.

Never is there a hint that Joseph, David, Daniel, or any other hero of the faith needed the therapies considered so vital and effective today. It was when Job got a glimpse of God that he said, "I abhor [hate] myself," and he repented in ashes (Job 42:5–6). Then he was restored by the Lord. It was when Isaiah also had a vision of God and cried, "Woe is me! for I am undone" (Isaiah 6:1–8) that God was able to use him. We need to turn from self-analysis to look at the Lord. This is the sure path to victory in His name and to His glory.

Develop an insatiable thirst for God! Get to know Him through His Word, meditating day and night on His person and love and what Christ suffered and accomplished for you on the Cross! Tell Him often that you love Him with your whole heart and ask Him to make this true in every way. The fruit of the Spirit does not come as the result of understanding ourselves through the use of humanistic analyses or techniques (though clothed in biblical language) but through the manifestation of the power of the Holy Spirit in our weakness. Some of us are too strong in ourselves for God to use us. Be weak enough to know you are helpless without Him, weak enough to cry out for His strength, and weak enough for Him to use you!

---

1. Martin and Deidre Bobgan, *Four Temperaments, Astrology & Personality Testing* (Santa Barbara, CA: EastGate Publishers, 1992), 6-7, 9, 30, 33, 50-51.

WEEP FOR YOUR CHILDREN!

— Dave Hunt —

BEING LED AWAY TO THE CROSS, Jesus turned to those lamenting among the mockers, and said to them, "Daughters of Jerusalem, weep not for me, but weep for yourselves, and for your children. . . . For if they do these things in a green tree, what shall they do in the dry?" (Luke 23:28, 31.) Under Bill Clinton and Al Gore, for the first time in its history, the United States had a president and vice-president who openly approved homosexuality, the murder of the unborn, and the pagan worship of Mother Earth. President Clinton's first official moves revealed a determination to elevate what for thousands of years had been known worldwide as "a crime against nature" to an honorable act that makes one a member of a favored new and powerful class in society. Today, no one dares to speak a word against that privileged "minority." Moral convictions based upon conscience and the Bible are now "hate and prejudice."

Years before, the United States had already turned moral standards (once accepted as clearly written by God in man's conscience) over to psychologists and psychiatrists to redefine for the rest of us. The new "Bible" became the *Diagnostic and Statistical Manual of Mental Disorders* (*DSM*) published by the American Psychiatric Association. Only those "disorders" listed within its pages became eligible for insurance coverage. The *DSM* has been revised five times since first published in 1952 and is now in the process of a further revision to be published in 2011. Each time, the list of "mental disorders" grows longer because new "disorders" are continually being invented and added to the official list. On some scientific basis? No. There is none. They are added by *vote*—as far from science as one could imagine. Are Americans getting crazier and crazier? Not exactly, but they have surrendered their common sense to psychologists and psychiatrists. The latter, by inventing new "mental disorders," claim control over ever-larger protions of society—and the church eagerly embraces this fraud.

The first edition listed one hundred six mental disorders; *DSM-II*, published in 1968, listed one hundred eighty-two disorders, one of them being homosexuality. Under threats from homosexuals, APA members attending the annual convention in San Francisco in 1974, voted 5,854 to 3,810 to change homosexuality from deviant/abnormal behavior to a "sexual preference." That change was immediately made official in the seventh printing of *DSM-II* in 1974. Later, homosexuality was removed from the manual altogether. This is not science—nor is it honest!

Are the Patients Running the Asylum?

Psychological theories come and go on a merry-go-round of confusion. For example, *drapetomania* was the official psychiatric diagnosis of a "mental illness" that was epidemic in early America. Afflicting only slaves, its symptoms were a compulsive urge to escape the plantation—a serious "mental illness" that was miraculously cured by the Civil War! Today, mental illnesses are created or cured *by membership vote*. Psychology would be laughable were it not devastating both the world and the church. One newspaper editor wrote sarcastically:

> Does your 10-year-old dislike doing her math homework? Better get her to the nearest couch because she's got No. 315.4, *Developmental Arithmetic Disorder*.
>
> Maybe you're a teenager who argues with his parents. Uh-oh. Better get some medication pronto because you've got No. 313.8, *Oppositional Defiant Disorder*. . . . I'm not making these things up. (That would be *Fictitious Disorder Syndrome*). . . .
>
> I know there are some cynics out there who . . . wouldn't be caught dead on a psychiatrist's couch. . . . Your unwillingness to accept professional help is itself a symptom of a serious mental problem. It's right here in the book: 15.81, *Noncompliance with Treatment Disorder*.[1]

Just as homosexuals have been given favored status, so those with these newly defined "disabilities" are falling heir to numerous benefits never before imagined. How is such madness possible? Thank psychology. This is what that pseudo-science has done for us, and it is getting worse. One of its stepchildren is the Americans with Disabilities Act of 1990 (ADA), which actually encourages irresponsible and obnoxious behavior. The authority behind ADA is *DSM-IV*'s nearly nine hundred pages of folly. George Will continues:

> Consider the DSM's definition of "oppositional defiant disorder" [ODD] as a pattern of "negativistic, defiant, disobedient and hostile behavior toward authority figures . . . often loses temper . . . is often touchy . . . or spiteful or vindictive.
>
> The *DSM*'s list of "personality disorders" includes "anti-social personality disorder" [APD] ("a pervasive pattern of disregard

for . . . the rights of others . . .); "histrionic personality disorder" [HPD] ("excessive emotionality and attention-seeking . . . inappropriately sexually provocative or seductive"); "narcissistic personality disorder" [NPD] ("grandiosity, need for admiration . . . boastful and pretentious . . . may assume they do not have to wait in line"), etc., etc.[2]

After years of controversy, including an attempt to delete the concept of neurosis amid the new popularity of the term "syndrome," *DSM-III* was finally approved and published in 1980. Mental illnesses had proliferated at an alarming rate so that the *DSM* listed two hundred sixty-five diagnostic categories. Seven years later, *DSM-III-R*, containing changes in terminology and categories, listed two hundred ninety-two diagnoses. In 1994, *DSM-IV* was published with two hundred ninety-seven disorders described in its eight hundred eighty-six pages (compared with one hundred thirty pages for *DSM-I*).

What has happened to the conscience? Much of what *DSM* deals with is neither neurosis nor syndrome but is simply selfish behavior or lack of self-control, once recognized as such by society at large. Self is at the root of all sin. Incredibly, *DSM* is designed to whitewash what used to be recognized as sin against God and one's fellows. Self-centered attitudes and actions have been reclassified as "mental disorders" or "addictions" that the presumed "victim" is helpless to overcome.

Just as we would not fault someone for catching a cold, we must not blame anyone for selfish and even harmful behavior toward others—they are the unfortunate victims of a "mental disease" that they are powerless to resist without "medication." The prevailing attitude in the Western world was explained and justified by Anglican priest and publisher David Guthrie, formerly of Auckland, New Zealand's Holy Trinity Cathedral:

> Whatever it means to be a Christian in today's world, it does not entail the acceptance of a legislating God. . . . As the world of global culture settles on its new tack, there will be a new set of "virtues". . . that the human community chooses . . . to espouse and adopt, not because they are legislated by divine authority . . . but because the community chooses them to be so.[3]

It couldn't be stated more clearly: *There is no God, there are no moral absolutes, and we are free to follow our own desires whatever they may be.* The guide for our behavior is whatever suits the "community" at the time. This is total rebellion against God and Christ.

Officially Sanctioned and Favored Rebellion Against God

Weep for your children! Such amorality can be traced directly to the influence of psychology and the fact that only on the ruins of Christianity could psychology's anti-God theologians construct their pagan religion. As early as 1969, *Psychology Today* declared that we must "face our own inner experiences without the guidance of traditional . . . foundation stones of Judeo-Christian experience. . . . We are compelled to erect our own morality, arrive at our own faith and belief. . . . "[4]

Carl Rogers admitted, "Yes, it is true, psychotherapy is subversive. . . . Therapy, theories and techniques promote a new model of man contrary to that which has been traditionally acceptable."[5] In *Psychology Today*, Rollo May exulted, "We have bid goodbye to the theologians at the wake for our dead God."

Pressured by that militant and tiny minority of no more than 2 percent (recently the largest random sex survey ever conducted—121,300—found that only 1.4 percent of adults engaged in homosexual behavior[6]), both the media and public schools present homosexuality as natural and acceptable. Children are being taught to experiment in order to learn their sexual "orientation" or "preference." Instead of concentrating upon teaching reading, writing, arithmetic, history, geography—the standard subjects that every child needs to learn—public schools are trying to undermine students' moral beliefs, starting in the earliest years. As a consequence, the United States (which spends more money on schools per pupil than any nation on earth, much of it to "raise students' self-esteem") ranks near the bottom, along with third world countries, relative to the effectiveness of its educational system.

In its 1983 report, the National Commission on Excellence in Education, set up by President Reagan, concluded: "If a foreign power had attempted to give America the bad education it has today, we would have viewed it as an act of war."[7] Much of the fault lies with psychology, which gave us the concept of low and high self-esteem and the necessity of raising it for everyone, especially children. That folly infiltrated the church as part of "Christian" psychology.

The election of Clinton and Gore introduced a new and frightening dimension to the moral degeneracy of our day that seems only to gather downward momentum under each succeeding administration. We have long known that liberals in the media and public schools have an anti-family agenda that would rob our children of their innocence and replace a God-given conscience with humanism's "If it feels good, do it!" Each edition of *DSM* gives added justification and license to the change agents and seducers of our children.

If God does not bring severe judgment upon America and the world, He would seem to owe an apology to Sodom and Gomorrah. The entire world, with America leading the pack, is racing down the broad highway to hell.

Because it was the homosexual community that brought it to crisis proportions—and because of the misinformation the homosexual lobby has persuaded the government and media to disseminate—AIDS enjoys a status never before granted to a highly contagious and deadly disease. Incredibly, instead of being treated like the fatal plague it is, AIDS has become a civil right that gives those carrying it a privileged status and even the prerogative to keep their infection secret. Health laws prevent anyone with such diseases as hepatitis from working in a restaurant, yet those with AIDS may do so. To bar them, which common sense would demand, is forbidden as "discrimination," even though it means sure death to those who, as a result of this insane policy, may accidentally contract the HIV virus. Insanity is imposed upon the rest of us because HIV is largely a homosexual disease and that privileged class must not be offended by telling the world the truth.

Such criminal folly, which has displaced true compassion and wisdom, threatens us all with unprecedented catastrophe. Only a few years ago, incredibly, it was denied that blood could be contaminated—and as a result large numbers of hemophiliacs are dead or dying of AIDS. Arthur Ashe is only one of many "transfusion" casualties. In spite of current precautions, medical personnel treating HIV patients have contracted AIDS. Recently an entire family (parents and children) was wiped out by AIDS, though they were heterosexuals. How it was contracted remains a mystery. The National Center for Health Statistics estimates that "within a few years" AIDS among heterosexuals, which increased 28 percent in 1991, will account for about half of all cases in America.

That Clinton and Gore both claimed to be Christians (Southern Baptists) was not surprising. That the label "Christian" can now be attached to almost any belief prepares the way for Antichrist. He will be worshiped by the entire world as Christ. Thus, his followers will be "Christians." A false and even antichrist "Christianity" must become the world religion. At least one phase of this prophecy is being fulfilled before our eyes.

The "Christianity" of Clinton and Gore and so many others still in leadership throughout the world is increasingly more indistinguishable from the prevailing trend in the church at large. Already Protestants are accepting as church members, and even ordaining, homosexuals and lesbians. While Roman Catholicism officially opposes homosexuality and abortion, it has covered up such deeds among its clergy for centuries. That shameful iniquity is now being exposed for the world to see through lawsuits by the hundreds that have bankrupted some dioceses. Doctrine and morals stand or fall together, and Rome has long been the major purveyor of false doctrine and a false gospel.

Psychology, Public Schools, and Homosexuality

Pope John Paul II, the world's leading ecumenist in his lifetime and probably in history, declared that snake worshipers, witchdoctors, Buddhists, Hindus, Muslims, et al., all worship the Christian God. Yet evangelical leaders, who knew better, continued to praise the pope as a great spiritual leader (heaping honors upon his memory at his death) and to accept Roman Catholicism as just another Christian denomination. John Paul II told voodoo leaders in Africa that "they would not betray their traditional faith by converting to Christianity."

Such Antichrist "Christianity" is in no position to say that anything is wrong, much less sinful, a term that has all but faded from today's vocabulary. If one can brush aside the Bible's doctrines, why not its morals? That is an easy next step. Both the Protestant and Catholic churches are preparing the way to make it a crime to call homosexuality, abortion, incest, or indeed, almost anything else sin. That three-letter word has almost been banished from the land, and many churches are leading the way.

Public schools, of course, are the major vehicle for transforming society. "Project 10," which began in Los Angeles schools in 1984 as a result of Virginia Uribe's research for her Ph.D. in psychology, is only one of several public school programs designed to open America's young children to homosexuality under the banner of "human rights" and open-mindedness. Gay crusaders work hard, are influential, and are making alarming inroads. First-grade readers being used across the country include *Daddy's Roommate* (promotes homosexuality as normal and wholesome), *Heather Has Two Mommies* (a child born through artificial insemination to one of two lesbians living together); and for the third grade, *Gloria Goes to Gay Pride*.

The assault on God's created order for the family through government schools has now reached ominous proportions, which, if not overturned by higher courts, will result in catastrophic—and prophetic—consequences.

On October 14, 2007, California Governor Arnold Schwarzenegger signed California Senate Bill SB 777, officially known as the California Student Civil Rights Act. This supposed anti-discrimination Bill will become law January 1, 2008. Critics are concerned that the terms "Mom and Dad [as well as] husband and wife . . . have been banned from California schools." Opponents go so far as to claim that the governor's signature has "ordered public schools to allow boys to use girls restrooms and locker rooms, and vice versa, if they choose." A broad interpretation would seem to do this, though such an application seems doubtful, at least at this time.

> "Arnold Schwarzenegger has delivered young children into the hands of those who will introduce them to alternative sexual lifestyles," said Randy Thomasson, president of Campaign for Children and Families, which worked to defeat the plans . . . Analysts have warned that schools across the nation will be impacted by the decision, since textbook publishers must cater to their largest purchaser, which often is California, and they will be unlikely to go to the expense of having a separate edition for other states. . . .

> SB 777 . . . bans anything in public schools that could be interpreted as negative toward homosexuality, bisexuality and other alternative lifestyle choices. There are no similar protections for students with traditional or conservative lifestyles and beliefs . . . resulting "in reverse discrimination against students with religious and traditional family values," said Meredith Turney, legislative liaison for Capitol Resource Institute. "These students have lost their voice as the direct result of Gov. Schwarzenegger's unbelievable decision. The terms 'mom and dad' or 'husband and wife' could promote discrimination against homosexuals if a same-sex couple is not also featured."

> CCF noted that now on a banned list will be any text, reference or teaching aid that portrays marriage as only between a man and woman, materials that say people are born male or female (and not in between), sources that fail to include a variety of transsexual, bisexual and homosexual historical figures, and sex education materials that fail to offer the option of sex changes. . . .

> AB394 promotes the same issues through state-funded publications, postings, curricula and handouts to students, parents and teachers. It also creates the circumstances where a parent who says marriage is only for a man and a woman in the presence of a lesbian teacher could be convicted of "harassment," and a student who believes people are born either male or female could be reported as a "harasser" by a male teacher who wears women's clothes, CCF said.

> Thomasson said Schwarzenegger also signed AB14, which prohibits state funding for any program that does not support a range of alternative sexual practices, including state-funded social services run by churches. Affected will be day cares, preschool or after-school programs, food and housing programs, senior services, anti-gang efforts, jobs programs and others.

Thomasson said it also forces every hospital in California—even private, religious hospitals—to adopt policies in support of transsexuality, bisexuality, and homosexuality and opens up nonprofit organizations to lawsuits if they exclude members that engage in homosexual, bisexual, or transsexual conduct.[8]

Of course these bills do not say in plain language what the critics quoted above interpret them as saying. Opponents go so far as to say that as a result of these laws students, whether male or female, must be allowed to use the restroom and locker room corresponding to the sex with which they choose to identify. While the alleged inevitability of this seems presently incredible, the bills do open the door to such extreme interpretations.

Someone will have to try to use the bills as an excuse for such behavior and the courts will have to decide based on the law—and that could open the door to a flood. This could take years, but the the current trend increasingly opposing biblical and traditional behavior and favoring behavior that a few years ago would have been unthinkable is quite clear. The heavy emphasis on protection from discrimination for persons with any kind of "sexual orientation" seems to justify the critics' concerns.

Just as evolution is taught as scientific fact, and the teaching of creation as an alternate possibility is barred from public schools, so it is with morality. Against the wishes of parents, condoms are given out and "safe sex" taught to young children, and "gay" as just one more "lifestyle" promoted in school, with the governments' blessing and backing. To recommend abstinence from premarital sex as a "preventive" is excluded as a religious idea—and religion is barred from public schools. No, that's not entirely true. Christianity is barred. Islam and witchcraft are allowed.

A "Homosexual Gene"?

Lies and cover-up abound. The search is on for the alleged "homosexual gene," in spite of the fact that as many as 70 percent in some Roman Catholic seminaries are homosexuals—obviously not caused by a special gene, unless the same gene also causes those who have it to seek the priesthood. Much of the British penal colony in the early days in Australia consisted of practicing homosexuals (letters of many to family and friends in England expressed revulsion but helplessness)—again hardly explainable by a "homosexual gene."[9] In both of these cases, the explanation is that these were/are all-male communities with no outlet for the normal sex drive.

Australia lends itself to perhaps the most thoroughgoing study of the proliferation of homosexuality. In the late eighteenth century, British lawmakers turned this far-off colony into a prison. England's felons (some as young as eight years old, convicted of stealing a handkerchief or crust of bread) were placed there, conveniently out of sight and forgotten. The peculiarities of their incarceration—two or three to a bed,[10] locked down between 6:00 PM and 6:00 AM,[11] the lack of female companionship—turned the barracks into brothels. Young boys were "claimed" by the older prisoners as they stepped off the ships. Their "protectors" were a necessity for their survival.[12] A prisoner declared that two-thirds of Norfolk Island convicts were practicing homosexuals.[13]

Of course, the much-sought "homosexual gene" could hardly explain this reality. Furthermore, the Aborigines had never practiced homosexuality until the convicts introduced them to it.[14] The Irish (mostly Catholics) among the convicts were never known to adopt this sinful way of life, in spite of the constant pressure to do so. Did they possess a negative gene? Or did a fear of the "hell-fire" they had been taught about restrain them? Certainly, no special gene played any part.

A "homosexual gene" is propaganda and myth. If there were one, its origin would be a mysterious copy error or cosmic ray, not likely to reoccur except perhaps in one person out of billions. Any occurrence would not be passed on but quickly eliminated because "gays" don't have children. The fact that even 1 percent of the population claim to be "gay" and lesbian could never be explained by a foul-up in the genome.

The only explanation is the biblical one: it is a sinful lust that can be passed on not by birth but by teaching. Its promotion in public schools, beginning in the earliest grades, is reprehensible. In fact, it ought to be a crime by law because it reduces average life expectancy by about twenty-four years, according to the latest statistics. Furthermore, these facts should be enough to block same-sex couples from adopting children because a gay couple of thirty-five is as close to death as a married heterosexual couple of fifty-five. These are the latest figures from Denmark and Norway, countries that have the longest records of "married" gays and lesbians—but these essential facts, which could serve to warn the public, are suppressed in order to protect homosexuals from "discrimination."

Psychology, the Perfect Ecumenical Bond

Just as a small minority of communists took over Russia, China and a host of other nations, so a dedicated minority has seized control of America's courts, public schools, and media and is determined to remold the thinking of our children. Schools are supposed to educate students in academic subjects. Instead, they are trying to remake them morally, emotionally, and psychologically. Parents who object to this breach of trust and calculated destruction of "family values" are denied the right to "interfere" in the moral training of their own children and are scorned as "fanatical fundamentalist Christians," now the most demeaning of labels.

A *Reader's Digest* poll across the country demonstrated conclusively that the courts, media, and public schools are forcing upon our children humanistic values to which not only their parents but an overwhelming majority of American citizens are opposed. For example, 80 percent disapproved the U.S. Supreme Court ruling that it is unconstitutional to offer prayer at a high school graduation (it never used to be), while only 18 percent approved. As for prayer in public schools (voluntary and personal, not regimented), 75 percent were in favor and only 19 percent opposed. William J. Bennett, Secretary of Education from 1985 to 1988, declared,

> The Founding Fathers intended [Christian] religion to provide a moral anchor for our democracy. Yet again and again as Education Secretary . . . I was attacked as an 'ayatollah' when I supported voluntary school prayer—and the posting of the Ten Commandments in schools.[15]

Although rejecting biblical moral values long accepted in American schools, those in charge of curricula are pushing substitute religions (Eastern mysticism, humanism, Islam, and open occultism) upon our children. "Pumsy [a dragon]: "In Pursuit of Excellence" (a self-esteem course used in the elementary grades) and "DUSO" (a dolphin) are a few examples of many. Pumsy and DUSO, through visualization and guided imagery, become the child's ever-present inner guides to be called upon through visualization for problem-solving and miraculous help, opening the door to the occult.

The techniques used by psychologists and psychiatrists in client therapy are taught to children in public schools, even though they are similar to those used by witchdoctors for contacting the "spirit guides" (demons) that give them their power. Even non-Christian parents are rising up to oppose the harmful effects of these courses. Yet similar visualization techniques are rampant in Christian schools and churches, while the follies of self-esteem, self-image, and self-talk are promoted by Christian psychologists.

Psychology, as justification, has become the common language of every change agent. It is, in fact, the common language that can bring the entire world together. To facilitate the establishment of the coming world religion headed by Antichrist, psychology, through its worldwide acceptance, is now the common language of every race, religion, and cult, from evangelical Christianity to Mormonism to Science of Mind. It is, in fact, proving to be the greatest ecumenical vehicle Satan has ever devised.

The Psychological Society

Whether one's concern is moral decline or the invasion of paganism, the major influence in effecting such changes in our schools and society comes from psychology. Investigative reporter Martin L. Gross warned in his book, *The Psychological Society*, that a revolutionary change in man "has taken place quietly, yet it has altered the nature of our civilization beyond recognition." He explained in shockingly clear terms:

> *The major agent of change has been modern psychology* [his emphasis] . . . an international colossus whose professional minions number in the hundreds of thousands. Its ranks include psychiatrists, psychoanalysts, clinical psychologists, psychotherapists, social workers, psychiatric nurses, school psychologists, guidance counselors, marriage and family therapists, educational psychologists . . . and assorted lay therapists. . . .
>
> Its experimental animals are an obliging, even grateful human race. . . . As never before, man is preoccupied with Self. . . . The contemporary Psychological Society is the most vulnerable culture in history. Its citizen is . . . dependent on others for guidance as to . . . the authenticity of his own emotions.
>
> As the Protestant ethic has weakened in Western society, the confused citizen has turned to the only alternative he knows: the psychological expert who claims there is a new scientific standard of behavior to replace fading traditions. . . . This new truth is fed to us continuously from birth to the grave. . . .
>
> Childhood, once a hardy time of adventure, is now seen as a period of extreme psychological fragility. . . . The nation's child guidance clinics have trebled in number. . . . The schoolhouse has become a vibrant psychological center, staffed not only by schoolteachers trained in "educational psychology" but by [tens of thousands of] guidance workers and school psychologists whose 'counseling' borders on therapy. . . . Perfectibility [of human behavior] was once sought through the intervention of God, but is now accomplished by supposed scientific adjustment of the psyche. . . .

It is now apparent that the Judeo-Christian society in which psychology began its ascendancy is atrophying under the massive impact of . . . modern psychology. . . .

When educated man lost faith in formal religion, he required a substitute belief . . . [to replace] Christianity. . . . Psychology and psychiatry . . . offer mass belief, a promise of a better future, opportunity for confession, unseen mystical workings and a trained priesthood of helping professionals devoted to servicing the pay-ing-by-the-hour communicants.

The traditional concept of sin is becoming obsolete . . . [and] the medico-psychological concept of sick has replaced it almost intact. We now speak glibly of murderers . . . as being 'sick' or 'neurotic'. . . .

Freud's atheistic ideas have paradoxically [influenced] min-isters, priests and rabbis [who] now flock to courses in pastoral counseling. . . . Only psychology, we are told, can divine our secret motivations and reveal the elusive 'why' of the strange human animal. . . .

To egocentric modern man, the prospect of Self instead of God seated at the center of a world philosophical system is exqui-sitely attractive.

The university has been invaluable in spreading the new gospel . . . [and] the popular communications industry . . . [has made] the jargon of psychology the currency of an entire civil-ization. . . . Natural emotions such as outrage, despair, grief, jeal-ousy, suspicion, disappointment and passing depression are made to appear not only undesirable but abnormal. . . .

The new Society flourishes on the belief that human technol-ogy can remake man as effortlessly as a computerized assembly line . . . offering its techniques as the hope for a scientific Utopia.[16]

Our children are being inexorably molded into the amoral citizens of humanism's planned Utopia. Paul warned that "evil men and seducers shall wax worse and worse" (2 Timothy 3:13). We are seeing this prophecy fulfilled before our eyes. Today's children face a world far more evil and occult than their parents could even have imagined a few years ago. Be warned!

What Can We Do?

In spite of all the protests parents may voice, the change agents are determined and will continue to press their agenda under the guise of "health education" or even "history" or "literature." Parents need to 1) have family devotions daily and teach their children to know Christ personally and be fully committed to Him; 2) see that their children are believers in and followers of the Lord out of genuine choice and not due to parental or church pressure to conform; 3) see that their children's honest questions are answered and that they know what they believe and why on the basis of God's Word; 4) know fully what is being taught at their children's school (public or Christian), arm them to stand against what is wrong, and, if necessary (particularly in the case of very young children), remove them from classes or programs calculated to undermine their faith and morals; 5) carefully supervise friendships, activities, and other influences upon their lives that can be as deadly as public school; 6) pray earnestly to God for wisdom; 7) love their children fervently; 8) be ready at all times with godly counsel, patiently and lovingly shared.

Christian schools once seemed the answer, but they are increasingly infiltrated with psychological/occult techniques. Depending upon circumstances, home schooling may be the only hope—but even that all too quickly comes to an end. The day inevitably arrives when the teenager must enter university or trade school in order to qualify for many professions and positions. Eventually, everyone must step out into the world to be exposed to the enemy's raw tactics. Christian employment or attendance at a Christian university is not always possible—and even there the influence of psychology and immorality is often rampant. Polls have shown that at some "Christian" universities the immorality of students exceeds even that at secular schools.

Psychology is as popular a subject and major, and sometimes even more popular, at Christian universities than at comparable secular institutions of "higher learning." And the course materials in the psychology departments of Christian universities are often scarcely distinguishable from those at secular universities. At Jerry Falwell's Liberty University, psychology is second only to a business major. Under "Some Helpful Web Resources," along with the American Association of Christian Counselors (AACC), the home page of the psychology department at Liberty lists the atheistic American Psychology Association, with no distinction between the two. The APA ought to be offended because the AACC has such lax standards that virtually anyone can become a member simply by paying the required fee.

The New Psychological Gospel

Symptomatic of what Christian psychology has done to the gospel is the fact that on his *Old Time Gospel Hour* weekly TV program, the late Jerry Falwell promoted the Liberty University School of Lifelong Learning (LUSLLL) as a means of improving one's self-esteem and said that "maybe a psychology degree is for you if you're interested in people and you want to help them." Written advertisements have said,

> Enroll today in LUSLLL, the Psych Connection, LUSLLL's Bachelor of Science in Psychology meets a number of needs with a variety of concentration—General Psychology, for example. Accreditation assures a sound reputation nation-wide for this degree. . . . These assets make LUSLLL your Psych Connection.[17]
>
> Stop reserving your gift for close acquaintances only. Get the training necessary to deal with others as a professional—ministering to a hurting world. . . . [18]
>
> In the past six months similar attitudes and experiences have motivated 2,400 students to enroll in LUSLLL's Bachelor of Science program in Psychology . . . which features concentrations in three important areas: General Psychology, Developmental Psychology, Clinical Psychology. . . . [19]

"Psych 200" is a required course for all Liberty students. The course text was for years *Introduction to Psychology* by Atkinson, Atkinson, Smith and Hilgard. That book boasts that psychology has been able to redefine morals for society, even changing what was once viewed as perversion to normal.[20] It treats humans as highly evolved animals, promotes situation ethics and neither acknowledges God nor sin. It exalts Self and legitimizes sodomy. A former student writes, "I have completed the entire General Psychology course [with a] grade of A (I add this to show that I closely listened to and studied the material presented) and never heard the professor even once, to my recollection, correct the false, devilish, unbiblical claims of the textbook."

The situation is virtually the same at other Christian colleges. Even seminaries, and not just the liberal ones such as Fuller but those with conservative reputations such as Talbot (now thoroughly integrated, like Biola, with Rosemead Graduate School of Psychology), promote the false gospel of psychology.

Sound doctrine is the only anchor for our faith and that of our families. Unfortunately, sound doctrine is increasingly neglected in favor of clever sermonettes (for "Christianettes") and entertaining programs that appeal to the flesh. While many evangelicals still oppose evils such as homosexuality, abortion, and pornography in secular society, few are willing to stand against false doctrine of any kind inside the church. Without sound doctrine, however, everything eventually is corrupted.

Lacking a firm doctrinal foundation, the church is being seduced into conformity with the world in subtle ways that inevitably lead to ever more serious compromise and error. Weep for your children, indeed—and take prayerful, decisive, biblical steps to rescue them from both this present evil world and from apostate "Christianity"!

1. Quoted in *Christianity Today*, March 6, 1995.

2. "Digging in the Walls," *O Timothy*, vol 12, issue 7-8, 1995, 35.

3. David Guthrie, "We're no longer bound by tradition," *New Zealand Herald*, October 1996, 18-19.

4. "Psychology Today, Psychology Tomorrow, Psychology Forever," in *Chronicles*, March 1986, 48.

5. Allen Bergen, "Psychotherapy and Religious Values," quoting Carl Rogers in *Journal of Consulting Clinical Psychology*, vol. 48, 101.

6. www.earned media.org/frireport.htm.

7. G. P. Gardner (chair), National Commission on Excellence in Education, *A Nation at Risk: The Imperative of Educational Reform* (Washington, DC: U.S. Government Printing Office, 1983), 5.

8. http://www.worldnetdaily.com/news/article.asp?ARTICLE_ID=58130.

9. Robert Hughes, *The Fatal Shore* (New York: Alfred A. Knopf, 1987).

10. Ibid., 268.

11. Ibid., 271.

12. Ibid., 267.

13. Ibid., 271.

14. Ibid., 272.

15. *Reader's Digest*, November 1992.

16. Martin L. Gross, *The Psychological Society: A Critical Analysis of Psychiatry, Psychotherapy, Psychoanalysis, and the Psychological Revolution* (New York: Random House, 1978), 3-5.

17. http://www.liberty.edu/index.cfm?PID=2573.

18. *LUSLL Update*, May 1989.

19. Ibid., April 1989.

20. Rita L. Atkinson, Richard C. Atkinson, Edward E. Smith, Ernest R. Hilgard, *Introduction to Psychology*, Ninth Edition (Harcourt Brace Jovanovich, Publishers, 1987), 5.

THE SUFFICIENCY
OF GOD'S WORD

— Dave Hunt —

CHRISTIANITY TODAY (CT) was founded in 1956 by Billy Graham (he remains Honorary Board Chairman) to "restore intellectual respectability and spiritual impact to evangelical Christianity [through] a new generation of highly trained scholars who were deeply committed to Christ and His Word."[1] Why "intellectual respectability" would even be desired for converting the unsaved is inexplicable.

Furthermore, "the preaching of the cross is to them that perish foolishness." Why should we try to change that when "it pleased God by the foolishness of preaching to save them that believe" (1 Corinthians 1:18, 21)? Why should Christians attempt to impress the world with their intellectual and academic qualifications and prowess? That ambition is not biblical nor has it proved to be fruitful—but it does pander to a pride that Christians are not supposed to have. Christian academia has been a major contributing factor in creating today's apostasy.

The Apostle Paul must have been one of the most powerful preachers and greatest soul winners in history. What was his "secret"? He eschewed intellectualism! Paul knew from painful experience that the message of "Christ crucified [was] unto the Jews a stumbling block, and unto the Greeks foolishness." Yet he told the Corinthians that he was determined "not to know anything among you, save [except] Jesus Christ, and him crucified" (1 Corinthians 2:2). Though he was well educated for his day, Paul declared:

> I was with you in weakness, and in fear, and in much trembling. And my speech and my preaching was not with enticing words of man's wisdom, but in demonstration of the Spirit and of power: that your faith should not stand in the wisdom of men, but in the power of God. (2:3–5)

Why aspire to competence in the very "wisdom" of this world, which is "foolishness with God" (1 Corinthians 1:20), and with which Paul refused to preach? We should not; we dare not!

The Intellectual Descent into Apostasy

Billy Graham was pleased that *CT* "has helped change the profile of the American church."[2] Unfortunately, the American church has been steadily changing not for the better but for the worse. Although that fact cannot be blamed entirely upon *Christianity Today*, *CT* has been a major contributor to this slide into ever-deepening apostasy—in spite of Billy's original good intentions. Even though it offers some good articles, *CT* has fostered decreasing confidence in God's Word and increasing reliance upon scholarly humanistic theories and methods, including psychology. David Wells points out,

> When *Christianity Today* began, advertising . . . [took] up a mere 3 to 7 percent of the space. . . . Three decades later . . . advertising filled anywhere from 30 to 48 percent of the space . . . [including] fund-raising businesses, Sunday School peanut butter . . . a gold-embossed ring that had been made . . . "to unite the body of Christ. . . ," etc.
>
> In 1959 . . . 36 percent [involved] . . . biblical doctrine. . . . Three decades later . . . doctrinal content was . . . 8 percent. . . .
>
> In 1959 . . . a regular section . . . explored . . . biblical revelation . . . the person and work of Christ . . . the gospel and Christian salvation. . . . By 1989, this column had been replaced by . . . success stories . . . pains of a mid-life crisis . . . marriage . . . struggling with homosexuality . . . with less money than we would like . . . with a diet.
>
> In these three decades . . . [*CT*] moved . . . to a therapeutically constructed faith the central concern of which was psychological survival. . . . Thus was biblical truth eclipsed by the self and holiness by wholeness. . . .
>
> By 1989 . . . *Christianity Today* . . . looked like a poor cousin to *Time* magazine . . . [though] a little more pious. . . .
>
> By 1989, gone was the vision in which the magazine was born, gone was its moral and intellectual fiber, and gone was its ability to call the evangelical constituency to greater Christian faithfulness. Reflecting the nostrums of the therapeutic society had been transformed from a vice into a virtue, and popularity had been transformed from something incidental to Christian truth to something central to it.[3]

The corrupting influence of Christian psychology is visible everywhere. Wells writes, "The psychological undertow of conformity . . . sets the limits on what kind of theological idea can take root in the evangelical Church [and] is redefining Christian theology."[4] In 1980, *CT* launched *Leadership* magazine designed especially for clergy. Of that venture, David Wells comments:

> Since this is an evangelical publication, it is quite stunning to observe that less than 1 percent of the material made any clear reference to Scripture. . . .
>
> The articles are single-minded in their devotion to the wisdom that psychology and business management offer and apparently as equally single-minded in their skepticism concerning what Scripture and theology offer for addressing the practical crises of pastoral life. . . . Even when the subjects being discussed were . . . subjects about which Scripture has much to say . . . the authors of the articles in *Leadership* thought it would be better to look elsewhere for help in their pastoral tasks![5]

Christianity Today devoted the entire back cover of at least one issue to promoting a Graham-endorsed three-hundred-page occult/science-of-mind manual: John Marks Templeton's *Discovering the Laws of Life*. *CT* supports theistic evolution and Roman Catholicism, and called the late Pope John Paul II "the successor of St. Peter . . . [whom] God has called . . . to forge a united church . . . [and whose] priority to the Christian message . . . endear[s] him to the hearts of evangelicals."[6] It has defended heretical teachers, refused to be corrected itself, misrepresented its critics, and failed to include substantive response in its pages.

Enemies of Truth

When *Christianity Today* featured a lengthy article titled "Exposing the Myth that Christians Should Not Have Emotional Problems," since I was its major target, I submitted an article in response. It was refused. Here is an adaptation of the response *CT* would not publish:

> The very title of the *CT* article misrepresents Christian psychology's critics and attacks a straw man. Even the quotation cited to support the title ("At the cross you can be made whole") offers a solution to emotional needs; it does not deny their existence.
>
> Claiming that the heretical "Health and Wealth Gospel [has] an insidious variation" in something he calls the "Emotional-Health Gospel," the author of the *CT* article accuses critics of Christian psychology of teaching that "if you have repented of your sins, prayed correctly, and spent adequate time in God's Word, you will have a sound mind." Paul said it: "For God hath not given us the spirit of fear; but of power, and of love, and of a sound mind"

(2 Timothy 1:7). The author says critics such as "John MacArthur and Dave Hunt" propagate views that "lead us to shoot our wounded." This is a serious charge, without any proof, which surely warrants a response, but *CT* would not allow one in its pages.

Much space is given to quoting alleged admissions by Luther and Spurgeon of serious emotional problems and citing scriptures that supposedly show that Moses, Elijah, Job, Jeremiah, and Paul "suffered from depression" and that even Christ had "negative emotions." Even if that were the case, it would not support the *CT* author's thesis. Moses, Spurgeon, et al., lived long before Christian psychology was invented and they triumphed gloriously without it! Comparing the lives of past Christians with "Christianity today" shows that Christians' lives have not improved with psychology but rather have deteriorated badly.

The *CT* author declares, "We must take seriously Paul's injunction to 'encourage the fainthearted, help the weak, be patient with all men' (1 Thessalonians 5:14)." Again, instead of supporting the view that Christians need specialized help from trained professionals, Paul's statement proves the opposite. He obviously believed that his injunction could be fully obeyed by Christians at that time, centuries before psychology appeared on the scene. So why should we need it today?

The issue is not whether Christians experience emotional difficulties but what God's remedy is. He created and redeemed us, and the Bible is His instruction manual for living. Believers throughout the ages have found God's Word and His remedies sufficient in every situation. Why turn to pitiful and destructive theories invented by humanists who can't help themselves? Psychologists and psychiatrists have the highest percentage of any profession under the care of psychiatrists, committing suicide, divorcing, and on prescription drugs. Consulting them is like asking directions of someone who is himself hopelessly lost.

If "Christian psychology" has anything of value to offer, then that means the church lacked it for nineteen hundred years, and the Holy Spirit, through ignorance or oversight, left out of God's Word part of what we need to live fruitful lives for Christ. The Bible, however, claims that Jesus Christ's "divine power hath given unto us all things that pertain unto life and godliness" (2 Peter 1:3–11); and that "love, joy, peace, longsuffering, gentleness, goodness, faith, meekness, temperance" are "the fruit of the Spirit" (Galatians 5:22–23), not the fruit of therapy.

Problems experienced today for which people seek the help of professional psychologists are not new. The Bible is all about those who victoriously endured rejection, hatred, misunderstanding, jealousy, persecution, uncertainty, and every other trial one could imagine, including martyrdom. Consider Joseph. His jealous brothers hated and sold him into Egypt. There, falsely accused of rape, he languished in prison. Did he (or any of the many other heroes and heroines of the faith) suffer for lack of psychological counseling, which the author argues is essential today? Obviously not! If not one of the millions of Christians who lived before the advent of psychology (and whose lives and martyrdoms put us to shame today) needed any help from psychology, how can anyone say that we need psychological help today?

What a contrast between the triumphant saints of old and today's struggling and self-centered victims of months or years of psychological counseling! Of his own personal suffering Paul testified,

> . . . in prisons more frequent, in deaths oft. Of the Jews five times received I forty stripes save one. Thrice was I beaten with rods, once was I stoned, thrice I suffered shipwreck, a night and a day I have been in the deep; in journeyings often, in perils of waters, in perils of robbers, in perils by mine own countrymen, in perils by the heathen, in perils in the city, in perils in the wilderness, in perils in the sea, in perils among false brethren; in weariness and painfulness, in watchings often, in hunger and thirst, in fastings often, in cold and nakedness. Beside those things that are without, that which cometh upon me daily, the care of all the churches. Who is weak, and I am not weak? who is offended, and I burn not? (2 Corinthians 11:22–29)

Who today endures such trials? Why turn for help to that which Paul never needed in spite of his almost unbelievable trials and difficulties? From prison he wrote, "I have learned, in whatsoever state I am, therewith to be content. . . . I can do all things through Christ which strengtheneth me. . . . My God shall supply all your need according to his riches in glory by Christ Jesus" (Philippians 4:11–13, 19). That same triumph can be ours today—not through psychotherapy but by faith through Christ our Lord living His life within us in the power of His resurrection.

"I've tried just following the Bible, and it doesn't work," is a common complaint. Is God then a liar? To the anxious, troubled, fearful, and depressed, Paul joyfully declares that God "always causeth us to triumph in Christ" (2 Corinthians 2:14). Only an uncrucified self prevents that victory. Paul testifies, "I am crucified with Christ: nevertheless I live; yet not I, but Christ liveth in me . . . " (Galatians 2:20). Surely Christ, who said, "Because I live, ye shall live also" (John 14:19) and, indeed, "who is our life" (Colossians 3:4), needs no psychological counseling! Let Him live His life through you!

One of Christ's names is Counselor (Isaiah 9:6). Could His counsel ever fail? Christian psychology rests upon the blasphemous, God-dishonoring claim that the Bible and the indwelling Christ are not sufficient. Its "professionals" promise to make up for that deficiency with therapy invented and practiced by atheists. Their boasted expertise (now claimed also by Christian psychologists) is an affront to God and His Word!

Peter calls us to "rejoice" in every "fiery trial" because we are sharing in "Christ's sufferings" (1 Peter 4:12–13). The first Christians rejoiced that they were counted worthy to suffer for his name (Acts 5:41). By the Holy Spirit, Paul commands us (with no exceptions for those who have been "abused," are "depressed," or have some new syndrome) to always rejoice and to be anxious for nothing; and he promises that "the peace of God, which passeth all understanding, shall keep your hearts and minds through Christ Jesus" if we will thankfully commit ourselves into His hands (Philippians 4:4–7). This is not theory. Christians through the ages have proved it to be true—and so can we, by God's grace.

The only justification for the existence of Christian psychology is the faithless claim that the Word of God and the power of the Holy Spirit, totally sufficient for multiplied millions of Christian in past ages, are insufficient for the followers of Christ today. Christian psychology fosters further unbelief. The *CT* author insists that churches and pastors relying solely upon God and His Word lack the expertise to deal with emotional problems; the help of professionals trained in psychology is required. Faith has fled and logic itself deserts him as he argues:

> If my car needs the transmission replaced, do I expect the church to do it? Or if I break my leg, do I consult my pastor about it? For some reason, when it comes to emotional needs, we think the church should be able to meet them all. It can't, and it isn't supposed to. This is why the emotional-health gospel can do so much harm. People who need help are prevented from seeking it and often made to feel shame for having the problem. Thankfully, more and more people in the Christian community are beginning to realize that some people need this extra help. If professionals and church leaders can recognize the value of each other's roles, we will make progress in helping the wounded. . . . Church leaders should get to know Christian therapists in their communities so they can knowledgeably refer people with persistent emotional problems.

So go the standard arguments. It is an insult to God to suggest that "people need this extra help" that He failed to provide in His Word—an oversight that must have deprived millions of believers of necessary help in past ages! There were no "Christian therapists" (because the atheists hadn't yet invented psychology) to whom leaders could refer their flocks in the early church. Why today? Why is God's Word, by which we live (Deuteronomy 8:3; Matthew 4:4; John 6:35, etc.), and which is "a lamp unto [our] feet, and a light unto [our] path" (Psalm 119:105), no longer sufficient for today's Christian?

Furthermore, it is completely irrational to equate the physical with the spiritual. It is nonsense to compare replacing a car's transmission or setting a broken leg with attending to one's spiritual and emotional needs. The Bible makes no claim to deal with the former, but it does claim to deal *fully* with the latter. Christian psychology undermines confidence in God and His Word. Indeed, it must, or it would have nothing to offer, and those who have devoted their lives to studying the humanistic theories of atheists to pass them along to clients in the name of "Christian" psychology would be out of a job.

We do not deny that there are hurting people in the church. Sadly, members of Christ's body are not providing the loving care and counsel to one another that they should. Emotional healing should take place within the context of the love and care of fellow Christians in a local body of believers. Instead, the troubled are being referred to "professionals" for whom they become a means of income and who see them only during brief encounters with a timer running.

Other professions deal with the physical world. Psychology claims to heal the *psyche*, or soul, and thereby intrudes into the realm that the Bible claims is its sole province. The brain, a physical organ, can suffer trauma requiring medical attention. The nonphysical soul and spirit can only function properly in a right relationship with God, who "is a Spirit" (John 4:24). "Repentance toward God, and faith toward our Lord Jesus Christ" (Acts 20:21) bring the needed spiritual solution.

"Christian psychology" has become so well accepted that anyone who questions its validity is accused of having no sympathy for those who suffer from emotional problems. That is a false accusation. We only say that real concern for those in need would cause one to recommend the biblical solution, which has been proved adequate by millions of believers for thousands of years. It would seem less than kindness to advise the hurting to draw instead upon worldly wisdom's contradictory theories, which many psychologists and psychiatrists have come to oppose because they don't work and, in fact, are often destructive.

But doesn't Christian psychology use the Bible? Again, it is an insult to God to integrate the theories of godless humanists with the Bible—as though the wisdom of this world, which Paul said is "foolishness with God" (1 Corinthians 3:19), is a worthy partner for God's wisdom. There are hundreds of schools of psychology and countless therapies that conflict with each other. Which are to be called *Christian*? None of them, because not one came from God's Word.

The Integration of Psychology and the Bible

Sadly, the integration of psychology and theology, which Christian psychologists have dreamed of for years, has been effected quite handily but dishonestly by changing the meaning of Scripture so that it seems to support psychology. We have already mentioned this fact in relation to "self-love . . . self-esteem . . . self-image," and a host of other selfisms. This modern perversion of Scripture is due to the influence of humanistic psychology in the church—a fact that is freely, even proudly, admitted by Christian psychologists.

Every psychologist or psychiatrist, whether Christian or atheist, must take the same courses, give the same answers to pass the same tests and be licensed by the same government bureaus. So one must immerse one's self in humanism in order to learn from anti-Christians theories that will then help one to counsel from the Bible! If this is not a huge contradiction—as well as contrary to God's Word—then what is it?

In refuting Christian psychology, we are calling the church back to the simple faith that was proved sufficient before psychology was invented. God's promises are still true today, and when, by faith, self is crucified with Christ and our Lord lives within, we experience the same triumph that such faith has always produced. Let us steadfastly oppose anything that claims to supplement or improve upon God's Word and thereby denies its sufficiency in all things that pertain to life and godliness.

1. Billy Graham, *Just As I Am: The Autobiography of Billy Graham* (San Francisco, CA: HarperSanFrancisco/Zondervan, 1997), 286.

2. Ibid., 287.

3. David F. Wells, *No Place for Truth: Or, Whatever Happened to Evangelical Theology?* (Grand Rapids, MI: William B. Eerdmans Publishing Company, 1993), 112-13, 208-11.

4. Ibid., 214.

5. Ibid., 114.

6. "A Man Under Orders," editorial, *Christianity Today*, September 6, 1985.

SCIENCE
FALSELY SO-CALLED

— *Dave Hunt* —

"FRIENDSHIP OF THE WORLD is enmity with God" (James 4:4). It would be both illogical and unscriptural to imagine that those in whom the One now lives who was "despised and rejected of men" and through whom He now expresses Himself on this earth would not themselves, exactly as He foretold, be despised and rejected by the world. Popularity with the ungodly requires a compromise of faith. Sadly, many church leaders are cultivating a popularity that forces them either to compromise or lose the good opinions of the ungodly—a friendship that they seem to value above God's approval.

It is an insult to God to modify Christianity to reflect worldly wisdom. He who does so forgets that "the wisdom of this world is foolishness with God" (1 Corinthians 3:19) and imagines that God's Word needs supplementation with human ideas. To adjust the gospel in order to make it appealing to the ungodly is dishonest and certainly not helpful, for such a "gospel" will not save those who believe it. Supplementing the Bible with worldly wisdom implies that Scripture's claim to be sufficient for every spiritual need is false. Yet this is exactly the position of Christian psychologists, which causes unbelievers to despise and ridicule Christians—not for our Christlikeness but for our folly.

The cause of Christ is not discredited by failure to keep up with modern science (which has nothing to do with spiritual reality) but by the substitution of "science falsely so-called" for God's unchanging truth. This is a modern abomination. Yet the foundational ambition of Christian psychologists is to enhance credibility and effectiveness of Christianity by bringing it up to date with an infusion of scientific theory. But psychotherapy is not a science, its theories are not scientific, and Christian psychology has brought folly into the church and dishonored Christ, who promised to *be* our life by living His life through us in the power of the Holy Spirit.

Christian Psychology and Folly

A prime example of such dishonor to the cause of Christ took place at the July 1988 Christian Booksellers Association (CBA) annual convention held in

Dallas. The scene was one of CBA's biggest events, the Evangelical Publishers Association banquet. Christian psychologist and author Gary Smalley, the featured speaker, was a humorous and a polished communicator, but his speech was humanistic psychology nonsense. His entire talk was based upon what was at that time a popular myth spawned by pop psychology and since relegated to the trash heap: the left-brain/right-brain fad. Brain researchers rather quickly refuted it and it became known as "whole-brain half-wittedness."[1] But at the date of that meeting, it was popular among Christian psychologists, who referred to it (and, amazingly, some still do) as though it had been scientifically proved to be true and of great value in living our lives for our Lord.

As his talk proceeded, I became increasingly embarrassed because of the many non-Christians present who knew that what this "Christian psychologist" was saying was ludicrous. Yet they observed hundreds of Christian leaders who supposedly represented the cream of evangelical publishing applauding in enthusiastic approval. I was angry because I knew this event could only make the nonbelievers there even more cynical of "Christianity." Moreover, instead of biblical truth that sets free, a deluding lie that would enslave was being passed off upon trusting Christians who thought that the "expert" addressing them knew whereof he spoke.

How bad was Smalley's misinformation? A subsequent *Omni* article said, "Everyone knows that the left [brain] hemisphere is rational, logical and Western, and the right is creative, intuitive, and Eastern. Everyone knows, that is, except the scientists who did the research on which the whole notion of left and right brains is based." The determined efforts by brain researchers such as Jerre Levy of the University of Chicago to undo the "mythology" that has sprung up around right and left brain have had little effect.[2] As one writer explains: "The left/right brain myth has a lot of pizzazz." Smalley used that "pizzazz" to dazzle and delude his audience.

Left Brain, Right Brain, Broccoli Brain

Showing the contempt with which brain researchers view this fad, another article in *Psychology Today* was titled "Left Brain, Right Brain, Broccoli Brain?"[3] In a third magazine, Sally P. Springer, co-author of *Left Brain, Right Brain*, writes, "The concept that the human brain is divided into two halves or hemispheres, each with specialized functions, is now firmly entrenched in popular culture. . . . [Yet] by all of our current measures . . . both hemispheres are active and involved in any situation. . . . Those who seek to modify our educational systems and implement assessment and training programs based on our knowledge of brain asymmetry are indeed on shaky ground. . . . [T]heir ideas receive no [scientific] support."

Then what must be said for those who reinterpret the Bible and counsel Christians based upon this humanistic myth! Second Timothy 4:3–4 warns, "For the time will come when they will not endure sound doctrine; but after their own lusts shall they heap to themselves teachers, having itching ears; and they shall turn away their ears from the truth, and shall be turned unto fables." The fulfillment of that prophecy seems to have come upon today's church with a vengeance. And nowhere is that more evident than in the field of psychology, which has literally hundreds of conflicting theories and therapies, that all work equally well and equally poorly, yet many of them have their advocates and practitioners among psychologists in the church. Chasing after psychology's latest fad is an abomination and a slap in the face to Christ, who promised to live His life in His own and to be all we need to live happily and fruitfully for Him to the glory of the Father.

Unlike some of the more devious theories of humanistic psychology honored in the church today, the left/right-brain error is obvious and easily refuted. It deals not with the soul/psyche but with the physical brain. That people favor or use only one side of their brains is as absurd as the notion (also promoted by "Christian psychologists") that we use only 10 percent (or less) of our brains and thus have a huge untapped potential. It is ludicrous to imagine that most brain cells lie unused—or that husbands need to "develop" or "activate" the right side of their brains in order to communicate with their "right-brained" wives, as we heard that evening from this psychological "expert." Sadly, such myths, couched in Christian terms, are more appealing to the carnal mind of many Christians than biblical truth, giving them excuses not to be bound in obedience to God's Word but to live by another "scientific" standard.

Christian Psychology—"A Lamp unto My Feet, A Light unto My Path"?

Instead of sound doctrine, Gary Smalley's talk offered a series of humorous anecdotes presenting an oversimplified perspective on the communication problems that husbands and wives experience. It was all cleverly "explained" by the supposed lately discovered scientific fact that males are left-brained while females are right-brained. Tragically, most of the laughing and applauding audience being brainwashed to apply this alleged wisdom in their lives were not aware that it was, in fact, a myth. The same could be said of most of the psychology that has become popular in the church.

The solution the speaker offered for communication problems between the two sexes was for husbands to paint "emotional word pictures," which would allegedly activate the dormant right side of men's brains and communicate with the dominant right side of their wives' brains. There was nothing of spiritual value, no teaching from God's Word. Men and women were depicted as stimulus-response mechanisms whose failures to love and forgive were simply due to poor communication caused by brain hemispheres being out of sync.

The only reference to Scripture was to tell us at the end of the talk that he had explained left/right-brain thinking so that we could fulfill the admonition in Ephesians 5 for husbands to love their wives. Then he prayed. For the first time in my life I did not close my eyes and could not join in a prayer. It seemed an insult to God to seek His blessing upon this deceitful and harmful mixture of misinformation and pop psychology.

Smalley's talk at the CBA Convention was based upon his (at that time) new book (co-authored with Christian psychologist John Trent), *The Language of Love*, published in 1988 by Focus on the Family and distributed by Word Books. The prestigious *Focus on the Family* magazine for November 1988 featured Chapter Four from that book, sending out to hundreds of thousands of trusting Christians such false statements as, "By using the power of emotional word pictures to open his right brain, a man can move beyond 'facts' and begin to achieve total communication with a woman. . . . If a woman truly expects to have meaningful communication with her husband, she must activate the right side of his brain. . . . Indeed, a world of colorful communication waits for those who learn the skill of bridging both sides of the brain."

This was pure nonsense and had already been condemned by the very brain research that Smalley and Dobson naïvely imagined supported it. Perhaps most tragic of all was the sad fact that James Dobson, looked up to as the greatest authority on the family in the entire Christian world, didn't know the truth and joined in the promotion of a harmful myth not only to the readers of the book but also to the trusting readers of his magazine. Nor is this the only example we could give of the misinformation that Christian psychologists have brought into the church and continue to promote to trusting audiences and readers.

Worldly Theories Reinterpreting and Replacing the Bible

There are almost no references to Scripture in the entire Smalley/Trent book. The very few that are in the book consist of attempts to use the Bible to support the fallacious humanism being presented. For example, it is suggested that Nathan the prophet activated the right side of King David's brain by using "an emotional word picture that would change the course of a kingdom and echo throughout the ages. . . . [S]hattered by the blow of one emotional word picture . . . [David] was forced . . . to feel. . . . "[4] Talk about a trivialization of Scripture! It was the Holy Spirit who convicted David in his God-given conscience that had already condemned him!

Not only does a technique (activating the right brain and thereby arousing the emotions through the use of "word pictures") become the key, but its appeal is not to conscience or truth but to feelings. The technique is self-centered and independent of the Holy Spirit's conviction of sin and the power of truth to reach the conscience. There is no biblical teaching to awaken moral obligation or motivation by the fear of God and His love, but it is all feelings and experience oriented. The fact that such techniques, like placebos, often work for a time makes them doubly dangerous.

Although Smalley's book did point out the necessity for communication, it promoted a feelings-oriented pseudo-spirituality unrelated to truth. The only "faith" it offered was divorced from fact and vulnerable to further delusion. From church leaders we are increasingly getting pop psychology under a Christian label but with basically no biblical content. Thinking non-Christians recognize this folly and belittle the gospel and Christianity on that basis.

Take for example the following from The Association for Humanistic Psychology's October 1988 *AHP Perspective*: "Christians claim to know that Jesus died for their sins because they experience relief and new life when they 'accept Jesus as Lord and Savior.' They fail to grasp that such a sense of renewal flows naturally from releasing guilt feelings and experiencing acceptance, no matter whether the belief that brings us to this new freedom is based on fact or fiction."

This is a valid criticism of a psychologized and self-centered "Christianity" that justifies itself not on the basis of the truth of God's Word but as a means of producing a more positive self-image and a greater sense of self-acceptance and self-worth. Such "Christianity" is an insult to our Lord, as though this is what He died to give us. Nor does it have any valid claim to superiority over other humanistic methods that produce similar placebo effects. Today's pop "Christian" psychology is setting a generation up for a huge fall. The only hope is a return to propositional truth from the Bible, which God's Word refers to as sound doctrine.

Exchanging God's Truth for Lies

The same issue of *AHP Perspective* also comments, "Many of us grow up with little or no awareness of how often and how much we adjust our perceiving to accommodate our needs for acceptance, approval and belonging." Certainly a valid point. Yet these very "needs" are placed ahead of objective truth in the church today—and catering to them is the foundation of much Christian psychology at the expense of "the word of life" (Philippians 2:16). Substituting psychology's latest fads for solid biblical exegesis will produce a new generation of "Christians" whose "faith" makes them feel good about themselves and may even temporarily help their marriages but has no moral/spiritual/biblical content. In times of real crisis, such "faith" will fail those who hold it.

The popularity and pernicious influence of fallacious humanistic theories in the church is indicated by the fact that even before publication, bookstores had ordered more than a hundred thousand copies of Smalley's book. Yet this "Christian" book, published by one of the most trusted and influential Christian leaders today, gave to millions the false impression that the reason husbands and wives have problems is not that their hearts are evil and selfish and that they have neglected the love of God in obedience to His Word but simply that there has been a failure to communicate one's feelings adequately. While communication is indeed important, it must convey not only feelings but *commitment* based upon God's truth.

Jesus was the perfect communicator, yet there were multitudes who heard His parables (which Smalley says are designed to activate the right brain), experienced His miracles, and rejected Him. He was crucified by those He healed and fed and taught because they would not accept His admonition: "If ye continue in my word, then are ye my disciples indeed; and ye shall know the truth, and the truth shall make you free" (John 8:31–32). That truth is absent from almost every aspect of Christian psychology.

Let us not just shrug our shoulders and go on about our business when we see obvious and serious error promoted by Christian leaders. Ask God what He would have you do in each specific instance, and do it! Remember, you have a responsibility not to just keep the truth to yourself but to deliver others from error.

The Cross of Christ and our crucifixion to the self-life, so missing from popular evangelicalism, is the only way to heaven and the only basis of joy and genuine victory in this life and of His "Well done" in the life to come. Let us remain true to our rejected Lord in spite of popular fads and the reproach attached to His cross.

Postscript: Dave Hunt met with Smalley and Trent and their pastor in Phoenix at their request as a result of this article. They subsequently removed from The Language of Love *the references to left-brain and right-brain mythology. Unfortunately, however, they have continued to promote other myths of psychology, as do James Dobson and other "Christian psychologists."*

---

1. Laurence Miller, "Neurobabble," *Psychology Today*, April 1986, 72.

2. Jerre Levy, "Right Brain, Left Brain: Fact and Fiction," *Psychology Today*, May 1985, 43.

3. "Left Brain, Right Brain, Broccoli Brain," *Psychology Today*, 1988.

4. Gary Smalley, John Trent, *The Language of Love*: *A Powerful Way to Maximize Insight, Intimacy, and Understanding* (Focus on the Family, Word Books, 1988).

ALL THE COUNSEL OF GOD

— *Dave Hunt* —

> I kept back nothing that was profitable unto you. . . . Wherefore I take you to record this day, that I am pure from the blood of all men. For I have not shunned to declare unto you all the counsel of God. — ACTS 20:20,26-27

B Y "PROFITABLE," PAUL DID NOT MEAN monetarily but all that is necessary and helpful for a joyful, fruitful, and triumphant Christian life, whenever in history, and wherever in this world in any culture one may live. Where would Paul find this wisdom? In the Scriptures, of course, already written and what he was being inspired of the Holy Spirit to add in completion of what the prophets had previously spoken as recorded in what we call the Old Testament.

How encouraging, comforting, and inspiring it must have been to those early Christians to know that "all the counsel" of the Creator of the universe was available to them! Surely we need no less in our day—and that is exactly what we have in the Word of God, which was completed by the Apostle John under the inspiration of the Holy Spirit a little over nineteen hundred years ago. As Paul reminded Timothy: "All scripture is given by inspiration of God, and is profitable for doctrine, for reproof, for correction, for instruction in righteousness: that the man of God may be perfect, thoroughly furnished unto all good works" (2 Timothy 3:16–17). But doctrine, with its objective, con-victing truth, is not popular with the present generation. Consequently, the Scriptures are being rewritten to please today's apostate church.

Paul's declaration is a stinging rebuke of much that is called "Christianity" today. How could Paul have kept back nothing that was profitable and have presented all the counsel of God when he never taught Christian psychology, Twelve-Steps programs, inner healing, visualization, positive confession, seed faith, the laughing revival, the binding of territorial spirits, Bible codes, and other inventions lately considered to be so exciting and vital? The conclusion is inescapable: either Paul was badly mistaken or these new teachings and prac-tices are neither profitable nor part of God's counsel! They are attempts to add man-made doctrines, supposed new understandings and alleged improvements to the Bible—strange doctrines, unknown to apostles and prophets and that contradict God's Word but which today's church loves.

Those who, on the authority of "new prophets," advocate teachings not found in the Holy Scriptures can hardly complain against NAMBLA (North American Man/Boy Love Association), outspoken advocate of pedophilia. After all, it was formed in a church (in 1978, under inspiration from "Boston's gay community"), with a number of "Christian" leaders, both Protestant and Catholic, participating and voicing their approval of this perversion.

Still going strong, NAMBLA's homepage promotes cooperation "with lesbian, gay, feminist, and other liberation [*sic*] movements . . . for the purpose of promoting 'the rights of youth as well as adults to choose the partners with whom they wish to share and enjoy their bodies.'" As Scripture says, "Their wickedness demonstrates that there is no fear of God before [their] eyes." (Psalm 36:1).

All manner of heresy has been introduced by men who were (and many who still are) looked up to as church leaders yet have led multitudes astray. The Scriptures alone, which warn us of these men who have "crept in unawares" (Jude 4), must be our guide, and we dare not deviate from them lest we fall into the same condemnation.

Concerned conservatives call for a "return to traditional moral values." But what "tradition" and by what authority? By the mutual consent of decent society? How is that defined? We desperately need to heed the counsel of God—and not just part of it but all of it! Christ did not accuse the two disciples on the road to Emmaus of completely ignoring prophecy. He chided them for not believing and heeding "*all* that the prophets have spoken" (Luke 24:25).

The Bible is one book, inspired by one Holy Spirit, and it interprets itself. We must take the time and expend the effort to see how it all fits together, from Genesis to Revelation, in order to understand fully what God is saying to mankind. But most Christians will not devote the time it takes to know the Bible well—and that fact is a major reason why we are in the midst of such confusion and departure from sound doctrine throughout even today's evangelical church.

Following Our Creator's Instructions

What could be more thrilling than having God himself as one's personal Counselor and to be assured that the Bible contains all the counsel of God! That perfect counsel, of course, does not offer business techniques or instruction in repairing an engine, flying an airplane, or operating a computer. It teaches us as spirit beings made in the image of God (Genesis 1:27; 9:6) but living in physical bodies and redeemed by Christ's blood (Galatians 3:13; 1 Peter 1:18–19; Revelation 5:9) to glorify Him in body and in spirit (1 Corinthians

6:20) here on this earth—and prepares us to be eternally with Him in His Father's house of many mansions (John 14:2).

The Bible has rightly been called "the Manufacturer's Handbook." "God our Maker" (Psalm 95:6; Proverbs 22:2; Isaiah 17:7; 45:11; 51:13; Hebrews 11:10, etc.) intended mankind, whom He had made to consult that detailed instruction manual continually, in faith, praying for wisdom and understanding (Proverbs 4:7), with the intention of obeying. Surely God our Maker included in His operating manual every instruction needed for His creatures to function holily (Leviticus 11:44–45; 19:2, 27; 1 Thessalonians 2:10; 1 Peter 1:16), happily (Job 5:17; Psalms 128:2; 144:15; 146:5; Proverbs 3:13,18; 14:21; 16:20; 28:14; 29:18; John 13:17; 1 Peter 3:14; 4:14), and fruitfully (Genesis 1:28; John 15:4, 8; Colossians 1:10). God has not overlooked any possible problem or malfunction that might befall us nor has He failed to provide complete instructions and the appropriate remedy!

Suppose the descendants of Adam become angry, frustrated, fearful, anxious, insecure, lonely; or suppose they feel misused and abused or useless and lacking in purpose or meaning. Let troubled or tempted souls turn for counsel and help to their Creator, who knows everything about them, and to the Manufacturer's Handbook, in which He has provided complete operating instructions—"all things that pertain unto life and godliness" (2 Peter 1:3). As David said, "What time I am afraid, I will trust in thee" (Psalm 56:3). Let those who feel that life's burdens are too great to bear turn to Christ, who indwells and empowers all who believe on Him and whose very name is Counselor (Isaiah 9:6). What further counsel or help could anyone require or desire?

Indeed, until the recent infiltration of the church by psychology, the people of God looked to Him alone for their spiritual and emotional needs—and triumphed gloriously by simple faith. Consider the suffering that Job endured without any counseling or therapy from a Christian psychologist. If *he* didn't need it, then surely those who suffer far less today don't need this newly invented ungodly counsel either! Job's trials and the remedy he found through faith in God and submission to His will teach us that trials must be endured for our own good, to refine and mature us. The assurance that God himself will be with us and be our very life and strength, as He promised, is surely all we need to carry us through any trial.

Or consider Joseph: misunderstood and criticized by his parents, hated by his brothers, who wanted to kill him but were persuaded instead to sell him as a slave into Egypt. Surely this young slave must have needed psychological help—right? Wrong! In Egypt he was falsely accused of attempted rape, imprisoned, and left to languish as a criminal in a hell hole, though he was innocent. How could he have survived, with no Minirth and Meier or Rapha clinics, no James Dobson, inner healing, or other kinds of psychotherapy to provide the help and support that so many now consider to be essential?

In fact, he triumphed gloriously, as did all of those alluded to in Hebrews 11—and many more besides! Logically, then, if today's psychological remedies weren't needed by Job, Joseph, Joshua, David, Jeremiah, Peter, Paul, and other heroes of the faith, they aren't needed by *any Christian* today. On what basis would anyone dare to contradict the previous sentence, backed by Scripture from Genesis to Revelation? Yet the denial of the sufficiency we have in Christ and in His Word is the very foundation of Christian psychology!

Compare any human suffering today to what Paul endured: "[I]n labours more abundant, in stripes [scourgings] above measure, in prisons more frequent, in deaths oft. Of the Jews five times received I [thirty-nine] stripes . . . [forty lashes could be fatal]. Thrice was I beaten with rods, once was I stoned, thrice I suffered shipwreck, a night and a day I have been in the deep; in journeyings often, in perils of waters, in perils of robbers, in perils by mine own countrymen, in perils by the heathen, in perils in the city, in perils in the wilderness, in perils in the sea, in perils among false brethren; in weariness and painfulness. . . hunger and thirst, in fastings often, in cold and nakedness . . . [and] that which cometh upon me daily, the care of all the churches" (2 Corinthians 11:23–28). And finally, under the false accusations of his fellow Jews, a martyr's death at the hands of Rome, in all of which Paul rejoiced that he was counted worthy to suffer for Christ.

What help did any of the biblical heroes and heroines of the faith receive from psychology, "Christian" or secular? None! Psychology hadn't even been invented. The same could be said of preachers, teachers, and missionaries of the more recent past: Livingstone, Moody, Müller, Spurgeon, C. T. Studd, Hudson Taylor, Wesley, Whitefield, et al.

Christian Psychologists' Self-Esteem Debacle

Of course it must have been Paul's sense of self-worth, his positive self-image, and his high self-esteem that carried him through. Wrong again! This pitiful humanistic theory, exceedingly popular in both the world and the church, has proved to be so false and harmful that even the secular world that invented it (followed eagerly by Christian psychologists) has turned against it. *Newsweek*'s cover of February 17, 1992, announced its feature article in large letters: "THE CURSE OF SELF-ESTEEM: WHAT'S WRONG WITH THE FEEL-GOOD MOVEMENT?" A November 23, 1995, article by a professor/researcher in

Oregon's *The Oregonian* newspaper was titled, "Note to California: Drop Self-esteem, Self-control is most important. . . . " (California, with its Self-Esteem Task Force, like the leading Christian psychologists who supported it, has unsuccessfully spent years and much money trying to prove that self-esteem or lack of it is the key to human behavior, especially of youth.) Based upon years of research, the article's author declared, "If we could cross out self-esteem and put in self-control, kids would be better off and society in general would be much better off."

That is precisely what the Bible has always said. Yet psychology's fallacious and harmful theory—that the major problems in families, schools, and in society are caused by low self-esteem—is the very bread and butter of the ministry of James Dobson and many other Christian psychologists. The same is true for multitudes of pastors who have been feeding it to their flocks for years, having been deceived by the authoritative declarations of a host of Christian psychologists.

Paul failed so miserably in the self-esteem department that he should have suffered from lifelong depression and been of no use at all to God. He called himself the chief of sinners (1 Timothy 1:15), considered himself "less than the least of all saints" (Ephesians 3:8), unworthy to be an apostle (1 Corinthians 15:9), and rejoiced in his weakness. Yet he claimed to be able to do "all things through Christ" (Philippians 4:13), and through Christ to be always victorious (1 Corinthians 15:57; 2 Corinthians 2:14; Philippians 1:20, etc.). Christ told Paul, "My grace is sufficient for thee: for my strength is made perfect in [your] weakness." Paul's response? "Most gladly therefore . . . that the power of Christ may rest upon me. . . . I take pleasure in . . . persecutions, in distresses for Christ's sake: for when I am weak, then am I strong" (2 Corinthians 12:9–10). What a well-deserved slap in the face to psychology, Christian and secular!

In contrast to Paul's joy and victory through Christ alone, many of today's Christians put their trust in Christ *plus* Christian psychology, the latter presumably able to make up for the failings of the indwelling Christ and Holy Spirit. Its false theories and therapies offer new comfort to the abused, confused, and depressed, making it the fastest growing and most monetarily profitable movement the church has ever seen. Incredibly, it is now generally accepted among evangelicals that God's counsel in the Bible is deficient and needs to be supplemented with psychology. This lie has probably done more to destroy Christians' faith in God's Word than anything else of Satan's devising. Psychology is surely Satan's master stroke of genius! A university professor and secular researcher in the field of psychology has written:

This belief that human distress can be traced to deficient self-esteem is widespread in our current society. Popular books such as Nathan Branden's *The Psychology of Self-Esteem* have propagated it, and poor self-esteem is often cited as the "root cause" for a failure to learn in elementary schools, to failure in business, to "overachievement," to divorce or even to "sexual codependency."

For example, Branden wrote. . . , "I cannot think of a single psychological problem—from anxiety and depression, to fear of intimacy or of success, to spouse battery or child molestation—that is not traceable to the problem of poor self-esteem. . . . There is overwhelming evidence, including scientific findings, that the higher the individual's level of self-esteem, the more likely he or she will treat others with respect, kindness, and generosity. People who do not experience self-love have little or no capacity to love others. . . . People who have "deep insecurity of self-doubts . . . have nothing to contribute to the world. . . . "

There are a number of flaws in Branden's reasoning [and] let me state categorically that there is *no* "scientific evidence" [for what he says]. . . many admirable people, like Abraham Lincoln, often suffered from "deep insecurities and self-doubts" . . . many less-than-admirable people suffered from no self-doubts whatsoever . . . until they were caught or disgraced.[1]

The issue is very simple: Either "all the counsel of God" (which is found in the Bible and nowhere else) is sufficient, or God has both lied to and failed us. If Christian psychology, inner healing, Twelve-Steps programs and today's other new techniques for deliverance truly have something of value to offer, then the Bible is deficient. Period. And if that is true, then for nineteen hundred years God left the church without the insights and tools it needed. Who would believe that? Sadly, this is exactly what Christians are saying to God when they turn to psychological counseling for help, whether secular or "Christian."

The Anti-Christian Fake "Science"

Like Adam and Eve, mankind still flees the voice of God, clothes itself with the makeshift garments of new theories no better than fig leaves, and hides behind the trees of its latest excuses for unbelief and rebellion. Providing those pitiful excuses is the role Christian psychology has played from its very beginning. There is nothing Christian about psychology. Its use of terms like "soul," "spirit," and even "God" deceive many Christians into believing that it is at least compatible with Christianity, but it is not. Psychology's meaning for such words comes from humanism and the occult, contradicts the Bible, and is irretrievably anti-Christian.

Psychology is, in fact, a rival religion with its own anti-Christian gospel, which offers unbiblical diagnoses and godless cures for the human condition. Even Rollo May, the best-known American existential psychologist and close friend of apostate theologian Paul Tillich, expressed concern about psychology's link to religion. Other secular psychologists such as Sam Keen and Philip Reiff have described psychotherapy as a "kind of national religion, with a gospel of self-fulfillment and with therapists as the new priests."[2] That description is accurate.

The diagnostic and treatment record of the psychological/psychiatric growth industry has not improved since its early days, which now seem almost laughable had the results not been so destructive. It was, however, no laughing matter (and still is not) for the many mentally and emotionally destroyed victims left in the wake of this tornado of error. In his book, *The Myth of Psychotherapy*, the famous Jewish psychiatrist, Thomas Szasz, called psychology "the clever and cynical destruction of the spirituality of man, and its replacement by a positivistic 'science of mind.'" Another of his books was titled, *The Myth of Mental Illness*. "Mental" refers to the mind, which is nonphysical and could therefore hardly have an illness, while the brain, of course, could have many physical problems. To turn sin into a sickness is psychology's false cure for guilt.

It is upon a host of similar myths, invented in the secular world by anti-Christians and often coming from the occult, that so-called Christian psychology has built its house of cards. Indeed, *House of Cards: Psychology and Psychotherapy Built on Myth* is the name of a book by another secular author, Carnegie-Mellon professor and researcher, Robyn M. Dawes. As for the destructive influence of psychology upon society, Dawes writes:

> The professional therapist . . . deals primarily with feelings. . . . While the New Age psychology begins with the music of Aquarius, it ends with the puerile harmony of pure selfishness. . . . Moreover, a failure to feel just right is to be explained in psychological terms. . . . Alcoholism and drug addictions became "diseases," criminality became a "product" of the social environment in which people were raised. . . . The mediating variable leading to behavior was how adult individuals felt about themselves and the world. . . .
>
> And since childhood experience is [supposedly] the determinant of adult feeling, we can only get better by allowing the selfish, bratty "child within" to come out, maybe even in group "therapy" sessions where we grasp teddy bears to facilitate communication with our "inner child". . . .

> Negative emotions such as guilt "cause" undesirable behavior and therefore should be expunged by whatever means possible, probably some new, unproven, often bogus, technique or other. . . . People shouldn't feel guilty, no matter what they do. There is something wrong with people who experience guilt. Thus, contrary to what people have believed for centuries, guilt following bad behavior is inappropriate. . . . [3]

The fact that psychotherapy turns the Bible on its head cannot honestly be denied by anyone even minimally acquainted with the Word of God. Nor can it be denied that any psychotherapeutic theories and practices that have any value simply reflect common sense. The fact that so many of them violate this human instinct is a further indictment of this wicked profession. Willard Gaylin put it bluntly, "All the pop psychologists are misleading people about things like guilt and conscience. Guilt is a noble emotion; the person without it is a monster."[4]

Yet the church eagerly accepts each new mythological theory, no matter how absurd and harmful, puts it into practice, and credits itself with being on the "science" of psychotherapy's "cutting edge." Tragically, the more clearly and widely the fallacies of psychotherapy are exposed, the faster the implicit faith that Christians trustingly place in unbiblical practices (which don't even work) continues to grow. There is almost no limit to the folly of Christian psychology or to the gullibility of Christians eager to embrace it as a rescue from the alleged inadequacy of the indwelling Christ and His Word.

As noted previously, Carl Jung, whose influence upon Christian psychology and thus upon the church is greater than that of Freud, declared, "In cases of difficult diagnosis I usually get a horoscope."[5] Absurd? Not for psychologists and psychiatrists, who grasp at anything that will increase their power over the masses who look to them for guidance.

Indeed, at the same time that they insist psychology is a science, "A surprising number of today's psychotherapists are following Jung's advice [about consulting a horoscope]."[6] R. Christopher Barden, psychologist, lawyer, and president of the National Association for Consumer Protection in Mental Health Practices, declared:

> It is indeed shocking that many, if not most forms of psychotherapy currently offered to consumers are not supported by credible scientific evidence.[7]

The Shameful Profession that's too Blind to Blush

One of the most astonishing and destructive delusions to enter the church through psychology (from the world, of course) was called Multiple Personality Disorder (MPD), later renamed Dissociative Identity Disorder (DID). This "remarkable discovery" by psychologists was unknown until its supposed symptoms suddenly began to appear with increasing frequency and became a virtual epidemic. As investigative journalist, Mark Pendergrast, documented as the result of a three-year investigation:

> Multiple personalities were considered rare until the publication of *The Three Faces of Eve* . . . in 1957 . . . the story of Christine Costner Sizemore, who ultimately graduated from 3, to 22 different internal personalities. But it was *Sybil,* published in 1973 and made into a popular movie in 1977, that really spawned the modern crop of multiples and provided the cornerstone for an assumed background of sexual abuse.[8]

Other investigators agree: "Before the 1980s, MPD had been one of the rarest disorders in the history of psychiatry. The first documented case may have been that of a sixteenth-century French nun who was 'diagnosed' as demonically possessed and successfully treated through exorcism. Few cases had appeared in the literature since then. But diagnoses of MPD skyrocketed in the post-*Sybil* era. Writing in 1986, Putnam and his colleagues observed that 'more cases of MPD have been reported within the last five years than in the preceding two centuries.' As many as six thousand patients may have received the diagnosis by 1986, most in North America."[9]

Once "discovered," MPD's supposed symptoms began to pop up nearly everywhere as psychologists and psychiatrists, secular and Christian, "learned how to find them" and eagerly jumped aboard this new money train just leaving the station. Christian psychologist James G. Friesen, who became a leading Pied Piper in this growing fad, wrote in a Here's Life Publishers (Campus Crusade for Christ) book: "The incidence is turning out to be much higher than anyone expected. The number of MPD therapists is lagging far behind the growing demand. . . . "[10]

One would think that this sudden epidemic of a "mental illness," previously unknown, would have alerted Friesen and other Christian psychologists eager to be on the cutting edge to at least *suspect* that something was rotten at the core of this whole mess. Instead, its proponents pressed enthusaiastically and blindly forward to uncover "multiples" at all cost—and the cost was heavy!

The MPD mania provided fervent diagnosticians one more opportunity to show how bogus psychotherapy really is. It is astonishing how much concern was stirred up and how many false accusations, which tore families apart and resulted in innocent fathers being sentenced to prison, came out of what later would prove to be embarrassingly false. Truth finally prevailed and burst the bubble that so many therapists had been sure was the latest big money winner for practitioners of this fake religion masquerading as a science. I make this accusation not only in relation to the MPD hoax but to all psychotherapy, both secular and Christian.

The Suspicious Rise and Location of MPD/DID

Multiple Personality Disorder was renamed Dissociative Identity Disorder (DID) in the 2000 *DSM-IV-TR* (Text Revision). So serious was concern over this "mental disease" when first "diagnosed" that some psychologists began to theorize that everyone has multiple personalities and that mankind could take a great evolutionary leap forward by learning to harness this power within. Others pointed out—and drew a variety of conclusions, some valid, some sensational—MPD's clear connection to occult experiences and the relationship of "multiples" to the "higher self" discovered in yogic trance.[11]

The validity of any MPD or DID diagnosis is questionable for a number of obvious reasons. First of all, this unbelievable phenomenon is largely confined to English-speaking countries, primarily to the United States, and only among patients who have undergone "regression therapy." If that were not suspicious enough, prior to the 1957 publication of *The Three Faces of Eve*, cases of dual personality and multiple personality were so seldom reported that they were looked upon as curiosities in the Western world and as anomalies elsewhere. Moreover, it was only after the 1974 book, *Sybil*, and the burst of publicity that followed it, that the *DSM* finally included Multiple Personality Disorder in its 1980 edition.

The exploding rise in diagnoses paralleled the rise in media coverage. From 1985 to 1995, about forty thousand cases were "diagnosed." Not surprisingly, as already noted, this folly rapidly became popular among Christian psychologists, only too eager to surf this new wave to profit. Some even carried the absurdity to astonishing new heights by attempting to win each "multiple" to Christ!

Following a New Instruction Manual Unknown to Our Creator!

Friesen earnestly tells us that the secret of dealing with MPDs (about which the Bible is totally silent) is the "perplexing [necessity of] uncovering . . . hidden memories." He admits that these alleged "memories" are "forgotten" and "usually are unbelievable." Yet, once dredged up through weeks,and sometimes months or even years of intensive hypnotherapy—accompanied by much coaxing, leading questions, and suggestions—these "memories" provide the entire "proof" that psychologists point to in support of this theory that has destroyed so many families and lives. Friesen admits:

> They are awful, painful, and even grotesque events that nobody wants to discover. "That didn't happen to me!" is a common response. . . . Friends and family can be in denial too. We all would like to believe those things didn't happen, but *maybe they did.*
>
> I often say, "Because it happened to another part of you, it does not feel real to you. . . ." [Emphasis added][12]

Maybe they happened? So thousands of lives have been shattered because of accusations based upon something that *might* have happened, about which neither the therapist nor hypnotized victim can be certain, and which is hotly denied by all those who know the intimate details of the alleged victim's life? What evil is this that has invaded the church?

And "it happened *to another part of you*"? Are we made up of separate "parts" that can only be put in touch with one another through "therapy"? What could that mean? Common sense would give no credence to "memories" that didn't exist until hypnotherapy "uncovered" (in fact created) them and that seem unreal to the patient and involve unbelievable events that family and friends insist never occurred! It even became popular to uncover alleged "satanic ritual abuse" (SRA)—a delusion that *Moody Monthly* supported in a major article. As we have noted, in that article *Moody* promoted the blasphemy that those "recovering" should not be left only to prayer and Bible study but *must* have psychotherapy.

What about the embarrassing fact that the alleged victims and closest friends and family all deny that the alleged abuse ever occurred? The standard psychological explanation is that everyone is "in denial." Larry Crabb, for example, claims that those who will not admit to suffering from "rejection" are the "tough cases" because they refuse to be persuaded of what psychologists say must be the case, even though the alleged victim knows it isn't true!

Psychology, in spite of overwhelming proof that it is *not*, persists in its claim to be a "science." Psychological theories, therefore, in spite of blatantly contradicting God's Word, are presumed to be correct, even though the foundation is obviously rotten. (Atheists also claim that "science" supports their rejection of God.) Consequently, those, too, who will not embrace the bogus theories of psychology are accused of being "in denial"—a psychological term invented to protect psychology from valid criticism.

Putting the Inmates in Charge of the Asylum!

Friesen developed a unique explanation and treatment for this fantastic phenomenon, which psychologists eventually discovered was not based in reality but in a fantasy created by therapy. None of Friesen's procedures was based upon the Bible, which has not a word to say about such a delusion, but upon his experiences with "multiples." Launching into space, he declared with great solemnity, "Distinguishing between [multiple] selves and demons is crucial. . . . " One wonders why Jesus, who cast out many demons, never mentioned or ever did what Friesen says is "crucial."[13] Nor did Paul ever utilize Friesen's procedure in his considerable experience of successfully casting out demons.

The contradiction that confronts us is both obvious and mind boggling. If Jesus and Paul were right—and they must have been—then Friesen and his fellow Christian psychologists have been dead wrong and have led many astray. A major problem in the church today (and Christian psychology is a root cause) is the loss of confidence in God's Word to instruct the believer in every area of spiritual life. In contrast to the early apostles, who obeyed God rather than men (Acts 4:19), the church today follows men rather than God. The practitioners who profit from this unbiblical growth industry summarily brush aside as an unscientific objection the clear biblical fact that "the whole counsel of God" contains none of today's psychological theories (indeed, contradicts them).

Having become the foremost Christian "expert" in this specialized field, Friesen insists that demons "are not removable until those [hidden] memories are uncovered."[14] Yet Jesus never engaged in uncovering memories (the very heart of psychotherapy), nor did Paul when he cast out demons. Far from teaching, much less approving, the recovery of "buried memories," Paul instructed us to forget what is past (Philippians 3:13).

Friesen adds that exorcism must be "carried out by people with experience in both the Christian and the psychological arenas."[15] Yet Christ and His apostles were very successful at casting out demons nineteen hundred years before psychology invaded the church! If Christian psychology is true, the

Bible is not! This statement applies to all of Christian psychotherapy, not only to MPD/DID fiasco theory.

Friesen suggested that when the numerous personalities had been "revealed," the therapist should "teach the client to live life from the strong [multiple] selves, and reserve work with the injured selves to be carried out in therapy. . . . Get every self to work for the common good. This usually means having the adult selves stay in charge most of the time, while the child selves are safely kept away from the stresses of adult living."[16] Can he be serious? We've dropped through the rabbit hole into Alice's Wonderland!

As if that were not foolish enough, Friesen goes on to earnestly advise with the utmost concern, "Sometimes there is no willingness to work for the [multiple] selves' common good until there is spiritual accord. . . . The rift between a group of Christian alters and a group with other loyalties needs to be overcome. The wounded, misled alters can use their strength to further God's kingdom after they have received His healing. When God is in the middle of the system, it is easier for all the selves to work for their common good. Their allegiance to Him and to His family creates health and safety."[17]

It sounds as though the "cure" has put the inmates in charge of the asylum! One wonders why these vital instructions are missing from the "Manufacturer's Handbook." To put it bluntly, Paul is being accused of lying! He told the Ephesian elders that he had kept back "nothing that was profitable" for them. How could he dare to say that, when, according to Friesen and other Christian psychologists, he left out essential help for MPD/DIDs!

It took a few years and some expensive lawsuits, but eventually, in increasing numbers, the psychologists and psychiatrists themselves (with varying degrees of reluctance) began to voice the opinion that true cases were extremely rare and that the majority reported were iatrogenic (i.e., created in therapy). The prevailing opinion became that MPD/DID simply reflected behavior that patients learned to adopt in response to what they knew the therapist wanted— or to gain some notoriety and attention and even reward for themselves.

Founded upon Delusion

Psychotherapists routinely engage in hypnotic regression to uncover alleged past traumas that supposedly influence the patient's present condition. For years, a major "scientific" justification was the fact that in alleged regression back to the moment of birth under hypnosis the client often accurately described doctors and nurses and even conversations that took place during the birthing process. Only later did the excitement at the power of this tool for reliving the past turn to bewilderment when it was learned that the myelin sheathing of the prenatal, natal, and early postnatal brain is not sufficiently developed to carry such memories. What could be their source? Could demons be creating false memories to further their lies? What other explanation could there be?

Furthermore, it has been discovered that almost any occult experience can be induced under hypnosis. For example, the suggestion that the subject is dying brings forth "memories" of going through a tunnel, coming out into a beautiful land, being met by a "Being of Light" who expresses acceptance and love without condemnation, no matter how selfishly and godlessly one may have lived. This is precisely what is reported by those who have suffered so-called "clinical death" and have recovered to tell about it yet have never heard such reports. Again we confront a common source of inspiration. So beautiful is this experience that when commanded by the Being of Light to return to their bodies the clinically dead are reluctant to do so until told that their mission will be to tell the living that there is nothing to fear in death! Of course, this was the serpent's lie to Eve.

The Supreme Court of Canada recently banned testimony by witnesses that was obtained under hypnosis as "not scientifically reliable enough to have a place in a court of law." One of the lawyers involved in the case that led to this decision declared, "The reality is that hypnosis is more than capable of generating completely unreliable evidence."[18] A number of States in America have long rejected testimony from anyone who has undergone hypnosis in relation to the court case at hand. Yet such testimony is the only basis for an MPD/DID diagnosis. Hypnosis is the only way to "recover" lost memories. In fact, it creates them! The same is true of many "memories" of being abused as a child that are "discovered" during therapy.

Paul had both spiritual and practical reasons for saying, "Forgetting those things which are behind. . . . " Numerous in-depth studies have established the weakness and unreliability of human memory at best and the fact that false memories are created in hypnotic regression. *"Created" in hypnotic regression?* Yes, indeed. The very purpose of hypnosis is to deceive the subject.

Hypnosis and Psychotherapy

Pierre Janet, the French master hypnotist from whom many of Jung's theories came, justified as quite acceptable the deception that is innate in hypnosis, a technique also used by Freud. After quoting Janet's justification of deliberate deception, the Bobgans declare:

> Hypnotic induction . . . consists of a system of verbal and non-verbal manipulation to lead a person into a heightened state of suggestibility . . . in which one will believe almost anything.[19]

Critics have pointed out that psychotherapy is basically a specialized form of hypnotherapy, in which it has its roots. Hypnosis was once called "Mesmerism," so named after Franz Anton Mesmer (1734–1815), one of Mozart's patrons who is often falsely credited with having been the discoverer and first practitioner of hypnotism. In fact, witchdoctors had been using it for thousands of years. Mesmer believed that it involved a mysterious fluid present in the body that was the secret to health and could be controlled by the motions of his hands, eyes, and mind, thereby curing the patient. Many were the believers who testified that it worked.

In 1784, King Louis XVI appointed a royal commission to investigate "Mesmerism." The verdict was that the power at work through what Mesmer called "animal magnetism" was the imagination of the patient. In modern terms, it worked like a "placebo"—a sugar pill that often produces in the patient the very effect that he has been told will follow its ingestion. Psychiatrist Arthur Shapiro has called psychoanalysis "a magical ritual based on primitive shamanism . . . an esoteric system not easily understood by even an educated patient [an] intellectually convoluted system . . . a disguise for its true method . . . the simple placebo effect . . . the most used placebo of our time."[20]

What can be wrong with Christian psychologists attempting to cure clients with the use of a placebo? They are lying—misrepresenting what they offer as both biblical and scientific, when it is neither. Lawrence LeShan, at the time president of The American Psychological Association, declared that psychotherapy would be known as "the hoax of the twentieth century."[21] So this is what Christian psychology really is? Indeed! In agreement, professor of psychiatry Thomas Szasz made some interesting observations relating psychotherapy to hypnosis:

> Insofar as psychotherapy as a modern "medical technique" can be said to have a discoverer, Mesmer was that person. . . . Mesmer stumbled onto the literalized use of [a] metaphor . . . for explaining and exorcising all manner of human problems and passions, a rhetorical device that the founders of modern depth psychology subsequently transformed into the pseudomedical entity known as psychotherapy.[22]

Martin Gross states, "Contemporary research and logical examination have shown [psychoanalysis] to be an anti-science and an illogical set of theories developed mainly out of the eccentric mind of Sigmund Freud . . . a highly respectable mass delusion born from the typical human tendency to invent, then worship, what we do not yet know."

The present volume has demonstrated that this condemnation is well deserved and that it applies not only to the MPD/DID delusion but to all psychotherapy, not only secular but "Christian," to which it gave birth.

Exposing a Wicked and Costly Scam

The Recovered Memory Therapy (RMT) industry involved thousands of psychotherapists using hypnosis, group therapy, and other means to help patients recover alleged "repressed memories." After enjoying its profitable (for the therapists) heyday, at the cost of many broken families and fathers sent to prison as a result of false memories created in therapy, the recovered memory industry "was dismantled over a five-year period by hundreds of malpractice lawsuits beginning with the Hamanne v. Humenansky trial of August 1995."[23] In that landmark case, the jury found therapist Humanensky liable and awarded the patient $2.6 million. Attorney and psychologist R. Christopher Barden commented,

> I think the effect is a stunning warning to therapists . . . and to insurance companies that they had better start obeying the informed consent laws and stop experimental treatments like recovered memory treatments on patients. . . . This is a huge warning shot to them.[24]

At RMT's peak in the mid-1990s, thousands of patients annually were reporting so-called recovered memories. The effect of this scam upon society and the church was devastating. "Thousands of patients' families were torn asunder by allegations of abuse produced in therapy. The recovered memory movement was ultimately decimated by a wave of successful malpractice lawsuits. . . . The final crushing blow . . . came in 1997 with a $10.6 million legal award to the Burgus family. . . . World-wide attention [to that case] exposed the glaring scientific, methodological, and ethical errors inherent in recovered memory therapy. . . . Following a series of high profile litigation losses, many of the professional leaders of the RMT movement suffered licensing prosecutions, license revocations, disciplinary actions and even criminal prosecutions. . . . By 2000, the 'memory wars' were largely over. . . . "[25]

Today one could hardly find "a therapist who will admit conducting any form of therapy to recover so-called repressed memories."[26] One of the most famous cases involved an accusation by former seminarian Stephen Cook, who charged Cardinal and Chicago Archbishop Joseph Bernardin with sexual abuse—but recanted of the false accusation shortly before his death of AIDS.

Trashing Paul's Holy Spirit-Inspired Counsel

Christian psychologists are the new authoritarian clergy in the church. Like the Catholic clergy, they cannot be questioned because they have a source of "truth" that supplements the Bible, and they possess an expertise lacking to the layman. The most popular authors and speakers at conferences, they glibly present a new interpretation of the Bible unimagined by those "holy men of God . . . moved by the Holy Spirit" whom God inspired to write His Word. And Christians by the millions sit at their feet looking up to them as the authoritative purveyors of this new "science of the mind."

How it must break God's heart to see His children seeking counsel outside of His Word! To do so is to accuse our Creator of either lacking understanding of the man and woman He made or of not caring enough to provide everything in His instruction manual that is needed for mankind's good. So Paul, after all, contrary to his pledge, actually did hold back much that was profitable, and God's counsel is deficient?!

Any genuine Christian with even an elementary understanding of the New Testament should have immediately seen the conflict between MPD and Christianity. As we have seen, the *sine qua non* of MPD/DID diagnosis and treatment was to search the victim's past through regression induced by hypnosis. But Paul, as we have emphasized, had written under the inspiration of the Holy Spirit, "Forgetting those things which are behind, and reaching forth unto that which is before. . . . "

To encourage a passion to know and to put to use all the counsel of God is a major purpose of The Berean Call's ministry. One must know the whole Bible and not merely favorite or "positive" parts of it. May nothing undermine our confidence that God's Word is a sufficient guide for "life and godliness" (2 Peter 1:3–9)! Only through heeding its "doctrine, reproof, correction, [and] instruction in righteousness" can we be "perfect [i.e., mature, complete], throughly furnished unto all good works" (2 Timothy 3:16–17)!

Such is God's desire for each of His children—but we must be willing and trust in Him alone and in His Word.

1. Robyn M. Dawes, *House of Cards: Psychology and Psychotherapy Built on Myth* (New York, NY: The Free Press, division of Macmillan, 1994), 234-35.

2. Miles Vich and Rollo May, "Debating the legitimacy of Transpersonal Psychology," *Common Boundary*, July/August 1986, 7-15.

3. Dawes, *House*, 231-33.

4. Willard Gaylin, in an interview, *Publishers Weekly*, March 23, 1990.

5. *Wholemind Newsletter: A User's Manual to the Brain, Mind and Spirit*, vol. 1, no. 1, 5.

6. Ibid.

7. The National Association for Consumer Protection in Mental Health Practices Press Release, Office of the President.

8. Mark Pendergrast, *Victims of Memory: Sex Abuse Accusations and Shattered Lives* (HarperCollins Publisher, 1996).

9. Richard J. McNally, *Remembering Trauma* (Cambridge, MA: Harvard University Press, 2003), 11-12.

10. James Friesen, *More Than Survivors: Conversations with Multiple Personality Clients* (Here's Life Publishers, 1992), 203.

11. Ray Grasse, *The Quest*, Autumn 1994, 38-44.

12. Friesen, *Survivors*, 17, 219-20.

13. Ibid., 220.

14. Ibid., 145-46.

15. Ibid., 220.

16. Ibid., 219.

17. Ibid.

18. Janice Tibbetts, "Supreme Court Bans Hypnosis Testimony," *CanWest News Service*, February 2, 2007; http://rickross.com/reference/false_memories/fsm117.html.

19. Martin and Deidre Bobgan, *Hypnosis and the Christian* (Minneapolis, MN: Bethany House Publishers, 1984), 17.

20. Interview, Martin L. Gross, *The Psychological Society: The impact—and the failure—of psychiatry, psychotherapy, psychoanalysis, and the psychological revolution* (New York: Random House, 1978), 230.

21. Lawrence LeShan, *How to Meditate* (Boston: Little, Brown, and Company, 1974), 150-51.

22. Thomas Szasz, *The Myth of Psychotherapy* (Garden City, NJ: Anchor Press [Doubleday], 1978), 43.

23. http://en.wikipedia.org/wiki/Repressed_memory.

24. "Doctor Loses False Memory Suit," *Chicago Tribune*, August 2, 1995, Section 1, p. 12.

25. http://en.wikpedia.org/wiki/Repressed_memory.

26. Ibid.

THE NEED FOR
A THOROUGH PURGING

— *Dave Hunt* —

ALTHOUGH THERE MAY BE SOME CHRISTIAN psychologists who use only Scripture in their counseling, their designation of themselves as "psychologists" is extremely unfortunate. That word has an established meaning. It identifies a godless system that does not merit any association whatsoever with the word "Christian." What confusion to link in any way "the faith once [for all] delivered to the saints" (Jude 3) with humanistic theories of anti-Christians! The very term "Christian psychology" gives honor where only reproof is due, and it sullies our Lord's name by dragging it into the muck of infidelity.

Christian psychologists embrace and practice virtually every kind of psychology and therapy ever invented, from primal scream to shamanism. By this means, godless beliefs and practices (which have already proved to be both dangerous and ineffective and have numerous critics even among secular psychologists and psychiatrists themselves) have been brought into the church to deceive the flock.

Are Christians now expected to rejoice that the Bible has been discovered at long last to be in agreement with atheistic humanism? Would this mean that we Christians no longer need to go about with a hangdog look and poor self-image but can now hold our heads high before the world, especially in academic circles? Should we all be grateful because a "new Reformation" that psychologizes Christianity has uncovered novel interpretations of Scripture never before known in the history of the church, thus bringing Christianity at last into agreement with the theories of anti-Christians such as Freud, Jung, and their disciples?

This "new and improved Christianity" is being welcomed with apparent disregard for the increasing admissions by secular psychologists themselves that psychotherapy is really bankrupt. R. D. Laing, one of psychology's most respected leaders, gave his opinion that not even one "fundamental insight into relations between human beings [had] resulted from a century of psychotherapy." Yet the thoroughly discredited theories of psychology are credited by Christians with having brought great blessing to the church through fundamental new insight into "God's truth"!

Before believing that suspicious scenario, we would do well to heed the many non-Christian psychologists and psychiatrists who are issuing warnings, such as the following by internationally respected psychiatrist and author E. Fuller Torrey:

> The techniques used by western psychiatrists are, with few exceptions, on exactly the same scientific plane as the techniques of witch doctors. Psychiatry . . . . is a false Messiah.[1]

Martin L. Gross comments: "Today, the M.D. psychiatrist and his first cousin, the Ph.D. psychologist, have appointed themselves the undisputed Solomons of our era. The new seer delivers his pronouncements with the infallible air of a papal bull, a stance which intimidates even the most confident of laymen."[2]

In order to return to biblical Christianity, the church must renounce psychological theories and terminology and completely separate itself from this rival religion to which it has been wed in an unholy alliance. How can there be a partnership between the wisdom of God and that of the world, which God unequivocally says is foolish (1 Corinthians 1:20)? Justification is offered in the blasphemous error promoted by Christian psychologists: that God's Word is lacking essential ingredients for guiding mankind to personal happiness and fulfillment. What other possible reason could there be for this unequal yoke with the world except the delusion that psychology provides the wisdom and enablement that the Bible lacks?

Instead of purging out the leaven, however, the church continues to give increasing trust and honor to psychology. Christians are asked to accept psychology as an additional source of "God's" truth and to put it on an equal footing with God's Word, which Christ said is alone "the truth" (John 17:17). The actual truth is, however, that psychological counseling has proven to be bankrupt. Its false gospel continually changes as its conflicting theories ebb and flow and its gurus come and go.

Lawrence LeShan, past president of the Association for Humanistic Psychology, suggested that psychotherapy would be known as the *hoax* of the twentieth century. He also pointed out that "The basic model of man that led to the development of [Eastern] meditational techniques is the same model that led to humanistic psychotherapy"[3]—yet the church loves it.

Today, even as many leading secular psychologists and pyschiatrists are debunking their own profession in books and articles with such titles as *The*

Myth of Mental Illness; *The Myth of Neurosis*; *Psychotherapy, The Dangerous Cure*; *The Death of Psychiatry*; *Psychoanalysis, The Impossible Profession*, etc., Christian psychologists wax ever more eloquent in praise of the very system that is being exposed as a harmful fraud by secular practitioners! As a result, discredited psychological theories and practices that have deceived and damaged almost the whole of mankind are being embraced within the church.

We do well to heed J. Vernon McGee's warning that if it continues to grow in favor, "Christian psychology could well be the death of the evangelical church." If biblical Christianity is to survive, it needs to purge itself completely of this viper that it has clutched to its breast.

---

1. E. Fuller Torrey, *The Mind Games: Witchdoctors and Psychiatrists* (Emerson Hall, 1972), 8.

2. Martin L. Gross, *The Psychological Society: The impact—and the failure—of psychiatry, psychotherapy, psychoanalysis and the psychological revolution* (New York: Random House, 1978), 56-57.

3. Lawrence LeShan, *How to Meditate* (Boston: Little, Brown, and Company, 1974), 150-51.

THE VANISHING GOSPEL

— Dave Hunt —

THE CONCEPT OF ONE TRUE GOD, who exists eternally in three Persons—Father, Son, and Holy Spirit—is rejected even by some who claim to be Christians. Yet this truth is taught throughout Scripture, in the Old Testament as well as in the New. Consider: "I have not spoken in secret from the beginning; from the time that it was, there am I. . . . " Surely the speaker, who has been in existence forever and is therefore without beginning, must be God himself, but He declares, "the Lord GOD, and his Spirit, hath sent me" (Isaiah 48:16).

In this one verse we have One who is God, another called the Lord GOD, and another who is the Lord GOD's Spirit. The first, who is clearly God, was sent (apparently to earth on a mission) by the other two, each of whom is God also. There is no escaping the Trinity in this verse as well as in many other places throughout the Hebrew Scriptures.

The fact that we cannot comprehend the Trinity is not a valid argument against it. We can comprehend almost nothing even of the physical universe, let alone the spiritual. What is space? What is gravity? What is an atom, an electron, neutron, or proton? What is energy, or time? We don't know, but we are sure of their existence. Neither can we explain or comprehend a Being without beginning or end who is all-powerful, knows all, is everywhere at once, and has created all—but we know He must exist or we would not exist. Nor would it make it easier to comprehend His infinite, eternal person if He were a single Being instead of three persons in One.

Furthermore, the eternal God, who not only created us but redeemed us, could not be a single being for a number of reasons. If God were a single being (as Muslims believe Allah to be and most Jews Yahweh), He would have been lonely, incomplete, and have needed to create other personal beings in order to experience love, fellowship, and communion. Such a "God" would embody unity but would lack the equally essential quality of diversity.

The biblical God, who is perfect in Himself and therefore unchangeable, does not have, nor ever had, such limitations. He was never lonely or without someone to love or someone who loved Him. He *is love* (1 John 4:8,14) in Himself, manifesting not only unity but plurality in the

Godhead: "The Father loveth the Son. . . " (John 5:20). God must be one; but He must also embody both singularity and plurality, unity and diversity.

Rebellion and Redemption

God created man "in his own image, in the image of God created he him" (Genesis 1:27). That fact meant that man—solemn thought—could never cease to exist. It also meant that God would be to him not only his Creator but His creature's best friend, companion—his very life and happiness, and the whole reason for his existence. But man joined Satan in the cosmic rebellion against the Creator and, in cutting himself off from the God who designed him to express Himself in flesh, died instantly spiritually! As a result, physical death immediately became inevitable. It took Adam's and Eve's bodies longer to wear out and die than it takes ours today, but death was just as inescapable for them as for us.

Why did man rebel? He wanted to be a god in his own right. Certainly he could never take credit for *creating* the universe, but he was determined to own it and use every part of it for his own purposes. Of course, the Creator could not tolerate such creatures in His universe. Man would have to be banned from God's presence. He couldn't just be annihilated, however, because God had made him in His own image to exist forever.

In spite of what man had done, God still loved and pitied this rebellious creature He had made, and He was willing to do whatever it cost to bring him back into a proper relationship with Himself. The penalty for sin was not only physical death but eternal death—not cessation of being but the agony of perpetually dying spiritually forever and ever. This eternal separation from God's life, with no hope of recovery, is described as "the lake of fire . . . the second death" (Revelation 20:14).

This penalty prescribed by God himself could not be set aside without making Him a liar. The only hope for man was for *someone*—but *who?*—to pay that penalty in his place. It is no secret that only the infinite God could pay the infinite penalty that His justice demands for sin. But that would not be just, because "God is not a man . . . " (Numbers 23:19) and could not represent mankind. The incarnation was therefore essential—but impossible if God were a single being. It was neither the Father nor the Holy Spirit, but the virgin-born, sinless Son of God, Jesus Christ, who died on the Cross and paid the full penalty for mankind's sins so that God "might be just, and the justifier of him which believeth in Jesus" (Romans 3:26).

What occurred on the Cross was not a last-minute emergency act by God.

It was foretold from the very beginning in hundreds of prophecies that we have detailed elsewhere. All through the Old Testament, Yahweh declares that He is the only Savior (Isaiah 43:3, 11; 45:15, 21; 49:26; Hosea 13:4, etc.). Thus, Jesus had to be Yahweh but also a man. When God the Son became a man, He did not and could not cease to be God. As both God and man, Jesus bridged in Himself the chasm between Creator and creature.

How could God become a man? Again, that is only possible through the Trinity. The Father didn't become man, nor did the Holy Spirit. Even though this is beyond our finite understanding, we know it must be so. The penalty for our sins is infinite because God and His justice are infinite. Consequently, those who reject Christ's payment on their behalf will be separated from God forever.

Where Is the Fear of God Today?

One of the greatest sorrows for lovers of God is the fact that the vast majority of mankind selfishly and ungratefully live day after day without even thinking of the Creator to whom they owe their existence and who holds their eternal destiny in His hands. So it is even with many who claim to know Him. How often do we tell God we love Him and thank Him for His love and grace and the salvation He has given us in Christ? When was the last time?

The opinion polls consistently show that from 90-95 percent of the people in the United States believe in God. It is obvious, however, that very few have been gripped by what this really means. Even most who call themselves Christians do not live as though they are not their own but belong to Him. If we are Christians, Christ has purchased our redemption, having bought us with His blood. Yet even Christians at times forget God and live for themselves as though He did not exist. They don't deny the truth mentally, but in their hearts and by their daily lives they do. That lack of faithfulness leads to many woes.

We live in a wicked world that hourly bombards us with its ungodly influences. Day and night, degrading us with its fleshly and often lewd entertainment, radio and TV belch out programs and even commercials that entice us to lust. Neither thought of God nor fear of His judgment impede the downward spiral.

The miracle of our bodies, with their trillions of unfathomable cells and chance-defying organs such as the eye and brain, the ingenious design displayed in nature, and the mystery of soul and spirit shout at us continually: "In the beginning God created the heaven and the earth" (Genesis 1:1), and He made man "in his image" (1:26–28). Yet most people—even many who call themselves "Christians"—dishonor God by embracing the outrageous fraud of evolution.

This world's contemptuous disregard of its Creator should cause every Christian to weep—for God's sake and for all mankind, which is blindly plunging itself and its world into judgment. In this evil world, who is really moved to "tremble, tremble, tremble," as the old song ("Were You There?") says, at the memory of the Son of God, despised and beaten, nailed to a Cross in satisfaction of a corrupt empire, and a mad mob demanding His blood? Who trembles in realization of the judgment that is coming upon mankind for its defiance of God?! "The wicked shall be turned into hell, and all the nations that forget God" (Psalm 9:17)—and forgotten God they surely have.

Man's rebellion and the accompanying wickedness that is engulfing the world today cannot be excused in any way. Nor can it be blamed upon any outside influences. Jesus described the problem's source: "For out of the heart proceed evil thoughts, murders, adulteries, fornications, thefts, false witness, blasphemies. . . " (Matthew 15:19). Therein lies the root of all of the personal, family, church, community, state, national, and international problems that vex us today. Psychology is the wrong place to turn for a solution. Its founders exemplified to the fullest degree the very problems it claims to mend.

Psychology has been called "the only profession that causes the disease of which it claims to be the cure."

A Horror Story Like No Other

The problem is sin. Man's evil heart produces every foul thought, word, and deed. Paul preached the only biblical solution: "repentance toward God, and faith toward our Lord Jesus Christ" (Acts 20:21). Such was the gospel held forth by evangelical churches for nineteen hundred years. That message brought the joy of forgiveness and peace with God, with oneself, and with others—and it really transforms lives.

Of course, not yet delivered from the bodies in which we live, Christians fall into sin at times. Always, however, because of Christ, we can resort to the promise, "If we confess our sins, he is faithful and just to forgive us our sins, and to cleanse us from all unrighteousness" (1 John 1:9). For centuries, the church preached that "His divine power hath given unto us all things that pertain unto life and godliness, through the knowledge of him that hath called us to glory and virtue (2 Peter 1:3). Souls were saved, lives were changed, missionaries were spreading the good news around the globe. Then—tragedy!

Psychology was invented by the godless, and the rest is a horror story like no other. That heretic of all heretics, Norman Vincent Peale, brought the "Trojan Horse" of psychology into his church and preached it from his pulpit and in his best-selling books. His chief disciple, Robert Schuller, followed suit a few years later. The entire evangelical church rejected the heresy of psychology for decades. Gradually, however, Christians succumbed to the enticement of getting degrees from secular universities that would allegedly give the "gospel" credibility with the world. Evangelicals tried to "integrate" psychology with the Scripture, insisting that it had always been there, but no one had realized it until Freud and his cohorts came along to show the way back to the God they didn't believe in. The claim was made and most of the evangelical church believed it: Jesus and Paul and the other disciples had taught "psychological principles" without even knowing it!

The Bible was given new interpretations by atheists—interpretations that the church accepted as light from God. For example, in 1947, *Man for Himself: An Inquiry into the Psychology of Ethics*, by Freudian psychoanalyst Erich Fromm, proposed a new interpretation of what the Bible called the sin of Adam and Eve, declaring that independent thinking, rather than submitting to God's authoritarian defining of moral values, was a virtue, not a sin. He reinterpreted Christ's command to love one's neighbor as oneself to mean that we all naturally hated ourselves and needed to learn to love ourselves before we could love God or others. A lack of self-love and self-esteem was mankind's major problem.

Robert Schuller popularized this lie in his 1969 book (introduction by Peale and published by occultist W. Clement Stone), *Self-Love: The Dynamic Force of Success*. Typical of its many sub-headings is "Self-Love is Being Proud of Who and What You Are."[1] It only takes a moment's reflection to realize that Schuller turned the Bible on its head. Compare Christ's command to "deny self" with the following self-*ad nauseam* that pours forth from Schuller's pen:

> Self-love is a crowning sense of self-worth . . . an ennobling emotion of self-respect . . . a divine awareness of personal dignity . . . an abiding faith in yourself. It is sincere belief in yourself. It comes through self-discovery, self-discipline, self-forgiveness and self-acceptance. It produces self-reliance, self-confidence and an inner security calm as the night.[2]

But what say the Scriptures? Paul warned against thinking too highly of oneself (Romans 12:3) and urged, "Let each esteem other better than themselves" (Philippians 2:3). Never does the Bible suggest the possibility that we might think too *poorly* of ourselves. The Scriptures, however, had not yet been integrated with the Epistles of the new apostles of psychology, nor had the church surrendered to the surrounding culture. Who led us to join the crowds on the broad road to destruction? There may be multiple answers to that question, but Christian psychologists deserve most of the blame—or credit, for those who look at it that way.

The Band-Aid® of Christian Psychology

As a result of Christian psychology's influence, both the gospel and today's church, which supposedly preaches and lives it, would scarcely be recognized by Paul, Wesley, Whitfield, Spurgeon, or any of the men and women of God of past centuries, were they able to drop in for a visit. It is staggering to realize that in the few years since its advent, Christian psychology, originally an alien invader that was resisted for decades by nearly every pastor, church, and seminary, spread like a contagious disease until today it is the most all-pervasive single influence in the church, exceeding even that of the Bible itself.

The new gospel of psychology has little to say about sin or repentance. It does not and cannot deal with the root of the problem in the human heart, a heart that "is deceitful above all things and desperately wicked" (Jeremiah 17:9). It deals with the symptoms rather than the disease. It attempts to put bandages on cancers that need to be surgically removed. The focus is on feelings rather than on truth. Instead of being denied, as Christ commanded, self is seen as the solution—if self can only be persuaded how good and worthwhile it really is.

It is not only disheartening for those who love sound doctrine but almost frightening to read the following description of the astonishing domain that Christian psychology has staked out for itself in the church. Here was the boast of two popular Christian psychologists/authors concerning the recognition and respect psychology had already achieved within the church nearly thirty years ago. They considered the triumph of psychology in the church to be a great advance for the Lord:

> Christianity is in the throes of an encounter with psychology. On academic and popular levels alike, psychology is making inroads into areas traditionally considered the domain of Christianity. And the signs of this encounter are everywhere about us.
>
> Religious bookstores are filled with volumes on psychology. A Christian periodical is incomplete without an article on some aspect of personal or family adjustment. And nearly every theological seminary offers courses in areas such as counseling, psychology, and mental health.

Psychologists are lecturing at Bible conferences. The "family-life week," with psychologically oriented speakers and seminar leaders, is fast replacing the church's revival meetings, evangelistic services, and prophetic conferences. . . .

Increasingly, our society is looking to psychology to shed new light on the problems of human existence. Questions concerning the nature of the human being and psychological health and happiness are being directed increasingly to the psychological community. In fact, in many quarters, the whole process of "curing sick souls" is rapidly moving from the church to the doorsteps of psychologists and other mental health professionals.

With the possible exception of the theory of evolution in biology, psychology has already had a greater impact on the church than any other scientific discipline.[3]

Pairing psychology with evolution is very accurate. Both are pseudo-sciences, and both deny God and His work. Freud considered Darwin's *The Descent of Man* one of the "ten most significant books" ever written.

The reason why psychology and evolution were embraced by the church and are steadily taking over Christian universities and seminaries is very simple: sound doctrine is neglected and not heeded even when token attempts are made to teach it. Few families come together for daily Bible reading and prayer—and many of those few who do use faulty "Bibles" such as *The Renovaré Spiritual Formation Bible* and *The Message* or paraphrases that likewise change the Bible's meaning in many places. Paul's description of idolaters in past ages fits our generation, including many who call themselves Christians:

> Even as they did not like to retain God in their knowledge, God gave them over to a reprobate mind . . . [to] all unrighteousness, fornication, wickedness, covetousness. . . . [They are] haters of God . . . inventors of evil things, disobedient to parents . . . without natural affection . . . who knowing the judgment of God, that they which commit such things are worthy of death . . . do the same, [and] have pleasure in them that do them. (Romans 1:28–32)

The connection is undeniable between the evil foretold for "the last days" (2 Timothy 3:1–7) and the godless "lifestyles" popularized on trendy TV shows that even Christian viewers love, to their everlasting shame. Believers have opened their homes to TV programs that they would have been ashamed to be found watching a few decades ago; and the children in many Christian homes spend much of their time totally absorbed in video games that have the players participating in occultism, violence, and murder.

Life has become one big fantasy game, with God relegated to watching from the sidelines. Many parents, even non-Christians, are concerned about their children who live in a world made real by video games. "He/she just can't concentrate on school work" is often the complaint of parents who have simply failed to discipline the child. And Christian psychology is very likely to partner with Ritalin or some other drug to solve the problem of alleged ADHD (Attention-deficit-hyperactivity disorder). This is only one of many "psychological" problems that never existed until some enterprising psychologist or psychiatrist invented the "disorder" in order to expand psychology's influence and control in the world and church.

The Megachurch Solution

Hollywood has long glorified and exported all manner of ungodly attitudes and behavior. The marketing of evil provides billions of dollars in profits by promoting youth rebellion; sexual "freedom" and wanton perversion; mutilation of the body; obscene, suicidal, and murderous lyrics; gangland and satanic clothing—and much more. Could Sodom and Gomorrah have been any worse?

Homes are invaded and families destroyed by immoral, corrupting media, leaving consciences "seared with a hot iron" (1 Timothy 4:2). Many Christians enjoy "family time" in their homes by watching programs that, as mentioned, would have shamed and embarrassed them only a few years ago. An estimated 50 percent of professing Christians have been hooked on internet pornography, among them a surprising number of pastors.

To attract those thus corrupted, many of the largest and fastest-growing churches mimic the world in "seeker-friendly" and "youth-oriented" services that exploit sensuality and compromise the truth. One newspaper investigation reported:

> Megachurches are good at reaching young people raised in an entertainment-saturated culture. . . . Many have . . . a rock-concert feel to them. . . . [At the] largest congregation in the United States, with more than 25,000 attendants each weekend . . . Victoria Osteen steps to the podium in front of 16,000 cheering Sunday worshipers and proclaims: "We're going to rock today!"[4]

A popular youth program on TBN is called *Jesus Rocks*. It is a scandalous perversion of everything godly and Christian—an abomination to God. How could the church have sunk so low so fast?

One analyst wrote, "The Jesus People erected [a] worship ritual . . . from the preeminent communal ceremony of their generation—the rock concert."[5] Out of this came "Christian rock." By embracing "contemporary Christian music" (CCM) and "contemporary worship," and failing to Heed the warnings of Apostasy, the church has been converted to the "religion" of the world.

Some of the largest presumably evangelical churches have designed their Sunday morning services based upon what the ungodly want. Missing are the fear of a holy God's wrath against sin, deeply felt repentance, and a genuine and humble faith in Christ, the eternal God who became man through the virgin birth to suffer the full penalty of God's judgment in our place. Seeker-friendly churches must not "offend" with the Truth but pamper with the flattering "gospel" of self-esteem, self-love, and positive thinking—a "gospel" that cannot save. As Paul foretold, "they will not endure sound doctrine. . . " (2 Timothy 4:3).

Creating large, rich churches is not new. In *A Woman Rides the Beast*, we show that the Roman Catholic Church—the world's largest and wealthiest—grew out of a marriage between the Roman empire and the church, making "Christianity" the state religion. It grew larger and increased in power worldwide by wedding itself to the dominant pagan religions in Italy, Spain, Latin America, Africa, the Philippines, etc. Haiti is said to be 85 percent Catholic and 110 percent Voodoun. New Orleans, "the most Catholic city in America,"[6] is also America's voodoo capital. Historian Will Durant describes the beginning of this process:

> Paganism survived . . . in the form of ancient rites and customs condoned, or accepted and transformed, by an often indulgent Church. An intimate and trustful worship of saints replaced the cult of pagan gods. . . . Statues of Isis and Horus were renamed Mary and Jesus; the Roman Lupercalia and the feast of purification of Isis became the Feast of the Nativity; the Saturnalia were replaced by Christmas celebration . . . an ancient festival of the dead by All Souls Day, rededicated to Christian heroes; incense, lights, flowers, processions, vestments, hymns which had pleased the people in older cults were domesticated and cleansed in the ritual of the Church . . . soon people and priests would use the sign of the cross as a magic incantation to expel or drive away demons. . . .
>
> [Paganism] passed like maternal blood into the new religion, and captive Rome captured her conqueror . . . the world converted Christianity. . . . [7]

Now "Protestantism" is creating megachurches by merging with the "new paganism" in today's culture—a culture that is becoming ever more anti-Christian and anti-Israel. And psychology, by undermining faith in the sufficiency of Scripture, has played a major role in this metamorphosis.

Blindsided by Satan's Master Stroke of Genius

We desperately need God's Word as a "lamp unto our feet and a light unto our path" (Psalm 119:105), but our adversary, "the great dragon. . . that old serpent, called the Devil, and Satan . . . " (Revelation 12:9) is a master at keeping the Word from believers. Modern translations and paraphrases have robbed the Bible of much of its power and have confused the truth. Entertainment has driven out the Holy Spirit, with His convicting and saving power. Satan's cleverest and most effective way of robbing the church of Scripture and "sound doctrine," however, is through psychology's lie that the Bible, though it may be *infallible*, is not *sufficient* to meet the needs of hurting and confused people today. Psychology has an amazing appeal to young and old, unbelievers and believers, carnal and spiritual. Its gospel has transformed the world and church in so many ways.

Today's world doesn't need more entertainment and "positive" messages assuring the "hurting" that God loves, forgives, "accepts them as they are," heals their "inner child," and has an exciting plan for their lives. Mankind needs the changeless convicting truth that leads sinners to repentance and salvation. God's holy character has not changed; the separation between man and God caused by sin—and the judgment to come—have not changed, nor has God's remedy in Christ been outdated and revised. On these basic facts the Bible is clear and uncompromising—and the megachurches have compromised.

We must preach the gospel everywhere to everyone (Mark 16:15), and it must be sincerely believed to effect one's salvation: "The gospel of Christ . . . is the power of God unto salvation to every one that believeth" (Romans 1:16); "There is none other name . . . whereby we must be saved" (Acts 4:12). "What must I do to be saved? Believe on the Lord Jesus Christ. . . " (Acts 16:30–31). The warning is solemn and clear: "He that believeth not the Son shall not see life; but the wrath of God abideth on him" (John 3:36).

Sadly, God's Word of truth is perverted continually by men such as Robert Schuller. There are many on radio and TV whose influence is staggering. Schuller is one of the leading promoters of pop psychology. His *Hour of Power* TV program reaches 20 million viewers weekly. He declares, "We have to find God in our own way. . . . "[8] Rewriting the Bible, Schuller turns God's solemn warning, "Thou shalt have no other gods before me," into *Believe in the God Who Believes in You*. The back cover copy of that book declares, "Pride, self-respect, peace of mind, love—God is waiting to give you all this and more! It's only a matter of trust, and Dr. Schuller guarantees: 'You can't go wrong if you will only choose to—Believe in the God who believes in You!'"[9]

The Apostle Paul had it right when he declared that he had "no confidence in the flesh" (Philippians 3:3). Yet God believes in *us*? What "God" is this? And how could Satan, the father of lies (John 8:44) persuade so many Christians to swallow this spiritual poison? The world has its pop psychology and this is the church's version—and Christians love it. "Christian psychology" is Satan's master stroke of genius. Christianity has been so thoroughly psychologized that it may never recover. It is surely time for our Lord to take the true believers to heaven and let Satan show what he can do with this world and the false church!

The Bible vs. Christian Psychology

"Christ Jesus came into the world to save sinners" (1 Timothy 1:15). Yet Schuller, self-proclaimed "founder of the church growth movement" (his annual Institute for Successful Church Leadership has attracted tens of thousands of pastors from around the world), claims that "attempting to make people aware of their lost and sinful condition" is an "unchristian strategy" that is "destructive [and] counterproductive to the evangelism enterprise. . . ."[10] David F. Wells writes:

> In another age, Robert Schuller's ministry . . . might well have been viewed . . . as comedy. . . . Sin, he says with a cherubic smile, is not what shatters our relationship to God [but] that we do not esteem ourselves enough. In the Crystal Cathedral, therefore, let the word sin be banished. . . . Christ was not drawing a profound moral compass in the Sermon on the Mount; he was just giving us a set of 'be (happy) attitudes'. . . ."[11]

Paul declares that the Bible is to be used "for doctrine, for reproof, for correction, for instruction in righteousness: that the man of God may be perfect [what God wants him to be], thoroughly furnished unto all good works" (2 Timothy 3:16–17). What higher ambition could one have than this: to be what God wants one to be and to be equipped and able to do every good work? This scripture, if the church really believed and followed it, would leave Christian psychologists without any following or a job. Thus, for self-preservation, they must perpetuate the lie.

If that should happen, what would they do with their degrees and expertise? What would happen to their prestige? No wonder they try so hard to "integrate" psychology with the Bible. This is their only hope for salvaging Christian psychology. Of course, they can't make it work, but they continue in the promise that one day they will be able to show that God's Word and the words of Freud et al. are indeed compatible and those who have trusted in man instead of God haven't been wrong after all.

God's Word is the foundation of our faith—yet that foundation is being undermined by Christian psychologists. Let us be careful to "preach the word" and "obey the word" and allow Christ the "living word" to live through us as we offer sinners the biblical "gospel of God" (Romans 1:1) that truly saves. Let us "earnestly contend" for this unchangeable faith (Jude 3).

1. Robert H. Schuller, *Self-Love: The Dynamic Force of Success* (New York: Hawthorne Books, 1969), 37.

2. Ibid., 32.

3. John D. Carter, Bruce Narramore, *The Integration of Psychology and Theology, An Introduction* (Grand Rapids, MI: Zondervan Publishing House, 1979), 9-10.

4. *The Christian Science Monitor*, December 30, 2003.

5. *Worship Leader*, November/December 2003.

6. *Our Sunday Visitor*, October 15, 1995.

7. Will Durant, *The Story of Civilization: Caesar and Christ* (New York: Simon and Schuster, 1940), vol. IV, 75; vol. III, 657, 672.

8. *Larry King Live*, December 19, 1998.

9. Robert H. Schuller, *Believe in the God Who Believes in You: The Ten Commandments, A Divine Design for Dignity* (Nashville, TN: Thomas Nelson Publishers), back cover copy.

10. *Christianity Today*, October 5, 1984.

11. David F. Wells, *No Place for Truth, or Whatever Happened to Evangelical Theology?* (Grand Rapids, MI: Wm. B. Eerdmans Publishing Co., 1993), 175.

Inerrancy, Sufficiency, and Authority

— Dave Hunt —

If ye continue in my word, then are ye my disciples indeed; and ye shall know the truth, and the truth shall make you free. —JOHN 8:31-32

All scripture is given by inspiration of God, and is profitable [to be used] for doctrine, for reproof, for correction, for instruction in righteousness: that the man of God may be perfect, thoroughly furnished unto all good works. —2 TIMOTHY 3:16-17

WE HAVE MANY TIMES NOTED what is clear to every God-fearing person: that the increasing evil of today's world stems from the tragic fact that mankind, following in the steps of Adam and Eve, is in rebellion against God. That rebellion, which only gets worse (2 Timothy 3:13) and is so brazenly displayed in the secular world, works most subtly under the cover of religion. It operates through false doctrines and the perversions and pious rationalizations that justify a calloused disobedience to God's Word. This disobedience, tragically, is steadily growing even among evangelicals. A major cause of this sad fact is the growing credibility given to Christian psychology.

Satan's primary tactic in opposing God and evading the "sword of the Spirit" (Ephesians 6:17) is not to foster atheism but religion; not to prove there is no God but to be worshiped as God and to promise a pseudo-god-hood to all mankind who will follow him. Satan's boast, "I will be like the most High" (Isaiah 14:14), admits God's existence but exalts Self to the same lordly level. Satan became, in fact, "the god of this world" (2 Corinthians 4:4). He damns far more souls with pride and the lure of power and success than with overt degradation. He didn't tempt Eve with alcohol or bestiality but with the highest ambition: to be like God. Satan's purpose is not to prove that Christ never existed but to have his own man, Antichrist, worshiped as Christ. Not being an atheist himself, Satan's primary goal is not to promote atheism but to pervert "Christianity" and make it his ultimate weapon against God.

Some Examples of Satan's Lie Believed

One example of Satan's subtle tactics is found in Masonry. Its influence permeates both the world and the church. A Masonic-dominated Supreme Court legalized abortion and put Christianity out of public schools. Masonry is an anti-Christian religious cult rooted in Hinduism, occultism, and other forms of paganism. Masonry assures members that through good works and obedience to its tenets they will reach the Celestial Lodge in the Sky presided over by the G.A.O.T.U. (Great Architect of the Universe), which is "God as you conceive him to be." Masonic authority Carl H. Claudy writes, "Masonry . . . requires merely that you believe in some deity, give him what name you will, any god will do."[1] Yet more than 1 million Southern Baptist laymen and clergy are in the "brotherhood," and most of them would defend it as "Christian." In fact, the 1993 annual convention of Southern Baptists declared that membership in a Masonic Order was to "be a matter of personal conscience."

Mormonism is another astonishing example. On June 8, 1873, speaking from the Salt Lake City Tabernacle, Brigham Young said, "The Devil told the truth. . . . I do not blame Mother Eve. I would not have had her miss eating the forbidden fruit for anything. . . . " Another Mormon president declared, "The fall of man came as a blessing in disguise. . . . We can hardly look upon anything resulting in such benefits [i.e., godhood] as a sin." Incredibly, Mormonism is based upon the belief that Satan's central lie is the gospel truth!

Psychology reflects the same satanic perversion. For example, in *The Courage to Create*, Rollo May, who had a B.A. from Union Theological Seminary, commends Eve for her self-assertive rebellion against God. What the Bible calls sin, May calls *felex culpa*, the "fortunate fall" that emancipated humanistic psychology's Self. As we have noted, Carl Rogers called self "the god within" and advocated worshiping at its altars. Such theories have been adopted by Christian psychology, creating its belief in self-love, self-image, self-esteem, etc.

Mankind's essential need, according to the Bible, is not self-esteem, as James Dobson and other Christian psychologists tell us, but deliverance from self, sin, and Satan. Human concern is for economic, political, or other physical freedoms. What man needs, however, is moral and spiritual liberation, both now and eternally. God's only and complete solution is redemption: the purchase of mankind with Christ's blood from sin's penalty and from Satan's slave market of sin. Christ declares that the practical outworking of this God-given freedom in the lives of the redeemed comes by obeying the truth (John 8:31–32).

Three Characteristics of "God's Truth"

Pontius Pilate, having faced so many liars standing before him for judgment, cynically asked, "What is truth?" (John 18:38). Prior to Pilate's question, Jesus had stated, "Every one that is of the truth heareth my voice." This tells us that God's truth, referred to in Scripture, differs from facts. Scientific facts are available to all mankind through observation of nature. *The* truth, which alone sets free, is known only by Christ's followers. Nobel Laureate Sir John Eccles wrote, "In the mindless universe of mere nature . . . there is neither justice nor mercy, neither liberty nor fairness. There are only facts; and no fact . . . seeks or requires a justification." What is merely factually true is not "the truth" of which the Bible speaks and that sets free those believing it.

Christ's words in John 8:31–32 reveal three things about truth and Scripture: 1) God's Word is 100 percent true without any error ("my word . . . the truth"); 2) All of what Christian psychologists call "God's truth" is in God's Word ("ye will know the truth," not part of the truth); and 3) Knowing the truth is contingent upon obedience to the authority of God's Word ("if ye continue in my word"—obviously not just reading or memorizing but obeying). These attributes of Scripture (inerrancy, sufficiency, and authority) are like the legs of a three-legged stool: remove any one of the legs and the stool cannot stand.

The Dire Consequences of Not Accepting the Truth

Once faith is lost in the inerrancy of the Bible, for example, the door is opened to all manner of error and perversion. Liberalism long ago abandoned this essential pillar of truth, and with it went sufficiency and authority. Biblical morals hung on for another generation, mostly as tradition, in a society that had lost its faith; but without that foundation, "traditional morals" are now generally passé and won't be recovered without submission to God's Word.

Roman Catholicism, which denies all three (inerrancy, sufficiency, and authority), provides an amazing example of the rationalizations that ensue. Although claiming to stand strictly against divorce, the Church grants, in the United States alone, "annulments" by the tens of thousands each year.[2] Rome's use of psychology is particularly self-serving. Many annulments are granted for "psychological" reasons, e.g., being raised in a "dysfunctional" family or being "psychologically unprepared" for marriage. Annulments often end long-term marriages (of twenty to thirty years or more) involving numerous children. Psychology is a willing accomplice in this scam, assisting the Catholic Church in its destruction of many families.

Although Rome outwardly stands firmly against fornication, thousands of its priests, unable to fulfill the unnatural and unbiblical pledge of celibacy, engage habitually in sex outside of marriage. A major Roman Catholic Newspaper reported, "Seven French women . . . companions of priests who . . . are forced to 'live clandestinely, for a lifetime, the love they share with a priest' [and who] represent thousands of women in similar relationships . . . arrived at the Vatican Aug. 20, 1993. [They] asked the pope to . . . look into the reality faced by 'thousands of priest's companions who live in the shadows, often with the approval of church superiors, and by the children who can't know their fathers and are raised by their mothers alone or are abandoned.'"[3] Of course, the pope would not hear them.

The only remedy for such immorality and corruption, as the Reformers well knew, is *sola scriptura*. The Bible alone is all we need to live joyful and fulfilled lives of fruitfulness pleasing to God. This is affirmed by Paul's assurance "that the man [or woman] of God may be perfect [all that God wants], thoroughly furnished unto all good works" (2 Timothy 3:17).

The Role of Christian Psychology

This sufficiency of Scripture is denied by the saying "All truth is God's truth"— the Christian psychologist's excuse for looking outside God's Word to Freud, Jung, et al., for "essential truth." Yet Christ declared that "the world cannot receive" (John 14:17) "the Spirit of truth [who leads] into all truth" (John 16:13). Hence, no unsaved person knows "God's truth," which can be revealed only by the Holy Spirit through His Word to those who open their hearts to Christ. Contrary to Catholicism's and Christian psychology's claim, there is no extrabiblical source of *the truth*.

Though many Christian psychologists affirm the inerrancy of Scripture, they all deny its sufficiency. If they didn't, they would have to abandon their profession. Consider a paper delivered by John Coe to conventions of both ETS (Evangelical Theological Society) and CAPS (Christian Association for Psychological Studies), entitled "Why Biblical Counseling is Unbiblical." In it, he denounces the belief that "the Bible is the only legitimate and authoritative source" of moral values and spiritual guidance for mankind. Astonishingly, Coe sat for sixteen years under the ministry of John MacArthur (who opposes Christian psychology). He taught apologetics and contemporary theology for five years at Talbot Theological Seminary, where he is currently Associate Professor of Philosophy and Theology.

So flagrant is Coe's denial of the sufficiency and thus the authority of Scripture as to claim that the Bible itself "mandates the church to develop a science of [moral and spiritual] values and human nature" from extrabiblical sources. Yet common sense recognizes that "good" and "evil" do not apply to nature. The indisputable fact that moral values are outside of science and thus human behavior cannot be explained by science has been stated by numerous Nobel Laureate scientists. Erwin Schrödinger, for example, declared that science "knows nothing of beautiful and ugly, good or bad, God and eternity."

In his attempt to justify Christian psychology's rejection of the sufficiency of Scripture, Coe declares that whatever is "natural" is good and that one can deduce a "science of [moral] values" simply from observing nature or by following one's natural impulses. Of course, nothing is more "natural" than to eat the fruit of a tree—and what could be more beneficial than to eat of a tree whose fruit is not only delicious and nutritious but will impart the knowledge of good and evil! As for making "natural" human behavior the standard, nothing seems more natural to modern man than fornication. Does that make fornication normal and thus "good"? Is human sacrifice normal and good because it has been practiced by many pagan societies? Homosexuals argue that homosexuality is "natural"—that they were born that way. This claim is false, but so-called social science is still in flux on this issue.

Dishonesty in Psychology's and Sociology's Theorizing

The Bible's declaration that the "natural man" cannot know God's truth, which is only revealed by the Spirit of God (1 Corinthians 2:14), thoroughly demolishes the Coe/Christian psychology thesis. Observation of nature reveals only that God is eternal and infinite in wisdom and power (Romans 1:20). A personal revelation from God by His Spirit is required to know more than that. Mankind's common recognition of moral standards comes not from observing nature but from acknowledging God's laws written in the conscience (Romans 2:14–15). As Herbert Schlossberg reminds us, "A system of ethics that says human beings ought to base their behavior on nature therefore justifies any behavior, because nature knows no ethic."

Far from establishing God's truth, as Coe and other Christian psychologists assert, "social science" has from its very beginning opposed God's Word and promoted an amoral lifestyle. For example, Margaret Mead's book, *Coming of Age in Samoa*, sold millions of copies in numerous languages, was the recognized standard in anthropology for decades, and provided a key "scientific" justification for the sexual revolution that is still perverting both today's world and much of the church. The book, however, was a fraud put forth to justify her own adultery and lesbianism. More recent research in Samoa has shown that Mead's representation of an idyllic native society, unspoiled by sexual restrictions, was totally false. The facts about Samoan life are exactly the opposite, yet the lie continues to provide "scientific" excuse for immorality worldwide.

We have elsewhere quoted Thomas Szasz, a Jewish psychiatrist, to the effect that Freud's primary motive was revenge against Christianity. Szasz adds, "The popular image of Freud as an enlightened . . . person who, with the aid of psychoanalysis, 'discovered' that religion is a mental illness is pure fiction." Freud's theories were founded upon his warped view that all thought, feeling, and motivation have their roots in sexual cravings. His "Oedipus complex," for which no evidence can be found in the general population, clearly reflected his own obsession with incest. It makes sense, as E. Michael Jones points out, only "when seen in the context of Freud's own life."

Indeed, some of Freud's case studies, put forth to support his theories, are disguised autobiographical sketches. His "discoveries" reflect his own perverted sexual fantasies and obsessions, as did Jung's. Early correspondence between them involved Jung's efforts to have Freud advise him regarding his seduction of a patient, Sabina Spielrein. Jung had other mistresses, just as Freud was not limited to his sister-in-law, Minna Bernays. Likewise, Carl Rogers' worship of Self, expressed in the theories of self-love, self-esteem, etc., which have so influenced the church, finds its roots in his rejection of Christianity and in his attempt to justify his own infidelity. There is no doubt that the entire structure of modern psychology/sociology, far from being scientific, springs in large part from rebellion against God and the sexual depravity of its honored "discoverers."

Corruption at the Highest Levels

Though professing Christian faith, the Clintons have long been in the forefront of dethroning God and putting a "new, liberated person" in His place. Hillary, a long-time fierce supporter of the radical Left, chaired the New World Foundation 1987–88, ranked by the Capitol Research Center as "one of the ten most liberal foundations in the United States." It has not hesitated even to support communist causes. From 1986–92 she chaired the Children's Defense Fund, which promotes an amoral approach to sex education and other means of destroying the very moral values that most parents want to pass on to their children.

The major social theories that revolutionized society during the last one hundred years were not, as claimed by academia, "scientific" advancements, but the popularizing of the immorality of their "discoverers" under a thin veneer of scientific language. In *Peace, Prosperity, and The Coming Holocaust* and *Global Peace and the Rise of Antichrist*, I documented the fact that Karl Marx, though Jewish, in his earlier years was a professing Christian who turned to Satan and became the sworn enemy of God. His socialistic theory was an attempt at revenge against the One he hated. In a poem, he wrote, "I wish to avenge myself against the One who rules above." A friend, Georg Jung, remarked, "Marx will surely chase [the biblical] God from His heaven!" Lenin became the Marxist god.

Most disturbing is the fact that many of today's leading evangelicals who affirm inerrancy undermine the Bible's sufficiency and authority. They seek "the counsel of the ungodly" (Psalm 1:1) and insist that to do so is biblical. Satan has perverted the church by appealing to the pride that desires to be respected by sinners and especially by the academic world. That world is hopelessly corrupt. Let us diligently look to God and His Word for guidance and stand firm for its inerrancy, sufficiency, and absolute authority.

---

1 Carl H. Claudy and other authorities: for example, *Little Masonic Library* (Macoy Publishing and Masonic Supply, 1977), Vol. 4, 32.

2. *National Catholic Reporter*, August 27, 1993.

3. Ibid., September 3, 1993.

"THEY HAVE
FORSAKEN THE LORD"

— Dave Hunt —

Ah sinful nation, a people laden with iniquity, a seed of evildoers, children that are corrupters: they have forsaken the LORD they have provoked the Holy One of Israel unto anger, they are gone away backward. — ISAIAH 1:4-7

MOST OF US FAIL TO GRASP THE DEPTHS of depravity into which the United States—and the world—are rapidly sinking, provoking a merciful and patient God to judgment. The evidence is so overwhelming that we're blinded to the truth like the proverbial frog in the pot that is slowly, by small degrees, being brought to a boil. Deceit is everywhere, and lies pass for truth. The major promoter of abortion calls itself *Planned* Parenthood. By what perverted logic can a husband and wife who deliberately murdered in the womb what would have been their baby be called its "parents"? Shouldn't the organization that promotes such foul deeds be called "Planned *No* Parenthood"?

The intent to commit murder in the womb cloaks itself under the innocuous label of "Pro-choice." The "Campaign for Healthy Families" was the group that defeated a proposed ban on abortions in South Dakota. To what "healthy family" do aborted babies belong? In 2006, the National Abortion Federation complained that the Child Interstate Abortion Notification Act "imposed additional harmful burdens on teens seeking abortion" by making it a Federal crime for "a person other than a parent to help a minor . . . obtain an abortion in another state if the minor had not first fulfilled the parental involvement requirements of her home state."[1] So to require minors to get parental approval for an abortion is imposing a "burden"!

Between 1960 and 1990, out-of-wedlock births in the U.S. increased more than 500 percent (from 5.3 percent to 28 percent), single-parent families tripled, about 50 million babies were murdered in the womb, and violent crimes increased 500 percent. About sixteen thousand crimes occur on or around school campuses each day! In 2005, 37 percent of births were to unwed mothers, up from 36 percent in 2004 and 28 percent in 1990. The report stated that "The overall rise reflects the burgeoning number of people who are putting off marriage or are living together without getting married." Are these "stable families" for building a sound society?

Oppression by Protected Minorities

Homosexuals not only flaunt their sin in public, they are fêted, wooed, indulged, and thanked by politicians for voting them into office. It's Sodom and Gomorrah again—or worse! In January 2007, Christian Vanneste, an MP in France's ruling party, under the country's "hate speech law," was fined nearly four thousand dollars for saying that homosexuality is "inferior to heterosexuality" and would be "dangerous for humanity if it became universal." Of course, he was merely stating the truth. But daring to express the simple truth often unleashes the wrath of police and courts in their zeal to protect the feelings of a favored class that complains of being offended.

Homosexuals and lesbians don't procreate as God commanded mankind to do. The Creator's very first commandment to Adam and Eve was "Be fruitful, and multiply, and replenish the earth. . . " (Genesis 1:28). "Gays" seek not children but pleasure, to the exclusion of all else. They defy God's very first words to mankind. And in their self-absorbed folly, they tauntingly boast of their "gay pride." Are they proud that their lifestyle is not only "dangerous" but that it would wipe out the human race if universally adopted? This is the madness of a celebrated perversion.

Vanneste is appealing his case to the European Court of Human Rights, a likely exercise in futility. As of June 2007, there was no forward movement with the case. Truth used to be a sure defense in a lawsuit. Today truth is irrelevant: the issue is whether a "protected minority" or a special interest group has been offended. In Brussels, Vladimir Bukovsky, a former Soviet dissident, warned that "the EU's enforcement of political correctness was a symbol of the Union's slide toward a similar [Soviet-like] oppressive regime."

On October 10, 2004, in Philadelphia, eleven evangelical Christians were arrested and jailed for "praying, singing, and reading Scripture during an annual 'gay pride' event known as 'Outfest.'" The charges were criminal conspiracy, ethnic intimidation, riot, and five misdemeanor charges. Their attorney, Brian Fahling of the American Family Association Center for Law & Policy commented:

> First, symbols of Christianity are removed from the public square. Now, Christians are facing years in prison because they preached the gospel in the public square. Stalin would be proud.[2]

On February 18, 2005, the Philadelphia County Court of Common Pleas dismissed the charges. The harassment of Christians, however, continues worldwide, and the cases are growing in number. "A German priest faces jail time for publicly criticizing abortionists, and in Holland, 'fornicators' and 'adulterers' are protected classes and cannot be criticized."[3]

On October 6, 2006, LifeSiteNews reported, "The gloves have come off, the Parliamentary debate in Canada has moved beyond homosexual 'marriage' and on to refusing freedoms for those with religious beliefs opposed to homosexuality and those with conscientious reasons for opposing it."[4] Hundreds of other examples of "political correctness" gone berserk in defense of immorality throughout the Western world could be cited if space permitted

Sobering Lessons from Europe and England

Visiting Holland, Germany, France, and England today, where the Protestant Reformation challenged Roman Catholicism (which had held the entire Western world in its iron grip for centuries), is inspiring but at the same time disheartening. It is thrilling to visit the Wittenberg Castle Church, where the Reformation began. It held one of Europe's largest collections of religious relics—some nineteen thousand accumulated by Frederick III. Pilgrims viewing all of them would receive indulgences that would allegedly shorten their time in Purgatory by 5,209 years[5]—the largest reduction obtainable in one place outside of Rome.

Of course, these poor souls never suspected that on January 1, 1967, over the signature of Pope Paul VI, as part of Vatican II, their infallible Church would issue its "Apostolic Constitution on the *Revision* of Indulgences," admitting centuries of false promises, undoing all the years of reduction of their purgatorial sufferings deceased Catholics thought they had purchased, and making new requirements they couldn't possibly fulfill, having been dead and presumably still in purgatory after four hundred years of torment in its flames.[6]

This was a different madness that ruled in the Middle Ages. There were tiny vials of "true milk from the Virgin Mary's breasts," preserved fingers and toes of this or that "saint," and enough pieces of wood in Europe venerated as parts of the "true cross" to build a cathedral. Even toenails of "saints" were worshiped by the deluded devout. Peter's toes were uncommonly prolific; enough "certified trimmings" could be gathered from Europe's cathedrals to fill a gunnysack. The big business in the church was selling "indulgences" to release deceased relatives from Purgatory—and who would be such a Scrooge as to refuse to buy Aunt Maria's release from the flames! From such blood money, St. Peter's Basilica was repaired and expanded to become almost what we see today.

No matter how well one knows the story, it is an emotional experience to stand in front of the Wittenberg door. It was there, on October 31, 1517, that Martin Luther nailed his Disputation of the Power and Efficacy of Indulgences, known as the 95 Theses. By 1518, copies had been printed and widely read throughout Europe, opening blind eyes and arousing a wave of rage against the Roman Catholic Church. Luther's brave challenge at the risk of death shook the church and world of his day. Could it happen again—not just to Catholicism (which hasn't changed its unbiblical dogmas and bogus gospel) but to Protestantism as well?

It is also thrilling to stand there and remember the impact of Luther's simple paper—but at the same time it is discouraging. Everywhere, one sees the wreckage that the Reformation has left in its wake: apostate state churches scarcely attended, mostly dead and ineffective and a reproach to Christ instead of being the centers for proclaiming the gospel they once were. "Christian" Europe, to what extent it ever knew Him, has assuredly forsaken the Lord and is beginning to reap in earnest the fruit of the rebellion it has been sowing for a long, long time.

The liberalism of England's universities, media, and courts undermined any sense of God-given morality that had barely survived from the Protestant Reformation. "Multi-culturalism" is the new standard for everything—a multiculturism that embraces every religion and creed. There is one exception: the culture of the host country, England. Why? Because it is Western and has a Christian heritage. That, above all, is not acceptable. Islam most assuredly is in, and Christianity absolutely is out.

In fact, it was the rejection of Chrisitanity that opened Britain to the amoral liberalism prevalent in its courts, media, and universities that now favors Islam above all and is sowing the seeds of its own destruction.

The Islamic Invasion and Delusion

It is more disheartening, if possible—even frightening—to see firsthand the evidence of the "new reformation" sweeping Europe and the world today. A fresh Islamic invasion that is already far more effective than the military invasion that was turned back at Poitier-Tours in 732 and Vienna in the eighteenth century is changing the face of England, France, Holland, Germany, and the other countries that supported the first Reformation. The new privileged "minority" are the Muslim immigrants, many of whom have come in obedience to Muhammad's command (which all Muslims everywhere are obligated to obey) for Muslims, in the name of Allah and Islam, to take over the entire world—by violence, if necessary. Most of them refuse to be integrated into the societies they invade, retaining their own customs and language while demanding "rights" (including welfare support, even of multiple wives) from the country they intend to destroy. The protection of Europe's liberal laws assists terrorists in planning and doing their mischief. Imam Abu Baseer, a leading religious supporter of al-Qaeda, confessed:

> One of the goals of immigration is the revival of the duty of jihad and enforcement of their power over the infidels. Immigration and jihad go together. One is the consequence of the other and dependent upon it. The continuance of the one is dependent upon the continuance of the other.[7]

Christians and Jesus Christ himself may be mocked in the West, but no word must be whispered (for fear of violent reprisals) against the new oppressive minority that is taking over and robbing everyone else of their rights as human beings. One city in England is already 75 percent Muslim and has a Muslim mayor. Of course, non-Muslims move out, property values plummet, allowing more Muslims to move in at bargain prices. Islamists boast that they will eventually have a string of Muslims-only cities in a crescent shape stretching across the heartland of England. They insist that this "crescent" will be ruled by *sharia* (Islamic law), as in Saudi Arabia, where women are stoned to death for "allowing" themselves to be raped, where no non-Muslim place of worship may be built, where those who convert from Islam to any other religion are beheaded, and where Islamic law rules an Islamic state. This is Islam's intent for the entire world.

The cost of opposing Islam or Muhammad far exceeds the judgments decreed by liberal courts against anti-abortionists or anti-gays. The cost that Islam has exacted from the West has already mounted into thousands of lives and billions of dollars. We've seen it in murder and destruction through riots in Paris, trains blown up in Madrid, subways and buses exploding in London, planes flown into the Twin Towers in New York—on and on, worldwide. Yet, in spite of such overwhelming evidence, the same old political correctness insists that all of this horror is in the cause of "peace" because Islam is *peace*— and woe to anyone who dares to speak the truth in correcting that lie!

In spite of the many lives already sacrificed in England to Muslim terrorism, "Britain's leading police officer, the Metropolitan Police Commissioner

Sir Ian Blair, was himself rebuked 'for hanging his own officers out to dry' to prove his anti-racist credentials." Though a tribunal ruled that he had disproportionately disciplined three white officers for what he called "Islamophobic" remarks, "he was 'unrepentant' . . . declaring that the Met had to 'embrace diversity.'"[8]

"Muslim sensitivities [are] uppermost in police minds." They will "go to almost any lengths to avoid . . . the charge of 'Islamophobia.'" Incredibly, after 9/11 and again after the London bombings of 2005, government instructions were for police "to avoid doing anything to alienate Britain's Muslims." As a practical matter, "this meant the police had to deny the nature of Islamist terrorism altogether.

"This was why, on the day that four Islamist suicide bombers blew themselves and more than fifty London commuters to bits, the Met's deputy assistant commissioner, Brian Paddick, stood before the television cameras and made the noteworthy comment: 'As far as I am concerned, Islam and terrorists are two words that do not go together.'"[9] Such whitewashing of Islam by high officials in the face of thirteen hundred years of terrorism by Muslims, which has killed millions, has become the scandal of the century. Nevertheless, "British police say they do not use the phrase 'Islamic terrorism' or even 'Islamist terrorism.'" Yet Mansoor Ijaz, a prominent Pakistani-American businessman and commentator warned shortly after the first London attacks:

> It is hypocritical for Muslims living in western societies to demand civil rights enshrined by the state and then excuse their inaction against terrorists hiding among them. . . . It is time to stand up and be counted as model citizens before the terror consumes us all.[10]

How Did This Happen?

Much of the fault lies with psychology and its creation of a society from which sin and blame have been banished and everyone has been turned into a victim: of childhood deprivation or abuse, of being raised in a "dysfunctional family," of "low self-esteem" or "poor self-image," especially "feelings of inferiority," the curing of which James Dobson suggests would solve everything from teen rebellion to suicide to drug addiction, pornography, and abortion.[11]

From secular psychology, Christian psychology has brought into the church the idea that the problem isn't really a sinful heart but one's victimhood: "People aren't actually sinners; deep down they're really 'good at heart,' and victims of circumstances beyond their control." This attitude, too, blinds

Britain and Europe to the true threat that it faces. As Melanie Phillips so perceptively points out:

> Britain is in Denial. Having allowed the country to turn into a global hub of the Islamic jihad . . . the British establishment is still failing . . . to acknowledge what it is actually facing and take the appropriate action. Instead, it is deep into a policy of appeasement of the phenomenon that threatens it . . . in a panic-stricken attempt to curry favor and buy off the chances of any further attacks. . . .
>
> The fervent embrace of "victim culture" means instead that this minority has to be treated on its own assessment as a victim of the majority and its grievances [as though they] are the cause of terrorism. . . . The deeply rooted British belief that violence always arises from rational grievances . . . created a widespread climate of irrationality and prejudice in which the principal victims of the war against the West, America, and Israel, are demonized instead as its cause. . . .
>
> Yet the vast majority of the French rioters were Muslims; the rioters screamed "Allahu akhbar" [Allah is the greatest], talked about jihad and expressed admiration for Osama bin Laden. . . . [12]

Astonishing and Enlightening

Though they knew that London had become a headquarters for Islamic terrorism worldwide, the British police, even after 9/11, still took no action against Islamist jihadists in London. The willful blindness to indisputable facts was incredible. "Security officials confessed they had no idea the youths . . . convicted in the Yemeni capital, Aden, of plotting terrorist attacks against British targets . . . had been recruited from mosques around England and were being trained at special 'terrorist camps' sponsored by Osama bin Laden. 'It was a complete shock to us, and it was a shock that chilled us to the bone,' a [security] source said." [13]

As one author remarked dryly, "British security officials seem to specialize in being 'shocked' time and again by such developments—then doing nothing about them." The Yemenis urged Britain "to do something about Abu Hamza [who] was masterminding the terror from the mosque in Finsbury Park [yet] the British did nothing." [14]

"Over the years, the governments of India, Saudi Arabia, Turkey, Israel, France, Algeria, Peru, Yemen and Russia, among others, lodged . . . protests about the presence in Britain of terrorist organizations or their sympathizers.

". . . Egypt denounced Britain as a hotbed for radicals. . . . Of its fourteen most-wanted terrorists, seven were based in Britain. . . . Many countries asked Britain to extradite radicals back to the countries they were threatening but were turned down, often by the courts. . . .

"Security officials in countries that for years had been watching the relentless development of 'Londonistan' with incredulity and exasperation . . . could not understand why successive British governments had allowed so many extremists and terrorist godfathers to enter Britain, take up residence and be left undisturbed to organize, recruit for, fund and disseminate the jihad against the West, often being paid generous welfare benefits to do so."[15]

The answer was in the multi-culturism (every culture and religion is equally good—except for Christianity, which must be jettisoned because of its narrow-minded claim that Jesus Christ is the only way to God) and the "victimism" promoted by psychology, which has translated into liberal politicians, universities, media, and churches. In a word, British society has lost its moral foundation, as even secular commentaries realized, because it had for all practical purposes thrown out its Judeo-Christian foundation based upon the Bible. As Melanie Phillips explains:

> In the early 1980s, Ray Honeyford, a Bradford [today a heavily Muslim area] headmaster at a school where languages such as Urdu, Gujurati and Hindi predominated over English, protested Bradford council's policy of educating ethnic minority children according to their own culture. . . . Honeyford wanted to teach English as a first language and teach the history, culture and customs of this country, so that children of all cultures and creeds could identify with and participate in the society of which they were a part. He was accused of racial prejudice and hounded out of education, retiring early to save his family from further harassment. . . .
>
> The underlying message in the classroom was that there was no historical truth at all, and whatever had happened in the past [including the crucifixion of Christ for our sins and His resurrection] was only a matter of opinion. . . . [A]t the heart of this unpicking of national identity lies a repudiation of Christianity, the founding faith of the nation and the fundamental source of its values, including its . . . profound love of liberty. . . . Britain's Christian identity is fast becoming notional. Few go to church; even fewer send their children to Sunday school. For the secular elite, Britain is now a "post-Christian" society; and insofar as this is not yet the case, this elite is determined to make it so. Under the rubric of multiculturalism and promoting "diversity," local authorities and government bodies are systematically bullying Christianity out of existence. . . .

The Christian outreach group Faith Works . . . run with a clear Christian ethos . . . has one of the smallest reoffending rates of any young offenders' program in the country. Yet discussions with local and central government about replicating it stalled because the councils wanted to do so without the Christian ethos—which was responsible for its success. . . .

In other words, "diversity" is a fig leaf. . . . What is clearly not part of "diversity," however, is to put the Christian faith into practice. The "diversity" agenda is thus a cover for an attack on Christianity, on the illogical premise that it is divisive and exclusive whereas minority faiths are not. At the same time, antireligion is being positively encouraged. Prison inmates are now allowed to practice paganism in their cells. . . .

And as multiculturalism thus unwittingly fomented Islamist radicalism in the sacred cause of "diversity," it simultaneously forbade criticism of Muslim practices such as forced marriages or polygamy, or the withdrawal of children from school to be sent for long periods to Pakistan. Even to draw attention to such practices was to be labeled a racist. . . . And so, as British identity was steadily eviscerated by multiculturalism, real human rights abuses on British shores were studiously ignored and its victims left abandoned in its name.[16]

In the Meantime, the Church. . .

"Ecumenism" has done to the church what "diversity" has done to the secular world. To speak of "right" and "wrong" doctrine is to express one's narrow-minded prejudices, according to the "positive thinking" that all must adopt. Through errors that "Christian" psychology has brought into "Christianity"— false doctrines that have wedded it to the world—something dreadful has happened to the church founded by Christ at Pentecost, having purchased it with His blood, shed on the Cross.

The Reformation recovered the gospel and opened the way for fiery preachers such as Moody, Billy Sunday, Wesley, Whitefield, et al. Led by souls aflame with Christ's love such as William Carey, Isobel Kuhn, David Livingstone, Robert Moffat, C. T. Studd, Hudson Taylor, and many others, the gospel spread around the world. In those early days, Britain was the leader, showing how far she has fallen.

Gradually apostasy set in. The fervent love for Christ, based on true gratitude for His death on the Cross for our sins, grew cold. Burning passion to "rescue the perishing" became a dying ember of memories of past missionary sacrifices for lost souls enshrined in cold stone and bronze memorials but no longer in hearts. To a new generation, these memories were embarrassing reminders of Britain's imperialism, which had "forced" native peoples to adopt Western culture. The truth of Christianity, the fear of God, and the solemn warning of "after death, the judgment" were seen as prejudicial accusations that some religions (no matter how hellish) were actually wrong—an *attitude* (truth no longer existed) that aroused prejudice against "minorities," causing them to react with "justifiable" violence.

By the latter part of the twentieth century, televangelists were preaching prosperity, psychologists were the leading influence in the church, personalities were followed instead of Christ, and entertainment was the secret of "church growth," which became the favorite excuse for all manner of errors to enter. The "leaders" looked up to by much if not most of the church in the late twentieth century were no longer men and women of God who stood vocally for, and with their lives modeled, sound doctrine. They were stars of stage and screen and popular athletes—personalities to be worshiped in the place of God, many of whose lives, beneath the show, were morally bankrupt. Even the secular world mocked them, while the church continued to be deceived. Of Jim and Tammy Bakker, one humorist wrote

How could such a grasping, shallow and flagrantly self-absorbed couple manage to acquire such a large and fervent [Christian]following. . . ? I think the Bakkers were successful because they personalized a very appealing, very convenient moral philosophy that flourished in the '80s, a philosophy that can be summarized as follows: You can't do good unto others unless you feel good about yourself, and you can't feel good about yourself unless you have a lot of neat stuff.[17]

It was precisely these values that "Christian psychology" had introduced and nourished in the church. One has to be blind indeed not to see the abandonment of God and His Word as the cause of what has happened in Europe and Britain. The rejection of the truth of the gospel created the unwillingness to speak the truth in order not to find fault with any culture (above all, Islam), no matter how paganistic or violent. One must be blind also not to realize that American culture, politics, education, and media are following in Britain's and Europe's staggering footsteps along the broad road to destruction.

God's pronouncement of pending judgment upon Israel cannot help but apply to America today: "They have forsaken the LORD, they have provoked the Holy One of Israel unto anger, they are gone away backward" (Isaiah 1:4–7).

Let each of us who still believe the truth, and love of Lord, fall on our faces before Him, cling, weeping, to His nail-pierced feet, and repent of our own sins of omission and commission and those of our country and the church at large. It may be that God's hand of judgment will be stayed from falling upon us long enough to afford one last opportunity to preach the gospel freely and to win many out of this morally bankrupt world to Christ and eternal life with Him in heaven.

1. http://www.prochoice.org/policy/policyreports/legislative_2006.html.

2. http://www.lifesite.net/idn/2004/dec/04/04121704.html.

3. http://www.wnd.com/news/article.asp?ARTICLE_ID=54260.

4. http://ca.altermedia.info/news/general/page/2/.

5. Martin Treu, *Martin Luther in Wittenberg: A Biographical Tour* (Wittenberg: Saxon-Anhalt Luther Memorial Foundation, 2003), 15.

6. *Vatican Council II: The Conciliar and Post Conciliar Documents*, General Editor Austin Flannery, O.P. (Northport, NY: Costello Publishing Company, 1988 Revised Edition), Volume I, 62-79.

7. Stephen Ulph, "Londonistan," *Terrorism Monitor* (Jamestown Center), vol. 2, no. 4, February 26, 2004.

8. Nicole Martin, *Daily Telegraph*, June 26, 2005.

9. Ian Herbert, *Independent*, July 8, 2005, cited in Melanie Phillips, *Londonistan* (New York: Encounter Books, 2006), 33.

10. Mansoor Ijaz, *Financial Times*, July 11, 2005.

11. James Dobson, *Hide or Seek* (Revell, 1974), 12-13.

12. Melanie Phillips, *Londonistan* (New York: Encounter Books, 2006), 182-84.

13. Kathryn Knight, *Mail on Sunday*, September 23, 2001.

14. Phillips, *Londonistan*, 38-39.

15. Ibid., 36-41.

16. Ibid., 64-69.

17. Dave Barry, "Jim and Tammy Faye Bakker: Their Game Was Jack-in-the-Pulpit, Their Downfall a Divine Comedy of Finger Pointing," *People Weekly,* Extra, Fall 1989, 70.

GOD AS YOU CONCEIVE HIM, HER, IT TO BE

— Dave Hunt —

ONE OF SATAN'S MOST SUCCESSFUL delusions, which many in both the world and church have welcomed with a sigh of relief as an escape from personal guilt, is psychology's redefinition of sin as sickness. This stroke of the pen is one of the major foundation stones of psychology, whether secular or Christian. It manifests itself almost everywhere.

Even those who have committed premeditated murder can be declared "not guilty by reason of insanity." Habitual fornicators and adulterers are no longer looked upon as willful sinners but are treated at Christian psychiatric facilities as "sex addicts" to be pitied rather than condemned. Of course there is no such thing as a "drunkard" anymore. The new word is "alcoholic." This relatively new "incurable disease" gives added respect to those who valiantly fight it all their lives, especially those honest enough to "come out of the closet" and join Alcoholics Anonymous (A.A.).

In society's eyes, there is now something almost admirable in declaring oneself to be a "recovering alcoholic" who bravely faces up to the alleged fact that the battle to stave off this horrible sickness of the psyche must be fought to the end of one's life. That diagnosis evokes sympathy rather than the contempt that habitual drunkenness used to arouse. Such is the "courageous" stance that Rick Warren's Celebrate Recovery program, which has spread to thousands of churches, encourages its participants to take—a brave "standing for Jesus" by another "oppressed minority."

The devastation wrought worldwide by A.A., founded in 1935, has been enormous through the spread of its 12-Steps program. One can scarcely keep track of the many 12-Steps groups A.A. has spawned: Adult Children of Alcoholics, Debtors Anonymous, Emotions Anonymous, Gamblers Anonymous, Sex Addicts Anonymous, Shoplifters Anonymous (to name a few)—and now even Fundamentalists Anonymous for "recovery" from fundamentalism. In a book that every Christian ought to read, *12 Steps to Destruction*, Martin and Deidre Bobgan point out, "Thousands of groups across America . . . and most codependency/recovery programs utilize the Twelve Steps in one way or another. . . . "

New Age psychiatrist M. Scott Peck (a pseudo-Christian promoted as a genuine Christian by many church leaders) has called the founding of Alcoholics Anonymous in Akron, Ohio, on June 10, 1935, "the greatest event of the twentieth century."[1] *Christianity Today* says, "The 12-Step movement has tapped a profound need in people.[2] Best-selling Christian author Keith Miller (who advocates visualizing Christ to become more intimate with him) calls the 12-Steps program "a way of spiritual healing and growth that may well be the most important spiritual model of any age for many contemporary Christians."[3]

Such praise for A.A. from Christian leaders is astounding. The truth is that its 12 Steps came by direct dictation from the demonic world. These "willingly ignorant leaders" (2 Peter 3:5) open the door to the occult by introducing members to a false god. *Step Two* says, ". . . came to believe that a Power greater than ourselves could restore us to sanity." Step 3 continues, ". . . made a decision to turn our will and our lives over to God as we [Hindu, Buddhist, Christian, Mormon, shaman, agnostic, et al.] understood Him."

A.A. Is Christian?

Nevertheless, in a featured article in *Christianity Today*, Tim Stafford says, "The 12 Steps are Christian."[4] Why would he say that? They contain no mention either of Jesus Christ or the gospel. In fact, they are thoroughly *anti-Christian*. An official A.A. publication says, "You can, if you wish, make A.A. itself your 'Higher Power.'"[5] Stafford himself admits that A.A. founder Bill Wilson "never pledged his loyalty to Christ, never was baptized, never joined a Christian church. . . ."[6] Instead, the Christian church has joined A.A!

Sadly, the greatest boost the "12 Steps" ever received was the spread into thousands of churches of Rick Warren's Celebrate Recovery (CR), which is based upon A.A.'s 12-Steps program, in spite of Rick's staunch denials. (See "A Way Which Seemeth Right" by T. A. McMahon in this book.)

Stafford and *Christianity Today* are pleased with A.A. to the point of suggesting that Episcopalian pastor Sam Shoemaker (who mentored Wilson) "may have made his greatest contribution through Wilson."[7] Yet Stafford also writes, "A.A. is pluralistic, recognizing as many gods as there may be religions. . . ."[8] Helping this heresy get started—a heresy that has corrupted the world and church—was a pastor's "greatest contribution"? To what? To Satan's coming world religion?

The Willow Creek Community Church of South Barrington, Illinois, pastored by Bill Hybels, is one of thousands of churches sponsoring 12-Steps programs. Willow Creek has been called "the most influential church in North America"[9] and a model of the church for the twenty-first century.

In an exhaustive study of Willow Creek, G. A. Pritchard writes,

> One of the first staff members I spoke with proudly told me
> how more than five hundred individuals met at the church each
> week in various self-help groups (e.g., Alcoholics Anonymous,
> Emotions Anonymous, Sexual Anonymous [etc.]). . . . One of the
> requirements of these organizations was that individuals could not
> evangelize or otherwise teach other participants about God.[10]

Of course. This is an A.A. official prohibition enforced everywhere. And
this is "Christian"? Stafford commends 12-Steps groups for being "tolerant."[11]
Should we commend a tolerance for false gods that denies the difference
between God's truth and Satan's lie? Note the "tolerant" rules for the 12-Steps
programs at Willow Creek:

> The Steps suggest a belief in a Power greater than ourselves, "God
> as we understand Him." The Program does not attempt to tell us
> what our Higher Power must be.
>   It can be whatever we choose, for example, human love, a
> force for good, the group itself, nature, the universe, or the tradi-
> tional God (Deity).
>   The code instructs, "We never discuss religion."[12]

All Christians are commanded to "earnestly contend for the faith which
was once delivered unto the saints" (Jude 3). How, then, can Willow Creek
sponsor the promotion of false gods and false gospels? Stafford says, "Christians
[in A.A. groups] can express their convictions." Yet he notes that A.A. does not
allow Christians to say anything that would suggest "that others' views of God
are misguided."[13] So, actually a Christian (like a Mason) is free to say that
Jesus is one, or his, "Higher Power" but not "the way, the truth, the life" (John
14:6). Why commend this intolerantly anti-Christian "tolerance"?

The truth is that the false gospel of A.A. suppresses the true gospel of Jesus
Christ; and the tolerance it professes is only of error, while it remains intolerant
of truth. Pritchard comments,

> Even church members could not talk about Christian truth in
> these meetings. . . . Although the programs give lip service to a
> "Higher Power," they function as practical atheism, teaching the
> categories of the contemporary psychological worldview. . . .
>   That Willow Creek would sponsor and advertise these pro-
> grams illustrates the church's lack of priority for educating its
> members in Christian truth.[14]

Nevertheless, in *Christianity Today*, Stafford writes with approval, "The 12 Steps penetrate every level of American society." That fact is all the more reason not to commend and call it "Christian" but to sound the alarm against A.A.'s false god and gospel. Referring to Bill Wilson, Stafford admits that after supposed deliverance from alcohol, "the rest of his life was morally erratic." Yet CT declares, "The 12 Steps are a package of Christian practices and nothing is compromised in using them."[15]

Words have lost their meaning. Truth has been drowned in tsunami of compromise. The gospel and the eternal destiny of souls are being sacrificed on the altar of appeasement of alcoholics and psychologists.

A New "Diagnosis" and False Label

Founder of A.A. Bill Wilson was what the Bible calls a "drunkard" (Proverbs 23:21; 1 Corinthians 5:11, etc.). Martin and Deidre Bobgan pick up the story: "After years of struggling with the guilt and condemnation that came from thinking that his drinking was his own fault and that it stemmed from a moral defect in his character, Wilson was relieved to learn from a medical doctor that his drinking was due to an 'allergy.'"[16] A.A.'s official biography of Wilson relates,

> Bill listened, entranced, as [Dr.] Silkworth explained his theory. For the first time in his life, Bill was hearing about alcoholism not as a lack of will power, not as a moral defect, but as a legitimate illness. . . . Bill's relief was immense.[17]

Dr. Silkworth's theory might have remained in obscurity had not Bill Wilson founded Alcoholics Anonymous upon it, and millions of drunkards, as happy as Wilson to be relieved of accountability to God and a guilty conscience, turned that theory into a universally accepted axiom. What a relief to exchange the God who judges man's sin for a "higher power" that judges no one! The fact is, however, that the theory that alcoholism is a disease is false.

A leading authority in this field, University of California professor Herbert Fingarette, has written an entire book[18] as well as numerous articles refuting the "alcoholism is a disease" delusion. Writing for Harvard Medical School, Fingarette refers to "a mass of scientific evidence . . . which radically challenges every major belief generally associated with the phrase 'alcoholism is a disease.'"[19]

Stanton Peele, author of *Diseasing of America: Addiction Treatment Out of Control*, offers research to show that multitudes have been "brainwashed" to believe they have the disease of alcoholism—and that the result has been to impede the normal recovery which otherwise takes place.[20] Why doesn't *Christianity Today* carry articles that give the careful judgment of science rather than promoting a false diagnosis that is so damaging to souls and jeopardizes their eternal destiny?

It is astonishing how Christian leaders can remain blindly ignorant of well-known and indisputable facts and how prone they often are to promote not only unbiblical but unscientific and occult techniques for personal improvement because they are recommended by psychologists. Here we have an "authority" that no one may question. To do so is to be banned from Christian radio and television because the truth "might offend some listeners or viewers."

Dale Ryan, Baptist pastor who became executive director of the National Association for Christian Recovery, claims that "the Christian community . . . is the source of the 12 Steps." He considers it a major tragedy that the "Christian wisdom that's embodied in the 12 Steps got separated . . . from the mainstream of the church."[21] Such ill-informed statements are not only destructive but inexcusable.

Harmful but Widely Accepted Misinformation

The facts refute Stafford's and *CT*'s false assurance, which, because of *CT*'s reputation as a leading Christian magazine, has been accepted by thousands if not millions in the church: "The 12-Steps . . . are Christian practices, and nothing is compromised in using them. We [Christians] ought to use them gladly. They belong to us originally. They are doing tremendous good."[22] So demonically inspired automatic writing was given to the church by God?

It is an irrefutable and alarming fact that 12-Steps programs are doing great harm by turning people away from the true God to a false "higher power" and by denying the sufficiency of God's Word and robbing multitudes of the Holy Spirit's transforming power. It is reprehensible for *Christianity Today*, Willow Creek, or anyone who claims to be a Christian, to encourage participation in 12-Steps programs. Yet Rick Warren's 12-Steps Celebrate Recovery, which is based upon A.A., is now in more than five thousand churches. Even though we have given him the irrefutable evidence that A.A.'s 12-Steps came out of the occult, nothing has changed in Celebrate Recovery to this date. Rick persists in the belief that Bill Wilson was a Christian.

There can be no question about the fact that A.A., with its higher-power-as-you-understand-it (i.e., "God as you conceive Him, Her, or It to be"), not only came from an occult source but opens the door to occultism. The official

A.A. biography of Wilson reveals that for years after A.A's founding, regular séances were still being held in the Wilsons' home, and other occult activities were being pursued:

> There are references to seances and other psychic events. . . . Bill would . . . "get" these things [from the spirit world] . . . long sentences, word by word would come through. . . .[23]
>
> As he started to write [the A.A. manual], he asked for guidance. . . . The words began tumbling out with astonishing speed.[24]

Encountering A.A.'s "Higher Power"

It's a matter of record that A.A.'s 12 Steps were actually received verbatim from the demonic world. It is not surprising, then, that the effect of A.A. upon many of its members has been to lead them into occult involvement. In 1958, Wilson wrote to Sam Shoemaker,

> Throughout A.A., we find a large amount of psychic phenomena, nearly all of it spontaneous. Alcoholic after alcoholic tells me of such experiences . . . [which] run nearly the full gamut of everything we see in the books.
>
> In addition to my original mystical experience, I've had a lot of such phenomenalism myself.[25]

Wilson's "original mystical experience" was his alleged "conversion"—a classic occult encounter: "Suddenly the room lit up with a great white light. I was caught up into an ecstasy . . . it burst upon me that I was a free man . . . a wonderful feeling of Presence, and I thought to myself, 'So this is the God of the preachers!' A great peace stole over me. . . ."[26]

This was not the "God of the preachers" but the one who transforms himself "into an angel of light" (2 Corinthians 11:14). This comforting, mystical light, accompanied by an overwhelming feeling of acceptance and love, is commonly encountered upon one's initial entrance into the occult. Those returning from "clinical death" testify to the same experience, which has given them the assurance that "acceptance by a Higher Power," not judgment, follows death, and that there is nothing to fear.

The experience was so profound that Wilson never touched alcohol again. Satan would be more than willing to deliver a man from alcoholism in this life if he could thereby ensnare him for eternity and inspire him to lead millions to the same destruction!

Wilson joined the Oxford Group and regularly attended its meetings at Calvary Church (NY), pastored by Episcopalian Sam Shoemaker. Shoemaker urged his hearers to "accept God however they might conceive of him. . . . "[27] Here was the origin of Step Three's "God as we understood him." It was a clever deception from the master of lies himself that A.A. would spread around the world—even into presumably evangelical churches.

The true God of the Bible does not respond to those who call upon false gods. Neither the conscience sensitive to the witness of the Holy Spirit nor basic common sense would accept this belief in a god who fits anyone's wildest imagination. God expects us to know Him for who He really is. Jesus said, "And this is life eternal, that they might know thee the only true God, and Jesus Christ, whom thou hast sent" (John 17:3). God's judgment comes upon them "that know not God, and that obey not the gospel of our Lord Jesus Christ" (2 Thessalonians 1:8). This is not "narrow-minded fundamentalism" but the solemn truth.

The Oxford Group and Moral Re-Armament Connection

The Oxford Group (no formal affiliation with the University of Oxford) was founded by American Missionary Frank Buchman (a Lutheran minister) and attracted student leaders and athletes at Oxford. From that small beginning it grew rapidly and spread to many countries. Sam Shoemaker became a leader in the Oxford Group movement in the United States, holding meetings at his Calvary Episcopal Church in New York. Bill Wilson had gone to many Oxford meetings but without receiving any real help.

Prior to World War II, the Oxford Group changed its name to Moral Re-Armament (MRA) through the mystical "guidance" that was a large part of Buchman's life. This belief that by "listening" one could receive directly from God divine direction for every part of life carried over both into MRA and Alcoholics Anonymous. Bill Wilson wrote, "Early A.A. got its ideas of self-examination, acknowledgement of character defects, restitution for harm, and working with others straight from the Oxford Groups and directly from Sam Shoemaker . . . and nowhere else."[28] Certainly not from God or His Word.

MRA emphasized a mystical reception of "guidance from God," which recipients would write down and follow as though their thoughts were God's Word to be obeyed. This unbiblical and dangerous procedure, widely practiced even by evangelicals today as an integral part of some Christian psychology, has led multitudes astray. "Listening" for direction makes one susceptible to misdirection either from one's own thoughts or from demonic intrusion, to both of which one easily becomes vulnerable when in a passive state of consciousness, "seeking guidance."

One former associate points out that the Oxford Group "Quiet Time" gradually became

> . . . less and less a time of Bible study and prayer and increasingly a time of "listening to God." This members did with their minds blank and with pencil and paper in hand, writing down the thoughts that came to them. In this way men received entirely irrational guidance . . . regarded as authoritative. . . . They tended to lose their concern for doctrine and to end up less definite about the gospel. . . . [29]

British author and former MRA member Roy Livesey writes, "MRA had been a stepping stone for me into the occult."[30] Vineyard members have been trained in much the same way by John Wimber and his successors to receive alleged words of knowledge and to prophesy—a major explanation of how occult phenomenon entered the Vineyard churches. Christian psychology played a major role in the first Vineyards in Santa Monica and the San Fernando Valley in the very beginning, under the direction of founder Kenn Gullikson.

The influence of this concept of receiving direct communication from the spirit realm (kept alive in the church today through charismatics, some pentecostals, televangelists such as Copeland, Hinn, Pat Robertson, Oral Roberts, authors such as Richard Foster, and many others) can be seen in A.A.'s Step Eleven. It calls for "meditation to improve our conscious contact with God as we understood Him. . . . " This MRA/A.A. relationship is acknowledged by Dick B., one of the biographers of the movement.[31] Moral Re-Armament eventually changed its name to Initiatives of Change. In 1965, members founded "Up With People," which sponsored singing groups that spread MRA teachings far and wide.

It was out of the Oxford Group that *God Calling* came, one of the best-selling "Christian" books of all time—and one of the most deceptive. Written by "two listeners," it purports to be the very words of Jesus dictated to them as they placed themselves in the proper "receptive" state and wrote them down as the words spontaneously "came." The relationship between this occult technique of getting messages from "Jesus" and Step Eleven and the openness in both to the occult is no mere coincidence. What this "Christ" says in *God Calling*, however, could not possibly have come from the historical Jesus Christ of the Bible because what He allegedly says contradicts the Bible repeatedly. Here is part of what this "Jesus" said:

> Our deliberate imagining of something with the intention of making that thing come into existence will produce the desired result. God is within every man. . . . Man needs only to quieten all sense distraction and turn inwards to commune with the 'God within.' By means of thought-power, word-repetition, and visualization, it is possible to contact and feel Christ's presence on earth beside us.[32]

"Experience" Instead of Truth

Being in part a step-child of psychology (Bill Wilson had consulted with Carl Jung), it is not surprising that A.A.'s emphasis is upon the "experience" of recovery. In contrast, Christ emphasized moral and spiritual freedom based upon truth as revealed in His Word: "If ye continue in my word, then are ye my disciples indeed; and ye shall know the truth, and the truth will make you free" (John 8:31–32). The mantra of Christian psychologists, however, as we have repeatedly explained, is "all truth is God's truth." By that view, the Bible does not contain all of the moral and spiritual truth we need. It appears we also need help from Jung, Freud, and other godless psychologists and psychiatrists who couldn't get their own lives in order. Interestingly, Jung advised Rowland Hazard, a wealthy drunk from Rhode Island who had come to Switzerland to consult him, that there was no hope for him unless he could find it in religion. He went back to America and was "cured" through the Oxford Group.

Satan cleverly uses mystical experiences for turning men from God's truth to his lies. Tragically, experience and emotion, more than the Word of God, seem to fuel the "revivals" that supposedly have occurred within the past thirty years. A good example is the "revival" that was all the rage for several years at the Brownsville Assembly of God in Pensacola, Florida, until it sputtered to a halt. Such a fizzle is inevitable, sooner or later, if experience rather than Holy Spirit conviction based upon the truth of God's Word is fanning the flames.

MRA founder Frank Buchman compromised the gospel and embraced new "revelations" through occult guidance. As a result, MRA helped to set the stage for the New Age movement. One of Buchman's close associates during the '40s and '50s writes,

> MRA was est and TM. It was consciousness raising and sensitivity. It was encounter and confrontation. Frank Buchman was drying

out drunks before A.A.'s Bill W had his first cocktail. He was moving hundreds of people in hotel ballrooms to "share" with each other before Werner Erhard was born. He inspired thousands on all continents to meditate . . . decades before Maharishi Mahesh Yogi left India. He was indeed Mr. Human Potential, ahead of his time. . . . Paul Tournier [originator of "the medicine of the person"] . . . has frequently expressed his debt to Buchman for much of his own approach to [psychological] counseling.[33]

Tournier and his connection to Buchman and MRA provide another link with so-called Christian psychology. MRA became active in more than fifty countries and achieved NGO (Non-Governmental Organization) status with the United Nations, which it enjoys today. The principal conference center of Initiatives of Change was formerly the largest and most luxurious hotel in Switzerland. Located in the village of Caux high above Montreux, it has been a mecca to which world leaders have been drawn for years. The setting, looking down from high above upon Lake Geneva far below and stretching out into the distance with the snow-clad French Alps rising alongside, is exceptionally magnificent even for Switzerland.

While living in that area, my wife Ruth and I with our four young children made several visits to Caux in 1966 and 1967. We met Gandhi's grandson, who was there with an "Up With People" singing group from India. We spoke with many whose lives had been "transformed" through impressive spiritual experiences and who had a compelling zeal to "change the world" through MRA principles. They used "Christian" phrases yet didn't seem to know Christ or His Word. MRA and A.A., which quickly went so far astray, are tragic reminders of the necessity of adhering to sound doctrine and the need for daily washing in God's Word (John 15:3; Ephesians 5:26).

Psychotherapy, as we have documented in this volume, offers false hope. Numerous clinical studies indicate that psychotherapy works best on "alcoholics" when combined with the A.A. program. The two are closely related in that both reject the sole authority of the Bible and focus on the patient's "self" to work the cure. Clinical psychologists, secular or Christian, are happy to partner with anything that seems to "work," and A.A. has proved to be very compatible. Of course, A.A. was never truly Christian as MRA appeared to be in its early days, nor did it take long until the latter had "changed the truth of God into a lie" (Romans 1:25), leading millions far from the truth as it "is in Jesus" (Ephesians 4:21).

Changing the World

Many Christian groups that seemingly started out well have departed from the faith because they didn't want to be perceived as narrow minded and felt that broadening their language would help them reach a wider audience. Each compromise (always, of course, for the worthy purpose of reaching more "key people") only gets worse. Such was the case with the YMCA and YWCA, which were originally Christian organizations. This same compromise that the flesh imagines surely would be the best way to "change the world for Christ" has afflicted most denominations and many Christian organizations. Of course, World Vision long ago ceased to be a Christian organization devoted to evangelism and now focuses on assuaging physical hunger and thirst rather than the spiritual counterpart. In the process, it turned against Israel. In the Middle East, it gives assistance to everyone but God's chosen people, the "apple of his eye" (Deuteronomy 32:10; Lamentations 2:18; Zechariah 2:18).

Christ called us to preach the gospel, not to "change the world." As soon as the latter ambitious and unbiblical goal becomes the motivation, the steeply downward path to further compromise, and even heresy, has begun. Already by the early 1940s, in his zeal to "change the world," Buchman, once a missionary devoted to the gospel, had become so blind to the truth that he declared that MRA was "the full message of Jesus Christ."[34] The comments of former MRA member Roy Livesey are instructive:

> Buchman was now poised to integrate people of other religions and faiths into MRA and to reach out to leaders and politicians like [Mahatma] Gandhi in India, Adenauer in Germany and many others.
>
> MRA was now more involved with the "universal religious experience" rather than Christianity. . . . Leading supporter Rajmohan Gandhi, grandson of the Mahatma . . . declared that MRA was the one thing on which Eastern and Western countries can unite.[35]

This broadminded and ecumenical promotion of generic "spirituality" has a strong appeal to the world and contributed greatly to Buchman's remarkable success. One piece of MRA literature was "believed to be the largest, simultaneous, global distribution of any single literary publication in history . . . 75 million copies."[36] An MRA film, *The Crowning Experience*, with endorsements from leaders such as a former prime minister of Japan and boxer Sugar Ray Robinson, was credited with playing a major role in "bringing a solution to [discrimination in] Little Rock [Arkansas]."[37] But who was receiving Jesus Christ as Lord and Savior?

This changing of the world for Christ seemed to be working with amazing success, but that success only created more compromise. Buchman even had a notable impact on diplomacy during the Cold War. The United States Ambassador to Moscow, Admiral William H. Stanley, declared, "The choice for America is Moral Re-Armament or Communism."[38] MRA's worldwide influence caused the Communists to strike back. Moscow radio broadcast,

> Moral Re-Armament is a global ideology with bridgeheads in every nation in its final phase of total expansion throughout the world. It has the power to capture radical revolutionary minds. It is contaminating the minds of the masses.[39]

There is nothing so deadly as false religion. Every false concept of God (from the *Star Wars* Force to A.A.'s "higher power as you conceive it to be") provides a front for Satan and his minions. Counterfeit miracles of the mind, mystical experiences, and false guidance act as enticements along the well-worn path to occult bondage that ensnares those who will not bow in obedient submission to God and His Word alone. Satan is not an atheist but the "god of this world" (2 Corinthians 4:4), the founder and leader of all of the world's religions.

The same compromise that seduced the Oxford movement (which was never firmly anchored in God's word) when "changing the world" became its focus is corrupting Youth With A Mission, InterVarsity Christian Fellowship, Campus Crusade for Christ, and other organizations in their equally zealous and well-meaning but equally misguided desire to "change the world for Christ." The compromise of ecumenism opens the door to what seems at first to be only a tiny trickle of error far outweighed by the "good" the compromise seems to produce. But that seeming trickle of error soon becomes a flood sweeping sound doctrine away altogether.

Psychology is a tsunami in itself. Its pretense of being scientific has a great appeal in an age that worships science. Christians by the millions are only too happy to have "science" on their side, imagining that more souls can be won with such backing. This religion of the mind with no scientific proof to support it and known as psychology is one of Satan's master strokes of genius. Its tentacles now reach into nearly every evangelical church, university, and seminary.

As J. Vernon McGee, about twenty years ago, declared concerning psychology's transformation of the church: "If this trend continues, it will be the destruction of the evangelical church." This book is a wake-up alarm and an appeal to all who love God's Word to stand against this evil in the world round about and especially in the church. It is not enough to declare that God's Word is inerrant and infallible. We must also prove from the Bible and with our lives that it is sufficient to guide and empower us in "*all* things that pertain unto life and godliness" (2 Peter 1:3).

---

1. Tim Stafford, "The Hidden Gospel of the 12 Steps: Understanding the origins of the recovery movement can help Christians know how to relate to it today," *Christianity Today*, July 22, 1991.

2. Michael G. Maudlin, "Addicts in the Pew," *Christianity Today*, July 22, 1991, 19-21.

3. Ibid.

4. Stafford, "Hidden," *Christianity*, 14-21.

5. *Twelve Steps and Twelve Traditions* (Alcoholics Anonymous World Services, Inc., 1953), 26-27.

6. Stafford, "Hidden," *Christianity*, 18.

7. Ibid., 15.

8. Ibid., 18.

9. G. A. Pritchard, *Willow Creek Seeker Services* (Baker Books, 1996), inside front cover; quotation of author Lyle E. Schaller.

10. Ibid., 273.

11. Stafford, "Hidden," *Christianity,* 18.

12. Pritchard, *Willow*, 273.

13. Stafford, "Hidden," *Christianity*, 18.

14. Pritchard, *Willow*, 273.

15. Stafford, "Hidden," *Christianity*, 18.

16. Martin and Deidre Bobgan, *12 Steps to Destruction: Codependency Recovery Heresies* (Santa Barbara, CA: EastGate Publishers, 1991), 72.

17. *Pass It On: The story of Bill Wilson and how the A.A. message reached the world* (Alcoholics Anonymous World Services, Inc., 1984), 102; cited in Bobgan, *12 Steps*, 72.

18. Herbert Fingarette, *Heavy Drinking: The Myth of Alcoholism as a Disease* (Berkeley, CA: University of California Press, 1988).

19. Herbert Fingarette, "We Should Reject the Disease Concept of Alcoholism," *The Harvard Medical School Mental Health Letter,* February 1990, 4.

20. Stanton Peele, *Diseasing of America: Addiction Treatment Out of Control* (Heath and Company, 1989), 27.

21. Maudlin, "Addicts" *Christianity*.

22. Stafford, "Hidden," *Christianity*, 19.

23. *Pass*, 275-79.

24. Ibid., 198.

25. Ibid., 374.

26. Stafford, "Hidden," *Christianity*, 14; see also *Pass*, 121.

27. Stafford, "Hidden," *Christianity*, 16.

28. A. A. Grapevine, *A.A. Comes of Age*, (Alcoholics Anonymous Publishing, Inc., 1957), 39.

29. Oliver R. Barclay, *Whatever Happened to the Jesus Lane Lot?* (InterVarsity Press, 1977), 98-100.

30. Roy Livesey, *Twelve Steps to the New Age*, (Bury House Books, 1995, unpublished manuscript), 21-22.

31. Dick B., *Anne Smith's Spiritual Workbook* (Good Book Publishing Co., 1992), 45.

32. Livesey, *Twelve*, 47-49.

33. Willard Hunter, *The Man Who Would Change the World: Frank Buchman and Moral Re-Armament* (unpublished manuscript, 1977), 110-11; cited in Livesey, 88-89.

34. Frank N.D. Buchman, *Remaking the World* (London, 1941), 1, 7.

35. Livesey, *Twelve*, 84.

36. Tom Driberg, *The Mystery of Moral Re-Armament* (London, 1964), 156-67).

37. Livesey, *Twelve, 21-22.*

38. Ibid.

39. *Ideology and Co-existence* (Toronto, Canada: Moral Re-Armament, 1959), 2.

VICTORY OVER SIN

— *Dave Hunt* —

TORN BETWEEN THEIR SINCERE DESIRE to serve and honor their Lord and the inner turmoil of fleshly lusts and the seductive pull of worldly pleasures and honors, many Christians struggle to live for Christ. For them, Christianity involves great effort, little joy, much frustration and disillusionment, and the loss (when they have enough will power to deny themselves) of so much they once enjoyed in life. They struggle to avoid Paul's list of "don'ts" in Colossians 3:5–8:

> Mortify therefore your members which are upon the earth; forni-
> cation, uncleanness, inordinate affection, evil concupiscence, and
> covetousness, which is idolatry . . . put off all these; anger, wrath,
> malice, blasphemy, filthy communication out of your mouth.

Failing repeatedly, they repent remorsefully and puzzle over their inability to live as they know they should—but seemingly can't.

They fare no better with Paul's list of "do's" that follows (vv. 12–25):

> Put on therefore, as the elect of God, holy and beloved, bowels of
> mercies, kindness, humbleness of mind, meekness, longsuffering;
> forbearing one another, and forgiving . . . put on charity. . . . Let
> the word of Christ dwell in you richly. . . . And whatsoever ye
> do in word or deed, do all in the name of the Lord Jesus, giving
> thanks to God and the Father by him. . . .

Is it really possible to be kind, humble, loving, and forgiving at all times? The spirit is willing, but the flesh proves ever to be embarrassingly weak in attempting to be like Christ. How can one live up to the high standards the Bible sets for Christian living? Is there some secret to victory we are overlooking? The fact that psychology is not the key to living for Christ is clear. Then what can the Christian do who sincerely wants to fulfill the command to "glorify God in your body, and in your spirit, which are God's" (1 Corinthians 6:20)?

For many, the two key expressions, "mortify" in verse 5 and "put on" in verse 12, only increase the bewilderment and sense of failure. Is it really possible to "put to death" ungodly desires and, shedding that body of evil, as it were, to be clothed in a resurrection body of godliness? Surely Paul, led of the

Holy Spirit, is not taunting us with goals that cannot be attained and that, in fact, are not at all practical. Was he not, himself, an example of this kind of life, and did he not say more than once, "Be ye followers of me even as I also am of Christ" (1 Corinthians 11:1, etc.)? Then why do we fail? From whence comes the motivation and the strength to accomplish what is at once so desirable and yet so seemingly impossible?

There is a general failure to recognize the importance of one little word that occurs in both verses 5 and 12. It holds the answer to our dilemma. Paul does not say, "Mortify your members," and "Put on . . . bowels of mercies, kindness. . . . " That would impose a "do-it-yourself" religion of gritting one's teeth in determination and struggling to live up to high moral standards—no different from the atheist's or Buddhist's attempt to do the same. That is not Christianity!

Paul carefully and pointedly says, "Mortify *therefore*. . . . Put on *therefore*. . . . " Clearly *therefore* refers to something that Paul is convinced gives the Christian the motivation and power to do what he is commanding and lifts the Christian above the impossible struggle of flesh trying to live a godly life. It is, therefore, the Christian's secret to a happy, fruitful, and holy life pleasing to God.

The mortifying of the old deeds and the putting on of the new is possible only because, as the previous verses declare, "Ye are dead, and . . . your life is hid with Christ in God" (Colossians 3:3). The same thing certainly could not be said of the followers of Buddha, Muhammad, Krishna, et al. Christianity is thus unique and separated from all religions. Herein lies the secret dynamic of the Christian life.

Why, then, doesn't every Christian experience this power in daily living? Sadly, many who call themselves Christians have a very superficial understanding of the gospel they claim to believe: "[H]ow that Christ died for our sins according to the scriptures; and that he was buried, and that he rose again the third day according to the scriptures " (1 Corinthians 15:3–4). They have given intellectual assent, but the powerful reality of this historical event has not gripped their hearts.

For many who believe that Christ died for their sins, this event is more mystical than historical. The horrible death of the Cross is something that happened to Christ but that has only a theoretical rather than practical connection to them. They have a faulty understanding of what Christ's death means, imagining that the death of Christ in their place delivered them from their deserved eternal punishment in hell, so that, like Barabbas, they can live as they please. They have never understood or even desired what Paul rejoiced in:

> I am crucified with Christ: nevertheless I live; yet not I, but Christ
> liveth in me: and the life which I now live in the flesh I live by the
> faith of the Son of God, who loved me, and gave himself for me.
> (Galatians 2:20)

Paul was not expressing an inspiring but empty platitude. For that great apostle, the Cross was no mere religious symbol. It was the place where he had died in Christ to life as he would have lived it and had begun to experience the very life of Christ being lived in him. He knew that Christ gives *resurrection* life; therefore, only those who have died can experience it. With wonder, amazement, and deep gratitude, he realized that Christ had actually taken his place before a righteous, holy God—and that God had put Christ to death in payment for his (Paul's) sins. Paul was, therefore, a dead man. Christ's death in his place was literally his own death, and he rejoiced in that fact. If he was to experience life thereafter, it must be the resurrected Christ living in him.

The transformation in Paul was at once remarkable, yet not surprising. The most seductive temptation Satan can devise will arouse no response from a dead man. Insult a dead man to his face and he will not retaliate in anger. As a dead man, Paul experienced a new freedom over sin that he had never known before! Yet, in spite of being dead, Paul was more alive than he had ever been: "I am crucified. . . nevertheless, I live." Dead to sin, he was alive to God through Christ. So real was this to Paul, that it was as though Christ himself were living in him—and, indeed, He was! By faith, Christ had become his very life—and this, said Paul for our benefit, is what Christianity is all about!

Paul reminded the saints at Colosse that victory over sin and self was not possible through willpower and fleshly struggle. True victory could come only through understanding and believing what it really meant that Christ had died for their sins and been resurrected for their justification. Paul declared that this was the secret of his own complete transformation—and so it must be with them and with us.

But how could Christ's death, burial, and resurrection be as real to them as it was to Paul—so real that their very lives would be totally transformed? Paul explained: They must believe that Christ was coming any moment to take them to heaven, where they would thereafter appear with Him in glory! It was the hope of Christ's imminent return that would make the difference between victory and defeat in the Christian life!

The fact that this hope is the key to victorious living is clear. Notice again Paul's staggering declaration: "When Christ, who is our life, shall appear, then shall ye also appear with him in glory[!] Mortify *therefore*. . . . Put on *therefore*. . . ." Such a vibrant hope was this and of such certain accomplishment that Paul began this entire section with the statement, "If ye then be risen with Christ, seek those things which are above, where Christ sitteth on the right hand of God. Set your affection on things above, not on things on the earth" (vv. 1–2). Herein lay the secret to the godly life that Paul himself lived and expected of the Colossians as well. They were to be so heavenly minded that the things of this earth would have no appeal and thus no power over them.

Nor was this orientation away from earth toward heaven to be merely a "positive mental attitude" such as psychology promotes, which they had adopted without any basis in reality. It was not wishful "positive thinking" but truth that would change their lives. Through Christ's Cross, Christians have been crucified to the world and the world has been crucified to them, as Paul had firmly declared (Galatians 6:14). A man who has just been taken down, dead, from a cross has no interest in this world nor does it have any claims upon him. The person crucified and those who crucified him have nothing further to do with each other.

So it is with the Christian and the world through the Cross of Christ. The vicious hatred this world has for Christ and its irreconcilable animosity against all that He stands for have been fully exposed in the rejection and crucifixion of our Lord. Christ declared that the world would hate and persecute us as it had Him (John 15:18–20; 16:2; 17:14). By His Cross we have been cut off from this world just as surely as He was.

Death, however, did not end it all. Christ rose triumphant from the grave and ascended to the right hand of the Father in heaven. Moreover, He is coming again in power and glory to judge and take vengeance upon those who have rejected Him—and we, who have identified ourselves with Him in His rejection and death, will participate in His triumph and glory. Nor is the glad day when Christ will return to catch up His own alive to heaven so far in the future that it has no practical meaning for us now. On the contrary, it could occur today. The glorious fulfillment of the hope that the gospel has instilled within our hearts could burst upon us at any moment! This fact causes eternity to invade the present and makes the Christian no longer of this world!

Hear Paul say it again: "For ye are dead, and your life is hid with Christ in God." Consenting to be dead and willing for Christ to be their life was not only the Colossians' basis for victory, but it was also the essential meaning of the gospel they must embrace. Otherwise, there could be no salvation. Without that, they were mere Barabbases, grateful that Christ had died in their place but mistakenly assuming that they had been "saved" from death in order to live for self. If they were not willing, however, to acknowledge Christ's death as their very own and to give up life as they would have lived it so that Christ could become their life, then they could not experience the victory over sin and self that Paul preached. Indeed, they had not consented to the message of the gospel!

And what made the fact of their death, burial, and resurrection with Christ the dynamic power that transformed their lives? It was this promise: "When Christ, who is our life, shall appear, then shall ye also appear with him in glory." Once that truth had gripped their hearts so that His "appearing" had become their daily expectation and hope, Christ's death and resurrection were so real to them in the present that they were changed into new persons. As such, Paul told them, they were to "seek those things which are above, where Christ sitteth on the right hand of God. Set your affection on things above, not on things on the earth" (vv. 1–2). May we each pursue that challenge wholeheartedly!

The "pretribulation Rapture" is thus no mere hair-splitting thesis for theologians to discuss or a theory without practical effect. It is the over-looked secret to victory in the Christian's life. John said, "Every man that hath this hope in him purifieth himself, even as he [Christ] is pure" (1 John 3:3). Paul indicated that it had been his love of Christ's appearing and the faith that it could occur at any moment that had motivated him to holiness and faithfulness and had made him victorious—and that the same "crown of righteousness" was for "all them also that love his [Christ's] appearing" (2 Timothy 4:8). On the other hand, Christ associated wickedness with fail-ing to love His appearing: "But and if that evil servant shall say in his heart, My lord delayeth his coming; and shall begin to smite his fellow servants, and to eat and drink with the drunken . . . " (Matthew 24:48–49).

Would "Christian" Psychology Help?

If what Paul held out to the Colossians is indeed the secret to victory in the Christian's life, where does psychology enter the picture? Will therapy help us to believe the promises of our Lord? Will some Freudian or Jungian principle make the fact that our "life is hid with Christ in God" more real and therefore strengthen us against trials and temptations? Could some other one of the hundreds of therapies now being practiced by Christian psychologists make more real the truth that we have been crucified with Christ and that He is living in us? If so, why are not these therapies part of Scripture? And if they are not (which is obvious), and Christians triumphed over the world, the flesh, and the devil without any help from psychology, why would any Christian need help from psychology today?

In fact, psychological therapies were devised by humanists. Even if their "Christianized" form brought into the church by Christian psychologists attempts to incorporate biblical truths, that would be altogether fruitless and clearly erroneous. Darkness cannot enhance the light; error cannot improve upon the truth. Certainly, no part of psychology, invented as it was by atheists and Christ-haters, has anything whatsoever to do with the death of Christ paying the penalty for our sins, with our being crucified with Him and He living in us, or with the hope of His any-moment return to take us to His Father's house. Nor would it be of any value to attempt to devise some psychological therapy to make these truths real to the heart. Indeed, it would be counterproductive because psychology not only has no relationship to these truths, but it mocks them.

Christian psychology, however, now an apparently irremovable fixture in the church, is based upon the rejection of the biblical promise that the power of the indwelling Christ, the Holy Spirit, and the Word of God provide all we need "for life and godliness" (2 Peter 1:3). We are told that we need much more, and that it is provided in psychology, God's new way to victory. This lie represents a clear rejection of God's promise in His Word. That was the astonishing basis for the founding in late 1989 of the Liberty Institute for Lay Counseling (LILC):

> There are simply not enough trained Christian Psychologists, Psychiatrists, and Pastors to meet the counseling needs of the teeming masses who are crying out for help. Liberty Institute for Lay Counseling will provide the necessary training so lay people can now be equipped to do something about the hurt, confusion, neglect, abuse, and suffering that is sweeping this nation like a sinister plague.

Christian psychology has brought an alien gospel into the church and it is being promoted by Christian universities eager for tuition from more students to meet mounting budgets. "Being born again . . . by the word of God . . . which by the gospel is preached" (1 Peter 1:23–25) so that "old things are passed away . . . all things are become new" (2 Corinthians 5:17) is no longer enough to meet the challenges of daily living. We need more—and humanists have come to our rescue through psychology. This is the "good news" we now have to offer to "the teeming masses . . . crying out for help." The promises of God were sufficient for past generations, but in our day, God has allowed atheistic psychologists to help Christians live godly lives in the power of a new truth. What theology was never able to do, therapy will accomplish.

This is a lie! Don't believe it for a moment.

Let us diligently and enthusiastically "seek those things which are above, where Christ sitteth on the right hand of God." Let us "set [our] affection on things above, not on things on the earth." Why? "For our conversation [citizenship] is in heaven; from whence also we look for the Saviour, the Lord Jesus Christ: who shall change our vile body, that it may be fashioned like unto his glorious body, according to the working whereby he is able even to subdue all things unto himself" (Philippians 3:20–21). With that perspective in our hearts and minds, the trials and temptations of this brief life on earth lose their power to discourage or hinder us from glorifying our Lord. Praise God!

THEREFORE IF ANY MAN BE IN CHRIST, HE IS A NEW CREATURE: OLD THINGS ARE PASSED AWAY; BEHOLD, ALL THINGS ARE BECOME NEW.... FOR HE HATH MADE HIM TO BE SIN FOR US, WHO KNEW NO SIN; THAT WE MIGHT BE MADE THE RIGHTEOUSNESS OF GOD IN HIM.

— 2 CORINTHIANS 5:17 & 21 —

PART THREE

TROUBLING QUESTIONS
BIBLICAL ANSWERS

— Dave Hunt —

QUESTION: I've been on the fence concerning your views of self-esteem and self-love, but I think you've really missed the mark when it comes to our self-worth. I recently read *The Secret of Loving* by Josh McDowell. He's no slouch when it comes to biblical apologetics, and he says we are worth the price God paid for us—the death of His Son. Doesn't that make us of infinite value to God?

RESPONSE: Where does it say in the Bible that mankind has value to God? Jesus did say that we are of "more value than many sparrows," but that doesn't support the humanist selfisms being promoted in the church today through its embrace of psychology. It is not our great value (self-worth) but the fact that God loves us *in spite of our unworthiness* that caused Him to give His Son and that caused Christ to die for our sins.

Scripture declares that "God so loved the world that He gave His only begotten Son. . . . " It doesn't say that "God so *valued* the world that He gave His only begotten Son. . . . " Love does not love because of the value of the object. That would not be genuine but a self-centered love (1 Corinthians 13) and would detract from the biblical teaching about redemption.

God did not get a bargain. He didn't exchange equal value. Is each of us worth as much to God as His Son because that's the price He paid? Is that what I am "worth"? The great cost at which I was redeemed gives no cause for me to have a sense of self-worth but of shame that my sin caused Christ to pay such a great price.

McDowell is promoting this heresy that "Christian psychology" has helped to spread in the church. Robert Schuller majors on this theme: "The death of Christ on the cross is God's price tag on a human soul . . . [It means] we really are Somebodies!" On the contrary, Christ didn't die for somebodies: He died for helpless, hopeless, ungodly sinners:

> For when we were yet without strength, in due time Christ died for the ungodly. For scarcely for a righteous man will one die: yet peradventure for a good man some would even dare to die. But God commendeth his love toward us, in that, while we were yet sinners, Christ died for us. (Romans 5:6–8)

The fact that the sinless Son of God *had to die upon the Cross* to redeem me should not make me feel good about myself but ashamed, for it was my sins that nailed Him there. How could that fact build up my self-esteem? Yet Bruce Narramore insists:

> What a foundation for self-esteem! The purchase price tells us the value of an object. . . . Of man alone it is said, "You were bought with a price" (1 Corinthians 6:20). . . . What a sense of worth and value this imparts. The Son of God considers us of such value that He gave His life for us.[1]

The shedding of Christ's blood, with which we were redeemed, did not occur because of our "worth" but because of our *sin* and the demands of God's justice. Thus, the greater the price, the worse the sin. To associate this "purchase price" with the "value" of an object to God and to make it the basis for self-worth is neither biblical nor logical. In fact, it shows the perversion that is caused by the influence of selfist psychology.

Even from a logical point of view, the price paid for an object does not determine its worth. It only represents what someone is willing to pay for it at a given time and under given circumstances. Everything fluctuates in price, from hay to gold. Price is determined by the market—not by the thing itself.

Nothing has an intrinsic value in and of itself, so the very concept of self-worth is wrong. A painting may have been bought at great price during times of plenty. In a famine, no one would give even a crust of bread for it. Value is set by circumstances independent and outside of the object. It is not an intrinsic quality of the thing itself. There is no way to attach the price paid to the object purchased. Thus, the entire idea of self-worth is self-deception.

QUESTION: If, as I have heard you say, the brain doesn't originate thoughts, what about dreams, which are visualized thoughts? What about insanity? What about drugs acting on the brain and changing behavior?

RESPONSE: Neuroscientists and brain surgeons have likened the brain to a computer that the real person within (soul and spirit) uses to operate the body. If the brain originated thoughts, we would have to do whatever it decided. We would be wondering what the brain might think of and cause us to do next. Absurd? Of course.

It is clearly not the brain that thinks and decides what we should or should not do. *We* decide. And when the brain is decomposing in the grave along with the body, the soul and spirit are no longer inhabiting it as they did while life was in the body. The soul and spirit that comprise the real person who lived in the body have either gone to be with Christ (if the person was saved) or are in hell, like the rich man (Luke 16:19–31), waiting to be called before Christ at the Great White Throne final judgment and sent to eternal punishment. We need to warn the unsaved, and we can use the fact of the distinction between the physical brain and the nonphysical person living inside who makes the choices and will be held accountable for every thought, word, and deed.

Solomon said dreams come "through the multitude of business" (Ecclesiastes 5:3). While we sleep, the "computer" plays back composites of what we have said, thought, or done. Insanity could represent a foul-up of the physicial brain mechanism. As a spiritual problem, apparent insanity could be rebellion against God or against the truth of God, an attempt to escape reality and its responsibilities, or a deliberate means (in one's warped thinking) to gain one's own selfish ends by manipulating others, etc.

Psychoactive drugs simply distort or destroy normal brain functions and thus change behavior. Neither insanity nor drugs negate the fact that the brain is like a super-computer that the person living in the body operates in order to function in the physical universe.

QUESTION: Although I agree with you that psychology has created more problems for the church than anyone could number, I think there are some areas of the field that can be helpful. What do you think?

RESPONSE: First of all, when the term "psychology" is used, most people think of psychotherapy. That's understandable because psychotherapy is the best-known field of psychology. There are, however, about fifty divisions of the American Psychological Association, and they run the gamut from mostly objective to extremely subjective. The most scientifically legitimate would be the former, and that would include those fields of research or experimental psychology that use the scientific method as they collect and evaluate tangible, observable, and predictable behavior.

The study of man/machine interface, e.g., the placement of knobs or keys on a machine or the choice of letter size or color for optimum use, would be a good example of a psychological field with varying degrees of objectivity. To the degree that researchers stick to quantifiable facts, evaluation, measurement, and verifiable statistics, that much of psychology has a chance of being a legitimate science. The testing of skills or abilities for placement (typing, math, hand/eye coordination, finger dexterity, etc.), where the information gleaned and reported is objective and quantitative, would be valid as a psychological endeavor.

However, testing that deals with personality types, personal feelings, or subjective views lacks the necessary statistical validity to be considered seriously. When evaluation mixes the objective "*what* has taken place" with the interpretive "*why* it has taken place," it has moved out of science and into subjective speculation.

Therefore, regarding whatever calls itself a psychological enterprise, we would consider it to be legitimate to the degree that it can demonstrate objectivity and verifiable and repeatable results. Clinical psychology (psychotherapy) is subjective, emotional, and relies upon the very wisdom of man that God warns us against (1 Corinthians 2:5). It is often harmful, and all of the evaluation tests declare that it either doesn't work or is no more effective than the talk-therapy of untrained nonprofessionals. After fifteen years of investigating his own profession, clinical psychologist Bernie Zilbergeld declared:

> One of the most consistent and important effects of counseling is a desire for more counseling . . . it is no longer unusual to meet people who are looking for . . . a therapist to resolve problems caused in a previous therapy. . . .
> There is absolutely no evidence that professional therapists have any special knowledge of how to change behavior, or that they obtain better results—with any type of client or problem—than those with little or no formal training. In other words, most people can probably get the same kind of help from friends, relatives, or others that they get from therapists.[2]

QUESTION: You say that the need for self-love is not taught in the Bible but that we naturally love ourselves too much. Yet Jesus Christ said, "Love your neighbor as yourself." How can we obey that command if we hate ourselves? Yes, I've heard people sincerely say, "I hate myself!" These people are miserable, deeply depressed, and some of them are suicidal. What can be done for them? Have you no sympathy?

RESPONSE: Genuine sympathy for such persons would cause us to try to help them to understand the biblical remedy, not offer them the false remedies of this ungodly world. Jesus was asked by critics attempting to trap Him, "Master, which is the great commandment in the law?" He replied, "Thou shalt love the Lord thy God with all thy heart, and with all thy soul, and with all thy mind. This is the first and great commandment. And the second is like unto it, Thou shalt love thy neighbour as thyself. On these two commandments hang all the law and the prophets" (Matthew 22:36–40).

Notice that Christ said that upon the commandments to love God and neighbor "hang all the law and the prophets." Since these two commandments are the essence of Scripture, nothing further need be nor can be added. Yet to these two commandments has been added a third: the love of self. It is now widely taught not only in the world but especially in the church that self-love is the great need: indeed, that it is actually the first and greatest commandment, thus contradicting Christ. Christian psychologists tell us that until we obey this new first commandment of loving ourselves, we can't fulfill the other two, of loving God and neighbor.

The fact that this modern perversion of Scripture is due to the influence of humanistic psychology is freely, even proudly, admitted by Christian psychologists. For example, Bruce Narramore (nephew of Clyde Narramore, the godfather of Christian psychology in America) declares, "Under the influence of humanistic psychologists like Carl Rogers and Abraham Maslow, many of us Christians have begun to see our need for self-love and self-esteem. This is a good and necessary focus."[3]

Narramore is admitting that no one studying the Bible on their knees in the past thirty-five hundred years ever got such an idea from there; this "new truth" came from humanists. And Christian psychologists seemingly have no sense of shame and see nothing wrong with the fact that their theories and practices have such a godless source. In the last two thousand years since Christ died for our sins and ascended to His Father's right hand, no one found the necessity for self-love or self-esteem or a good self-image *anywhere in the Bible!*

Calvin, Luther, Wesley, Spurgeon, Moody, et al., found just the opposite in God's Word, which Jesus said "is truth" (John 17:17). It was the atheistic humanists who discovered this "new truth." Incredibly, through the influence of Christian psychology in the church, even Christian leaders find the lie appealing and pass it on to their flocks in books and sermons.

Far from teaching self-love, when Christ said, "Thou shalt love thy neighbour as thyself," He was in essence saying, "You feed and clothe and care for yourselves day and night. Now give to your neighbors some of the loving attention that you lavish upon yourselves. Love your neighbor as you excessively love yourselves." Christ would not tell us to love our neighbors *as we love ourselves* if we did not love ourselves enough. He surely wasn't saying, "Love your neighbor as you inadequately love yourselves"!

Tragically, the first commandment, love for God, is not only neglected but is given a secondary position, and self-love is made preeminent. Instead of being convicted of our failure to love God with our whole heart, soul, and mind as the gravest of sins and the root of all personal problems, we are urged to focus upon loving and esteeming and valuing ourselves as the solution to depression and other signs of unbelief. What a perversion of Scripture! And God laments, "My people love to have it so" (Jeremiah 5:31).

Yes, there are people who sob, "I hate myself!" Common sense, however, tells us it isn't true. They may hate their status, stature, physique, ineptness, appearance, job, salary, academic record, or the way others treat them, but they don't hate *themselves*. If they truly hated themselves they would be *glad* they were unattractive, poorly paid, abused, etc. Psychology has convinced millions of a lie. The Bible tells the truth: "For no man ever yet hated his own flesh [i.e., himself]" (Ephesians 5:29). When Christ said, "Love your neighbor as yourself," He was not correcting an imagined rejection and hatred of self. He was putting His finger on the obsession with self—the selfishness and self-centeredness that is our natural bent. And who of us does not need to heed our Lord's exhortation? Tragically, few do give heed.

Instead, this heresy grows in popularity. Robert Schuller has been praised by Billy Graham and by other evangelical leaders. Instead of the rebuke it deserves, his blasphemous book, *Self-Love, the Dynamic Force of Success*, has been selling steadily for nearly forty years in Christian bookstores, with the backing of church leaders. The front cover promises, "Learn to LOVE YOURSELF— the secret of happiness in life, in love, in everything you do." One wonders how what Jesus called "the first and great commandment" (Matthew 22:37–38) fell through the cracks in Schuller's theology and doesn't even merit mention in this book?

The book is not about God but all about me, myself, and I—exactly what those in hell will be stuck with for all eternity.

Among the sub-headings are the following, which pretty much explain what this anti-biblical book is about:

- To Love Yourself Is to Be Truly Religious
- You Are Going to Be a Different Person after Reading This Book
- The Universal Will to Self-Love
- Self-Love Is Discovering the Greatness Deep within You
- Self-Love Is Being Proud of Who and What You Are
- Self-Love is Experiencing God at Work in You and through You
- Love Yourself and Come Alive
- Love Yourself and Your Dreams Can Come True
- Love Yourself and Enjoy a Great Soul-Expanding Experience
- Is the Breakdown of the Family the Breakdown of Self-Love?
- Self-Confidence is Real Security

The Bible commands us to love God, neighbor, and even enemies, but never does God's Word command or even encourage us to love ourselves. We are encouraged to be loving, kind, merciful, patient, to preach the gospel to every creature, etc.—but never to be "truly religious."

Discover "the greatness slumbering deep within you"? Try that in the presence of God! Job said, "Now mine eye seeth thee. Wherefore I abhor myself, and repent in dust and ashes" (Job 42:5–6). Isaiah said, "Woe is me . . . for mine eyes have seen . . . the LORD of hosts" (Isaiah 6:5). Schuller apparently hasn't "seen the Lord of hosts," nor have those who find his ideas appealing!

"Real security" comes through "self-confidence"? Paul said he had "no confidence in the flesh" (Philippians 3:30); Solomon advised, "Trust in the LORD with all thine heart . . . " (Proverbs 3:5), and David repeatedly said, "O God . . . in thee do I put my trust . . . (Psalms 11:1; 16:1; 25:2, etc.).

Schuller seems intent upon contradicting the Bible and offering the advice of the Serpent to Eve to replace God with Self. The fact that so many Christian leaders commend him and his anti-biblical books and that so many hundreds of thousands of ordinary Christians find him appealing is a sad commentary on the state of Christianity today.

QUESTION: A.W. Tozer said that the church of his day didn't need a "revival" but a new Reformation. Would you agree with that? In one of his many books, Robert Schuller also called for a "new Reformation." Was he on the right track, at least this time?

RESPONSE: Schuller was certainly correct in saying that we need a "new Reformation," but he was dead wrong about the reason we need it and the kind of Reformation it must be. The book was titled, *Self-Esteem: The New Reformation.* He begins the Introduction by quoting a University of Pennsylvania Associate Professor of Psychiatry who congratulates Schuller with these words: " . . . you have pursued a religious route and I have pursued a scientific path, and we have both arrived at the same bottom line: unconditional self-esteem . . . I would say man's deepest flaw is to mistrust himself. . . . Perhaps we are at an era where psychiatric and religious thinking can be synergistic. . . . "

Schuller, of course, agrees, as do nearly all "Christian" psychologists. Their hope and dream for years has been to "integrate" psychology with theology so as to justify the delusion that psychology or any part of it could be called "Christian." Though a university professor, this psychiatrist apparently is ignorant of the fact, which we have documented several times, that psychology/psychiatry is not scientific and, indeed, never can be, for obvious reasons.

As for "self-esteem" being the great need around which the "new Reformation" would be built, those believing this couldn't be more wrong.

Some years ago, I stood by the huge stone in Constance, Germany, marking the place where Jan Hus was burned at the stake. Overcome with grief, I wept as I thought of the martyrs who died in Rome's attempt to destroy the Reformation in the sixteenth century. That Reformation was worth dying for. I wept, too, for my own generation that, led by Christian psychologists, is undergoing what Robert Schuller calls a "new reformation," which, he says "the church needs, more than anything else . . . nothing less will do."[4] He says that "Where the sixteenth-century Reformation returned our focus to sacred Scriptures as the only infallible rule for faith and practice, the new reformation will return our focus to the sacred right of every person to self-esteem!"[5] I asked myself, *Who would die for that?* Whoever did would regret it for eternity.

Schuller wrote that book more than twenty-five years ago. Tragically, the stranglehold that psychology has on the church has only strengthened, while the church's hold on Scripture has weakened to the point where professing Christianity can hardly last much longer. We need a Reformation that will return the church to God and to submission to His Word and will.

QUESTION: Your ministry seems to me to be far too negative. You can't attract the lost to Christ with "doom-and-gloom" predictions about the end of the world and coming disasters. There are so many positive things that Jesus taught! You could major on those. Why not?

RESPONSE: "Negative" and "positive" are words that have some meaning if one is referring to electricity, chemical bonding, magnetism, etc. However, they have absolutely no meaning regarding God, the truth of His Word, or the gospel. Was Jesus always "positive"?

If you think so, you haven't read the Gospels. More than anyone else, He warned of eternal punishment in a fire that is never quenched. The gospel may have what you would call a "positive" side, but to get to that, one must be willing to confess one's need as a sinner and repent of one's sins. No one can get "saved" until he realizes he is "lost" and condemned by God's justice—and that his only hope is forgiveness on a righteous basis.

Christ had many false followers who claimed to believe in Him but didn't really understand who He was and would not have been willing to deny themselves to truly follow Him had they understood. We learn from the way our Lord dealt with these false disciples how to deal with the many who claim to be Christians today but who really are not. Did He encourage them with "positive reinforcement" as Christian psychology would do? Hardly.

In Jerusalem, "many believed in his name, when they saw the miracles which he did" (John 2:23). That sounds wonderful! What was our Lord's reaction? The next two verses tell us: "Jesus did not commit himself unto them, because he knew all men . . . for he knew what was in man." In other words, He knew their hearts and that they only believed that He could indeed do miracles, but they did not want to receive Him as the One who would deliver them from sin and self. Of course, we can't look into new converts' hearts as Christ could. Therefore, we must see evidence that they are truly saved before we accept them as such.

Many came running to Christ to tell Him that they would follow Him anywhere He would lead them. When someone did that, Christ did not say, "Quick, Peter, sign him up for the choir! John, make him a deacon! Judas, he owns a business, so he must have some money. See if he would like to be your assistant—or maybe a member of the board. Give him something to do. We don't want to lose him!"

Jesus certainly did not soften His message in order to gain or keep new converts. What did He say to those who came running to follow Him? Was he interested in numbers, as the church is today, or did He desire reality? By today's standards, and especially by the wisdom of Christian psychology, Christ's response was too negative to build a following.

Here is what He said: "The foxes have holes, and the birds of the air have nests; but the Son of man hath not where to lay his head . . . " (Matthew 8:20); "If any man will come after me, let him deny himself, and take up his cross, and follow me" (Matthew 16:24); "Whosoever doth not bear his cross, and come after me, cannot be my disciple" (Luke 14:27). In the language of our day, Christ was saying, "So you want to follow me? Let's be sure you understand that I'm heading for a hill outside Jerusalem called Calvary. There they will nail me to a cross. If you desire to be true to me to the end, deny yourself, pick up your cross right now, and follow me—because that's where I'm going."

Do we hear *that* message from pulpits, Christian radio, Christian TV, or in popular Christian books? Rarely. You say that wouldn't gain any disciples. On the contrary, it would gain *genuine* disciples and prevent false ones from deceiving themselves into imagining that they were Christians. Today, however, we call such preaching "negative" because Christian psychology has deceived us with this label.

So Christ was wrong, and the new "positive" gospel is the true way to heaven? After all, isn't this what the really popular churches preach? Or could it be that Christian psychology, in following the world, has brought directly into the church the "broad . . . way" that is crowded with those heading to "destruction" (Matthew 7:13)?

Today we're far too sophisticated to present the gospel in such unappealing terms as Christ used. We've studied success motivation, psychology, and Dale Carnegie courses in How to Win Friends and Influence People. Of course, we think our motives are good, and we've believed the lie that "positive" tactics are ideal for "winning people to Christ." As a result, churches are growing as never before in history.

Is this at last the sign of great revival, which we've been hoping and praying for—or is it proof that Christian psychology appeals to the fallen Self? Is Christ pleased that we are able to gather far more disciples in this new way than He ever did His way? Or are we filling our churches with multitudes who imagine, as Robert Schuller and others teach, that Christ died on the Cross to make them feel good about themselves by building up their self-esteem, answering their selfish prayers, and fulfilling their self-centered agendas? Each one must decide whether to follow Christ in denial of self—or to honor self as do many Christian leaders in attracting the ungodly into church attendance without their being truly born again.

QUESTION: As I understand it, one of the major cries of the sixteenth-century Reformers was "Sola Scriptura!" They were Catholic priests and monks who did not want to leave the Church but wanted Rome to follow only Scripture instead of its traditions. It seems to me that Christian psychologists have appointed themselves the new infallible priesthood class but are even worse than Rome. In their rejection of Scripture, they don't just follow church tradition (in fact they have introduced something entirely new), but they follow the very doctrines of devils Paul warned about that pervade the world around us. Is there some connection between the Roman Catholic images and the visualization taught by Christian psychologists today, or am I just becoming a narrow-minded fanatic? I would value your opinion.

RESPONSE: Christian psychologists have indeed taken a position in the evangelical church similar to that of priests in the Roman Catholic Church. They have their own "confessional" through therapy, and they cannot be corrected from Scripture because they claim another source of truth in addition to the Bible ("all truth is God's truth"). They look to Freud, Jung, Rogers, Maslow, Adler, et al., as the new sources of God's truth, though they were all anti-Christians. Christian psychologists have deceived multitudes into following the "wisdom of this world [which] God made foolish . . . " (1 Corinthians 1:20).

In his important book, *The Way of the Shaman*, Michael Harner explains that the word "shaman" is what the Tungus tribe in Siberia call their medicine men, or witchdoctors. It has been adopted by anthropologists worldwide to describe those involved in such practices. Harner, himself a practicing shaman as well as leading anthropologist, mentions six elements that he says have always been at the heart of shamanism, are still common to its practitioners today worldwide, and have been embraced by today's secular society as part of the New Age Movement.

These six elements of shamanism are at the heart of humanistic and transpersonal psychologies and have invaded the church through "Christian" psychology. Harner describes these ingredients as: visualization, hypnosis, psychotherapy, positive thinking, positive speaking (self-talk), and Eastern meditation techniques.[6] Paul warns of these practices as "doctrines of devils" that will characterize the "latter times" (1 Timothy 4:1).

These are all occult practices, and it is significant that Harner lists visualization first. It is the most powerful occult technique and the fastest and easiest way to contact demons. Yes, there is indeed a connection between images and psychology's practice of visualization. The Reformers objected to the images of the Catholic Church because they considered them to be a form of idolatry. But the Council of Trent (1545–1563,)rejecting the reforms that were so desperately needed, justified the retention of those images. They are still an important part of Catholicism today. The fact that so many of the "saints" had found images helpful in prayer and worship was considered enough justification for the Council of Trent to continue their use in spite of the clear biblical prohibition.

Such idolatry was bad enough, but something even worse was added. A man who would be made a "saint" in 1622, Saint Ignatius of Loyola (1491–1556), took images one step deeper into blatant occultism. He was the founder of the Society of Jesus, whose members are known as Jesuits. His *Spiritual Exercises* involve visualization of biblical events and of Jesus Christ himself. He advises followers, for example, "to picture . . . Christ our Lord . . . standing in a lowly place in a great plain about the region of Jerusalem, His appearance beautiful and attractive."[7]

Of course, no one can picture Christ because we don't know what He looked like. And even if we did, He doesn't look today, in heaven, in His resurrected, glorified body, as He did when He lived on earth. I know former Jesuits who confess that they were demonized through these "spiritual exercises." Yet these practices are recommended in the *Renovaré Spiritual Formation Bible* (Richard Foster, Editor-in-Chief), and are widespread in evangelical circles today through "Christian psychology."

Following the lead of Ignatius of Loyola, Richard Foster says visualization will lead one to Christ and God:

> Take a single event [from Scripture]. Seek to live the experience, remembering the encouragement of Ignatius of Loyola to apply all our senses to our task. . . . You can actually encounter the living Christ in the event, be addressed by His voice . . . touched by His healing power. . . . Jesus Christ will actually come to you."[8]

This is a demonic delusion—the fastest and surest way to step through a door into the occult. The resurrected, glorified Christ will not leave heaven to appear in response to our desire. Demons, however, are only too eager to masquerade as "Christ" and give a mystical experience that will entice the visualizer to enter deeper into the occult.

Visualization of Christ is a principal element of inner healing, which is being taught today among evangelicals as well as among Catholics. Every image formed in clay, wood, or stone is first of all visualized in the mind and then built according to that mental picture. This is idolatry, forbidden in Scripture.

It is also the most powerful occult technique. Incredibly, this demonic practice, standard among witchdoctors, is today a key part of the therapy used by many Christian psychologists.

QUESTION: **If psychology is as unscientific, irrational, and unbiblical as you say it is (and I agree), how is it that the world embraces it so enthusiastically and the church in general loves it? This really puzzles me!**

RESPONSE: The first part of your question is easy to answer: "The god of this world hath blinded the minds of them which believe not, lest the light of the glorious gospel of Christ, who is the image of God, should shine unto them" (2 Corinthians 4:4). As a result, "the whole world lieth in wickedness" (1 John 5:19). The unsaved naturally love Satan's lies. As Jesus said to the Jews who rejected Him, "Ye are of your father the devil, and the lusts of your father ye will do" (John 8:44).

This is another reason why it is so wrong for pastors and their churches to attempt to become popular with the world. Watering down the gospel to "reach the world for Christ" may fill churches, but it will only hasten on their way to hell those who join the crowds. And if those who preach these unbiblical versions of the gospel really believe what they teach, they are going to the same place as those who trust them.

Christians are so enamored by the same delusion as the world for two reasons. First of all, in thoughtless disobedience of God's command, "Love not the world, neither the things that are in the world" (1 John 2:15), the lives of most professing Christians could hardly be distinguished from the lives of the ungodly all around them. They watch the same movies, laugh at the same jokes (even the off-color ones), love the same entertainment, admire, honor, and avidly follow the careers of the same sports and entertainment personalities in spite of the wickedness of their lives.

Sadly, they lead their children on the same downward path. Yet, in all of this, they manage to maintain what they imagine to be a clear conscience. Since they embrace almost everything else of the world, why would they reject the world's wisdom in psychology, particularly since it tells them what they want to hear and "scientifically" releases them from living truly sanctified, separated, and Christ-honoring lives?

Secondly, both Christian leaders and their followers feel a sense of inferiority when they are accused of being "unscientific." That accusation first arose

Catholicism Supports Evolution as Scientific (handwritten)

from the church's almost unanimous rejection of evolution for decades, from the very beginning of Darwinism being embraced by the world and for decades after. (Here we have one more reason for not classifying Roman Catholicism as an aberrant Christian denomination but as a cult: it never rejected Darwinism and continues to accept evolution as "scientific" to this day.)

Sadly, so-called Protestants have now almost totally surrendered even to evolution, though some call it "theistic evolution." It is taught in one form or another in most "Christian" universities and seminaries. Christians no longer want to be considered "unscientific" (and thus backward) by continuing to reject evolution. After all, Pope John Paul II claimed that it has been fully proved scientifically, *Christianity Today* and Promise Keepers went along with the pope, and Billy Graham, too, accepted it as a possibility.

At the same time, along came psychology, claiming to be a new "science" of the psyche/mind—ridiculous on the very face of it because the psyche/mind is nonphysical. Of course, following Freud's medical model, psychologists tried to make the mind part of the brain. At any rate, having been labeled "unscientific" because of its earlier rejection of evolution, the church wanted to be scientific like the world and was determined not to miss the boat again.

Christians jumped on the bandwagon and signed up to get Ph.D.s in the new "science" of psychology. Christian psychologists and psychiatrists became the new heroes and heroines of the faith and the most popular authorities in the church. They could boast of acceptance in the academic world, wave their degrees, claim to be scientific, and command the respect of both the world and the church.

Of course, nearly everyone today recognizes that the brain is distinct from the mind and that the latter is certainly not physical. Psychology has been proved not to be a science (in fact unsuited to be scientific) and has moved largely into pseudo-spirituality and occultism. This is most obvious in Transpersonal and Humanistic Psychologies, but the trend is throughout.

So here we are, with Christian psychologists into everything from hypnosis and dream analysis to the pitiful delusion of multiple personalities, which, unless faked, are demonic. But through relentless propaganda, the fantasy that psychology is scientific has metamorphosed into accepted fact, especially among Christians. The church has caught up with the world in its anti-God follies. Christians can hold their heads up even in academia, and those who dare to point out that the Emperor has no clothes are laughed to scorn.

This is an incomplete explanation, but I think it comes close to describing the present charade and how and why it came about.

QUESTION: I am the director of a Christian pro-life crisis pregnancy center and I am increasingly aware of, and uncomfortable about, testimonies and literature that come across my desk that insist upon the importance of "forgiving yourself." This is especially so in the area of counseling a client in the aftermath of abortion. It doesn't seem scriptural to me. My hope is that you would respond by telling me what you would say to someone who says, "I just can't forgive myself."

RESPONSE: Thankfully, we don't look to psychology for its answer to such questions. We look to God and to His Word. That is where we find truth and peace. When a counselee has confessed her sin to God, knows she's forgiven because of Calvary, yet says that she "just can't forgive herself," it may be that she's overwhelmed with remorse for a sinful act that she is ashamed to have committed. She now wishes desperately that it hadn't happened, but the clock cannot be turned back.

All of us do things that offend God, hurt others, and hurt ourselves, and that could haunt us for a time. What can we do? Whenever the shameful memory returns, we must refuse to grieve over it and remind ourselves that God has said "Their sins and iniquities will I remember no more" (Hebrews 8:12; 10:17). We can come to deeply regret our sins for many good reasons and may not be able to escape the memories for a time. There is nothing wrong with that (Romans 6:21) as long as guilt is no longer involved. It is unbelief to keep returning to something that took place in the past and has been confessed and forgiven. Paul said, "Forgetting those things which are behind, and reaching forth unto those things which are before, I press toward the mark for the prize of the high calling of God in Christ Jesus. Let us therefore, as many as be perfect, be thus minded: and if in any thing ye be otherwise minded, God shall reveal even this unto you" (Philippians 3:13–15).

Those who regard "forgiving themselves" to be more than an expression of remorse and who believe it to be a necessary condition in order to erase guilt have been duped by humanistic psychology and are ignorant of the truth. They need to be informed of the following:

1) We sin against God and others, and are sinned against by others. The Word directs us to ask God and others for forgiveness and to forgive them. While I may figuratively "sin against myself" in the sense that I've harmed myself, it is impossible to literally sin against myself since it is "myself" doing the sinning. Therefore, I have no basis for "forgiving myself."

2) Only God can forgive sin (Mark 2:7); only He can remove true guilt.

3) Thinking that I must or can forgive myself is a form of self-deification, especially when one says, "I know that God forgives me, but I just can't forgive myself." Am I a higher authority than God?

4) The delusion of self-forgiveness can also be a convoluted form of rebellion. It says, "Although God forgave me, I won't forgive myself." It says that although God will hold my sin against me no more, *I'm* going to hold it against me.

5) It can also be a form of self-righteousness or pride in the sense that I have overridden God's forgiveness with my decision that my sin is too grievous for me to forgive.

6) Except in cases where restitution is feasible, there is little we can do about sins of the past beyond confessing them and receiving God's forgiveness and cleansing (1 John 1:9; Psalm 51:2, 7). That's why Paul writes, "Forgetting those things which are behind . . . " (Philippians 3:13–14). Believers in Christ are to cast off any imagined bondage to the past so that they may serve the Lord with all joy and in the grace He provides.

The woman who washed the feet of Jesus with her tears and dried them with her hair remembered her sins; but her tears were those of joy for the forgiveness she received; and her act was an act of love for the One who had forgiven her. We're told that she loved much because she was forgiven much. Guilt ends with forgiveness; love increases with the recognition of and thankfulness for forgiveness. Yet even the joy of forgiveness would be nothing had there been nothing to forgive. So even in that joy there is remembrance of the sin. It is not a remembrance of guilt and remorse, however, but of gratitude that Christ has paid the penalty in full and we are forgiven.

One of the many benefits of being a Christian is that we are not bound to the sins of the past (1 John 1:9) and we can start each day (or hour or moment) with a clean heart before the Lord. Those under the delusion that they can't forgive themselves are rejecting what Christ has done for them and what He will do for them.

QUESTION: In his book, *Megashift,* James Rutz writes: "A megashift of spiritual power . . . is about to . . . put [the world] into vastly better shape. . . . A whole new form of Christianity promises to bring a far greater impact than the Protestant Reformation. . . . " Is this what the Bible promises? I don't think so, but now I'm confused because so many Christian leaders have hailed this book as a message of encouragement from God for the church today.

RESPONSE: This sounds like what one would hear on TBN or CBN: that the great sign of the last days will not be apostasy, as Christ, Paul, and other biblical prophets foretold. Instead, there will be a last-days worldwide revival. Of course, the Latter Rain movement has been preaching this for nearly one hundred years. We hear it from all the Positive Confession preachers, from Oral Roberts to Kenneth Copeland to Robert Schuller to Joel Osteen, et al.

But what is the reality that we see all around us in today's church? Churches are getting larger but generally only by compromise with false doctrine and even with the world. Sadly, Christian leaders in increasing numbers are falling into immorality that denies their professed faith. What *Megashift* is this?

Ted Haggard preached a message on the "last-days great revival and triumph over Satan" through new techniques of spiritual warfare at New Life Church, the megachurch he founded in Colorado Springs. It had been for years the headquarters for the unbiblical Spiritual Warfare Movement that John Wimber started and that C. Peter Wagner (until recently a member of New Life) has long directed. Satan apparently had little problem attacking this supposed bastion of "spiritual power" and taking out Haggard, its top man. That seems odd indeed. "Binding demons" all over the world, only to have them invade Spiritual Warfare's headquarters? Something isn't right!

Haggard's shocking fall into grievous sin (reportedly homosexuality and drug abuse) shook the evangelical church early in 2007. How could this happen, and how could he carry on this deceit at the same time that he was the shepherd of a 14,000-member congregation and the President of the 30-million-member National Association of Evangelicals? We all grieved! But even the world was surprised by the "cure" he intends to take: going back to school to study *psychology*. The following leaked email from Haggard explains:

> Jesus is starting to put me back together. . . . As part of New Life's efforts to help me, they sent Gayle and me to Phoenix for a three week psychological intensive that gave us three years worth of analysis and treatment. We all wanted to know why I developed

such incongruity in my life. Thankfully, with the tools we gained there, along with the powerful way God has been illuminating His Word and the Holy Spirit has been convicting and healing me, we now have growing understanding which is giving me some hope for a future.

Gayle and I have decided to move from Colorado Springs to go back to school [to get] our masters in Psychology so we can work together serving others the rest of our lives. Since we are taking our classes on-line, we can live anywhere that's affordable. Then we'll travel to location for short in-class requirements.

So, once again, we are forced to accept the shattering "truth": the Bible can't really live up to its promise to be "a lamp unto [our] feet and a light unto [our] path" (Psalm 119:105). It is not enough to be born again of the Holy Spirit through faith in Christ; and it is not enough that Christ has become our very life, expressing His resurrection life through us. The Bible has lied to us. Its promises are not true—at least the promise of victory over the world, the flesh, and the devil without the additional help we need from psychology. Most disillusioning of all is the fact that the Bible hid these essential truths from the church for nineteen hundred years, and Satan (who seems to be on our side after all!) has only lately revealed them by his new prophets of truth, Freud, Jung, Rogers, Maslow, Adler, et al.—sworn enemies of God and Christ, every one of them.

Contrary to what the Holy Spirit promises through Peter, tragically, our Lord and His Word, by His "divine power," have *not* "given unto us all things that pertain unto life and godliness, through the knowledge of him that hath called us to glory and virtue. . . that by these ye might be partakers of the divine nature, having escaped the corruption that is in the world through lust" (2 Peter 1:3–4). That was apparently a bogus promise. Something vital has been missing from Christianity all of these centuries since Christ died and resurrected. It is a mystery why so many more Christians through history, without psychology to help them, have not succumbed (as have so many in our day) to seducing spirits and doctrines of devils and wicked practices.

If the pastor of New Life Church discovered that the New Life he received from Christ and preached to his congregation failed him, what hope is there for the rest of us who have been relying upon promises that Christ and the Holy Spirit apparently can't keep? This is a solemn question. If there is a *Megashift*, it seems to be shifting in the wrong direction.

Fortunately, we are told, there is hope—not entirely in Christ, the Holy Spirit, and His Word, but in *psychology*! Haggard desperately cried out for help, and Christian psychologists came to the rescue. What the Holy Spirit apparently failed to include in Scripture (or lacked the power to fulfill), the emissaries of Satan have, in an ecumenical gesture of goodwill, graciously decided to share with the befuddled followers of Christ. Godless humanists have been able to supply the essential missing "psychological intensive . . . analysis and treatment" that the Holy Bible and Holy Spirit were not able to pass on to Haggard and other professed followers of Christ. That revelation awaited the coming in the nineteenth century of the new prophets of psychology, who were all anti-Christians.

Christian psychologists hailed Haggard's brave and enlightened determination to join their ranks. After all, many of them confessed, "It was our own personal problems that led us to study psychology." One can only marvel that the apostles and prophets upon whom the Church was built (Ephesians 2:20) and the martyrs described in Hebrews 11 were able to triumph over the world, the flesh, and the devil without any help whatsoever from psychology. Perhaps Ted Haggard could have managed that also by the same confidence *they* had in God's promises in His Word and by the power of the Holy Spirit—and so could we. Now that would be good news!

Indeed, this is exactly what the Scripture promises to those who will live by faith. That the simple gospel is "the power of God unto salvation to every one who believes" and that through faith God "always causeth us to triumph in Christ" (2 Corinthians 2:14) has been demonstrated fully in lives ablaze with the love of Christ through the ages. Nor is there any more clever way for Satan to prevent Christians from triumphing over him and his deceit than to get them to believe that, in addition to the Bible, they need psychology in order to live victoriously by faith in Christ. Perhaps this will be James Rutz's "whole new form of Christianity" that will usher in this last days great revival—or is it apostasy?

QUESTION: I believe you have stepped out beyond your depth by dealing with a subject on which you are not an expert. There are people who really need and benefit from Prozac, lithium, and other drugs; and for you to say they don't need them and that they are just not trusting the Lord enough is going to give many of them a sense of guilt. A lot of people will be hurt. Why don't you also suggest that diabetics give up their insulin? If we are exempt from brain disorders just because we are Christians, then we should also be exempt from the flu! I agree that there are "no chemical solutions to spiritual problems," but the drugs referred to are not primarily given to deal with spiritual problems. They are used to deal with serious affective mood disorders. For you to accuse those of us who, through no fault of our own, are afflicted with these disorders of having spiritual problems is cruel and unfeeling—a dangerous and sinful act on your part. It is not your place to diagnose diseases of the mind (which do exist, regardless of what you say). Although I would never tell anyone else to take these drugs, I have indeed been helped by them.

RESPONSE: We discover again how difficult it is, no matter how careful we are, to avoid serious misunderstandings. First of all, I have pronounced no judgment on anyone taking medication, nor have I said they didn't need it and should stop. (In fact, I said, "A word of caution: we are not advocating that anyone now taking medication should abruptly stop [which] could have serious consequences.") I did not suggest that Christians are immune to having brain disorders or that brain disorders are due to lack of faith or to a spiritual problem of the individual. (In fact, I said, "There is no doubt that much can go wrong with the brain as a physical instrument.") I did not attempt to "diagnose diseases." (In fact, I have said, "Any change in medication should only be under the supervision of a physician.")

I do believe that all of mankind's problems are the result of his separation from God and are therefore at their root spiritual. Had Adam and Eve (and all of their descendants) not sinned, none of today's *physical* ailments/diseases would exist, nor would death. Without sin, there would be no behavioral problems. I do not, however, suggest that every problem on earth today is due to some sin on the part of the individual experiencing it.

Yes, I have often pointed out the difference between the brain as a physical organ, which can therefore suffer trauma or disease and needs medical help, and the mind, which is not physical. Consequently, "mental illness" is a misnomer that can be used to excuse sin as sickness, avoid moral responsibility, and thus "treat" sin as a "psychological problem" needing therapy instead of repentance and God's help. Even non-Christian psychologists and psychiatrists have pointed this out. For example, Thomas Szasz, a leading research psychiatrist and nonpracticing Jew, said that psychology had mistakenly turned sin into a disease of the mind.

(Please, there is no comparison between insulin, which operates below the neck, and drugs that affect the brain. And remember, no one knows exactly how harmful these drugs are, much less what they actually do to the brain!)

It is true that I am neither a medical doctor nor an expert on drugs, nor did my conclusions require such knowledge. I simply suggested that in at least some cases dependence upon a drug or drugs could become a substitute for dependence upon the Lord; and I tried to encourage greater trust in God. I would expect Christians to agree with that.

Even the secular world recognizes the problem with pharmacological alleviation of stress or distress. For example, influential psychoanalyst Elizabeth Zetzel, M.D. (now deceased), author of *The Capacity for Emotional Growth*, considered a person's endurance of anxiety and depression essential to proper emotional growth. She warned that to improve mood artificially with a pill could deny the person the very strengthening experience needed for a real solution.[9] How much more could this be true for Christians who may too readily succumb to the temptation to take the easy way out through a drug and thus may miss the lesson of endurance and faith God wants to teach them! I neither diagnose nor accuse anyone. I simply exhort everyone to consider this possibility and act upon it as the Lord leads.

I have also issued some warnings because the alleged "wonder drugs" are so highly touted and so seldom are any cautions given except in fine print. Remember, there was a time when cocaine was as highly acclaimed by the medical profession (and its benefits sworn to by users) as Prozac has been in our day. Freud took cocaine himself, sang its praises, and prescribed it for others. Only later was it banned. We lack space to provide the long list of drugs that in more recent times have been praised for a few years, only to be banned or greatly restricted as their destructiveness has been reluctantly admitted.

LSD was hailed by many psychiatrists as a "miracle drug." It was in use for years before it was banned by the government in 1966, and some M.D.s still petition for its restoration.

There have been numerous cases of suicide, murder, and other problems traced to Prozac. It was only licensed in 1988; by February 1990, *American Journal of Psychiatry* research psychiatrist Dr. Martin Teicher "documented the cases of six depressed patients who became obsessed with violent suicidal thoughts two to seven weeks after starting treatment with Prozac. Four tried to hurt or kill themselves. The compulsion subsided after the patients went off the drug."[10] By 1991, a multitude of those damaged or destroyed by Prozac, or their heirs, had formed "Prozac Survivors Support Groups" all over America. By the end of 1992, one hundred seventy lawsuits had been filed against Prozac manufacturer Eli Lilly. Doesn't this information call for caution?

I have also reminded readers that the brain is the most complex mechanism in the universe. No one knows how psychiatric drugs work or the full effect, especially long-term, that they have on the brain. For a physician to prescribe Prozac (or Ritalin, or other similar drugs) is not like a mechanic fine-tuning an engine. The prescription is not based on a diagnosis of the brain but most often on a behavioral profile. Thus, Prozac is prescribed for everything from "low self-esteem" and "winter blues" to obesity, anorexia, bulimia, phobia, anxiety, chronic fatigue syndrome, premenstrual syndrome, migraines, and arthritis. It is not given to "balance" the brain (in fact, it causes *imbalance* by disrupting serotonin and dopamine) but rather to artificially improve one's feelings about oneself.

Peter Breggin (*Your Drug May Be Your Problem*) is not the only psychiatrist to criticize "biological psychiatry," i.e., the use of drugs to adjust mood. There are many others, such as the authors of the eight essays in the 1995 book *Pseudoscience in Biological Psychiatry*. Critical articles have appeared in professional journals of psychiatry and psychology. For example, *Psychology Today* contained a lengthy article that concluded that "two-thirds of the cases [in all studies] do as well with placebo as with active medication."[11]

Thus, the efficacy of psychotropic drugs is open to question, a question that has not been settled. Elizabeth Wurtzel, author of *Prozac Nation*, writes, "A strong hardy depression will outsmart any chemical. Even on Prozac and lithium I have had severe depressive episodes."

Nor is it true that drugs are an inappropriate subject for *The Berean Call* and unrelated to Scripture. The New Testament mentions sorcery four times, condemns it, indicates that it will be revived in the last days, and that men will refuse to repent of it (Revelation 9:21; 18:23; 21:8; 22:15). The Greek word translated "sorcery" is *pharmakeia,* from which we get the word "pharmacy," or "drugs." Psychoactive drugs have long been associated with the occult, and Prozac is now very popular as a recreational drug for youth. Surely, at least a warning is in order.

We desire to be helpful. We certainly do not want to cause offense or pain, but rather to encourage a careful consideration of the medical factors and dangers involved and also a deeper trust in God.

QUESTION: Why don't you ever speak out and take leadership against the political and social problems we face today? It seems to me that this is a great lack in your ministry.

RESPONSE: I have spoken out and written against sin in its various manifestations all around us. To give political and social problems more attention than we have would not be biblical. Furthermore, it would take time and effort that ought rather to be invested in rescuing souls for eternity.

Evangelicals who lead the fight against immorality in society rarely oppose false doctrine in the church. This is a simple and consistent fact. Yet Christ and His apostles gave no time to crusading against the evils outside the church but concentrated upon correction of error within. Jesus neither specifically opposed nor taught against the evils of the Roman Empire nor the general wickedness of society in His day. How could we justify spending time and effort on what our Lord did not? We find no example to follow in the apostles or early church that would cause us to lead a crusade against the political, social, and moral evils of our society.

Ironically, the one culprit that has been the major cause of the rapid and deep slide into immorality in both the world and church in the last forty years is generally promoted rather than opposed by those leading the crusade against political and social evils. That culprit is psychology.

Psychology has redefined sin as sickness. This has excused immorality, thereby encouraging it. Now, the sinner is diagnosed as in need of "therapy" rather than being held accountable and called upon to repent. Every kind of failure, from eating too much to murder is excused as some kind of addiction. Adulterers are now "sex addicts." Their insurance policies pay for extended "treatment" at "Christian" psychiatric hospitals. Jesus said to "Go and sin no more" (John 8:11). This is far "too simplistic" for today's psychological, sophisticated world and church. It is rejected by very definition by Christian psychology. How could they charge for therapy if repentance and faith are the effective cure?

The explosion of crime, rebellion, and immorality has coincided with the exponential growth of psychology since the early 1950s. So has the increase in the number of psychiatric beds in hospitals. As we have often pointed out, psychology has been rightly called the only profession that "creates the diseases that it claims to cure."

The Bible commends firm discipline (Proverbs 13:24; 22:15; Hebrews 12:6, etc.). It is exactly what children need, but it is now called "child abuse." Children have even been removed from Christian parents who lovingly "applied the rod." People wonder why we are raising a generation of rebels against God and all authority. What once was called laziness or stubbornness or rebellion is now excused as some new "syndrome." As mentioned in an earlier chapter, the number of children diagnosed as having "learning disabilities" nearly tripled from 1977 to 1992! Common sense would declare that children are not less intelligent; they are being trained to be less willing to honor parents and other authorities.

"Difficult" children are placed on Ritalin after they and their parents have been convinced by some therapist of their abnormality, a stigma (and excuse) that could be with them for life. In spite of its addictive nature, disputable evidence of its helpfulness, and many reported incidents of violence and suicide brought on by withdrawal from it, the prescribing of Ritalin rises continually. More children are diagnosed with attention deficit hyperactivity disorder (ADHD) in North America and given drugs to "help them behave" than in all the rest of the world.[12] "The United States accounts for approximately 90 percent of total world manufacture and consumption of the substance."[13] Whatever did we do without it—and why isn't the rest of the world similarly affected?!

Inventing new varieties of "mental illnesses" has increased the power of psychiatrists and psychologists over society. Americans now suffer by the millions from alleged maladies that were unknown a few years ago. Again, these are defined in the "bible of mental illness," the American Psychiatric Association's *Diagnostic and Statistical Manual for Mental Disorders* (*DSM*). The most popular and abused "diagnosis" is "biochemical imbalance in the brain." Notice what Peter Breggin, psychiatrist, leading expert, and outspoken critic of psychiatric drugs has to say:

> Some theoreticians would urge us to focus on the molecular level by looking for biochemical imbalances. But that's sheer speculation. . . . Besides, whose biochemical imbalance are we looking for? That of the child who is out of control or the caregiver who has difficulty disciplining? That of the child who isn't learning or the teacher who hasn't figured out how to reach this child. . . ? In short, whose brain isn't working right?
>
> In our own experience, most people with depression and anxiety have obvious *reasons* for how they feel. . . . But even if some people do turn out to have subtle, undetected biochemical imbalances, there is no reason to give them drugs like Prozac or Xanax that *cause* biochemical imbalances and disrupt brain function. . . .
>
> We have no techniques for measuring the actual levels of neurotransmitters in the synapses between the [brain] cells. Thus all the talk about biochemical imbalances is pure guesswork . . . [in fact] psychiatric drugs *create* imbalances. . . .
>
> The notion that Prozac corrects biochemical imbalances is sheer speculation—propaganda from the biological psychiatric industry. But disruption of biochemical reactions in the brain, causing severe biochemical imbalances and abnormal firing among brain cells, is a proven fact about Prozac. . . .
>
> How does the brain react to the intrusion of psychiatric drugs such as Prozac, Ritalin, or Xanax? The brain reacts as if it is being

invaded by toxic substances; it tries to overcome or compensate for the harmful drug effects. In the process, the brain . . . numbs itself to the drug and, in so doing, actually kills some of its own functions. So when a doctor tells us that Prozac is putting our biochemicals into balance, we are being badly misled. In actuality, Prozac is profoundly disrupting the function of the brain.

The approach taken by psychiatrists and other medical doctors . . . is both simple-minded and destructive. In contemporary psychiatry, the doctor almost always assumes that the problem lies in the "hardware" of the brain (i.e., in "biochemical imbalances"). . . . It is impossible to reduce a person's emotional suffering to biochemical aberrations without doing something psychologically and morally destructive to that person. We reduce the reality of that individual's life to a narrowly focused speculation about brain chemistry.[14]

Is it because so many of those Christians leading the crusade against immorality in society are themselves supporting "Christian" psychology that they fail to sound the alarm that psychology (this includes "Christian psychology") is the major contributor to today's growing immoral and rebellious behavior? If you are looking for a worthy political and social cause, you might research and report on the growing numbers of pre-school children that are being given drugs such as Ritalin. This is a crime of massive proportions that is going to impact generations to come if Christ does not return very soon! One researcher reports:

The federal government wants to perform mental health screening on infants and get them started on drugs which they will take for their entire lives, if the drugs don't kill them first. . . . Already, children as young as three who wind up in the foster care system are receiving psychiatric drugs for such disorders as schizophrenia, bipolar disorder or depression, with over 60% of foster children in Texas, nearly two-thirds in Massachusetts, and 55% of foster children in Florida on as many as 16 different psychiatric drugs. . . .

Based on current Bush administration policy, the government wants to "fundamentally alter the form and function of the mental health service delivery system in this country" by implementing the recommendations of the President's New Freedom Commission on Mental Health.

One of these programs, which is already in operation, is Foundations for Learning, which was added into the No Child Left Behind Act at the last minute by the conference committee. According to Dr. Karen R. Effrem, of the International Center for the Study of Psychiatry and Psychology, it "provides federal funds in the form of grants to states and other agencies to provide preschool screening, parent education, social services, home visits, transportation and curriculum to support 'social and emotional development' for children from birth to age seven. . . .

"The criteria for diagnosing mental disorders are very vague in general, but are extremely vague and inaccurate for children," says Dr. Effrem. "These grants will further subsidize the labeling and drugging of an alarmingly large population of young children with potent medications that have not been studied in that age group. . . . "

The NFC recommendations include a wide variety of mental health programs targeted at children as young as age three, and early intervention for some children from birth.

Michael Ostrolenk, a licensed psychotherapist and public policy consultant who founded the Medical Privacy Coalition, wrote, "Their influence [of the mental health establishment over government] causes our children to be labeled in infancy, and it creates a never-ending market for psychiatric drugs. The long term effects of these drugs on the brains of our children are unknown. They also create a market for other drugs used to treat the chronic side effects like obesity and diabetes, and they will be needed throughout the lives of those affected, enhancing drug company profits while bankrupting taxpayer funded programs. As these programs multiply, the use of politically motivated labeling and drugging for children who do not comply with the indoctrination of the federal curriculum will increase. Brave New World will appear less and less like fiction unless these programs are stopped."[15]

If you want to take on a social or political cause, here is something to go after. In the final analysis, however, by example and teaching, Christ, the apostles, and the early church showed that calling those who will heed out of the world for citizenship in heaven through the gospel is the only solution with proven and lasting results, and it is what we are to focus upon. The gospel is the power of God unto salvation not only from the penalty of sin but from its power in our lives. The church has lost confidence in God and His Word to meet our needs. The Christian mission—yes, Christianity itself—has been redefined. Let us return to the Lord and to His Word in obedience to our original and biblical mission!

QUESTION: You and Tom both wrote good, factual articles in *The Berean Call* and did ten radio programs about Rick Warren and *The Purpose-Driven Life*. Then, at his invitation, you [Dave] attended a pastors conference at Saddleback, and when you returned you seemed to have softened your position. As you know, Warren has had a column in the *Ladies' Home Journal* for nearly a year. I have yet to find the gospel in any of them! What he does present is pop psychology exactly like Robert Schuller, yet you say he has broken all ties with Schuller. Here is just one example from his March 2005 column: *"Self-esteem still wobbly. . . ? These five simple truths will show you that you don't need to be perfect to be priceless. . . . To truly love yourself, you need to know the five truths that form the basis of a healthy self-image: 1) Accept yourself; 2) Love yourself; 3) Be true to yourself; 4) Forgive yourself; 5) Believe in yourself."* This is typical of the non sequiturs Warren offers. He promises five "truths" but gives five things to do, none of them a truth. This is pop psychology that even numerous secular psychologists and psychiatrists have refuted—and it contradicts the clear teaching of Scripture. Warren's "accept . . . love . . . be true to . . . forgive . . . believe in yourself" blatantly opposes Christ's "except a man deny himself, and take up his cross, and follow me, he cannot be my disciple" (Matthew 16:24; Mark 8:34; Luke 9:23, etc.). How can you say Warren loves the Lord and has a passion for souls when his actions do not support such a claim? I think many people have been confused by your apparent change from criticizing Rick Warren to apparently supporting him.

RESPONSE: Thank you for your concern. Hearing Rick in person and talking with him face to face gave me a different opinion from the one I had formed by reading his books and watching him on video. I would still say that he is a sincere Christian who genuinely desires the salvation of souls. The fact that he so seldom, and then usually only obliquely, presents the gospel is an inexcusable contradiction—but that can be said of many Christian leaders. Joel Osteen has built the largest church in America (thirty thousand each weekend) by doing the same thing! The popularity of such leaders among Christians today is a sad commentary on the apostate condition of the church and the counterfeit "Christianity" flooding the world.

Rick's defenders told me that he wanted to gain the attention and trust of *Journal* readers before giving them the gospel. That excuse can no longer be used. His column ran in *LHJ* over a span of two years, and at the time of this writing, he has yet to give readers the gospel! Instead, as you say, he has given them the lies of pop psychology—again inexcusable. He can't be that ignorant—certainly not after reading the Bible for years.

Yes, he did tell me that he had broken with Schuller entirely. Yet not just his *LHJ* column but his writings and preaching in general continue to be filled with "Schullerisms." I had hoped through personal contact with Rick to help him. That opportunity seems to have passed. His huge success makes any admission of error increasingly difficult.

Rick is not alone among high-profile Christian leaders in the promotion of psychology's deadly selfisms. They are now common fare in the church. Nor is he alone (and perhaps not the worst) in partnering with Roman Catholics and promoting A.A.'s occult 12 Steps. That does not excuse Rick. But shouldn't we question the commitment to Christ and the gospel on the part of Billy Graham, Chuck Colson, and Bill Bright (all three praised Sir John Marks Templeton and his prize for progress toward the Antichrist's world religion and failed to give the gospel to the vast and needy audiences when they accepted that prize); J. I. Packer and every other signatory to ECT; Josh McDowell, David Jeremiah; James Dobson and every Christian psychologist, and all who accept and promote their lies?

Sadly, Rick is merely a reflection of the church of today. Almost every pastor of a large church, and Christian leaders from Billy Graham and the late Jerry Falwell down, have had nothing but praise for Christian psychology. James Dobson is still one of the most popular Christian leaders in the world. Rick gives lip service to understanding and opposing psychology, but in practice he teaches and supports it.

I am not excusing Rick Warren. I believe he is a genuine brother who has been led into compromise in order to reach a wider audience—but with what? He seems to be only part of a compromise of biblical truth that has enlisted Christian leaders as never before in history and is playing into Satan's plans to produce a false church for Antichrist.

In his December 2005 article, Warren encouraged *Journal* readers to "offer a taste of God's peace to those who've lost hope by following the example of Jesus." It was good advice for Christians but deadly deception for unsaved readers. *The Ladies' Home Journal* is one of the ten largest magazines in America with about 14.5 million readers. Millions of women who desperately need the gospel that will take them to heaven were instead treated to Warren's P. E.A.C.E. plan to improve life on earth:

1) Plant faith communities* [any 'faith' will do whose adherents are willing to follow the plan] *Changed in 2007 to "Promote reconcilication" (man-to-God, -governments, -earth, and each other, regardless of creedal conflicts).*

2) Equip leaders [for earthly secular tasks]

3) Assist the poor [for a better life on earth]

4) Care for the sick [bodies—but what about the soul?]

5) Educate the next generation [for this brief life]

We credit Rick and his wife, Kay, with having tender hearts for the physical needs of the poor, the uneducated, the diseased and dying, and for good works that put many of us to shame. But we fault them for hiding the gospel from those who need it and who without it will perish for eternity!

A search of *LHJ* issues reveals that Rick is still writing his column, though not every month. Tragically, through April 2007, he has yet to give his readers the gospel. He refers to "God" often, but never explains who the true God is. Yet he must know that many if not most of *LHJ* readers embrace one false God or another.

Much of what he writes is sound advice for sensible living. Christians would apply what he says about "God" to the true God of the Bible. To leave others with their false gods and the impression that any god will do is both tragic and heartless. Even when he has an easy opportunity to refer to Christ, he avoids that word. For example, in his December 2006 column he advises: "Do what the Wise Men did that very first Christmas: Seek God."

In fact, they sought Christ, and our Lord clearly declares that no one can come unto the Father except through Him. At the time of this printing, Rick has yet to provide this essential truth to trusting readers!

QUESTION: **The enclosed article by John H. Coe from R. C. Sproul's Ligonier Ministries' *Tabletalk* doesn't ring true to me. It blatantly states that the Bible "alone is insufficient" and elevates what it calls "natural revelation" to the level of Scripture. That contradicts my understanding of the Bible. Could you comment on this?**

RESPONSE: John H. Coe is currently Associate Professor of Philosophy and Theology at Talbot School of Theology, which is part of Biola University. In order to justify "Christian" psychology's borrowing of the "wisdom of this world" (1 Corinthians 1:20; 2:6; 3:19) from Freud, Jung, et al., and calling it part of "God's truth" to supplement the Bible, Coe must show that the Bible is insufficient or abandon his profession.

This he attempts to do in a paper titled "Why Biblical Counseling is Unbiblical," reprinted in Sproul's *Tabletalk*—demonstrating that Sproul is no less deceived by "Christian psychology" than most other leaders. Coe declares that whatever is "natural" is good and that one can deduce a "science of [moral] values" simply from observing nature. This is obviously not true.

Nature has no morals nor can science reveal morals, which are not physical and thus not subject to scientific analysis or evaluation. Neither can there be a science of human nature because man is not a robot, and human qualities such as love, joy, peace, choice, a sense of right and wrong, etc., cannot be explained in scientific cause-and-effect terms. Einstein confessed that science has nothing to do with religion. Sir Arthur Eddington, astrophysicist who helped to experimentally verify Einstein's theory of general relativity, declared that to imagine that consciousness is ruled by scientific laws "is as preposterous as the suggestion that a nation could be ruled by . . . the laws of grammar. . . . 'Ought' takes us outside chemistry and physics."[16]

The universe in which we find ourselves bears witness to the power, wisdom, and genius of its Creator but does not tell us of His love, His purpose for mankind, nor could it teach any moral lessons. Humanity's common recognition of right and wrong comes not from nature but from God's laws written in the conscience (Romans 2:14–15).

In the article, Coe accuses those who affirm the sufficiency of Scripture of having "retreated, particularly from the light of reason and natural revelation, to the island of faith, clinging desperately and unfortunately to the illusion of a Bible-alone approach to wisdom which is solely 'from above.'" He sounds like a humanist! He declares that without natural revelation "the Bible alone is insufficient." Of course, he includes in natural revelation the part of "God's truth" that secular psychologists have allegedly discovered, and which is therefore needed to supplement Scripture.

Yes, the Bible is insufficient when it comes to flying an airplane, repairing an engine, transplanting a kidney—but not when it comes to those "things that pertain to life and godliness," all of which Peter says have been given to us in Christ (2 Peter 1:3–4). Paul says that through Scripture alone the man or woman of God is "thoroughly furnished unto all good works" (2 Timothy 3:17). Christ said that the Holy Spirit is "the Spirit of truth, whom the world cannot receive" (John 14:17) and who guides believers "into all truth" (John 16:13). He said that those who continue in His word, which "is truth" (John 17:17), know "the truth" (John 8:32)—not *part* of the truth—and are thereby set free, not partially free and still in need of psychological/psychiatric help, much less from drugs!

The Bible's declaration that the "natural man" cannot know God's truth, which is only revealed by the Spirit of God (1 Corinthians 2:14), is proof that Freud et al. had nothing of God's truth to impart. That fact alone thoroughly demolishes Coe's thesis and the foolish notion that any part of God's truth is to be found in secular psychology. It isn't there.

Inasmuch as all of God's truth is contained in God's Word, Christian psychology has nothing to offer and leads into gross error. Preventing God's people from believing in the sufficiency of Scripture is essential for Christian psychologists if they hope to remain in business, and John H. Coe is determined to prove this thesis. The fact that R. C. Sproul's *Tabletalk* would join in promoting it tells us volumes about Sproul and his Calvinistic ministry.

QUESTION: I have some Christian relatives who are involved with Amway. Besides "bugging" me to sign up, is there anything I should be concerned about for their sakes?

RESPONSE: Our knowledge and experience with some aspects of Amway (now called Quixtar in North America) has given us concerns of which you should be aware. Although the corporation makes the disclaimer that it is a business and does not endorse a particular religion, there is an overt Christian emphasis among most of its leading "independent" distributors, who individually may have as many as three hundred thousand distributors under them. Amway's business orientation and high-powered sales techniques, when intermingled with evangelizing, inevitably combine reaching people for Christ with reaching them for profit—an impossibility in view of Christ's clear declaration, "Ye cannot serve God and mammon" (Matthew 6:24).

Many "Christian" Amway/Quixtar distributors concentrate their recruiting among evangelical Christians. Their instructed approach to potential sub-distributors expressly avoids mentioning the name Amway in initial get-togethers (why is that?), and the pitch directed at Christians emphasizes that "by increasing their financial base they can be more effective for the Lord, in terms of time and money." What happens in numerous cases, however, is that the faith of those involved becomes intermingled with pop psychology, positive mental attitude (PMA), and positive-confession beliefs. The required investment in the business of a great amount of time in the initial years often results in devastated families already lacking time together.

Of course, the intention is that eventually—when the business becomes profitable enough—there will be more time for the Lord and family than ever before. That day rarely comes because there is always the pressure to make more money and attend conventions, and much hype imposes new goals. Soon success becomes an overwhelming obsession in spite of original good intentions to the contrary.

An Amway/Quixtar distributor becomes a teacher/model/trainer/sponsor of those whom he recruits. Although this may seem to offer good opportunities to present Christian principles in a discipleship format, the training materials and particularly the reading lists promote a dangerous mixture of "Christianized" success and PMA concepts, mind-science beliefs, self-oriented psychology, and occult techniques and methods. The recommended book list includes such authors as occultist Napoleon Hill, PMA theologians Robert Schuller and NormanVincent Peale, motivational speaker Zig Ziglar, motivational psychologist Denis Waitley, and positive confession writer/preacher Charles Capps.

Those in Amway/Quixtar make money not primarily by selling products but from a percentage of the Amway income of those they have recruited. Their recruits become subdistributors who, in turn, recruit others to become their subdistributors. The more subdistributors, the greater the financial return. Therefore, though the company may have a diversity of good product, in effect Amway sees *people* as its most important product.

Second Peter 2:3 says, "And through covetousness shall they with feigned words make merchandise of you" (2 Peter 2:3).

Whereas covetousness can attract anyone to any business opportunity, Amway/Quixtar, through its ostentatious display of material success (clothes, jewelry, cars, luxurious homes, yachts, exotic vacations) in its promotions and *Amagram* magazine (now called *Achieve)*, seems to major on a theme that has caused many Christians to stumble in their faith.

QUESTION: Why do you speak of Pentecostals and charismatics in such a derogatory manner? You sound as if you have a chip on your shoulder. It's very demeaning. I resent the fact that you categorize all Pentecostal charismatics as believing in the "name-it-and-claim-it" movement. You have also stated that charismatics love the book *Quenching the Spirit* by Wm. De Arteaga. This book sounds like it's straight from the pit of hell!! Neither we nor any of our charismatic friends would ever touch anything recommended by Rita Bennett because she's into such error herself, nor would we read anything recommended by anyone from Fuller Seminary. You don't have to be a super-Christian to know that Christianity and psychology don't mix!

Please, please stop categorizing Pentecostal charismatics as being ignorant of Satan's devices.

RESPONSE: I did not intend to "categorize all Pentecostal charismatics as believing in the 'name-it-and-claim-it'" movement and as being deluded by De Arteaga, Rita Bennett, et al., as you suggest. If that was the impression given, then I apologize, for that was not intended. On the other hand, in spite of your own aversion to false doctrine, the Assemblies of God are not as clean as you imagine. Is it not true that Oral and Richard Roberts, positive confession, or word-faith teachers, and similar heretics, are popularly received in many large Assemblies of God?

As for the Pentecostal/charismatic movement in general, does it not provide most of the support and followers for those who hold to serious false doctrines, such as Oral and Richard Roberts, Kenneth Hagin, Kenneth Copeland, David Yonggi Cho, Benny Hinn, Joyce Meyer, Joel Osteen, T. D. Jakes, Rod Parsely, Robert Tilton, et al.? (I'm not suggesting that each of these individuals holds *all* false doctrines, but they *all* hold many.) Nor is this true only among the fringe fanatics. Is it not the case also with the mainstream Pentecostal churches? Don't nearly all of them promote "Christian psychology," with its deadly humanism?

Hasn't the AOG honored its own hero psychologist, Dr. Richard Dobbins, for the past fifty years? Isn't he a long-time member of the American Psychological Association, which is atheist/humanist dominated? Hasn't his goal long been to integrate psychology with Scripture; and isn't that based upon the belief that the Bible may be inerrant, but it is not sufficient to deal with the Christian's "mental health"?

Why don't the Assemblies of God vigorously oppose the false doctrines and practices and outright heresies so prominent in the Pentecostal/charismatic movement? Why is there not a strong voice raised from your Springfield, MO, leadership against the excesses and heresies promoted by Paul Crouch around the world? (Crouch was raised in the AOG, is really a product of Springfield, and, though no longer ordained, is very popular in AOG churches.) On the contrary, there seems to be confusion and compromise within the AOG's own ranks, right up to the top. Let me give some examples.

Glen D. Cole of Sacramento has served at the top level of AOG leadership as an executive presbyter, and is presently the district superintendent of Northeren California/Nevada, yet he is deeply involved with much that you say the AOG stands against. He has even had a Catholic bishop perform the Mass in his church at which Cole gave the sermon and said he had "never felt a greater presence of the Holy Spirit at a meeting." Yes, officially the AOG Bylaws, Article VIII, Sec. 11, seem to oppose the ecumenical movement and forbid participation in it, but the language leaves loopholes. Large enough loopholes, apparently, for the AOG itself to have engaged for some years in official "dialogue" with Roman Catholics, reported upon favorably in the *Pentecostal Evangel*!

Not only Cole, but AOG pastors Paul Radke and Karl Strader have served on the highly ecumenical North American Renewal Service Committee along-side numerous Catholic leaders and ecumenists. While the AOG seems to deny that David (formerly Paul Yonggi) Cho of Korea is officially affiliated with it, he is very popular with pastors of some of the largest AOG churches. For example, Cho was a featured speaker at the Grand Rapids First Assembly of God, along with AOG Assistant General Superintendent Everett Stenhouse. One of Cho's close friends and supporters, AOG pastor Tommy Reid, has been involved in pushing the occult practice of visualization of Jesus and two-way dialogue with God for years. Cho also was appointed an original committee member of the AOG's worldwide "Decade of Harvest."

The past (until his retirement in 1993) General Superintendent, G. Raymond Carlson, has been on the Board of Reference of Richard Foster's Renovaré, along with Catholics, ecumenists, and inner healers. Renovaré is pushing, worldwide, Foster's brand of mysticism, which includes visualization and advocates the "spiritual practices" of Catholic mystics and the integration of psychology and theology.

You say that you don't know anyone in your "charismatic circle" who believes in integrating psychology and theology, but I guarantee you that most charismatics, like most noncharismatics, do believe in it.

The AOG has its own involvement in "Christian psychology," and some of the leaders and pastors of its largest churches are involved in promoting the lies of self-esteem and self-love. You remind me that "there are people of all denominations who do believe in Christian psychologists—why don't you pick on some of the other believers?" Apparently, you haven't read my books and newsletters. I don't "pick on" anyone. However, I do point out error as I see it in comparison to the Word of God, and I have not been selective in those whose beliefs I hold up to the light of God's Word.

Were not the Bereans commended for testing Paul's teachings against the Bible? Isn't that what every Christian should be doing with every teaching, no matter how popular or how highly regarded the teacher? We at TBC feel compelled to follow the Berean example, which the Bible commends (Acts 17:11).

QUESTION: I've been given a couple of books by Brennan Manning, and although I had some trouble with *A Ragamuffin Gospel*, I was shocked by *The Signature of Jesus*. My impression is that he is a Catholic mystic in evangelical "wool." Is he trying to pull that wool over our eyes or what? And these are by trusted Christian publishers!

RESPONSE: *The Signature of Jesus* passes off popular psychological ideas (such as "unconditional love"—an unbiblical term that provides shelter for all manner of false doctrine and sins) under the guise of deeper spirituality. It is an emotionally charged and very persuasive primer for attracting Christians to the mystical contemplative way of spirituality. The modern contemplative approach has its roots in the Catholic and Orthodox mystics from the fourth century through the Middle Ages. Although its theology is foundationally Roman Catholic, the emphasis of contemplative prayer is on mystical experiential methods rather than the more common devotional activities of Catholicism. For example, where most Catholics stress liturgical acts in order to draw nearer to God (pray the rosary, make novenas, attend Holy Hours, perform acts of penance, etc.), contemplatives emphasize techniques of practicing silence before God in order to experience His presence. Through his books and speaking, former Catholic priest Brennan Manning has taken contemplative concepts and techniques (along with his Catholic beliefs) to increasing numbers of unsuspecting evangelicals, who are his main audience.

Throughout *The Signature of Jesus*, Manning takes biblical tenets and spins them in the direction of his mystical worldview. Faith, for example, is seen as a "journey across the chasm between knowledge and experience" (p. 18), with the experiential being preferable. Faith is advocated as belief in one's subjective spiritual experiences. The objective content of the faith through adherence to biblical doctrines is denigrated. An anti-doctrinal attitude pervades his book: "Instead of remaining content with the bare letter [of Scripture], we should pass on to the more profound mysteries that are available only through intimate and heartfelt knowledge [read "experience"] of the person of Jesus" (p.189).

Manning's own "salvation" testimony reflects his contemplative perspective: "On February 8, 1956, I met Jesus and moved from belief [meaning Catholic doctrine] to faith [meaning trust in his experience]. In this first-ever-in-my-life experience of being unconditionally loved, in one blinding moment of salvific truth, it was real knowledge calling for personal engagement of my mind and heart. Christianity was being loved and falling in love with Jesus Christ" (pp. 28–29).

Manning offers no declaration of the gospel that must be believed for salvation. Many have "fallen in love" with Jesus, as Gandhi did, while rejecting the gospel—the gospel that we never find in *Signature of Jesus*. This is as far as Manning takes his readers. His shunning of sound doctrine as inadequate is like an echo from Christian psychology, which either neglects Scripture or "integrates" it with so much humanism that its meaning is obscured.

Abusing the Genesis account and leaning on Thomas Aquinas, Manning claims that man is "flawed but good" (pp.100, 126–27, 178)—again an echo of the gospel of self-esteem, self-image, self-acceptance, etc. This unbiblical belief is then developed into a Schullerian gospel of universal acceptance and love based upon people realizing "their own belovedness" (p. 171). A key aspect of this gospel includes realizing the "divine" within everyone, to which the "prayer" technique will lead its practitioners: "The task of contemplative prayer is to help me achieve the conscious awareness of the unconditionally loving God dwelling within me [i.e., within every reader]" (p. 211).

Manning doesn't hide the ecumenical and universal prospect of his contemplative gospel: "Many devout Moslems, Buddhists, and Hinduists [who] are generous and sincere in their search for God have had profound mystical experiences" (p. 170). In other words, the gospel of salvation is not objective truth that I must believe but a mystical experience that I can have. It gets worse. His belief that God dwells within everyone he makes doubly clear by quoting (Catholic priest and spiritual mystic) Thomas Merton's answer to the question, "How can we best help people to attain union with God? We must tell them that they are already united with God" (p. 211). This is heresy at its worst.

Although in *A Ragamuffin Gospel* Manning gives lip service to the biblical doctrine of justification by faith alone, it is indisputable that his "unconditionally loving" God and "universal gospel" are psychological detours around God's justice. He writes, "We experience the forgiveness of Jesus not as the reprieve of a judge but the embrace of a lover" (p. 212). His "lover," however, is not the "just God," whose conditions for salvation must be satisfied, but a psychological fiction.

God's justice, according to Scripture, demands that the death penalty for sin be paid; yet because of God's infinite love, He gave His only begotten Son to die in our place. This is not the psychologically appealing "God" Manning presents. Furthermore, God's love relationship with man is not unconditional: "He that believeth on the Son hath everlasting life: and he that believeth not the Son shall not see life; but the wrath of God abideth on him (John 3:36). Manning is leading his readers far away from the truth.

In *Signature of Jesus* he credits the "Spirit of Christ" with inviting people "across the land" to [the occult technique of] centering prayer (p.149), and leads the reader in an occult exercise of "centering down" (pp. 94, 112, 218–19). His large cast of supporting characters throughout the book are nearly all Catholic mystics, ancient and contemporary. He presents Christian psychological fallacies such as "genetic predisposition to alcoholism" (p. 61), self-forgiveness, self-acceptance, and the humanistic classic, "If you love yourself intensely and freely, then your feelings about yourself correspond perfectly to the sentiments of Jesus" (pp.105–107, 128, 174–75). This is not only pure sentimental drivel—it is destructive of truth and the repentance that leads to salvation.

Psychospiritual inner healing is affirmed (p. 62, 233); visions of his "Jesus" are described (pp. 181, 235); and vain repetitions in prayer are introduced before a forbidden image of the One who condemns such a practice: "The overhead spotlight shines on the crucifix, and [I] stare at the body naked and nailed. Prostrate on the floor, I whisper 'Come, Lord Jesus' over and over" (pp. 47, 218). Finally, we are to "seek within" ourselves this indwelling "God" about whom he speaks, including when we pray and worship (pp. 94–95, 111, 150).

Of course, true believers are indeed temples of the Holy Spirit. Never, however, does the Bible direct man to look within himself to find God. As one analyst who spent hundreds of hours studying Manning's books in detail, attending his conferences, and meeting him personally, concluded: "Speaking at a conference, Brennan Manning summed up his view of the essence of his ministry and the core of the good news: 'In healing our image of God, Jesus frees us of fear of the Father and dislike of ourselves.' This is a radical departure from the good news of Jesus Christ. Eternal life and the forgiveness of sins is replaced with psychological healing."[17]

That a trusted Christian publisher such as Multnomah (purchased by secular publisher Random House in 2006) would print—and then *keep* in print, such heresy is symptomatic of the last days.

QUESTION: **Would you please respond to CRI's *Journal* articles on biblical counseling by the Passantinos? Thank you!**

RESPONSE: Although warning that Christianized psychology isn't without fault, the Passantinos, in fact, promote it and deny the sufficiency of the Bible. (Similar confusion is expressed in the December 1995 *New Covenant*, a leading Catholic charismatic magazine.) In their final article, the Passantinos state, "The Biblical Counseling Movement (BCM) falls short of a comprehensive program." In other words, the Bible isn't enough for counseling but needs some help from Freud, Jung, Rogers, et al.

"[Dave] Hunt and some other BCM advocates take 1 [*sic*] Peter 1:3 out of context. The verse reads, 'His divine power has given us everything we need for life and godliness.' Its context is salvation, not the details of daily human living. [*TBC: Dave is not part of the BCM movement.*]"

On the contrary, one could hardly say that "life" means only eternal life in heaven, and surely "godliness" involves our behavior here on earth. The context continues: "Whereby are given unto us exceeding great and precious promises: that by these ye might be partakers of the divine nature, having escaped the corruption that is in the world through lust" (2 Peter 1:3–4). Peter then exhorts to diligence, virtue, knowledge, temperance, patience, godliness, and brotherly kindness, which are to characterize the very "daily human living" that the Passantinos claim is not Peter's subject.

Does the "divine nature" within us need psychological help? No! Peter assures us that "if ye do these things, ye shall never fall" (v. 10). Paul agrees that through heeding biblical "doctrine, reproof, correction, [and] instruction in righteousness . . . the man [or woman] of God may be perfect, thoroughly furnished unto every good work" (2 Timothy 3:16–17). The Bible is sufficient. Even the watered-down NAS says, "adequate, equipped for every good work."

The Passantinos assure us that the Bible, lacking the new wisdom of Freud et al. is deficient in its understanding of "human nature" and therefore needs to be supplemented with psychology. They offer Christian psychology's new "good news" for the troubled heart: humanist apostles of psychology have discovered new truths to make up for biblical deficiency and to provide the church at last with the understanding and tools it has lacked for nineteen hundred years. They write,

> [N]ot everything about human nature is completely explained in Scripture. We can come to a more complete, comprehensive understanding of human nature by a variety of [lately discovered] truth-gathering activities, including observation, rational evaluation, assessment, and application of what we already know to be true.

The CRI articles reflect a tragic misunderstanding of what Jesus meant by "truth" when He said, "If ye continue in my word, then are ye my disciples indeed; and ye shall know the truth, and the truth shall make you free" (John 8:31–32). The Passantinos consider anything factual to be part of "God's truth": "100 times 100 equals 10,000, and we can count on that as 'God's truth' because it corresponds to reality."

On the contrary, the Jews would have readily acknowledged that 100 x 100 = 10,000. Yet Christ said they would not believe the truth—so He certainly was not referring to mathematical or scientific facts but to something entirely different. Furthermore, Christ said that "the truth will set you free"—hardly the case with the mathematical facts the Passantinos offer as an example of what Christ meant.

Jesus promised that through obedience to His Word His disciples would know the truth—all of it, not part of it. It takes just three verses to expose the folly of the Passantinos' (and Christian psychology's) position: "Even the Spirit of truth; whom the world cannot receive" (John 14:17); "[The] Spirit of truth will guide you into all truth" (16:13); "But the natural man receiveth not the things of the Spirit of God: for they are foolishness unto him: neither can he know them, because they are spiritually discerned" (1 Corinthians 2:14).

If the Spirit of truth guides into all truth, and the world cannot receive or know Him, nor can the natural man receive His truth, then the world knows not the truth. When Jesus said to Pilate, "I came to bear witness unto the truth" (John 18:37), He didn't mean science, much less psychology. Nor did He mean worldly wisdom when He said, "Because I tell you the truth, ye believe me not" (8:45).

The article clearly reflects a false view of what Christ meant by the truth. Only the Holy Spirit teaches *the truth* and only to those whom He indwells and guides. This truth alone can set men free from fear, anxiety, insecurity, selfishness, anger, frustration, a sense of hopelessness, inadequacy, and the other symptoms of sin. To supplement the truth of Scripture with the wisdom (folly, actually) of the world is an insult to God! Yet this is the very foundation of all Christian psychology.

Paul writes, "Now we have received, not the spirit of the world, but the spirit which is of God; that we might know the things that are freely given to us of God" (1 Corinthians 2:12). The "things that are freely given to us of God" are sufficient for "life and godliness" and to make us "perfect, thoroughly furnished unto every good work." Paul continues: "Which things also we speak, not in the words which man's wisdom teacheth, but which the Holy Ghost teacheth" (v. 13).

In contrast to Paul, the Passantinos consider at least some of "the words which man's wisdom teacheth" to be an essential supplement to the truth of God's Word. God promises, however, that "love, joy, peace, longsuffering, gentleness, goodness, faith, meekness, temperance" (as we have often pointed out) are the "fruit of the Spirit" (Galatians 5:22–23), not the fruit of psychotherapy.

QUESTION: I have enjoyed your books and also your column in *The Berean Call.* There is a phrase, however, that you use regularly and that I feel is not exactly a proper use. The phrase is "Christian psychology" or "Christian psychologist." I am not splitting hairs. I think this is theologically and biblically incorrect. If you can have a Christian psychologist, why can't there be a Christian prostitute? Or, why not a Christian automobile? There can possibly be a psychologist who is a Christian, but using the phrase "Christian psychologist" gives biblical support or acceptance to psychology, does it not? Without being dogmatic, I ask you to consider this carefully.

RESPONSE: I have so often said that there can no more be a "Christian psychologist" than a "Christian Hindu" that I am surprised you would now suggest that I believe the contrary! This only shows how careful we must be with not only what we say but exactly how we say it. Usually I put quotation marks around the phrases "Christian psychology" or "Christian psychologist" to show that they are misnomers. However, editors like to keep quotation marks to a minimum. So I may have acquiesced and allowed the quotation marks to be dropped in some cases. Also, I may have used these phrases because they are so well accepted today and expected that what I said about psychology would make it clear that I was not giving it any legitimacy.

I have also said that there is no such thing as Christian psychology. Anyone can easily find out if there is indeed such a thing by going into any university or public library and trying to find a listing for "Christian psychology" in the index of psychology textbooks. There is no such heading. Why? Among the hundreds of psychologies listed (Humanistic, Behavioristic, Freudian, Jungian, Transpersonal, Abnormal, etc.), "Christian psychology" does not appear, simply because there is no psychology invented or developed by a Christian. The psychology "Christians" teach was borrowed from the world. For decades, the goal of "integrating" psychology with the Bible has been pursued as though God's Word were deficient. "Integration" has failed, as it should, because psychology was invented by atheists. It cannot be shoehorned into Scripture. Consider the following from a paper presented at a professional conference of Christian psychologists:

> We are often asked if we are "Christian psychologists" and find it difficult to answer. . . . We are Christians who are psychologists but at the present time there is no acceptable Christian psychology that is markedly different from non-Christian psychology. . . . As yet there is not an acceptable theory, mode of research or treatment methodology [in psychology] that is distinctly Christian.[18]

The astonishing fact is that the unsaved recognize what has happened while Christians remain blind to the horror that has taken place. Great confusion has been caused by the careless use of this unbiblical term, "Christian psychology." What it represents has been a Trojan Horse bringing destruction into the evangelical church. Thank you for reminding me to be more careful both with what I say and how I say it.

QUESTION: I've read that the greatest success the early church achieved was within 200 years after Christ's resurrection. At that time, so history says, about 10 percent of the Roman Empire's citizens were Christians. Today there are several times that percentage of Christians in the United States. Yet you say that "apostasy" is the number-one sign that Christ gave of the last days before His return. How can you explain that?

RESPONSE: Christ did not promise His disciples the kind of "success" that the statistics to which you refer and that today's megachurches seem to indicate. If the Bible is true (which we know it is, in every word), then many (and probably most) of those today who claim to be "Christians" are tares that the devil has sown among the wheat in the church, as Christ foretold (Matthew 13:24–30, 36–43).

But let us consider briefly the truth about those early days in the history of the church. Christ promised His disciples, "If they [unbelievers] have persecuted me, they will also persecute you" (John 15:20). And so it has always been. Clement reported "roastings, impalings and beheadings" of Christians before he fled Alexandria about A.D. 203.[19] Even so, the church grew stronger. Seeing that "the heathen temples began to be forsaken and the Christian churches thronged," the Emperor Decius, around A.D. 250, massacred thousands of believers.[20] In A.D. 303 came the "Great Persecution" under Diocletian. All Bibles and churches were to be destroyed, Christian worship was banned, and all citizens were to sacrifice to pagan gods or die. The whole town of Christian Phrygia was wiped out.[21]

Yet Tertullian's saying proved true: "The blood of the martyrs is the seed of the church." So Satan changed his tactics. He seduced Constantine, a young general, with a positive false gospel of success. In response to a "voice" that said, "In this sign thou shalt conquer," accompanied by a vision of a cross in the sky, he put a Mythraic cross on his soldiers' shields because many of them worshiped the god Mythras. Constantine foolishly credited Christ with the crucial victory that made him emperor (though Christ's servants were not to fight–John 18:36), stopped the persecution, and even favored Christians in government, the military, and in business.

This was not a triumph for the church but its undoing. Although continuing to head the pagan priesthood (the Pontifical College, which still exists in Roman Catholicism today), Constantine gave himself the title Vicar of Christ (which the popes as his successors took to themselves when the emperor moved his capitol from Rome to Constantinople—now Istanbul). Here was the beginning of worldly apostasy in the church—and the ecumenical movement. Historian Will Durant comments:

> Statues of Isis and Horus were renamed Mary and Jesus . . . the feasts of purification of Isis became the Feast of the Nativity; the Saturnalia were replaced by Christmas . . . [paganism] passed like maternal blood into the new religion . . . the world converted to Christianity.[22]

"Christianity" eventually became the official state religion and began to be called Roman Catholicism. Every citizen in the empire was required by law, under pain of death, to belong to the state church. The true church, which had been persecuted and slaughtered as Christ had foretold, became the false, worldly, popular, and growing church (the "whore of Babylon–Revelation 17–18)—and the new persecutor of those who would not conform to its dogmas. The foundation for the massacre of millions by "Christian" Rome was laid as early as A.D. 380 with the "Edict of the Emperors Gratian, Valentinian II, and Theodosius I":

> We order those who follow this doctrine to receive the title of Catholic Christians, but others we judge to be mad and raving . . . nor are their assemblies to receive the name of churches. They are to be punished not only by Divine retribution but also by our own measures. . . . [23]

As the apostasy grew, new heresies were invented and became official Church dogma. The history of the church became the history of growing unbiblical teaching and traditions and the persecution and martyrdom of those who opposed them. Historian Peter de Rosa, himself a Roman Catholic, admits that Catholicism became "the most persecuting faith the world has ever seen. . . . [Pope] Innocent III murdered more Christians in one afternoon . . . than any Roman emperor did in his entire reign."[24] Will Durant writes candidly, "Compared with the persecution of heresy [by the Roman Catholic

Church] . . . the persecution of Christians by [pagan] Romans . . . was a mild and humane procedure."[25] (Of course, Catholicism's murders of millions have long since been exceeded by Islam. Yet Christian and secular leaders, from the President down, continue to insist that Islam is a religion of peace!)

Satan has had to change his tactics again. Unable to destroy the evangelical church through Rome's persecution, this arch enemy of God's truth is engineering a return of all Christians to the Catholic fold. Leading evangelicals have now joined in partnership with the Church that not only killed their brethren by the millions for centuries but sends its own members to hell with a false gospel! Robert Schuller, one of the champions of Christian psychology and its false gospel of "positive/possibility thinking," went to Rome to get the Pope's blessing upon his Crystal Cathedral before building it.[26] He advocates the return of all Protestants to Rome and papal authority.[27]

One of the Satan's major weapons is psychology. This provides a common language of heresy that not only has seduced true Christians but is spoken by the world and thus provides another entrance into evangelical circles rivaling what happened in the days of the Caesars. Roman Catholics, Protestants, atheists, and cults such as Mormonism and others all speak this same language now. Psychology was one of Satan's master strokes of genius, and its influence is all-pervasive in both the world and church.

On his *Hour of Power* show (the most watched religious TV program in the world each Sunday morning, provided his son, mimicking his father, can keep the audience), the senior Schuller has defined sin as a "lack of faith in yourself." He declared that "Jesus Christ . . . has saved me from my sin, which is my tendency to put myself down and not believe that I can do it. . . . Negative thinking is the core of sin. . . . Jesus died to save us from our sins to change us from negative thinking people to positive thinking people. . . . [28] Christ died to sanctify his self-esteem. And he bore the cross to sanctify your self-esteem . . . *the cross will sanctify the ego trip*! [Emphasis in original]"[29]

Multitudes have been led astray by Christian psychology's positive gospel of self-esteem, positive thinking, and worldly success. How appealing it is to the unsaved, how it encourages false professions of faith, and how destructive it is of souls for eternity! And how tragic that many evangelical leaders, influenced by Christian psychology, have changed the gospel to conform to current ideas about how to build a larger church.

The following warning from J. Vernon McGee has gone unheeded by today's most popular preachers and Bible teachers: "This matter of psychologizing Christianity will absolutely destroy Bible teaching and Bible churches."[30]

Today's ecumenical "gospel," which appeals to the ungodly and gives them false hope, owes much to godless psychology and to those who have brought it into the church. Earthly success is confused with salvation, gain has become godliness, and truth is trampled under the heavy boots of a proud Self, seeking its own glory. Where are those who will "reprove, rebuke, and exhort" and turn us back to the unchangeable truth of God's Holy Word?

QUESTION: I started to read *The Gospel According to Judas* by Ray S. Anderson. He is a pastor and also Professor of Theology and Ministry at Fuller Theological Seminary in Pasadena, CA. The book came highly recommended, but it bothered me after reading only fifty pages. Do you know the book, and if so, what is your opinion?

RESPONSE: Endorsements on the back cover by Eugene H. Peterson and M. Scott Peck should be enough to warn any evangelical that the book would have an unbiblical and even anti-Christian twist to it. Peterson authored *The Message*, a badly perverted paraphrase of Scripture that he nevertheless promotes as a "translation." Peck, although his books are highly praised by some evangelical leaders, is a blatant New Ager who, though he deceives many with "Christian" terminology, denies the essentials of the faith, as does Professor Anderson in *Judas*.

Anderson seems to psychoanalyze Judas and his fellow disciples, uncovering the "good" in Judas that the Bible fails to mention. The alleged prejudice of the disciples is uncovered by Anderson's "analysis" to correct "misinformation" in the Scripture. This is a terrible indictment of God's holy, Spirit-inspired Word. How much else in the Bible is not really true?

The book is outrageously heretical from beginning to end. It denies that the gospel writers were inspired of the Holy Spirit (at least in what they said about Judas) and accuses them of promoting their own prejudices: "Perhaps the other eleven needed a scapegoat. Judas gained his reputation as a betrayer through the selective memory of his former friends. In telling his story, they excised whatever good he had done and told us only of the bad."

What arrogance! How does Anderson know the "good" Judas did? He not only accuses the apostles of lying but also denies that they were inspired of the Holy Spirit. If what they wrote about Judas wasn't inspired, how can we be sure of what they wrote about Jesus?

Anderson says, "John remembers Judas as the one who protested the actions of the woman who anointed the feet of Jesus. Then, to make sure we see the evil motive behind the action, John adds, 'This he said, not that he cared for the poor but because he was a thief.'" (p. 34). Anderson faults Christ for declaring that Judas was "a devil" (John 6:70). So Anderson, who wasn't there, knows more than Jesus Christ, who was, and who as God knows everyone's heart! It seems that only Anderson knows the truth about the good side of Judas—a truth that the Holy Spirit dishonestly failed to reveal in the New Testament.

The book presents an imaginary conversation between the resurrected Christ and the dead Judas in which he is commended by Christ for his love and loyalty, his sin is excused as arising from that love, and the betrayer is given a place in heaven. In the Bible, however, Christ calls Judas "the son of perdition" (John 17:12), and we are told that he went not to heaven but "to his own place" (Acts 1:25). Concerning this traitor, whom Anderson excuses and places among the redeemed in heaven, Christ declared, "Woe to that man by whom the Son of man is betrayed! Good were it for that man if he had never been born" (Mark 14:21).

Had you read as far as pages 91–92, you would have found these blasphemous words: "Thus, when Jesus died, it was His own death that He died, the death that truly belonged to Jesus of Nazareth as a descendant of Adam. It was not the cross that introduced death for Jesus; He carried His own death with Him, as we all do from the moment of conception and birth."

What heresy! The only way Christ could have had "His own death" to die would have been for His sins, so Anderson is accusing Jesus of being a sinner! In that case, He could not have died for anyone else's sins. Anderson is a pastor and seminary professor, yet doesn't seem to know that the Bible says Christ "knew no sin" (2 Corinthians 5:21); He "did no sin" (1 Peter 2:22); and in Him "is no sin" (1 John 3:5)?

According to Anderson, Jesus would have died of old age like the rest of us had He not gone to the Cross! On the contrary, the death Adam's sin brought into the world is experienced by all of his descendants because "all have sinned" (Romans 5:12). Jesus, being without sin, could not possibly have died unless He chose to "lay it [His life] down" for the sins of the world. Indeed, Christ couldn't even be killed unless He allowed it: "No man taketh it [my life] from me, but I lay it down of myself" (John 10:18).

It gets worse on the next page, where the influence of psychology becomes even clearer. Under the heading "An Unhealthy View of the Cross," we find:

> If our sin is viewed as causing the death of Jesus on the cross, then we ourselves become victims of a "psychological battering" produced by the cross. When I am led to feel that the pain and torment of Jesus' death upon the cross is due to my sin, I inflict upon myself spiritual and psychological torment. Instead of the cross

being a liberation from the consequences of my sin, it becomes a burden that I bear. My spiritual life can then only be trusted when it has risen out of the ashes of my own self-immolation through remorse and "death to self." With this kind of theological understanding of spiritual piety reinforced through psychological "self abuse," it's not hard to find scripture texts that seem to support the 'death to self' approach to spiritual life. Under the influence of this tradition, self-esteem is considered to be rooted in sinful pride, not in authentic human selfhood.

Wow! For Anderson, the theories of godless humanistic psychologists are accepted as true, while the Bible is not to be trusted because it violates psychological principles. Yet the gospel, which "is the power of God unto salvation to everyone that believes" (Romans 1:16), clearly says that Christ died for our sins. Had He not died for our sins, we could not be saved.

Furthermore, the Bible states that rather than loving and esteeming self, we are to deny it. Many scriptures don't merely *seem* to support "death to self"; they proclaim it in great clarity! Surely Paul's declaration, "I am crucified with Christ" (Galatians 2:20), is one of triumph, not psychological battering, showing that Anderson has missed the Cross entirely! Anderson argues that Christ's death was because of grace and love and not because of our sin: "We're mistaken when we think that it was our sin, not the love of God, that brought Jesus to the point of His own death." Of course, it was both—but not "His own death." Anderson forgets the obvious: that grace and love would not have led Christ to die unless we were sinners and He desired to rescue us from the penalty of eternal death that God's perfect justice demanded for sin.

Anderson is simply wrong again. A flood of heresy flows fluently from his pen! Here is a pastor and seminary professor who either hasn't read (that couldn't be) or pays no attention to the Bible, which clearly said "Christ died for our sins according to the scriptures" (1 Corinthians 15:3). Christ's death for our sins is so elementary and foundational that we are shocked by Anderson's words. Indeed, that Christ died *for our sin* and rose again is the gospel that saves (1 Corinthians 15:1–4). Anderson, by his own confession, does not believe this gospel—therefore, he is not a saved man! Until he repents, we can come to no other conclusion.

Much more could be said of Anderson's other heresies. The above, however, should be sufficient to show that here is another book sold in Christian bookstores that offers further proof that the apostasy is gathering frightening momentum. *Judas* was published by NavPress. They discontinued it due to heavy criticism, but it is back in print with a new publisher.

QUESTION: You and the Bobgans are about the only Christian authors that I am aware of who reject the biblical teaching taught by most pastors and Christian leaders that high self-esteem and a positive self-image are essential to our emotional well-being. Dr. Dobson and other Christian psychologists aren't the only ones who emphasize the need to acquire a positive self-worth, self-esteem, self-love, and self-image. Many preachers teach the same, such as Josh McDowell, Chuck Swindoll, Charles Stanley, and others. Who are you to disagree with them?

RESPONSE: Any Berean comparing such teaching with God's Word will find that it doesn't pass the test. For example, Philippians 2:3 says, "In lowliness of mind let each esteem other[s] better than themselves." Romans 12:3 warns us not to think of ourselves "more highly than [we] ought to think." Nowhere does the Bible warn us against thinking too poorly of ourselves. Human beings don't have that problem.

For example, Samuel Yochelson, a psychiatrist, and Stanton Samenow, a clinical psychologist, spent six and one-half years investigating hundreds of hardened criminals and had to throw out almost everything they had learned about psychology academically as simply wrong. They could not find one person in prison who did not think highly of himself even when plotting a crime. They reported the results of their research in their book, *Inside The Criminal Mind.*

No wonder the Bible frequently reminds us that we are sinners and unprofitable to God in and of ourselves. How reluctant we are to admit that truth! As Horatius Bonar wrote in his classic *God's Way of Peace* one hundred fifty years ago, "It takes a great deal to destroy a man's good opinion of himself [and] even after he has lost his good opinion of his works, he retains a good opinion of his heart." Note the difference between what Christians used to believe, based upon the Bible, and today's opinions, influenced by humanistic psychology!

You mention Josh McDowell. He has devoted two entire books to helping Christians develop their self-image, self-esteem, and sense of self-worth: *Building Your Self-Image*, Tyndale, 1978, and *His Image, My Image*, (Here's Life, Campus Crusade for Christ), 1984. Josh is a *magna cum laude* graduate of Talbot Theological Seminary and the author of some excellent books on apologetics; yet his ready acceptance of psychology has caused him to embrace unbiblical beliefs and even to try to use Scripture to support them. In *His Image*, he presents three psychological essentials for a normal person: 1) a sense of belonging (acceptance by others); 2) a sense of worthiness (feeling good about oneself); and 3) a sense of competence (confidence in oneself). He didn't learn these ideas from the Bible but from humanistic psychology. In fact, most if not all of the heroes and heroines in the Bible lacked all that Josh says we need.

Moses, for example, was rejected by his own people and considered himself to be both unworthy and incompetent. If there was ever a man with an abysmal self-image and self-esteem and one who, by today's views, desperately needed help from psychology, it was Moses. Instead of prescribing months of psychological counseling to raise his self-image, however, God said, "I will be with you!" Millions are being robbed of the presence and power of God in their lives by being turned to self: self-love, self-image, self-acceptance, self-worth, etc.

Look at Paul. Hated by the Jewish community and rejected by most of the church ("No man stood with me"–2 Timothy 4:16; "All they in Asia be turned away from me"–2 Timothy 1:15), he considered himself the chief of sinners (1 Timothy 1:15) and "less than the least of all saints" (Ephesians 3:8). Like Moses, Paul doesn't come up to Josh's criteria at all. Did God seek to build up Paul's self-image and self-esteem? On the contrary, Christ declared that His strength was made perfect in Paul's weakness (2 Corinthians 12:9).

Try to reconcile Paul's self-evaluation, "When I am weak, then am I strong" (v. 10) and "In me dwelleth no good thing" (Romans 7:18), with psychology's three essentials! Josh supports psychology's self-esteem, self-worth, and self-acceptance with a blasphemous paraphrase from the Living Bible: "I want you to realize that God has been made rich because we who are Christ's have been given to Him" (Ephesians 1:18, TLB). Elaborating on this erroneous interpretation, Josh says we should feel good about ourselves because God was enriched through gaining us as His children. The context, however, is all about the blessings we receive from God. Clearly, the "riches of his inheritance in the saints" refers to what God has given the saints, not to an inheritance they have bequeathed Him. Nowhere in the Bible is God enriched by man. It is man who is always benefited by God. Common sense makes that clear. God, being infinitely rich and needing nothing, cannot be enriched by anyone or anything.

Christian psychology has promoted the lie that God loves us because of some value He sees in us and even that Christ's death proves we are of infinite value to God. In fact, He died for our *sins*. Spurgeon said it well:

> Jesus did not come to save us because we were worth saving, but because we were utterly worthless, ruined, and undone [nor] out of any reason that was in us, but solely and only because of reasons which He took from the depths of His own divine love. In due time He died for those whom He describes as ungodly, applying to them as hopeless an adjective as He could.

Tozer likewise wrote, "Until we believe that we are as bad as God says we are, we can never believe that He will do for us what He says He will do. Right here is where popular religion breaks down."

Two hundred years earlier, the seventeenth-century Scottish preacher, Samuel Rutherford, so well known for his inspiring letters, wrote:

> But alas! That idol, that whorish creature myself is the master-idol we all bow to. . . . Every man blames the Devil for his sins; but the great devil, the house-devil of every man [that] lieth in every man's bosom, is that idol that killeth all, himself. Oh! Blessed are they who can deny themselves, and put Christ in the place of themselves! O sweet word: "I live no more, but Christ liveth in me!"[31]

Such has been the unanimous opinion of Christians for nineteen centuries. It is only since psychology entered the church that the selfisms of today became popular. Let us get back to the Bible!

1. Bruce Narramore, *You're Someone Special* (Zondervan, 1978), 25-26.

2. Bernie Zilbergeld, "The Myths of Psychology" in *Discover,* May 1983, 66, 71.

3. Narramore, *Special*, 22.

4. Robert H. Schuller, *Self-Love: The Dynamic Force of Success* (New York: Hawthorne Books, Ind., 1969), 37.

5. Robert Schuller, *Self-Esteem: the New Reformation* (Waco, TX: Word Books, 1982), 25.

6. Michael J. Harner, *The Way of the Shaman: A Guide to Healing and Power* (Harper & Row, 1980), 57.

7. *The Spiritual Exercises of St. Ignatius*, 138, Second Prelude.

8. Richard Foster, *Celebration of Discipline* (Harper & Row, 1978), 26.

9. Elizabeth Zetzel, M.D., *The Capacity for Emotional Growth—Theoretical and Clinical Contributions to Psychoanalysis 1943-1969* (International Universities Press, Inc., 1979).

10. *Time*, July 30, 1990, 54.

11. *Psychology Today*, September/October 1995.

12. http://www.health24.com/child/ADHD/833-3442,14016.asp.

13. http://www.pbs.org/wgbh/pages/frontline/shows/medicating/backlash/un.html.

14. Peter R. Breggin, M.D., David Cohen, Ph.D., *Your Drug May Be Your Problem: How and Why to Stop Taking Psychiatric Medications* (Reading, MA: Perseus Books, 1999).

15. http://www.homelandstupidity.us/2006/03/24/drugged-from-birth/.

16. Sir Arthur Eddington, *Science and the Unseen World* (Kessinger Publishing, LLC, 2004), 54-58.

17. John Caddock, "What Is Contemplative Spirituality and Why Is It Dangerous?—A Review of Brennan Manning's *The Signature of Jesus,*" *Journal of the Grace Evangelical Society*, Autumn 1997, Vol 10:19.

18. J. Sutherland and P. Poelstra, "Aspects of Integration," a paper presented to the Western Association of Christians for Psychological Studies, Santa Barbara, California, June 1976.

19. Clement of Alexandria, *Miscellanies*, II:2, 125.

20. William Byron Forbush, ed., *Foxe's Book of Martyrs* (Zondervan, 1962), 14-17.

21. Philip Hughes, *A History of the Church* (London, 1934), 172.

22. Will Durant, *The Story of Civilization*, (Simon and Schuster, 1950), Vol IV, 75; Vol III, 657.

23. Sidney Z. Ehler and John B. Morall, *Church and State through the Centuries: A Collection of historic documents with commentaries* (London, 1954), 7.

24. Peter de Rosa, *Vicars of Christ* (Crown Publishers, 1988), 35 and jacket.

25. Durant, *Civilization*, IV, 784.

26. From tape of TBN's *Praise the Lord* program, March 7, 1990.

27. *Los Angeles Herald Examiner*, September 19, 1987, Religion page.

28. *Hour of Power*, April 12, 1992.

29. Robert Schuller, *Living Positively One Day at a Time* (Old Tappen, NJ: Fleming H Revell Company, 1980), 201; *Self-Esteem, the New Reformation* (Waco, TX: Word Books, 1982), 115.

30. J. Vernon McGee, personal letter to Martin Bobgan dated September 18, 1986.

31. *The Letters of Samuel Rutherford* (Moody Press, 1951), 277.

AFTERWORD

TOWARD THE PRIZE

— *Dave Hunt* —

PAUL WAS A MAN OF FERVENT PRAYER, with a seemingly endless prayer list of fellow Christians on his heart. To the believers in Rome, even before he had been there, Paul wrote, "without ceasing I make mention of you always in my prayers" (Romans 1:9). Likewise, to those at Ephesus whom he knew well, "I . . . cease not to give thanks for you, making mention of you in my prayers" (Ephesians 1:16). The number of believers he mentioned by name in his epistles and for whom he daily prayed supported his statement: "Beside those things that are without, that which cometh upon me daily, the care of all the churches. Who is weak, and I am not weak? Who is offended, and I burn not?" (2 Corinthians 11:28–29).

Of course, Paul's prayers expressed much that he desired God to provide for various believers. First and foremost in his heart, however, was one passion he had for all believers everywhere and in every time of history—and that would include us today. He expressed it in various ways in his epistles. Here it is in his prayer for the Ephesians:

> That the God of our Lord Jesus Christ, the Father of glory, may give unto you the spirit of wisdom and revelation in the knowledge of him [to] know what is the hope of his calling [and] the exceeding greatness of his power to us-ward who believe, according to the working of his mighty power, which he wrought in Christ, when he raised him from the dead. . . . (Ephesians 1:17–20)

Paul wanted believers everywhere to know and understand God's ultimate eternal purpose for them. His prayer was not that this purpose would be accomplished one day in eternity. There was no question about that, nor could Paul's prayer play any part in its ultimate realization. God had already determined to accomplish this goal for every Christian without fail, and He would do it by the very power with which Christ was raised from the dead.

That it will be realized for every true Christian is as certain as our salvation. What was it, then, for which Paul prayed? That we would here and now, in this present life, know and understand "the hope of his [God's] calling."

What is this hope? And if it unfailingly will be realized for eternity in glory, no matter what we may do or not do, why is it so important that we understand it ahead of time? Herein lies one of the key elements in a victorious life of fruitfulness to the glory of God and fullness of Christ's joy and ours.

The Apostles understood this hope well. Paul declared that we "rejoice in hope of the glory of God" (Romans 5:2). This passage and many others make it clear that "the glory of God" is not only something that will surround us in heaven, but it will be revealed in us: "Christ in you, the hope of glory" (Colossians 1:27). He calls it a "mystery which hath been hid from ages and from generations, but now is made manifest to his saints" (1:26). The fact that this promised "glory" is future and as yet unseen is likewise clear: "What a man seeth, why doth he yet hope for? But if we hope for that we see not, then do we with patience wait for it" (Romans 8:24–25).

Paul referred to "the glorious appearing of the great God and our Saviour Jesus Christ" as "that blessed hope" (Titus 2:13). How does that relate to "the hope of our calling?" Why would the hope of Christ's appearing at last to His own, in glory, be specially blessed?

We don't look to our own reasoning and speculation in seeking to understand the Christian's ultimate hope. We search the Scriptures, and the more deeply we understand, the more clearly we see that the Bible is indeed the Word of the true and living God, one integrated love letter to mankind from Genesis to Revelation.

"In the beginning God created the heaven and the earth. . . . " On the sixth day, "God created man in his own image" (Genesis 1:1, 27). That statement has nothing to do with man's physical body, male or female, for "God is a Spirit" (John 4:24). We can only conclude that man was made in the spiritual image of God to manifest to the universe the beauties of God's holy character: His selfless love, compassion, grace, gentleness, patience, holiness, and moral purity—as well as the power of choice. The latter, of course, was essential if man was to love God and his fellows—but that power, necessarily, opened the door for man to choose for himself rather than for his Creator!

In Adam's irrational and unthinkable rebellion against the God to whom he owed his very existence, Self (the autonomous self as "god") had its awful birth and, in partnership with Satan, has been trying to take over mankind's destiny ever since. Battles rage within and without as each individual Self competes not only with God but with every other Self for supremacy: conflict between husbands and wives, children and their siblings, parents and children, in a cacophony of "I, My, Me, Mine."

The moment man rebelled, the Spirit of God departed from man's spirit, and the image of God in which man had been created was shattered. Self was left to the unhappy loneliness of its insane, self-centered pride. Imagine worms boasting of their power and glory, and one gets a picture of the pitiful creature called man, mired deeply in sin, parading his positive self-image and self-esteem before the throne of God! Yet such selfisms are the very foundation of humanistic psychology, from which "Christian" psychology derives its basic ideas.

Jesus declared that the only hope for any man was to "deny himself [that wicked Self born in Eden], and take up his [individual] cross, and follow me" (Matthew 16:24–26; Mark 8:31–34; Luke 9:23). In defiance of our Lord's command, Christian psychology (which is trustingly looked to for guidance by almost the entire evangelical church) declares that man's great need is, instead, to nourish and cherish the Self. Rejecting Christ's command, the evangelical church now follows Christian psychologists, who have become the new infallible priesthood. They have brought into the evangelical church the foolish wisdom of the world (1 Corinthians 1:20), with the excuse that "all truth is God's truth." That mantra confuses mere facts of logic or science with "the truth" found only in "the word of truth" (Psalm 119:43; 2 Corinthians 6:7; Ephesians 1:13; Colossians 1:5; 2 Timothy 2:15; James 1:18), which alone "shall make you free" (John 8:32). As Jesus said to the Father, "Thy word is truth" (John 17:17).

Rather than denying self, "Christian psychology," thinking it can improve God's infallible and all-sufficient Word with the theories of atheistic anti-Christians, coddles rebellious Self with the offer of "self-esteem, self-love, self-acceptance, self-image, self-improvement, self-assertion," and all the other selfisms, *ad nauseam.* Bruce Narramore admits that these theories are not found in "the word of truth," but Christian psychologists have borrowed them from Christ-defying humanists:

> Under the influence of humanistic psychologists like Carl Rogers and Abraham Maslow, many of us Christians have begun to see our need for self-love and self-esteem. It is a good and necessary focus.[1]

James Dobson's ministry is built upon this same humanist foundation. We have quoted him saying that Christian psychology is a good career for any young Christian to aspire to, "provided their faith is strong enough to withstand the humanism to which they will be exposed." So the evangelical church, under the influence of Christian psychologists, has been reduced to reliance upon humanists for instruction in how to provide essential moral and spiritual counsel, which the Holy Spirit somehow failed to include in the Word of Truth, even though it claims to give us "all things that pertain unto life and godliness" (2 Peter 1:3).

How can so many Christians turn from the clear teaching of Scripture to Satan's lies? There is widespread ignorance of God's Word in the evangelical church. Even worse is the eagerness to follow the world in contemptuous disregard of what the Bible unmistakably teaches. Much of the blame must be placed upon Christian psychologists, who have led the way in this rebellion. The effect is everywhere. Robert Schuller (who for years has had the largest TV audience each Sunday morning), in a book with an introduction by his mentor, arch heretic Norman Vincent Peale, boldly defies God:

> Self-love is a crowning sense of self-worth. It is an ennobling emotion of self-respect . . . an abiding faith in yourself. It is sincere belief in yourself.
>
> It comes through self-discovery, self-discipline, self-forgiveness and self-acceptance. It produces self-reliance, self-confidence and an inner security, calm as the night.[2]

Self has taken the place of God. Christ's declaration, "Have faith in God" (Mark 11:22) has been replaced by "Have faith in yourself." Sadly, the specious belief that humanists can teach us how to counsel from the Bible through psychological techniques is widely accepted among evangelicals today. Church leaders are taking their flocks into one false teaching after another (from the avid pursuit of "signs and wonders," to numerical growth at the expense of sound doctrine, to a revived social gospel). Many such errors have been exposed in TBC's newsletters over the years. Here again Self, inflated by Christian psychology, is the culprit. Jesus said, "If any man will [i.e., wills to] do his [the Father's] will, he shall know of the doctrine, whether it be of God, or whether I speak of myself " (John 7:17). Scripture will not be understood nor sound doctrine valued and defended as long as Self has not been denied in surrender to the will of God.

In our lives, we need God. We need the Holy Spirit. We need Christ as our very life itself, allowing Him to restore in and express through us the image of God in which we were created. We have forgotten heaven and become enamored of this world, living our lives as though the only plans God has for us pertain to earth. Yes, some of our works seem good and spiritual: preaching the gospel and giving out tracts, writing Christian books and making Christian films, building missionary organizations, larger churches, and Christian universities, doing charitable deeds—and on and on it goes, keeping us so busy serving the Lord that we can scarcely find time to love and worship Him.

Believing the lie that one can become so "heavenly minded" as to be of "no earthly good" (surely Christ was the most heavenly minded man who ever lived, yet He was also the most earthly good!), we have lost sight of "the hope of his calling." I do not minimize the lust, self-indulgence, entrapment in sin, failure to pray, neglect of Bible study, the forsaking of Christian fellowship, and the carnality that is rampant today among those who claim to be born-again evangelicals. These failings, however, are easily recognized by anyone who knows the Lord and has a modicum of conscience.

It is a deadly error, however, to imagine that victory over these sins comes through getting "busy for God." No matter in what we are falling "short of the glory of God," the problem is the same: we have lost sight of (or perhaps never understood) what Paul says is "the hope of our calling."

Perhaps no one served Christ as wholeheartedly as Paul. At the same time, no one loved Him more. Consider carefully Paul's explanation of the secret of his life: "Forgetting those things which are behind, and reaching forth unto those things which are before, I press toward the mark for the prize of the high calling of God in Christ Jesus" (Philippians 3:13–14). Paul then exhorts, "Be followers together of me. . . " (3:17). What is this prize that we should all be pressing toward, as Paul did?

Clearly, it is not an individual award given to a "winner" in competition for excelling others. The prize is "the high calling of God in Christ Jesus" itself that Paul desired for all Christians to understand and press toward. This "high calling" is why Christ died and rose again for us! Peter explains that "the God of all grace . . . has called us unto his eternal glory" (1 Peter 5:10). Falling short of that glory is the biblical definition of sin (Romans 3:23). The restoration of that glory is fully assured in eternity for every true disciple of Christ, yet we are to pursue it even now. Laying everything else aside for this goal was the secret of Paul's remarkable life!

Of Christ it is written, "Who for the joy that was set before him endured the cross, despising the shame, and is set down at the right hand of the throne of God" (Hebrews 12:2). That joy was twofold: knowing that He had faithfully accomplished what the Father had given Him to do; and "bringing many sons unto glory" (Hebrews 2:10) in His very image. The "hope of his calling" is the joy set before us: the joy of at last fully becoming all that the Father's heart of love desires for us so that Christ will "see of the travail of his soul [and] be satisfied" (Isaiah 53:11).

The "hope of his calling" is beautifully expressed in this old hymn (excerpted here) written by John Nelson Darby, one of the founders in the early 1830s of the so-called "Plymouth Brethren":

> And is it so? I shall be like thy Son? Is this the grace which
> He for me has won?
>
> Father of Glory (thought beyond all thought), In glory to
> His own blest likeness brought!
>
> O Jesus, Lord . . . myself the prize and travail of Thy soul!
> Yet it must be!
>
> Thy love had not its rest were thy redeemed not with
> Thee, fully bless'd.
>
> That love that gives not as the world but shares all it
> possesses with its loved co-heirs.
>
> Nor I alone: Thy loved ones all, complete, in glory round
> Thee there with joy shall meet
>
> All . . . for Thy glory like Thee, Lord: object supreme of
> all, by all adored. . . .
>
> The heart is satisfied, can ask no more: all thought of self
> is now, forever, o'er.
>
> Christ, its unmingled Object, fills the heart: in bless'd
> adoring love its endless part.
>
> Father of Glory, in Thy presence bright all this shall be
> unfolded in the light!

The angel Gabriel told Daniel, "They that be wise shall shine as the brightness of the firmament; and they that turn many to righteousness as the stars for ever and ever" (Daniel 12:3). John explained when and how this transformation would occur: "When he shall appear, we shall be like him; for we shall see him as he is" (1 John 3:2).

Though that transformation will not be fully realized until we see Him face to face, yet even now, though "we see through a glass, darkly" (1 Corinthians 13:12), we are, as we keep our eyes upon Him, being "changed into the same image from glory to glory . . . as by the Spirit of the Lord." Let us lay all else aside to press on toward the prize "of the high calling of God in Christ Jesus!"

1. Bruce Narramore, *You're Someone Special* (Grand Rapids, MI: Zondervan Publishing House, 1978), 22.

2. Robert H. Schuller, *Self-Love, The Dynamic Force of Success: Learn to Love Yourself—the secret of happiness in life, in love, in everything you do* (New York, Hawthorne Books, W. Clement Stone, 1969), 32.

APPENDIX A

TRANSCRIPT OF THE DVD "PSYCHOLOGY & THE CHURCH"

From interviews (voice-over):

MAN #1: "The Bible works for me. I don't think Christians need to go outside God's Word for solving their problems."

WOMAN #1: "Well, what did Bible-believing Christians do anyway before these so-called experts on life's problems like Sigmund Freud or Carl Rogers came along? I think they probably did quite nicely with just the Word of God and the power of the Holy Spirit!"

WOMAN #2: "People have issues today that are beyond the scope of the Bible. I thank God for the insights of modern psychology."

MAN #2 "I think that pastors who attempt to counsel without professional training are doing a disservice to their church members!"

MAN #3: "Well, it's a simple formula…our pastor sees to our spiritual needs, a doctor our physical needs…and a psychologist our mental needs."

WOMAN #3: "There are times when folks have a very deep problem—it might be deeply seated, and I think you need professional help for that."

WOMAN #4: "My church doesn't do counseling so it's not really an option to us. We do have a list of recommended professionals that we can use if we need to."

Introduction

T. A. MCMAHON: I'm T. A. McMahon, executive director of The Berean Call, and I'll be your host for the next hour as we consider the very important subject of *PSYCHOLOGY & THE CHURCH.* It's an extremely vital topic because in the history of contemporary Christendom no secular enterprise has had such a profound influence on Christianity as has psychological counseling.

In the last fifty years, multitudes of pastors have added clinical counseling degrees to their theological credentials. Psychological theories have been preached so often and from so many pulpits that they are accepted without question by increasing numbers of Christians as biblical doctrines. As a result, the Christian church in the United States has become a major referral service for clinical psychologists and psychiatrists. The critical question raised by these developments is: Have they been helpful or harmful to the body of Christ? Crucial answers to that question will be the focus of this program, as we consider the effect of psychological counseling upon the church.

For nearly two thousand years prior to the rise of modern psychiatry and psychotherapy, the church has ministered to believers experiencing mental, emotional, and behavioral problems through the teachings of the Scriptures and in the power of the Holy Spirit. That, then, raises a question we all need to ponder: Was there an insufficiency on the part of God's Word and His Holy Spirit during those two millennia that made it necessary for the church to turn to modern psychotherapy in order to more effectively address a Christian's problems of living?

VOICE OVER: Joining T. A. in evaluating this very important subject are Dr. Martin Bobgan and his wife and co-author, Deidre Bobgan. Together they have written more than a dozen books addressing psychotherapy and biblical ministry. Psychologist and internationally recognized critic of psychotherapy, Dr. Tana Dineen is the author of *Manufacturing Victims.* Dave Hunt is the author of numerous books addressing movements and trends within evangelical Christianity, including the best-selling *The Seduction of Christianity* with T. A. McMahon.

T. A.: Perhaps the most influential and certainly the most recognized name in psychological counseling is Sigmund Freud. Born in Austria in the mid-1800s, and trained as a medical doctor, he developed psychoanalysis, a theoretical method that he used for treating patients suffering from "hysteria." In applying his theories, he employed techniques such as hypnosis, dream interpretation, and free association in order to investigate how elements in the unconscious mind supposedly brought about mental disorders.

Freud's many unproven yet generally accepted theories include **psychic determinism**, the supposition that our conscious thoughts and activities are determined by traumatic incidents repressed in our unconscious minds.

DR. MARTIN BOBGAN: Freud developed this idea that when we experience life in the zero-to-five-year-old stages, that there are certain psychosexual stages of development that occur, and he named those. And then, while we are passing through those stages, there's the repression that occurs—we repress material into our unconscious, and when we do this, the unconscious becomes the reservoir out of which we act in later life, and so because of the huge amount of repression into the subconscious or unconscious, Freudian psychology is know as "psychic determinism"—our behavior is determined by the early life activities.

T. A.: Freud's theory of **Infantile sexuality** proposed that mental disorders are caused by sexual desires resident within all children from birth to age five or six.

DEIDRE BOBGAN: Freud felt that all of our problems come from our childhood. We don't get through certain stages of development, and one of the ideas that people believe that is totally a myth is that the first five years of a person's life— from that they determine the rest of the life. And a lot of ideas that Freud had just have come into ordinary thought, like the id, the ego, the superego, and so forth—these came from him, and they were totally his ideas. They were just his opinions.

T. A.: The Oedipus complex is a foundational theory of Freudian psychoanalysis. The hypothesis was erroneously drawn from a Greek drama in which Oedipus unknowingly marries his own mother. Freud saw the mythological story as symbolic of a universal lust/hate relationship between children and their parents.

Alfred Adler and Carl Jung were disciples of Sigmund Freud. Although they were schooled in psychoanalysis, they developed their own theories and methods, some quite at odds with those of their mentor, and each other. Alfred Adler, also an Austrian physician, is best known for his focus on the individual himself rather than abstracted concepts such as the Id or the Oedipus. Like Freud, he believed mental disorders were rooted in childhood experiences, particularly inferiority complexes.

Carl Jung, a Swiss psychiatrist, was a protégé of Freud's who expanded his beliefs about the human psyche to a link between all psyches in his theory of the Collective Unconscious. In his concept of archetypes, Jung took psychoanalysis from biological urges to the non-physical realm of the spirit.

Freud, Adler, and Jung are considered the founding fathers and pillars of modern clinical psychology. Their theories and methods influenced latter-day psychotherapists such as Abraham Maslow and Carl Rogers, who further expanded them into humanistic concepts of needs, self, and self-actualization.

Another stream of psychology distinct from that of the psychoanalytical and the humanistic approach is behavioral psychology. B.F. Skinner is perhaps the best known in this methodology. Skinner taught that the thoughts and actions of humanity are all responses to stimuli external to each person. A person's genes, biological makeup, and environmental factors determine how he or she will act. Free will and personal responsibility are negligible in this theoretical system.

There are more than 500 psychological therapies. Most of them are variations of prior theories, expanding or modifying them—and, in many cases, abandoning prior concepts altogether.

[see list on next page]

T. A.: These many psychotherapies range from the mundane to the bizarre, from the innocuous to the dangerous, yet they all have at least two things in common: 1) they are merely speculations and have no scientific validity, and 2) no particular method is any more effective than any other. Dr. Tana Dineen provides some insights into how the psychotherapeutic process has become so influential in our society:

TANA DINEEN: In the 1960s, we thought of psychology—psychological treatment— as something that some people required, some people who were mentally ill, or who had serious problems. And in the 1960s, 1970s, the idea became prevalent that psychology's really too good to be wasted on the sick—it can help us all. And we're clinging to that idea. And as we've gone into this twenty-first century, we have the idea that psychology can help us not only in our pursuit of happiness but in the achievement of it. It's for getting over all problems. And all of life has become a problem. The public image, which psychology cares very much about, is that psychology is a scientifically based helping profession. We know how best to raise your kids, how best to recover from some trauma you've experienced, how to deal with your depression. We have all the answers. And I think it's this pretense that psychology has all the answers that concerns me most about psychology, because it's entirely false.

MARTIN BOBGAN: I would object to churches referring people to psychotherapists. I would object to denominations using psychotherapy of any kind, or psychological tests. I would object to the seminaries that have the psychology departments, and I could go on and on. And the reason I object to that is, there is no scientific evidence that gives a pass to that kind of activity, and if you look in the research you will find researcher after researcher after researcher says essentially the same thing: there is no positive support for psychotherapy in the literature.

T. A.: Given the significant influence it has had on the church, the *psychological way* compared to the *biblical way* should be an issue of critical concern for Christians — that is, those who believe that the Word of God is their authority and that it is completely sufficient for knowing and doing "all things that pertain to life and godliness." How then do they compare?

Foundationally, they couldn't be more at odds. The basic premises of psychological counseling are contradictory to what the Bible teaches about the nature of man and how he can solve his mental, emotional, and behavioral problems. Psychotherapeutic concepts regard humanity as intrinsically good. The Bible says that other than Jesus Christ, humanity is *not* good, but rather everyone has a sinful nature: *"For all have sinned, and come short of the glory of God"* Romans 3:23.

Partial List of Psychological Therapies

Adlerian Therapy
Analytical Psychology
Art Therapy
Autogenic Psychotherapy
Behavior Therapy
Biodynamic Psychotherapy
Bioenergetic Analysis
Biosynthesis
Brief Therapy
Catharsis
Classical Adlerian Psychotherapy
Coaching
Co-Counselling
Cognitive Analytic Psychotherapy
Cognitive Behavioural Psychotherapy
Concentrative Movement Therapy
Contemplative Psychotherapy
Core Process Psychotherapy
Dance Movement Therapy
Daseins Analytic Psychotherapy
Depth Psychology
Developmental Needs Meeting Strategy
Dream Analysis
Dialectical Behavior Therapy
Eclectic Therapy
Emotional Freedom Techniques (EFT)
Empathy
Encounter Groups
Eye Movement Desensitization and
    Reprocessing (EMDR)
Existential Analysis
Family Systems Therapy
Feminist Therapy
Focusing
Freudian Psychotherapy
Gestalt Therapy
Gestalt Theoretical Psychotherapy
Group Therapy
Hakomi
Holotropic Breathwork
Hot Seat
Human Givens Psychotherapy
Humanistic Psychology
Hypnotherapy
Integrative Psychotherapy
Internal Family Systems Model
Interpersonal Therapy (IPT)
Journal Work

Jungian Psychotherapy
Lifespan Integration
Logotherapy
Marriage and Family Therapy
Method of Levels (MOL)
Minimal Encouragers
Multicultural Counseling and Therapy
(MCT)
Multimodal Therapy
Narrative Therapy
Neuro-linguistic Programming (NLP)
Object Relation Theory
Paradoxical Intention
Person Centered Psychotherapy
Personal Construct Psychology (PCP)
Positive Psychotherapy
Postural Integration
Primal Integration
Process Oriented Psychology
Primal Therapy
Provocative Therapy
Psychedelic Psychotherapy
Psychoanalysis
Psychodrama
Psychodynamic Psychotherapy
Psycho-Organic Analysis
Psychosynthesis
Pulsing (bodywork)
Rational Emotive Behaviorpsychotherapy
Re-evaluation Counseling
Reality Therapy
Reflective Listening
Regression
Reichian Psychotherapy
Rogersian (or Rogerian) Psychotherapy
Role Play
Rolfing
Sand Play
Solution Focused Brief Therapy
Sophia Analysis
Self Relationship (or Sponsorship)
Systemic Therapy
SHEN Therapy
T Groups
Transactional Analysis (TA)
Transpersonal Psychology
Unconditional Positive Regard
Validation
Working Through Projections
Working Through Transference

Psychological counseling promotes the belief that problems adversely affecting a person's mental and emotional welfare are caused—even determined—by actions external to the person, such as by parents, his environment, his circumstances, and so forth. The Bible tells us that a man's evil heart and his sinful choices cause his mental, emotional, and behavioral problems: *"For from within, out of the heart of men, proceed evil thoughts, adulteries, fornications, murders, Thefts, covetousness, wickedness, deceit, lasciviousness, an evil eye, blasphemy, pride, foolishness: All these evil things come from within, and defile the man."* Mark 7:21-23

Psychotherapy regards one's self as the key to solving his problems, devising concepts such as self-love, self-esteem, self-worth, self-image, and so forth, as remedies. The Bible teaches that self itself is humanity's main problem, not the solution to humanity's ills: *"This know also, that in the last days perilous times shall come. For men shall be lovers of their own selves"* 2 Timothy 3:1-2

The Bible teaches that reconciliation to God through Jesus Christ is the only way for man to truly remedy his sin-related mental, emotional, and behavioral problems: *"And you, that were sometime alienated and enemies in your mind by wicked works, yet now hath he* [Jesus Christ] *reconciled In the body of his flesh through death, to present you holy and unblameable and unreproveable in* [God's] *sight"* Colossians 1:21-22

Psychological counseling methods and concepts include secular, atheistic, and spiritual beliefs—all of which contradict the biblical way of ministering. (It needs to be understood that this program is not addressing all fields of psychology—only psychotherapy, more commonly referred to as psychological counseling, which is far and away the largest discipline of psychology.)

MARTIN BOBGAN: People generally think about psychotherapy and its underlying psychologies—they don't think about some of the other divisions that are quite distant from and in some cases actually scientific, whereas psychotherapy is obviously not. And so we generally use the term "psychology," but we say in advance that the type of psychology we're talking about is psychotherapy, and the reason we want to talk about that is that's the type of psychology that has invaded the church—started out like a small leaven, and then, all of a sudden, you find it in practically every nook and cranny of the church. You see it in denominations, you see it in seminaries, Bible colleges, you see it in sermons that pastors put together because they're so influenced by the psychology of the day.

T. A.: In evaluating psychological counseling, it's important to recognize the medium that is central to its implementation. It's simply "conversation." A counselor engages the counselee or counselees in conversation. As one research psychiatrist puts it: "In plain language, what do patient and psychotherapist do? They speak and listen to each other."

DAVE HUNT: Psychotherapy has been called the "talking cure": you talk back and forth with one another and, of course, they're not going to get inside your heart. They are dependent upon what you say. "Well, let's talk about your problems, okay?" Well, maybe you're not expressing yourself accurately, you may not have a full understanding, or maybe you're not honest, not even honest with yourself. That's what it means that "the heart is deceitful." So you can't possibly get inside of a person and know everything about them, and then, somehow, you are going to change that person. No, only God can do that and He says it.

DEIDRE BOBGAN: The common factors that happen with any kind of interaction with people, they are talking together, they are interacting. Now, why would we send anybody out to a professional, rather than just having another believer who believes the same thing, who knows the Word, in whom the Lord is working—why can't a believer come alongside and minister to that person? You don't need the techniques; you don't need anything but the Lord in you, to work this out. And to encourage that person to go the direction the Lord would have them go.

TANA DINEEN: When I went to graduate school and did my doctoral thesis, when the other kids were studying rats and undergraduate students, I studied psychiatrists. And what I did was look at the extent to which their belief systems influenced how they diagnosed and treated people. And at that point—I should have quit—at that point, what my research and what a whole *body* of research was saying was that all you needed to know was what a psychiatrist believes, and you can determine from that what is going to happen to a patient. You don't need to know anything about the patient.

T. A.: That, basically, is the psychotherapeutic process that has displaced believers biblically ministering to one another, a function which the Body of Christ has performed for 2,000 years. How and why did the church surrender its biblical mandate from Galatians chapter six to Sigmund Freud and company and their offspring?

During the middle of the twentieth century, there were two developments that were instrumental in helping the fledgling enterprise of psychotherapy make inroads in Christendom. Local associations of mental health professionals began holding luncheons for ministers and priests in order to offer their counseling services.

DEIDRE BOBGAN: In the 60s, the local psychotherapists would have mental health meetings to which they would invite the pastors. The pastors would come, and they would talk about how they dealt with problems of living and the psychotherapists let the pastors know that they really were not qualified. And this was one place where the referrals started in, because the pastor—he's not trained in that. How can he deal with this kind of problem? And the therapists talked as if they certainly knew how to do it, and they had all of their terminology and their theories and so forth.

T. A.: The sales pitch featured a holistic approach—body, mind, and spirit: medical doctors attend to the body, ministers address issues related to the spirit, and of course, psychologists, the domain of the mind. That seemed to make sense to many.

Also, in 1952 the American Psychiatric Association produced a book titled *Diagnostic and Statistical Manual*, commonly called the *DSM*; it is considered the "Bible of mental illness." Originally it listed 106 Mental Disorders.

MARTIN BOBGAN: And as you use the *DSM*, you'll find that all of us fit into one or more of the categories of the *DSM*. It just depends on how you use the *DSM*, but I would say the *DSM* is a categorizer of people that began with a small beginning but it has expanded to literally hundreds of individual designations that would label us as mentally ill and erroneously so.

T. A.: The *DSM* list grew to 182 in 1968 then to 265 in 1980 and to 292 in 1987. The count in today's fourth edition *DSM* manual is 374 mental disorders. They include alleged dysfunctions of the mind such as:

OPPOSITIONAL DEFIANT DISORDER—classifying a child or adult who demonstrates "hostile behavior toward authority figures" as mentally ill. The symptoms include "losing one's temper," "arguing with adults," "deliberately doing things that will annoy other people," and "blaming others for his or her own mistakes or misbehavior."

NARCISSISTIC PERSONALITY DISORDER is a mental illness demonstrated by those who, ironically, nurture their self-esteem beyond the norm set by psychology.

DEIDRE BOBGAN: You remember what people used to call…people were "shy," now it's "social anxiety disorder," so that if you're shy and you want to be able to take psychotherapy to help you get over your shyness, or you want to talk to a therapist because you need someone to talk to because maybe you need a paid friend. You just can have anything, any ordinary thing like shyness, and that's turned into one of the categories.

TANA DINEEN: In 2004, in Canada there was a…"Statistics Canada" did a survey of the entire Canadian population and determined that two million people are suffering from debilitating shyness, which is now defined as a "social anxiety disorder," and claiming in the…the Canadian media has reported that survey, to indicate that that means that two million of us in Canada are…maybe didn't go to school long enough, didn't get good jobs, had our marriages fail because of this debilitating problem. I end up being speechless, as I am right now, because we can turn shyness, we can turn virtually *anything*—we can label it, we can transform it from something that might just say, "OK, I'm a shy kid," into "No, you're someone with a serious problem, and you need help or your whole life is going to be destroyed."

T. A.: If a person has an antagonistic view of psychological counseling, refusing to subject himself to therapy, he's classified as suffering from **NONCOMPLIANCE WITH TREATMENT DISORDER**. Then there is **UNSPECIFIED MENTAL DISORDER**, which, for purposes of health insurance coverage, gives a code for "specific mental disorder[s] not included in the *DSM-IV*."

TANA DINEEN: Psychology's handling of normal is quite bizarre. You know we have thermometers that measure what the temperature is, and we can define a range of normal. And we have an instrument that defines it. With psychology, normal is basically whatever a psychologist says is normal. And abnormal is whatever a psychologist might say is abnormal. So the standard doesn't exist other than in the mind of a psychologist, which means that virtually everything can become abnormal.

T. A.: Just how the mental disorders qualified for listing or were later disqualified was not exactly a rigorous scientific process. It's called a vote.

The most notorious example of this process had to do with homosexuality. Prior to 1973 it was listed as a mental disorder. However, the National Gay Task Force began pressuring the American Psychiatric Association and was successful in getting the organization to change its view of homosexuality from a deviant/abnormal behavior to a "sexual preference." The APA subsequently "voted" to remove homosexuality from its "mental disorder" list.

As the list grew over the years from 103 to 374 mental disorders, so did the number of those who would need help, and, consequently, there would be greater need for professionals to help them.

The Myths of Psychotherapy

T. A.: First of all, psychotherapy is not now, and can never be a scientific endeavor. An individual is made up of body, mind, and spirit. Of those three components, only the body can be studied by science.

DAVE HUNT: This is delusion, that man is scientifically predictable, that human behavior can be scientifically understood and adjusted, programmed, and so forth. That psychology is even scientific—we need science to help us—that has been laid to rest long ago. The American Psychological Association in conjunction with the National Science Foundation made an extensive study of human behavior. They engaged 80 eminent scholars to work on this, and over a period of years they examined this question very carefully and they came to the conclusion that psychology IS NOT scientific and it CANNOT be scientific.

T. A.: Dr. Sigmund Koch sums up the panel's findings, published in a seven-volume series entitled *Psychology: A Study of a Science*, in these words: "I think by this time [it should be] utterly and finally clear that psychology cannot be a coherent science."

TANA DINEEN: Psychiatry was never scientific. Psychoanalysis was never scientific. Social work came from, basically, a let's-get-out-there-and-help-people kind of basis—it wasn't scientific. The only little core of science was psychology. And I also find it interesting that the word we use now—my profession likes to think that we hold the reigns on it. And virtually everyone who does counseling or bizarre therapies of every form will be saying that they're doing psychology. It's all psychology now. And I think we use that word partly because it has that mystique of science about it.

T. A.: Major contributors to the delusion that psychotherapy is scientific are the misnomers of MENTAL HEALTH and MENTAL DISEASE. The terms are generally accepted because of Sigmund Freud's background as a physician. That led to the unwarranted assumption that his theories had a medical basis. Dr. Martin Bobgan comments:

MARTIN BOBGAN: Well, mental illness is a term that should never be used because when you're dealing with mental, you're dealing with mind. When you're dealing with illness, you're dealing with the body. And people very casually…and medical doctors use the term "mental illness," but there is no such thing as a mind that is ill. There's a *brain* that can be ill. But to put in "mental" with "illness" is just an incongruity that shouldn't exist. Mental illness is not a disease. You have illness, and you have mind, and you don't have a disease of the mind.

Counseling Is Not for Professionals Only

T. A.: Related to the intimidation of pastors regarding their inadequacy to effectively counsel is the myth that only a professionally trained counselor can be effective.

To the contrary, it has never been established that advanced degrees or training in psychology have contributed to the effectiveness of a psychotherapist.

No research studies have ever demonstrated the effectiveness of professional psychotherapists over nonprofessionals. In fact, the very opposite is true.

MARTIN BOBGAN: When you look into the research there are several things you find out. One is that in order to have effectiveness, if it exists at all, it's unrelated to credentials. It doesn't matter if you're an M.D., Ph.D., or no degree at all. That's very clear, in the research. And when you look into this area you find out there are a number of studies having to do with amateurs and professionals, and what happens is you get startled by the results, because the results are fairly equivalent.

At Vanderbilt University, Dr Hans Strupp conducted a research study in which he had long-experienced psychotherapists, degreed and licensed and all, compared to some amateurs that he brought in—these amateurs were other professors in the institution who had no training in psychotherapy at all, and gave, as nearly as they could, equivalent groups of students to these two groups of, in quotes, "therapists"—I say in quotes because obviously the other professors were not therapists by license. And what happened is the results were relatively equivalent.

T. A.: Consider the conclusion of a lengthy research project conducted by Dr. Joseph Durlak:

VOICE OVER: "Overall, outcome results in comparative studies have favored [non] professionals…. There were no significant differences among helpers in 28 investigations, but [non] professionals were significantly more effective than professionals in 12 studies."

"The provocative conclusion from these comparative investigations is that professionals do not possess demonstrably superior therapeutic skills, compared with [non] professionals. Moreover, professional mental health education, training, and experience are not necessary prerequisites for an effective helping person." [PH180]

MARTIN BOBGAN: The number one ingredient in change, recovery—whatever you want to call it—is the individual himself. The number two ingredient if somebody's brought into the situation is the therapeutic alliance. And it's interesting, there is a psychiatrist who has looked into this, and what he says is that the person has to share—have the same worldview—as the person who comes to him. And now, when we're dealing with worldview, why do we send people away from the church (we have a biblical worldview) to the world—*they* don't have a biblical worldview!

Psychology As Religion

DAVE HUNT: Thomas Szasz, a non-practicing Jew, one of the world's leading research psychiatrists said, "Psychotherapy is a fake religion that seeks to destroy true religion." In fact, he said that Freud's major motive in life was revenge against Christianity. Why is it called a religion? You've got to take it by faith. There is no evidence to support this. All the evidence is to the contrary, in fact. They've come up with *theories*, and now I'm going to believe their theories—now it's going to transform my life, it is going to give me the motivation to become the kind of a person that I want to be, and so forth. All of these things really infringe upon religion, morals. How do I live? What do I really believe? What is worthwhile in life? This is what psychology claims to deal with. Furthermore, it's the knowledge of the *pseuche*, the psyche, the soul. Carl Jung said "Yes, psychology is all about the soul, but we don't know what the soul is." So it claims to be dealing…in fact, psychology is getting more and more into what they call the transpersonal, the spiritual, the nonphysical side. They've kind of left Freud's medical model in the dust, and now they're getting more into the feelings and the spiritual side. This is *religion*.

T. A.: In the *Diagnostic and Statistical Manual of Mental Disorders*, under the heading of "Other conditions That May Be a Focus of Clinical Attention," is code V62.89 "Religious or Spiritual Problem." Examples include distressing experiences that involve loss or questioning of faith, problems associated with conversion to a new faith, or questioning of spiritual values. One wonders what part of a psychotherapist's training prepared him or her to deal with issues of faith and spiritual values.

Christian Psychology

T. A.: What about Christian Psychology? Wouldn't that be beneficial to the counseling process by adding a biblical worldview? Based upon the premise that "all truth is

God's truth," many psychotherapists who profess to be Christians have attempted to mix psychological concepts with their Christian beliefs, convinced that they have the best of both the temporal and spiritual worlds.

DAVE HUNT: This common phrase or excuse for looking to Freud or Jung or Rogers or Maslow or somewhere for "truth"—it says, "All truth is God's truth." Well I guess Buddha had some of it too, Freud or Jung or whoever—*no*! What do we mean by *truth*, first of all? All truth *is* God's truth, OK? But what do we mean by truth? Jesus said, "You will know the truth—you continue in my word" (this is John 8:31) "… you continue in my word, then are you my disciples indeed and you will know *the* truth—*the* truth will set you free." *The* truth is not "10 X 10 is 100." In John 8:45, Jesus said, "Because I tell you *the* truth you believe me not." Now you know that *the* truth must be something very special. He wouldn't say, "Well, because I tell you 10 X 10 is 100, you don't believe me," or "Because I give you some facts of science, you don't believe me."

No, *the* truth is something very special. Well, what is it? In John 14:17 Jesus said, "I'm not going to leave you comfortless. I will send the Comforter to you, even the Spirit of truth." And He says, "Whom the world cannot receive, because it seeth him not, neither knoweth him." And then if you went to John 16:13, Jesus said, "When he, the Spirit of truth is come, he will lead you into all truth." Well, if the Spirit of truth leads into all truth, and the world cannot receive Him, because it doesn't even know what this truth is—this is *God's* truth—Jesus said, "Thy word is truth;" "I am the truth." Then we're not talking about something that Freud or Jung or Rogers or Confucius or anybody else could come up with. We're talking about something that only comes from God. It is understood by His Holy Spirit indwelling the believer, and this is from His Word, and this is what we need.

MARTIN BOBGAN: Well, Christian psychotherapy, if you're really dealing with a professional who is a Christian, that's really a contradiction in terms, because what's happening here is you're having a Christian—if he's truly a believer, he's been brought up in the faith as a converted individual, the Bible is the truth—and he's dealing with psychology, which is not truth, it's just guesses and opinions. And so you can't really put together "Christian" and "psychology" or "Christian" and "psychotherapist." It's just two terms that should not be put together, and, as a matter of fact, we did a research study once, for CAPS—the Christian Association for Psychological Studies. We found there was almost the same diversity of orientations among these Christians who are practitioners as there were among the secularists who are practitioners. Lots of diversity—Freudian, Adlerian, Jungian, Rogerian, etc. And so we have this great variety of practices and yet these people, whenever they put together Christianity and the term "Christian" and "Psychologist"—we get pretty upset about that because it should never be done.

DAVE HUNT: Let me put it like this: psychology, human wisdom, the wisdom of this world, has nothing to offer unless it has picked it up from the Bible. There are some of these things that have slipped into psychology from the conscience that God has given us, but why am I going to take it from them? Why should I dredge through the muck and mire of all the humanistic theories that don't work in order to find a...I might find a gem of real truth that originally came from the Bible. Why don't I just get it from the Bible first of all? You know the poem that says, "Who would leave the noonday bright, to grope mid shadows dim, and who would leave the fountainhead to drink the muddy stream? Where men have mixed what God has said with every dreamer's dream?" That doesn't make sense.

DEIDRE BOBGAN: It's just like the Israelites did in the Old Testament. They were continuing to do the outward service to God, but they were relying on the idols of their neighbors for their problems of living. And God said these two things cannot be mixed. They were doing both—they were trying to mix them. But God withdrew His hand of protection, and I believe that happens with Christian psychology. People have turned away from the living God and all that He has given, and when they turn away from the living God, and all that He has provided in His Word, through His Son, through His Holy Spirit, through the Body of Christ, then people are left, basically, to their flesh.

DAVE HUNT: It's very clear what the Bible says. We are "new creatures in Christ Jesus"; "Christ Jesus has become my life"; "I am crucified with Christ, nevertheless I live." I'm being transformed! Second Corinthians 3:18 says I'm being transformed into the *image* of Christ. The fruit of the Spirit is love, joy, peace, and so forth. I'm to be Christ-like, I'm to be conformed to Him, I'm to be filled with the Spirit, I'm to be what God wants me to be. Now, then, it doesn't make sense—I'm going to go *to psychological counseling*? I'm going to go to the theories of *godless men*?

They were all godless men, right down the line from Freud, Jung, Rogers, Maslow—you name them—these are atheists. They were against Christianity, and now I'm going to go to them so that I can learn some techniques so that I can better counsel people so they can become more Christ-like? It doesn't make sense. It is not right. It isn't biblical, and we ought to stay away from it.

MARTIN BOBGAN: Psychotherapy is questionable at best, detrimental at worst, and a spiritual counterfeit at least. If you look at the first part of that, "questionable at best," look at the research studies. The research studies reveal it all, but the practitioners aren't listening. They are practicing because, as far as they're concerned, they are licensed, educated, and they're proceeding. They are not listening to the scientists and researchers. It's "detrimental at worst," because when you look at the detriment that it has caused—and everybody admits that there is a harm side to psychotherapy—but from a Christian point of view, there's even way beyond that: a detriment to the faith part of this, in which their theories, their ideas, their guesses, their hunches, their opinions are eroding "the faith once delivered unto the saints."

And it's a "spiritual counterfeit" at least, merely because it is a religion and it does have spiritual aspects to it, even though unsaid, and it is a counterfeit to

Christianity in many instances. They talk about some of the same things but not in the same way. They talk about love, they talk about commitment, and on and on, but these things are not *biblical* love, *biblical* commitment, and so on.

T. A.: How, then, does the Bible tell us we are to go about addressing our mental, emotional, and behavioral problems—in other words, everyday issues of living?

The answer is, simply, "God's way!"

DAVE HUNT: If a Christian has what they call emotional problems, or mental problems, whatever it may be—they feel depressed, they think they lack self-esteem, or they have…they're given to fits of anger, or overwhelming sexual temptations, unhappiness, can't get along with other people, whatever it may be—where do you go? You go to the *Bible*. You go to the Lord. You talk to the Lord in prayer.

Now that seems extreme to people today, but where did David go? David really had some problems. Where did Paul go? Paul was beaten and stoned and shipwrecked and hated and persecuted. What about the heroes of the faith in Hebrews 11? They wandered about in sheepskins and goatskins; they were destitute, tormented, afflicted; they dwelt in dens and caves of the earth. You think *you've* got problems!

Why don't you read about some of the problems that these people had. Where did they go? Who did they find counsel from? I mean, was there some psychological counselor nearby that they went to? No! They counseled with the Lord. They counseled from His Word. Read the Psalms and see what these men went through. And they trusted in God, and this is how they triumphed. And that is one of the problems today. You see, when you have problems like this—Peter calls it "the trial of your faith, much more precious than of gold that perishes"—you don't go running to somebody every time you've got a problem. You're not going to learn. You have to (even secular psychologists acknowledge), you need to suffer through these problems. That's how you learn, that's how you mature. It's like a soldier in basic training. They don't send them out to the front lines until they've at least gone through some obstacle courses. So this is an obstacle course. You trust God. You walk by faith. And you will triumph! It's called the victory of our faith.

T. A.: God's way begins and is centered upon an individual's relationship with Him through the person of Jesus Christ.

In order for that relationship to come about, Jesus said a person must be "born again" spiritually. This takes place when one believes the gospel, the good news of Jesus Christ reconciling us to God by paying the full penalty for our sins as He hung upon the Cross. Since all are under sin's condemnation—destined to be separated from God forever—because all have sinned, it is only through our turning to Jesus by grace through faith that we can receive salvation, the free gift of eternal life.

Once we place our trust in Him we become spiritual children of God, transformed as new creatures in Christ, sealed with the Holy Spirit, the Spirit of Truth who abides in us and enables us to overcome the world, the flesh, and the devil. As our lives are now in Christ, all issues of living are related to and dependent upon our relationship with Him. For the Christian, then, solving destructive mental, emotional, and behavioral problems is not a matter of applying methods or techniques but rather growing in righteousness through his or her relationship with Jesus.

MARTIN BOBGAN: When we're in a fellowship, a church, a group of believers—the qualifications are that we understand the essential elements in dealing with problems of living are first and foremost to the individual himself. We don't need some expert to come alongside; we don't need some certificated or licensed individual to come alongside. We need those in the church to realize that this is an excellent opportunity to deepen someone in the faith, and the elements of deepening someone in the faith are there. It's the Word of God, it's the work of the Holy Spirit, and it's the fellowshipping with the saints. And so you have a person with a problem—you want to accentuate those facets of the faith that we all know about. In most cases, people take care of problems themselves, but when someone needs help, then we can come alongside and encourage them in these areas.

DEIDRE BOBGAN: And in the Body of Christ you don't just have a therapist in an office—you have many people. You have the pastor who is preaching; you have, perhaps, a teacher—a Sunday School teacher—who is teaching the Word; you have, perhaps, some who can come alongside in certain ways to encourage; you have others who can come alongside and maybe take care of some of the needs that you might have. For instance, a widow needs to have her house painted, or something like that. I mean, a woman could get very depressed if things are beyond her taking care of things. But the body of Christ can come alongside, and I think that a lot of the working together of the body of Christ has been undermined by this professionalism of caring for people.

T. A.: As our knowledge of Jesus and love for Him grows, as well as our thankfulness for all He has done for us, our willingness to submit to Him in all things increases, thereby allowing *Him* to do the work of transforming our lives. This is God's way for every redeemed child of His. Scripture calls it the Spirit-led and empowered life. Any other approach, no matter how sincere or "Christianized," is a work of the flesh at best and therefore profits nothing.

For biblical Christians, whether shepherds or individual sheep, the challenge in today's heavily psychologized culture and church is to return to the ways and means of ministering to one another that God has provided in His Scriptures, through His Holy Spirit, and through the equipping of believers in Him. God's Word is completely sufficient. We simply need to be willing to do things His way.

Then said Jesus to those…which believed on him,
If ye continue in my word, then are ye my disciples indeed:
and ye shall know the truth, and the truth shall make you free.
—JOHN 8:31–32

SELECTED BIBLIOGRAPHY

American Psychiatric Association. *Diagnostic and Statistical Manual of Mental Disorders.* Washington, D. C., Third Edition, 1980.

Atkinson, Rita L., Atkinson, Richard C., Smith, Edward E., Hilgard, Ernest R. *Introduction to Psychology*, Ninth Edition. Harcourt Brace Jovanovich Publishers, 1987.

B., Dick. *Anne Smith's Spiritual Workbook.* Good Book Publishing Co., 1992.

Barclay, Oliver R. *Whatever Happened to the Jesus Lane Lot?* InterVarsity Press, 1977.

Baron, Will. *Deceived by the New Age.* Nampa, ID: Pacific Press Publishing Association, 1990.

Bloom, Allan. *The Closing of the American Mind.* New York: Simon Schuster, 1988.

Bobgan, Martin and Deidre. *12 Steps to Destruction: Codependency, Recovery Heresies.* Santa Barbara, CA: EastGate Publishers, 1991.

———. *Four Temperaments, Astrology, and Personality Testing.* Santa Barbara, CA: EastGate Publishers, 1992.

———. *Hypnosis and the Christian.* Minneapolis, MN: Bethany House Publishers, 1984.

———. *Psychoheresy.* Santa Barbara, CA: EastGate Publishers, 1987.

———. *The End of Christian Psychology.* Santa Barbara, CA: EastGate Publishers, 1997.

Braden, Charles S. *Spirits in Rebellion: The Rise and Development of New Thought.* SMU Press, 1966.

Breggin, Peter R., M.D., Cohen, David, Ph.D. *Your Drug May Be Your Problem: How and Why to Stop Taking Psychiatric Medications.* Reading, MA: Perseus Books, 1999.

Buchman, Frank N. D. *Remodeling the World*. London, 1941.

Carter. John D., Narramore, Bruce. *The Integration of Psychology and Theology*. Grand Rapids, MI: Zondervan Publishing House, 1979.

Cho, Paul Yongghi. *The Fourth Dimension*. Logos International, 1979.

Clement of Alexandria. *Miscellanies*. II:2.

Cloud, David. *Flirting with Rome*. Way of Life Literature, 1993.

Coleman, Lee. *The Reign of Error*. Beacon Press, 1984.

Collins, Gary. *Can You Trust Psychology?* InterVarsity Press, 1988.

Dawes, Robyn M. *House of Cards: Psychology and Psychotherapy Built on Myth*. New York: The Free Press, 1994.

Dawkins, Richard. *The Selfish Gene*. Oxford, England: Oxford University Press, 30th Anniversary Edition, 2006.

De Rosa, Peter. *Vicars of Christ*. Crown Publishers, 1988.

Dineen, Tana, Dr. *Manufacturing Victims: What the Psychology Industry Is Doing to People*. Westmount, Quebec: Robert Davies Publishing, 1996.

Dobson, James. *Dr. Dobson Answers Your Questions*. Wheaton, IL: Tyndale, 1989.

————. *Hide or Seek*. Revell Publishing, 1974.

————. *What Wives Wish Their Husbands Knew About Women*. Wheaton, IL: Tyndale House, 1979.

Driberg, Tom. *The Mystery of Moral Re-Armament*. London, 1964.

Durant, Will. *The Story of Civilization: Caesar and Christ*. New York: Simon and Schuster, 1940.

Eddington, Sir Arthur. *Science and the Unseen World*. Kessinger Publishing, LLC, 2004.

Ehler, Sidney Z., Morall, John B. *Church and State through the Centuries: A Collection of Historic Documents with Commentaries*. London, 1954.

Ellenberger, Henri. *The Discovery of the Unconscious*. Basic Books, 1970.

Feynman, Richard et al. *The Feynman Lectures on Physics*, Vol 1. Addison-Wesley, 1963.

Fingarette, Herbert. *Heavy Drinking: The Myth of Alcoholism as a Disease.* Berkeley, CA: University of California Press, 1988.

Flannery, O. P., General Ed. *Vatican Council II: The Conciliar And Post Conciliar Documents.* Northport, NY: Costello Publishing Company, Revised Edition, 1988.

Fodor, Nandor. *Freud, Jung, and Occultism.* University Books, 1971.

Forbush, William Byron, ed. *Foxe's Book of Martyrs.* Zondervan, 1962.

Foster, Richard. *The Celebration of Discipline.* San Francisco: Harper, 1978.

Friesen, James. *More Than Survivors: Conversations with Multiple Personality Clients.* Here's Life Publishers, 1992.

Gardner, G. P. National Commission on Excellence in Education. *A Nation at Risk: The Imperative of Educational Reform.* Washington, D.C.: U.S. Government Printing Office, 1983.

George, Carol V. R. *God's Salesman: Norman Vincent Peale and the Power of Positive Thinking.* New York, NY: Oxford University Press, 1993.

Graham, Billy. *Just As I Am: The Autobiography of Billy Graham.* San Francisco, CA: New York, NY: HarperSanFrancisco/Zondervan, 1997.

Gross, Martin. *The Psychological Society: The Impact—and Failure—of Psychiatry, Psychotherapy, Psychoanalysis, and the Psychological Revolution.* New York: Random House, 1978.

Harner, Michael J. *The Way of the Shaman: A Guide to Healing and Power.* Harper and Row, 1980.

Hart, Archibald D. *Me, Myself & I: How Far Should We Go in Our Search for Self-Fulfillment?* Ann Arbor, MI: Servant Publications, 1992.

Hughes, Philip. *A History of the Church.* London, 1934.

Hughes, Robert. *The Fatal Shore.* New York: Alfred A Knopf, 1987.

James, William. "A Plea for Psychology As a Natural Science." Collected Essays and Reviews. 1982.

Jeans, Sir James. *The Mysterious Universe.* Cambridge University Press, 1931.

Jones, Ernest. *The Life and Work of Sigmund Freud,* Volume I (1856-1900). New York: Basic Books, 1953.

Jung, C. G. *Memories, Dreams, Reflections.* Pantheon Books, 1963.

Kreeft, Peter. *Ecumenical Jihad.* San Francisco: Ignatius Press, 1996.

LeShan, Lawrence. *How to Meditate.* Boston: Little, Brown, and Company, 1974.

Livesey, Roy. *Twelve Steps to the New Age.* Bury House Books, 1995.

McGee, Robert S. *The Search for Significance.* Pasadena, TX: Robert S. McGee, 1985.

McNally, Richard. *Remembering Trauma.* Cambridge, MA: Harvard University Press, 2003.

Miller, Calvin. *The Table of Inwardness.* InterVarsity Press, 1984.

Narramore, Bruce. *You're Someone Special.* Zondervan, 1978.

Noll, Richard. *The Jung Cult: Origins of a Charismatic Movement.* New York: Simon & Schuster, 1994.

Paulk, Earl. *That the World May Know.* K. Dimension Publishers, 1987.

Peale, Norman Vincent. *Positive Imaging: The Powerful Way to Change Your Life.* New York: Fawcett Crest, 1982.

———. *The Power of Positive Thinking.* Fawcett Crest, 1983.

———. *The Power of Positive Thinking.* New Condensed Edition, Center for Positive Thinking, 1987.

Peele, Stanton. *Diseasing of America: Addiction Treatment Out of Control.* Heath and Company, 1989.

Pendergrast, Mark. *Victims of Memory: Sex Abuse Accusations and Shattered Lives.* HarperCollins Publishers, 1996.

Phillips, Melanie. *Londonistan.* New York: Encounter Books, 2006.

Popper, Karl. *Scientific Theory and Falsifiability*, Perspectives in Philosophy. Robert N. Beck, ed. New York: Holt, Rinehart, Winston, 1975.

Pritchard, G. A. *Willow Creek Seeker Services.* Baker Books, 1996.

Samenow, Stanton E., Ph.D. *Inside the Criminal Mind.* New York: Times Books, 1984.

Schuller, Robert H. *Believe in the God Who Believes in You: The Ten Commandments: A Divine Design for Dignity.* Nashville, TN: Thomas Nelson Publishers.

————. *Living Positively One Day at a Time.* Revell, 1981.

————. *Self-Esteem, the New Reformation.* Word Books, 1982.

————. *Self-Love: The Dynamic Force of Success.* New York: Hawthorne Books, 1969.

————. *The Power of the Inner Eye.*

Smalley, Gary, Trent, John. *The Language of Love: A Powerful Way to Maximize Insight, Intimacy, and Understanding.* Focus on the Family, Word Books, 1988.

Szasz, Thomas. *The Myth of Psychotherapy: Mental Healing as Religion, Rhetoric, and Repression.* New York: Anchor Press/Doubleday, 1978.

Templeton, John Marks. *Discovering the Laws of Life.* The Continuum Publishing Company, 1994.

The Letters of Samuel Rutherford. Moody Press, 277.

Torrey, E. Fuller. *The Mind Games: Witchdoctors and Psychiatrists.* Emerson Hall, 1972.

Treu, Martin. *Martin Luther in Wittenberg: A Biographical Tour.* Wittenberg: Saxon-Anhalt Luther Memorial Foundation, 2003.

Van Leeuwen, Mary Stewart. *The Sorcerer's Apprentice.* InterVarsity Press, 1982.

Wells, David F. *No Place for Truth: or Whatever Happened to Evangelical Theology?* Grand Rapids, MI: William B Eerdmans Publishing Company, 1993.

Wood, Garth. *The Myth of Neurosis: Overcoming the Illness Excuse.* New York: Harper & Row, 1987.

Zetzel, Elizabeth, M.D. *The Capacity for Emotional Growth—Theoretical and Clinical Contributions to Psychoanalysis 1943-1969.* International Universities Press, Inc., 1979.

Zilbergeld, Bernie. *The Shrinking of America: Myths of Psychological Change.* Little, Brown, 1983.

INDEX

AUTHOR-SUBJECT

A

Not needed by heroes and heroines of
the faith, 85
Offers excuses for Christians not to trust
and obey God, 87, 90, 105, 114-15,
257
Of very recent origin, 10
Only possible justification for, 7
Popular in Christian academia, 9
Preaches a false Christ, 64
Presents a "positive gospel," 304
Principles of "hidden from church" until
now, 312-13
Promoted by Bruce and Clyde Nar-
ramore's Rosemead School of
Psychology, 12
Promotes visualization, 171-72
Promotes "victimhood," 101, 105
Redefines sin as sickness, 75-76
Replaces God's truth with humanistic
theories, 29, 67, 80-81, 105, 152,
165-66, 255
Required in most Christian colleges, 179
Robs church and world of God's Word,
93, 98
Same as secular, 69, 98, 105, 107, 108,
212
Same techniques as those being aban-
doned as false by secular psycholo-
gists, 240-41
Satan's lies promoted by in the church,
64
Schuller a major promoter of, 72
"Science falsely so-called," 214
Scoffs at the power of God's Word to
transform the heart, 75, 108
Scripture sufficient without, 7-8
Self esteem a foundational doctrine of,
72, 90, 130, 337
Self-love basic thesis of, 32
Shamanism, 78, 305
Teachings of introduced by deceiving
spirits, 48
Undermines confidence in Christ,
84-86, 290
Undermines Christianity, 80, 86, 93,
270
Unscientific and could not be otherwise,
100, 115, 180-81
Why didn't Christ use it? 102
Youth rebellion encouraged by, 100-1
CHRISTIANIZED 12-STEPS GROUPS—
Celebrate Recovery, 34-39, 51, 272-73,
276

No scientific support for, 38
Problems inherent within, 38
CHURCH, ROMAN CATHOLIC (SEE ROMAN
CATHOLICISM)—
CHURCH, THE PROFESSING EVANGELICAL—
Allows governmental agencies to as-
sume discipline of their children, 317
Attempts to integrate psychology with
Bible, 41, 302
Believes that psychology is scientific,
40
Captivated and intimidated by lies of
psychology, 41, 46
Destructive influence of psychology
on, 46
Embraces theories of anti-Christians,
40, 46, 109, 137
False faith promoted by, 40, 93
Failure to exercise biblical discipline,
317
Failure of leaders to counter heresy, 40
Former rejection of Darwinism turning
to acceptance, 307-8
Gospel is psychologized, 40, 93, 108
Has abandoned Bible, 46, 100-1, 303
Immorality increasing, 93
Influence of psychology, 42
Lack of separation from world, 307
Licensed psychologists on staff of
many, 40
Neglects contending for the faith, 40,
93-94, 104
Primary referral service for professional
counselors, 40, 46
Refuses to correct heresy, 40, 104
Sinking deeper into compromise and
apostasy, 93, 108
Teaching on loving God virtually miss-
ing, 122
Views Bible as insufficient for counsel-
ing, 40, 209
Willow Creek, 42
CLAUDY, CARL H.—
Authority on Masonry, 255
CLINTON, HILLARY—
Chaired the Children's Defense Fund,
259
Chaired the New World Foundation,
259
CLINTON, PRESIDENT BILL—
Approval of immoral practices, 190

Promoted by Smalley, Trent, Dobson, 186-87

FRANKL, VIKTOR—
Christian psychologists follow his extra-biblical "truth," 109

FREEING YOUR MIND FROM MEMORIES THAT BIND (FRED AND FLORENCE LITTAUER)—
Uncovering hidden memories, 184

FREUD, SIGMUND—
And spirit entities, 50
Anti-Christian, 44, 108-9, 118
Anti-religion, 48
Altered states of consciousness, 49
Blasphemy to claim that God inspired him, 175-76
Claimed that everything is rooted in sex, 259
Claimed sexual freedom was necessary for mental health, 50
Considered Darwin's *Descent of Man* as one of the ten most significant books, 248
Developed technique of "free association," 49
Founded "religion of psychoanalysis," 48-49
Freudianism an important element in evolution, 145
Had hatred for Christianity, 44
His atheism influences ministers, 201
Some of his case studies are autobiographical, 259
Sought to destroy Christianity, 108-9, 118
Theories based on his own sexual perversions, 49
Theory of psychic determinism, 48
"Unconscious" replaces God, with no laws or judgment, 50
User of cocaine, 49

FREUD, JUNG, AND OCCULTISM (NANDOR FODOR)—
Claimed that Jung's story was unbelievably occult, 170

FRIESEN, JAMES G.—
Hidden memories key to deliverance from demonic influence, 232
None of his procedures based upon Bible, 232
Tells how to deal with Christians suffering from MPD, 233

Wrote on Multiple Personality Disorder (MPD), 229, 231

FRUIT OF CORRECTION—
Furnished for good works, 25
Perfection in Christ, 25

FULLER THEOLOGICAL SEMINARY—
School of Psychology, accredited by unbelievers, 9-10, 116

G

GAY GENES (*SEE* HOMOSEXUAL GENE)—

GENOCIDE TREATY,—
A crime to call homosexuality a sin, 74
Attempt to convert anyone is a crime under, 74
Effect has been nil ever since, 73-74
Psychology's rejection of "negative" largely responsible for, 74
Signed by President Reagan, 73
Undermines Scripture, 74-75

GEORGE FOX UNIVERSITY (*SEE* COLLEGES, CHRISTIAN)—

GIBSON, MEL (SEE *THE PASSION OF THE CHRIST*)—

GLORIA GOES TO GAY PRIDE—
Third-grade reader promoting homosexuality, 195

GOD—
About to judge world, 113
Alone knows the heart, 303, 339
Alone can cleanse heart, 161, 310
As you conceive Him, Her, It, 112, 272-73
Creates love for Him in the willing heart, 122
Christians have little time for, 111
Failure to love with whole heart is man's greatest sin, 120, 123
Glimpse of His glory obliterates all thought of self, 349-50
Ignored by humanity, 244
Man's rebellion breaks heart of, 237
Love for should continually overflow our hearts, 123, 299
Most people prefer false ideas to knowing Him, 111
Must be known in hearts, 126
Must be sought for Himself, not for what we get from Him, 111
Not contacted by visualization, 111

S

T

W

Y

Z

About The Berean Call

TBC is a nonprofit, 501(3)c organization which exists to:

ALERT believers in Christ to unbiblical teachings and practices impacting the church

EXHORT believers to give greater heed to biblical discernment and truth regarding teachings and practices being currently promoted in the church

SUPPLY believers with teaching, information, and materials which will encourage the love of God's truth, and assist in the development of biblical discernment

MOBILIZE believers in Christ to action in obedience to the scriptural command to "earnestly contend for the faith" (Jude 3)

IMPACT the church of Jesus Christ with the necessity for trusting the Scriptures as the only rule for faith, practice, and a life pleasing to God

---

A free monthly newsletter, The Berean Call, *may be received by sending a request to: PO Box 7019, Bend, OR 97708; or by calling*

1-800-937-6638

To register for free email updates, to access our digital archives, and to order a variety of additional resource materials online, visit us at:

www.thebereancall.org

Bend • Oregon